BEHNISCH, BEHNISCH & PARTNER

GÜNTER BEHNISCH, STEFAN BEHNISCH, GÜNTHER SCHALLER

BEHNISCH, BEHNISCH & PARTNER

BAUTEN UND ENTWÜRFE | BUILDINGS AND DESIGNS

BIRKHÄUSER

VERLAG FÜR ARCHITEKTUR | PUBLISHERS FOR ARCHITECTURE

BASEL · BERLIN · BOSTON

Inhalt | Contents

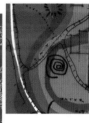

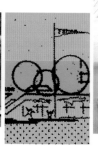

Das Büro | The Office

Das Büro Behnisch, Behnisch & Partner wurde 1989 als Zweigbüro von Behnisch & Partner gegründet und arbeitet seit 1991 eigenständig. Es hat bereits eine Reihe von Projekten in Deutschland und im Ausland realisiert und zahlreiche Wettbewerbe gewonnen. Die Bandbreite der Projekte reicht von Bürobauten über Schwimmbäder und Schulen bis zu Museen. Erste Preise erhielt es für Sportstadien, Archivbauten, Konzerthallen etc.

Heute arbeiten die Büros weitgehend unabhängig voneinander, beide in Stuttgart. Das Büro Behnisch, Behnisch & Partner wird von Stefan Behnisch gemeinsam mit Günther Schaller geleitet, der 1997 in die Partnerschaft eingetreten ist.

GÜNTER BEHNISCH

GÜNTHER SCHALLER

The office of Behnisch, Behnisch & Partner was established in 1989 as a branch office of Behnisch & Partner, and has functioned independently since 1991. It has already realised a series of projects in Germany and abroad, and won numerous awards. The range of projects involved extends from office buildings to swimming halls and from schools to museums. The office has received first prizes for sports stadiums, archive buildings, concert halls, etc.

Today, the offices of Behnisch & Partner and of Behnisch, Behnisch & Partner, both located in Stuttgart, function largely independently of one another. Behnisch, Behnisch & Partner is directed by Stefan Behnisch together with Günther Schaller, who joined the partnership in 1997.

1999 wurde ein Zweigbüro in Venice, Kalifornien, gegründet und 2002 ein Projektbüro bei unseren Kollegen architects Alliance in Toronto. Das Büro in Venice betreut und akquiriert unabhängig von Stuttgart Projekte auf dem nordamerikanischen Kontinent. Wie auch im Stuttgarter Büro werden hier Wettbewerbe bearbeitet.

Wir Architekten sind eng eingebunden in das Zusammenspiel vieler Disziplinen während des Planungsprozesses. Vor allem am Anfang sind wir auf eine gute, inhaltlich tragende Zusammenarbeit aller Disziplinen angewiesen. Nicht nur bei Architekten, sondern ebenso bei Ingenieuren, Beratern und Fachplanern gibt es jene, die zu etwas Besonderem beitragen wollen und auch am Innovativen interessiert sind. Für uns alle dürfte gelten, dass eben die Aspekte unserer Arbeit, die über den reinen Broterwerb hinausgehen, die interessantesten, riskantesten und auch die tragfähigsten sind.

Beleuchtet man den kreativen Prozess, so lässt er sich grob in drei Phasen einteilen. Die erste Phase ist die der freien Ideen und Konzepte. Oft heuristisch aus vielen verschiedenen Ansätzen gefunden, müssen diese gehegt und gepflegt werden. Sie sind empfindlich,

benötigen eine positive Umgebung, um sich entwickeln zu können. In der zweiten Phase wird die Idee an den Realitäten gemessen und überprüft. Oft wird sie verworfen, um dann wieder von vorne zu beginnen. In der dritten Phase wird die erfolgreiche Idee schließlich umgesetzt. Je stärker eine Idee bzw. eine Konzeption ist, desto unbeschadeter wird sie die kalte Welt der Realisierung durchstehen. Vor allem in den ersten zwei Phasen des kreativen Prozesses entscheidet sich, ob etwas Gutes entstehen kann oder nicht.

In Deutschland, jedoch vor allem auch im Ausland, wo unsere Urteilsfähigkeit durch fremde Traditionen und Kulturen eingeschränkt ist und wir auf den guten Willen der anderen angewiesen sind, braucht das Büro offene und positiv arbeitende Partner. Diejenigen, die immer nur auf die Probleme und Risiken, jedoch nicht auf Chancen und Möglichkeiten hinweisen, agieren zerstörerisch. Im Idealfall helfen Mitplaner, scheinbare Grenzen zu überschreiten und die Konzepte voranzutreiben.

Ein weiterer wichtiger Aspekt der Projektarbeit stellt die Zusammenarbeit mit Auftraggebern dar, dem Bauherrn in seiner Funktion als treibende Kraft. Private Bauherrn verfolgen zu Recht ihre eigenen Ziele.

BEHNISCH, BEHNISCH & PARTNER, VENICE
KALIFORNIEN | CALIFORNIA

STEFAN BEHNISCH

PROJEKTBÜRO BEI ARCHITECTS ALLIANCE |
PROJECT OFFICE AT ARCHITECTS ALLIANCE, TORONTO

In 1999, a branch office was established in Venice, California; in 2002, a project office was opened by our colleagues at architects Alliance in Toronto. The Venice office consults on and acquires projects in North America independently of Stuttgart. As in the Stuttgart office, competition entries are also prepared here.

During the planning process, we architects are tied closely in an interplay with numerous disciplines. Especially at the start, we are dependent upon positive, substantive collaboration among all the disciplines involved. There are those — not only among architects, but also among engineers, consultants and advisors, who want to contribute to something special, and who are interested in innovation. For all of us, it may well be that precisely those aspects of our work that transcend concerns with earning a livelihood are the most interesting, the most fraught with risk, but also the most rewarding.

The creative process can be divided, very approximately, into three phases. The first is that of free ideas and concepts. Often founded heuristically on a variety of points of departure, the results of this phase must be sustaining and cultivated. They are sensitive, and require a positive environment in which to develop. In the second

phase, an idea is measured against reality and tested. Often, it is discarded, and the process must begin all over again. In the third phase, finally, the successful idea is implemented.

The stronger the initial idea or conception, the better the chances it will survive the cold world of practical realisation undiminished. It is mainly the first two phases of the creative process that determine whether anything viable will emerge or not.

In Germany, but even more so abroad, where our powers of judgment are limited by the strangeness of foreign traditions and cultures and where we are dependent on the good will of others, the office needs open and positive working partners. Those who forever remind us of problems and risks, but never of opportunities and possibilities, behave destructively. Ideally, co-planners help us to transgress apparent limits in order to advance a given conception.

Another critical aspect of project work is represented by collaboration with the commissioning party, with the client in his role as a driving force. Private clients pursue, with justice, their own objectives. These are not invariably congruent with those of the architect.

Diese sind nicht immer deckungsgleich mit denen des Architekten. Nur da, wo man überzeugen kann, dass auch die schwächeren Aspekte der Architektur dem Wohle des Bauherrn dienen könnten, wird man erfolgreich im architektonischen Sinne sein und das Übergewicht der pragmatischen Aspekte begrenzen.

Bei der Entwicklung von Architektur kommen viele Aspekte zum tragen; viele Disziplinen arbeiten zusammen, und diese werden vertreten von verschiedenen am Projekt planerisch Beteiligten. Es gibt die starken Aspekte, diejenigen, die schon aus ihrer Stellung in unserer Kultur heraus für sich selber sorgen können. Das sind in der Regel die Bereiche des Quantitativen, der einfachen Wahrheiten; diese sind leicht messbar. Auch diese sind Teile der Architektur, jedoch lediglich einige von sehr vielen. Da sie leicht zu erfassen sind, mathematisch begründbar, scheinen diejenigen, die sie vertreten, immer die Wahrheit auf ihrer Seite zu haben. Kosten, Termine, rechtliche Bestimmungen, Flächen, Volumina, absolute Temperaturen zur Definition eines sogenannten Komforts sind solche Wahrheiten. Die Aussagen derjenigen, die sie vertreten, werden kaum angezweifelt. Es ist das Feld der vielen Berater, der Quantity Surveyors, Manager, Quality Surveyors, Code Consul-

tants, Steuerer etc. Diese Disziplinen haben letztendlich wenig Einfluss auf den kulturellen Wert von Bauten. Es sind Aspekte, die weitgehend im Prozess der Planung eine Rolle spielen, nach Fertigstellung sind sie dann weitgehend unbedeutend.

Der Architekten Aufgabe muss es sein, eben jene Kräfte zu stärken, die nicht für sich selber einstehen, die nicht dem gesellschaftlichen »Mainstream« entsprechen. Diese werden meist als Kür, und nicht als Pflicht betrachtet. Quantitativ kaum erfassbar, werden sie in Value Engineering Sessions schnell geopfert. Dabei sind doch jene schwachen Aspekte diejenigen, die die architektonische Bedeutung der Werke ausmachen.

Einen weiteren Gesichtspunkt sollte der Architekt nicht aus dem Auge verlieren: Seit die Nachhaltigkeit auf quantifizierbare Themen im öffentlichen Bewusstsein verkürzt wurde, eben auf reinen Energieverbrauch, ist sie salonfähig geworden und als Disziplin weitgehend anerkannt. Die vielen Facetten und subtilen Aspekte der Nachhaltigkeit, eben z.B. die Einheit von Natur und Mensch oder die längst überfällige Neudefinition von Komfort sind dabei weitgehend abhanden gekommen. Auch hier scheint man sich ausschließlich am Quantifizierbaren zu orientieren. Diese Entwicklung gilt es zu wenden. ◄

BEHNISCH & PARTNER, BÜRO REITHALLE |
REITHALLE OFFICE; 1989–1991

Only when we are able to persuade clients that architecture's "softer" dimensions can serve their well-being are we successful in the architectural sense and are we able to restrict the disproportionate weight of pragmatic concerns.

Many aspects contribute to the development of architecture; many disciplines work in concert, represented by the various parties who together plan a given project. There are the strong aspects, which, already by virtue of their position in our culture, can take care of themselves. As a rule, these occupy the realm of the quantitative, the simple facts of the case; they are readily measurable. They too form a component of architecture, albeit one of very many. However, because they are easily graspable, mathematically verifiable, those representing them always seem to have the "truth" on their side. Costs, deadlines, legal conditions, surfaces, volumes, absolute temperatures in the definition of so-called comfort are such "truths." Pronouncements by those representing them are seldom doubted. It is the field of the many consultants, the quantity surveyor, manager, quality surveyor, code consultants, supervisors, etc. These disciplines, ultimately, have limited bearing on the cultural value of a building. These aspects play a far-reaching role in the planning

process, but once a project has been completed, they recede to insignificance.

The task of architects must be to reinforce precisely those forces which cannot stand up for themselves, those failing to correspond to the social "mainstream." The cultivation of such forces is generally regarded as an optional exercise, not a duty. Hardly graspable in quantitative terms, they are those quickly sacrificed in value engineering sessions. And yet it is just these "soft" aspects that constitute the rank and significance of a work of architecture.

An additional perspective should be kept in view. Ever since sustainability became foreshortened as a quantifiable term in public consciousness, i.e., reduced purely to measurements of energy use, it has become fashionable, achieving wide recognition as a discipline. The many facts and more subtle aspects of sustainability, for example the unity of nature and the human being, or the long overdue redefinition of "comfort," are essentially lost in the shuffle. Here too, the prevalent orientation is apparently exclusively to the quantifiable. It is important to counter this development. ◄

Zum Zeitpunkt der Planung des St. Benno-Gymnasiums kurz nach der deutschen Wiedervereinigung waren die politische, die gesellschaftliche und auch die wirtschaftliche Situation zumeist nicht geklärt, schon gar nicht gefestigt. Unklare Eigentumsverhältnisse behinderten oder verhinderten viele notwendige Neubauten oder auch Renovierungen.

During the planning of the St. Benno Secondary School, shortly after German reunification, the political, social and even the economic situation had to a large extent not yet been clarified, let alone firmly fixed. Unclear ownership status hindered or even prevented much new construction and renovation work.

WETTBEWERB UND REALISIERUNG | COMPETITION AND REALISATION

ST.BENNO-GYMNASIUM | ST. BENNO SECONDARY SCHOOL

DRESDEN, DEUTSCHLAND | DRESDEN, GERMANY; 1992–1996

1

2

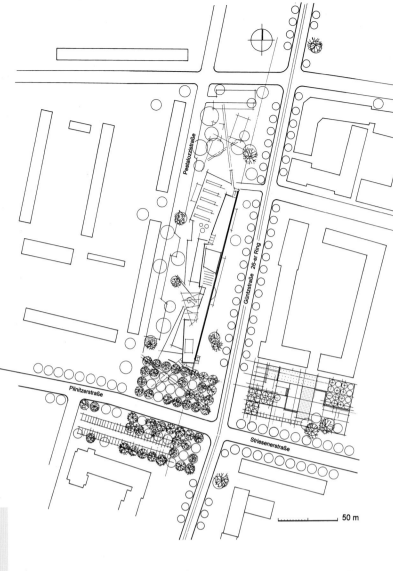

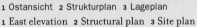

1 Ostansicht 2 Strukturplan 3 Lageplan
1 East elevation 2 Structural plan 3 Site plan

ST. BENNO-GYMNASIUM | ST. BENNO SECONDARY SCHOOL | 1992–1996

Dem Bistum Dresden-Meißen war es gelungen, ein Grundstück in zentraler Lage von Dresden zu finden, bei dem wenigstens die Besitzverhältnisse geklärt waren. Tatsächlich wirkte das Grundstück auf den ersten Blick für eine Schule angesichts der Zwänge wenig geeignet. Der Zuschnitt schien zu schmal, und die Belastung durch den Verkehr war hoch. In dieser Situation ist das Gebäude für das St. Benno-Gymnasium entstanden. Es folgt der schmalen Länge des Grundstücks. Die Unterrichtsräume wenden sich vom Lärm der Straße ab und öffnen sich nach Westen zur ruhigeren Wohnbebauung. Eine große, blau gefärbte Wand schützt die Schüler und Lehrer in den Unterrichtsräumen und den davor liegenden Pausen- und Aufenthaltszonen vor dem Verkehrslärm.

The Bishopric of Dresden-Meißen succeeded in locating a building site in a central location of Dresden, one at least with clear ownership status. In view of its constraints, the site seemed, at first glance, ill-suited for a school. Its dimensions were too narrow, and excessive traffic represented a significant disturbance. The building for the St. Benno Secondary School has its origins in these circumstances. It follows the long, narrow axis of the site. Classrooms turn away from the noise of the street and open to the west, toward a tranquil residential area. A large, blue wall shelters students and teachers inside the classrooms, as well as the recess and common areas lying before them, from traffic noise.

4 Blick von Süd-Westen 5 Ostfassade 6 Haupteingang 7 Westansicht
4 View from south-west 5 East facade 6 Main entrance 7 West elevation

ST. BENNO-GYMNASIUM | ST. BENNO SECONDARY SCHOOL | 1992–1996

Im Westen, an der Pestalozzistraße, liegen die Klassenräume den hohen Wohnblocks gegenüber. Das Beengte der Situation wurde aufgehoben bzw. verringert, indem die Unterrichtsräume zu den gegenüberliegenden Wohnblocks sowie zueinander etwas verschwenkt wurden. Sie liegen nicht parallel zu den Wohnblocks, sondern lösen sich von diesen.

Zwischen den Gruppen der Unterrichtsräume haben sich funktional weniger gebundene Flächen ergeben. Diese sind zu besonderen Attraktionen ausgebildet worden, z.B. die gläserne Pausenhalle mit ihren offenen Galerien, die alle Geschosse verbindet und in der Schulveranstaltungen stattfinden können, oder an anderer Stelle ein mehrgeschossiger, dicht begrünter Wintergarten.

To the west, on Pestalozzistraße, the classrooms lie across from tall housing blocks. The constrictions presented by the site were attenuated by rotating the classrooms somewhat, both in relation to the residential buildings across the way, and to one another. They do not lie parallel to the housing blocks, but instead lean away from them.

Between the clusters of classrooms, there are spaces less devoted to functional requirements. These were developed as special attractions, for example the glazed recreation hall with its open galleries, which unites all stories and serves as a space for school events; another special feature is a multi-story, densely-planted winter garden.

5

6

8

9

8 Haupteingang 9 Südansicht 10 Grundriss Erdgeschoss
8 Main entrance 9 South elevation 10 Plan, ground floor

ST. BENNO-GYMNASIUM | ST. BENNO SECONDARY SCHOOL | 1992–1996

Man betritt das Gebäude von Süden her kommend über eine großzügige Freitreppe, die etwas zurückgesetzt von der großen, vom Verkehr belasteten Straßenkreuzung ansetzt. Hier ist ein städtischer Vorplatz entstanden, ein Baumhain markiert und stabilisiert diesen Ort.

Aufgrund des Zuschnitts und der beschränkten Grundstücksfläche ist eine viergeschossige Anlage entstanden. Kinder jedoch finden sich in Häusern mit drei Geschossen besser zurecht. Bei drei Geschossen können sie sich an Himmel, Erde und dem Raum dazwischen klar orientieren. Auch deshalb wurde beim St. Benno-Gymnasium die Eingangsebene in das erste Obergeschoss gelegt. So entstand eine funktional tendenziell dreigeschossige Schule, unter deren Eingangsebene, aber ebenerdig, die Fachklassen, Kapelle, Schulküche und Sporthalle liegen.

The building is entered from the south via a generous outdoor stair set back somewhat from the wide intersection with its high volume of traffic. Here emerges an urban forecourt, one accented and stabilised by a small grove of trees.

In response to the site's dimensions and restricted surface area, a four-story layout was planned. Children, however, are more at home with three-story buildings, in which they are able to clearly orient themselves successfully in terms of sky, earth and the space between. For this reason, the entrance level at the St. Benno Secondary School was placed at the second floor. The result was a school tending toward a three-story functional plan. Below the entrance level, at ground level, lie science classrooms, a chapel, and the school's kitchen and sports hall.

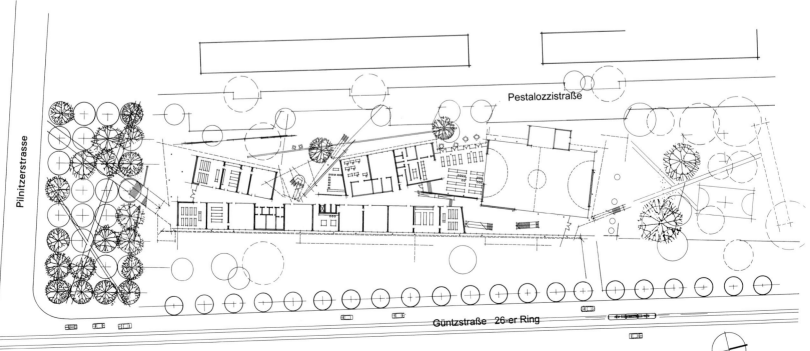

Pilnitzerstrasse

Pestalozzistraße

Güntzstraße 26-er Ring

10 20 m

10

11

12

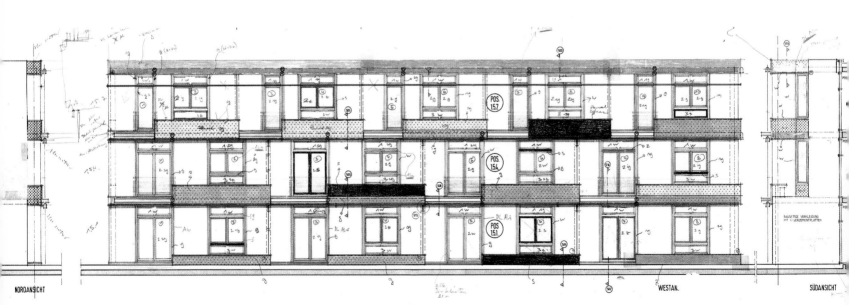

NORDANSICHT

WESTAN.

SÜDANSICHT

13

14

15

11 Süd-Westansicht: Blick auf verglaste Pausenhalle 12, 14 Fassadenausschnitt
13 Farbgestaltung der Fassade mit Erich Wiesner 15 Blick von Nord-Westen
11 South-west elevation: glazed recreation hall 12, 14 Facade, detail
13 Color design of the facade with Erich Wiesner 15 View from north-west

ST. BENNO-GYMNASIUM | ST. BENNO SECONDARY SCHOOL | 1992–1996

Die Farbgestaltung – vom Berliner Künstler Erich Wiesner konzipiert – und die Bewegtheit des Grundrisses haben sich in der Auseinandersetzung mit den Gegebenheiten entwickelt. Das Gebäude setzt sich in seinem Ergebnis von den eher stereotypen Elementen und den starren Ordnungen des Städtebaus der Umgebung ab. Frei von solchen Zwängen kann die Gestalt des Gebäudes sensibler auf Wünsche, Anforderungen und auch Ideale, die in der Regel vernachlässigt werden, reagieren.

The color design – conceived by Berlin artist Erich Wiesner – and the animated quality of the floor plan were developed via interaction with external preconditions. The result is a building that sets itself off from the rather stereotypical elements and stiff organisation of its urban surroundings. Freed from such constraints, the building's shape is capable of responding with sensitivity to desires, requirements and ideals, which are often neglected.

16

17

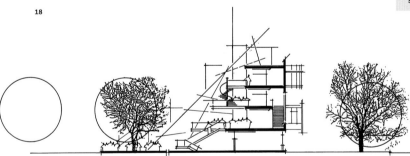18

19

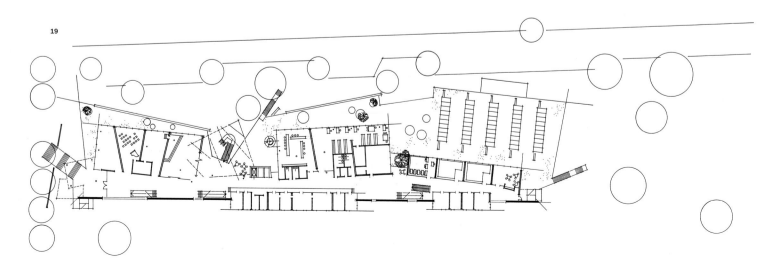

16, 17, 20 Pausenhalle   18 Schnitt Pausenhalle   19 Grundriss 1. Obergeschoss
16, 17, 20 Recreation hall   18 Section, recreation hall   19 Plan, 2nd floor

ST.BENNO·GYMNASIUM | ST.BENNO SECONDARY SCHOOL | 1992–1996

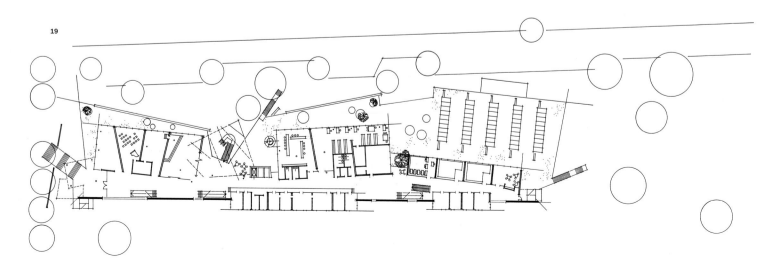

20

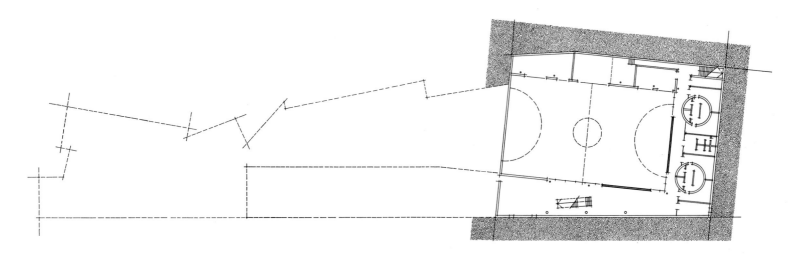

21

23

22

21 Grundriss Sporthalle **22** Blick aus der Cafeteria **23** Sporthalle **24, 25** Erdgeschoss: Blick in die Sporthalle **26** Schnitt Sporthalle | **21** Plan, sports hall **22** View from cafeteria **23** Sports hall **24, 25** Ground floor level: view into the sports hall **26** Sports hall, section

ST.BENNO-GYMNASIUM | **ST.BENNO SECONDARY SCHOOL** | 1992–1996

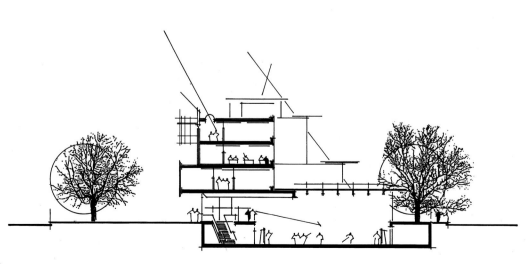

27

27 Eingänge zu den Klassenräumen im 3. Obergeschoss 28 Farbkonzept mit Erich Wiesner
29 Eingang zur Kapelle 30 Blick aus der Cafeteria 31 Klassenraum
27 Entrances to the 4th floor classrooms 28 Color concept with Erich Wiesner
29 Chapel, entrance 30 View from the cafeteria 31 Classroom

ST. BENNO-GYMNASIUM | ST. BENNO SECONDARY SCHOOL | 1992–1996

28

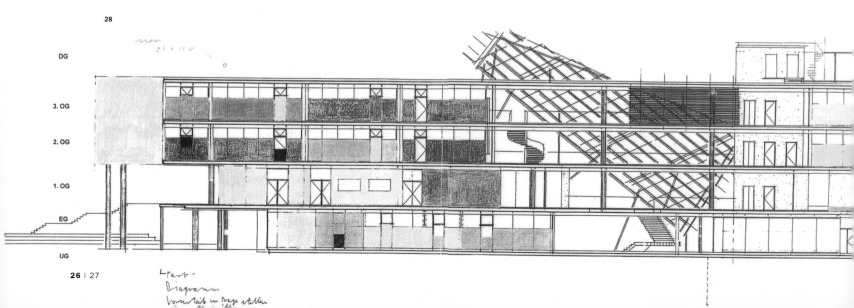

DG

3. OG

2. OG

1. OG

EG

UG

Einige Bemerkungen zur Gestalt des St. Benno-Gymnasium – Dresden

DAS FARBLICHE VERLANGEN

Jede Phase einer Entfaltung ist ein Aspekt des Ganzen unter den besonderen Bedingungen der Zeit und der Umstände. Konstellationen von farbigen Energiefeldern wirken multidimensional und können vielerlei Assoziationen wecken, je nach den individuellen Erfahrungen der Menschen, die ihnen begegnen. Während die Logik mit feststehenden Begriffen operiert, mit Begriffen, die wir durch unseren Intellekt von ihrem Hintergrund isolieren, haben Färbungen, die lebendige Eigenschaft, unmittelbare Verbindungen mit Menschen und Orten herzustellen. Ich habe fünf Wochen vor Ort gearbeitet. Dazu eine chassidische Legende:

Ein Sänger wurde gefragt:
»Für wen singst Du?«
»Ich singe immer einem Punkt zu.«
»Warum?«
»Ich mache das so lange, bis der Punkt zu mir singt.«
»Machst du das immer?«
»Ja, bis alle Punkte singen.«

Berlin, den 14. Oktober 1996, Erich Wiesner

◂

Remarks on the design of the St. Benno Secondary School, Dresden

THE NEED FOR COLOR

Each phase of a development is an aspect of the whole under the special conditions of a particular time and its given circumstances. Constellations of colored fields of energy are effective multi-dimensionally, and can awaken a variety of associations, depending upon the individual experiences of those encountering them. While logic operates by means of fixed concepts, isolated from their backgrounds by means of the intellect, colors possess the lively quality of establishing immediate connections between people and places. I worked on site for five weeks. This experience reminds me of a Hasidic legend:

A singer was asked:
"For whom do you sing?"
"I always sing toward a point."
"Why?"
"I do it until the point sings to me."
"Do you always do so?"
"Yes, until all of the points sing."

Berlin, 14 October 1996, Erich Wiesner

◂

32 Cafeteria 33 Treppe 34 Im 3. Obergeschoss 35 Treppenverbindungen 36 Kapelle 37 Tabernakel und Altar
38 Haupteingang und Verbindungstreppe 39 Bereich Wintergarten
32 Cafeteria 33 Stair 34 Interior, 4th floor 35 Connecting staircase 36 Chapel 37 Tabernacle and altar
38 Main entrance and connecting staircase 39 Area of the winter garden

ST. BENNO-GYMNASIUM | ST. BENNO SECONDARY SCHOOL | 1992–1996

36

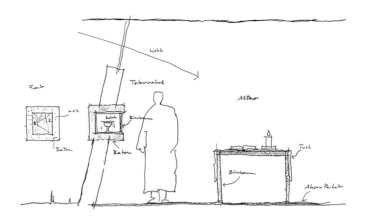

37

38

39

Architektonische Vielfalt   EXKURS 1

Architectural Multiplicity   DIGRESSION 1

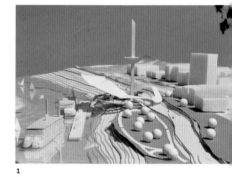

1

Viele architektonische Betrachtungen und Architekturen sind heute gültig. Man mag über Sinn und Unsinn einzelner Entwicklungen klagen, die Vielfalt an sich jedoch ist schon von großer Qualität, nicht nur in der Architektur. Vielfalt mit Beliebigkeit gleichzusetzen, scheint zur Zeit üblich zu sein. Dies ist falsch und ignorant, verkennt diese Betrachtung doch die Wurzeln der Vielfalt in den architektonischen Strömungen.

Im Büro Behnisch, Behnisch & Partner wird Vielfalt und Innovation gefördert. Allein die verschiedenen Interessen und Erfahrungen der Beteiligten führen zu immer neuen Ansätzen und Ideen.

2

3

4

5

Many views on architecture — and many architectures — are valid today. We may debate the reasonableness or absurdity of individual developments, but multiplicity alone is a quality, and not only in architecture. Multiplicity is often equated with arbitrariness. This is wrong and shortsighted; such attitudes ignore the sources of multiplicity in the various tendencies of contemporary architecture.

In the office of Behnisch, Behnisch & Partner, multiplicity and innovation are promoted. The divergent interests and experiences of the participants lead constantly to new ideas and points of departure.

Natürlich gibt es stets die Versuchung, sich auf das zu besinnen und zurückzuziehen, was man schon kennt. Dies führt jedoch zwangsläufig zum Wärmetod der Architektur, einem geistigen, kulturellen und auch physikalischen Endzustand.

Unsere modernen Kulturen entwickeln sich schnell weiter, sind lebendig und wandlungsfähig. Auch hier neigt das Alter natürlich dazu, alle neuen Entwicklungen erst einmal schlecht, unsittlich, auf Faulheit begründet, oder schlicht ungezogen zu finden. Sie werden zudem erstaunlicherweise fast ausschließlich der Jugend zugeschrieben. Das war schon vor Beginn unserer Zeitrechnung so, wie schriftliche und bildliche Zeugnisse belegen.

Unsere Kulturen werden von den Gegensätzen getragen, in der Sprache, der Kunst, der Literatur, den Moden und auch in der Architektur. Es gibt sicherlich keine Pflicht des allgemeinen Gefallens, jedoch die Pflicht zur Toleranz.

Die ehemalige DDR ist ein gutes Beispiel dafür, was geschieht, wenn eine Gesellschaft endlich einen kulturellen Konsens gefunden hat und diesen einfriert. Der ewige Charme der 60er Jahre blieb erhalten bis in die 90er Jahre. Vieles, was kulturell anspruchsvoller war, wurde als bourgeois angesehen. So ist es, wenn Kultur, politisch vorgegeben, über ethische Maßstäbe definiert ist, d.h. wenn ihr eben scheinbar allgemeingültige Kategorien oder auch nur Eigenschaften zugewiesen werden. Solch ein gesellschaftlicher Konsens ist kaum mehr aufkündbar, Beispiele hierfür gibt es in allen modernen Kulturen. Man muss

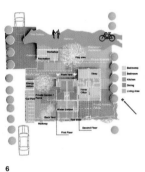

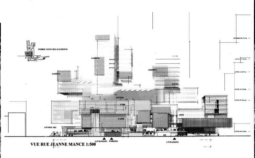

6 7 8 9

Of course, there is always the temptation to counsel caution and retreat to the already familiar. This leads inexorably to architectural entropy, to intellectual, cultural and even physical atrophy.

Our modern cultures continue to develop at high tempo, they are lively and versatile. Here too, old age automatically tends at first to stigmatise novelty as bad and ill-bred, the product of laziness, or simply as indecent. Astonishingly, it is attributed almost exclusively to the young. This was already the case before the beginning of the Christian epoch, as textual and sign evidence testifies.

Our cultures are propelled by contraries, in language, in art, in literature, in fashion and in architecture too. To be sure, no obligation to be appreciated by everyone exists, but certainly the obligation to cultivate tolerance is in order.

The former East Germany is a good example of what can happen when a society has finally discovered a cultural consensus and has frozen it into place. There, the eternal charm of the 1960s remained transfixed all the way into the 1990s. Much that was culturally demanding was regarded as bourgeois. So is the case when culture, accompanied by political pretensions, is defined according to ethical standards, that is to say, assigned to seemingly universally valid categories. Such a social consensus is most difficult to revoke; examples are to be found in all modern cultures. We must be aware of the fact that precisely this social consensus also excludes, other cultural manifestations are viewed by it as "non-culture." Architecture, as a part of everyday life, is caught up in this conception of culture. Architecture is defined in political terms and comes to embody certain political influences.

sich vergegenwärtigen, dass eben dieser gesellschaftliche Konsens auch ausgrenzt, andere kulturelle Erscheinungen sind dann »Unkultur«. So ist die Architektur als ein Teil unseres täglichen Lebens in diesem Kulturbegriff mit gefangen. Architektur wird politisch definiert, sie steht auch für bestimmte politische Einflüsse.

So wie wir uns eine vielfältige Kultur und Gesellschaft wünschen, so wünschen wir uns auch eine Architektur, die die Vielfalt unserer kulturellen Möglichkeiten auslotet, eben nicht beliebig, sondern wohl spielerisch, aber begründet und gezielt. Und so muss auch die Gruppe derjenigen, die bei uns im Büro an Architektur arbeitet, heterogen sein.

Eines der großen Privilegien, die einem die internationale Arbeit beschert, ist die Arbeit mit Ingenieuren, Beratern und Bauherrn aus vielen verschiedenen Ländern. Persönliche Bekanntschaften entwickeln sich, bis hin zu Freundschaften. Zudem kann man in Bereichen lernen, die einem im eigenen Kulturkreis verwehrt waren. Diese Orientierung nach außen wiederum erlaubt es, auch in der architektonischen Arbeit im Büro freier und innovativer zu sein. ◄

1 Anleger für Mississippi-Dampfer, Memphis, USA 2 Schweizer Landesmuseum, Zürich, Schweiz 3 Architektur-/Kunstobjekte am Aegidientorplatz, Hannover, Deutschland 4 Landeszentralbank, Chemnitz, Deutschland 5 Städtebaulicher Wettbewerb, Osaka, Japan 6 Wohnbau-Konzepte, Monterey, USA 7 Landesmesse, Stuttgart, Deutschland 8 Kultur- und Verwaltungszentrum, Montreal, Kanada 9 Schwimmhalle, Leipzig-Grünau, Deutschland 10 Sportanlagen, Singapur 11 Synagoge, Dresden, Deutschland 12 Messe, Hannover, Deutschland 13 Neue Elbbrücke, Dresden, Deutschland

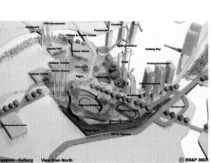

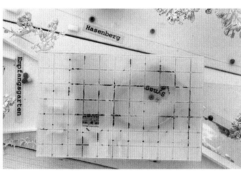

10   11   12   13

Just as we wish for a diverse culture and society, we also want to see an architecture that takes the measure of the diversity of our cultural potentialities. Not an architecture of the arbitrary, but instead one that is playful while also well-grounded and purposeful. And so too, the groups working on architecture in our office must be of heterogeneous composition.

One of the greatest privileges afforded by international work is the opportunity to collaborate with engineers, consultants and clients from many different countries. Personal acquaintanceships are developed, even friendships. Moreover, it is possible to gain knowledge in fields that might be closed in one's own cultural sphere. In the architectural work of this office, too, such an outward-directed orientation permits us to be freer and more innovative. ◄

1 Mississippi vessel landing, Memphis, USA 2 State Museum Switzerland, Zurich, Switzerland 3 Architectural/artistic objects at Aegidientorplatz, Hanover, Germany 4 Landeszentralbank, Chemnitz, Germany 5 Urban planning competition, Osaka, Japan 6 Concepts for residential housing, Monterey, USA 7 State trade fair, Stuttgart, Germany 8 Cultural and administrative complex, Montreal, Canada 9 Swimming pool complex, Leipzig-Grünau, Germany 10 Sports facility, Singapore 11 Synagogue, Dresden, Germany 12 Trade fair center, Hanover, Germany 13 New bridge over the Elbe River, Dresden, Germany

REALISIERUNG | REALISATION
NEUBAU | NEW DEVELOPMENT FOR THE
VEREINIGTE SPEZIALMÖBELFABRIKEN (VS)

BÜRO- UND AUSSTELLUNGSGEBÄUDE | OFFICE AND EXHIBITION BUILDING
TAUBERBISCHOFSHEIM, DEUTSCHLAND | TAUBERBISCHOFSHEIM, GERMANY; 1998

In Tauberbischofsheim an der Romantischen Straße, an der Grenze von Baden-Württemberg zu Bayern, wurden vor rund 100 Jahren die Vereinigten Spezialmöbelfabriken (VS) gegründet, zunächst zur Produktion von Schulmöbeln, später auch von Büromöbeln und -ausstattungen.

About a century ago, on the Romantische Straße in Tauberbischofsheim, on the border separating Baden-Württemberg from Bavaria, the "Vereinigte Spezial-möbelfabriken" (United Special Furniture Factories, or VS) were established, at first to produce school furnishings, and later for office furniture and furnishings as well.

1 Blick von Norden 2 Lageplan
1 North elevation 2 Site plan

VEREINIGTE SPEZIALMÖBELFABRIKEN (VS) | 1998

Die Firma VS hat in ihrer Geschichte immer schon Wert auf die Zusammenarbeit mit namhaften Gestaltern gelegt, sei es für die Entwicklung von Möbeln oder für die Errichtung von Produktionsstätten und Verwaltungsgebäuden. Anfang des 20. Jahrhunderts entstanden in enger Zusammenarbeit mit Richard Riemerschmied und Bruno Paul sowie dem Werkbund bei VS die ersten ganzheitlich ausgerichteten Schuleinrichtungen. Karl Nothelfer errichtete in den 50er Jahren neue Produktionsstätten und ein neues Verwaltungsgebäude in Tauberbischofsheim.

Throughout its history, the firm VS has always given priority to collaborations with reputed designers, whether for the development of furniture, or in setting up production facilities and administration buildings. At the start of the 20th century, in close collaboration with Richard Riemerschmied and Bruno Paul, as well as with the German Werkbund, the VS introduced the first integrated school furnishings. In the 1950s, Karl Nothelfer set up new production facilities and a new administration building in Tauberbischofsheim.

2

3

3 Haupteingang 4 Nordansicht 5 Südansicht
3 Main entrance 4 North elevation 5 South elevation

VEREINIGTE SPEZIALMÖBELFABRIKEN (VS) | 1998

5

Im Jahre 1987 entwickelten Behnisch & Partner in Zusammenarbeit mit VS für den Neubau der Leybold-Heraeus Werke in Alzenau einen neuartigen Schreibtisch. Der Entwurf entzieht sich bewusst einer rationalen Ordnung, er orientiert sich vielmehr an der Individualisierung des einzelnen Arbeitsplatzes und an der Eigenständigkeit der Mitarbeiter. Dieser Gedanke bildete den Ausgangspunkt für das Büromöbelsystem Serie 900.

Wunsch des Bauherrn war es, Mitarbeiter, deren Arbeitsplätze über das gesamte Firmengelände verteilt waren, in einem Gebäude zu versammeln. Der Bau sollte Platz für 100 Beschäftigte bieten, außerdem neue Ausstellungsflächen zur besseren Präsentation der Möbel, Konferenz- und Besprechungsräume sowie ein neues Restaurant beherbergen. Das neue Haus sollte einen Bezug zur Identität der Firma herstellen.

In 1987, in collaboration with VS, Behnisch & Partner developed an innovative writing desk for the new building of the Leybold-Heraeus Werke in Alzenau. The design consciously avoided any rational order, and was oriented instead to the individualisation of work stations and to employee autonomy. This consideration provided a point of departure for the development of the office furniture system, the Series 900.

The client wanted to assemble all employees, whose work stations were distributed throughout the extensive site, in one place. The new building was to provide space for 100 employees, in addition to new exhibition areas for improved display of furniture, rooms for conferences and meetings, and a restaurant. The new building was also to respond to and complement the company's corporate identity.

6

6 Am Löschteich 7 Blick von Süden 8 Restaurantterrasse 9 Schnitt
6 At the safety pond 7 View from the south 8 Restaurant terrace 9 Section

VEREINIGTE SPEZIALMÖBELFABRIKEN (VS) | 1998

7

8

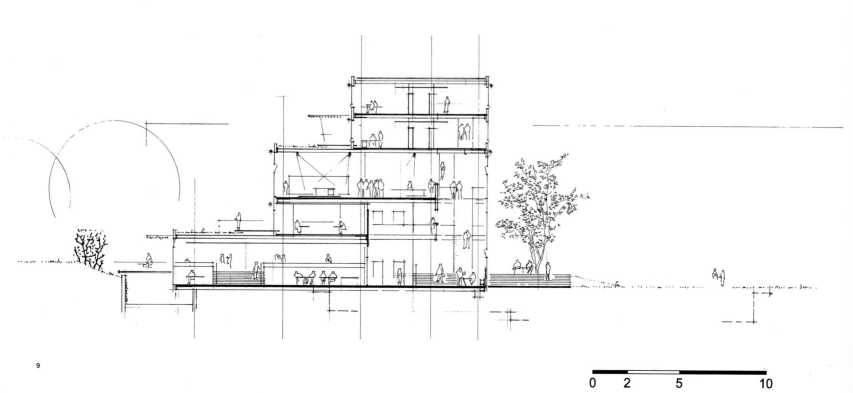

9

0   2   5   10

Der 110 m lange, klar und sachlich strukturierte Bau erstreckt sich zwischen zwei vorhandenen Gebäuden. Es entstand ein Hof, der später als Park ausgebaut werden soll, um somit die grüne Mitte der gesamten Anlage zu bilden. Das Gebäude überspannt, ähnlich einer Brücke, einen vorhandenen Löschteich. Nach Norden, zum Hof, erscheint es glatt und flächig, es bildet einen Rücken zu den Werkshallen und zum Park. Nach Süden, zu den dort angrenzenden kleineren Einfamilienhäusern und Wohngärten, wird die Gebäudemasse aufgelöst: Hier wurde der Baukörper terrassiert und erscheint dadurch kleinteiliger gegliedert. Das Grün der Gärten geht über in das Grün der Terrassen. Farbflächen an den dortigen Fassaden unterstützen diese Beziehung und erzeugen eine eher heitere und lässige Atmosphäre. Die Fassade zum Hof dagegen erscheint formeller und sachlicher. Eine mäandernde weiße Fläche, nach formalen Gesetzmäßigkeiten entwickelt,

The 110-meter-long clearly structured building stretches between two existing buildings. This arrangement produces a courtyard, to be developed later as the complex's green center. The building, somewhat like a bridge, spans a preexisting safety pond. To the north, toward the courtyard, it appears smooth and planar, offering a backbone to the workshops and park. Toward the south, where it faces toward adjacent smaller single-family homes and household gardens, the building's mass is broken down: terraces contribute to a more finely articulated appearance. Now the green of the garden flows onto the terraces. Colored surfaces on the facades emphasise this relationship, producing a cheerful, relaxed atmosphere. In contrast, the facade looking onto the courtyard appears more formal and neutral. A meandering white surface, developed according to the dictates of formal criteria, shapes the image of the north facade. The functional grid of the office

10

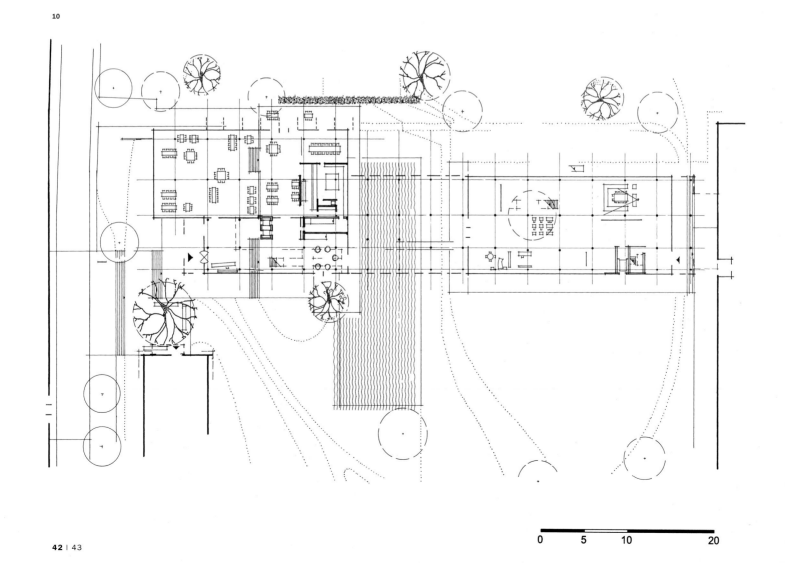

0   5   10   20

10 Grundriss Erdgeschoss 11–12 Mitarbeiterrestaurant
10 Plan, ground floor 11–12 Staff restaurant

VEREINIGTE SPEZIALMÖBELFABRIKEN (VS) | 1998

13 Eingangsbereich mit Empfang 14 Zwischengeschoss 15 1. Obergeschoss 16 Längsschnitt
13 Entrance area with reception 14 Mezzanine 15 2nd floor 16 Longitudinal section

VEREINIGTE SPEZIALMÖBELFABRIKEN (VS) | 1998

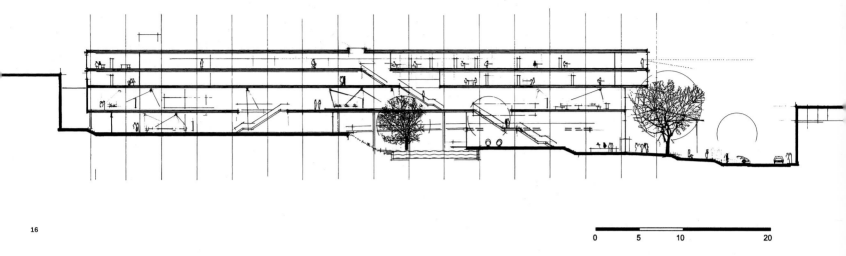

0   5   10   20

bestimmt das Bild der Nord-Fassade. Die
funktionale Ordnung, das Raster der Bürofassade, wird überspielt und formal überhöht. Es ensteht ein eigenständiges Bild,
welches sich scheinbar unabhängig von
den räumlichen und funktionalen Nutzungen
entwickelt.

Das Gebäude wird von der östlich verlaufenden Hochhäuser-Straße erschlossen. Ein
neuer großzügiger Vorplatz ist entstanden,
der auch die Verknüpfung zum bestehenden
Verwaltungsgebäude herstellt. An der Eingangshalle liegen der Empfang, das Mitarbei-
ter-Restaurant und Wartebereiche. Von der
Eingangshalle aus öffnet sich ein Blick durch
alle Geschosse und Bereiche des Hauses.
Offene Treppen führen auf die Galerieebene
mit den Konferenzbereichen, in die Ausstellungshalle im 1. Obergeschoss, sowie in die
Bürobereiche im 3. und 4. Obergeschoss.
Der offene Charakter stärkt die interne Kommunikation zwischen den Mitarbeitern. Es
war dem Bauherrn ein Anliegen, dass jeder
Mitarbeiter zwanglos mit der zentralen Aus-
stellungsfläche in Kontakt treten kann,
um eine intensive Auseinandersetzung mit
den einzelnen Produkten, aber auch die
Identifikation mit der Firma zu fördern. Die
Ausstellung ist für VS von übergeordneter
Bedeutung, da die Firma ihre Möbel ausschließlich direkt vertreibt.

facades is disguised and formally surpassed.
The result is an independent image, one
developing apparently unconstrained by
spatial and functional imperatives.

Access to the building is from Hochhäuser
Straße, running to the east. There is a
spacious new forecourt that provides a connection to the existing administration
building. Located at the entrance hall are
the reception area, staff restaurant and
waiting areas. From the entrance hall the
visitor is afforded a view up through the
entire height of the building. Open staircases lead to the gallery level with its conference areas; to the exhibition hall in
the second floor; and to the 3rd and 4th
level offices. Internal communication
between staff members is fostered by this
open character. The client made a point
of granting each employee unconstrained
access to the central exhibition area, allowing an intensive contact with individual
products while promoting the firm's identity. For the VS, the exhibition remains
of paramount importance, since the firm
markets its own furniture directly.

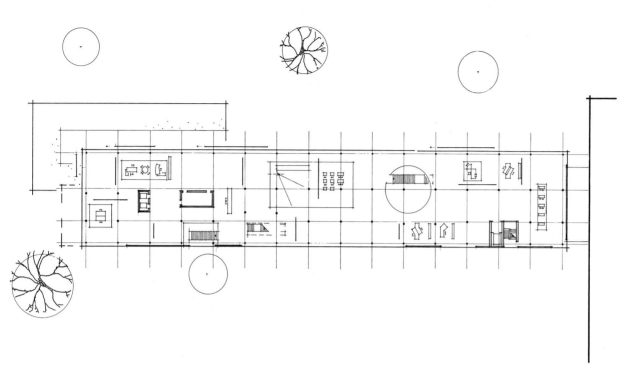

17

18   19

17 Grundriss 1. Obergeschoss 18 Konferenzraum 19, 20 Ausstellungsebene 1. Obergeschoss
17 Plan of 2nd floor 18 Conference room 19, 20 Exhibition level, 2nd floor

VEREINIGTE SPEZIALMÖBELFABRIKEN (VS) | 1998

Die ca. 3000 m² große, auf zwei Geschossen verteilte Ausstellungshalle ist formal zurückhaltend bearbeitet, sie erinnert an eine Werkstatt. So kann das sorgfältig und fein gearbeitete Mobiliar in den Vordergrund treten und sich frei entfalten. ◄

The approx. 3,000m² exhibition hall, extending over two stories, is formally restrained in appearance, and recalls a workshop. This allows the finely manufactured products to be taken to the center stage. ◄

21

21 2. Obergeschoss 22 Sekretariat des Vorstands 23, 24 Büroarbeitsplätze
25 Grundriss 2. Obergeschoss | 21 Office level, 3rd floor 22 Executive secretariat
23, 24 Work stations 25 Plan, 3rd floor

VEREINIGTE SPEZIALMÖBELFABRIKEN (VS) | 1998

24

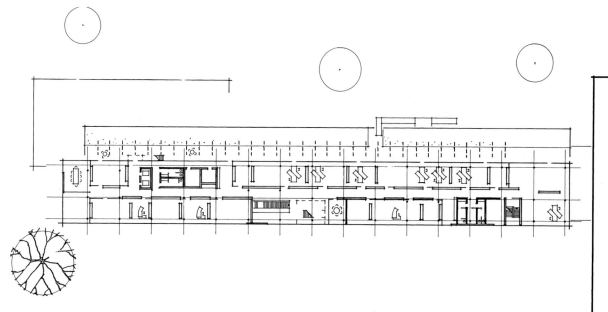

25

Der ursprüngliche Entwurf für das Museum
der Phantasie sah den Standort in Feldafing
westlich des Starnberger Sees vor. Wir meinten, an jenem Ort hätte sich die Sammlung
Buchheim in der Art, in der sie dort stets
gelebt hat, weiterentwickeln können. Teile
der Sammlung hätten in der vorhandenen
Maffai-Villa, andere in den Eigenbau-Pavillons
gezeigt werden können; und nur für diejenigen Teile, die in den vorhandenen Gebäuden
keinen bzw. einen nicht angemessenen Platz

The original design for the Museum of
Fantasy foresaw a location in Feldafing on
the western side of Lake Starnberg. We
believed that there, the Buchheim collection could have been further developed
where it has always resided. Parts of the
collection could have been displayed in the
existing Villa Maffai; others in self-con-
struction-pavilions; only parts of the
collection that could not be housed in the
available buildings, at least not suitably

WETTBEWERB UND REALISIERUNG | COMPETITION AND REALISATION

MUSEUM DER PHANTASIE, SAMMLUNG BUCHHEIM
MUSEUM OF FANTASY, BUCHHEIM COLLECTION

BERNRIED AM STARNBERGER SEE, DEUTSCHLAND |
BERNRIED AT LAKE STARNBERG, GERMANY; 1996–2001

hätten finden können, wären Neubauten geschaffen worden. Die vorhandenen Bauten mit ihren Gärten hätten ihren Charakter behalten und wären lediglich der neuen Situation angepasst worden. Die neuen Bauten dagegen wären modern gewesen. Das Museum Buchheim wäre eingestimmt auf die örtliche Situation, in Jahrzehnten gewachsen, vielleicht auch durch Zufälle mitbestimmt gewesen – in jedem Falle nicht ausschließlich durch Museumstechnik definiert und auch nicht betont modern. Das Museum hätte zwischen den Villengrundstücken gelegen, es hätte entdeckt werden müssen und sich nicht in den Vordergrund gedrängt. So wäre die Anlage vielfältig verknüpft mit Ort, Zeit und Aufgabe gewesen.

would have been provided with new structures. The existing buildings with their gardens would have retained their character, and would simply have been adapted to the new arrangement. The new buildings, on the other hand, would have been contemporary. The Museum Buchheim would have been attuned to the physical situation, growing up over a period of decades, perhaps also influenced by happenstance – in any event, not defined exclusively by museum technology, nor emphatically modern. The museum would have been inserted between the plots of the villas, requiring their active discovery, and hence hardly propelling itself into the foreground. The complex, thus, would have been linked in diverse ways with locale, time and the task at hand.

1

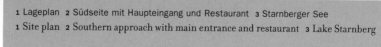

1 Lageplan 2 Südseite mit Haupteingang und Restaurant 3 Starnberger See
1 Site plan 2 Southern approach with main entrance and restaurant 3 Lake Starnberg

MUSEUM DER PHANTASIE | MUSEUM OF FANTASY | 1996–2001

4 Ansicht Süd-Ost 6 Grundriss Eingangsebene
4 South-east elevation 6 Plan, entrance level

MUSEUM DER PHANTASIE | MUSEUM OF FANTASY | 1996–2001

Das war das Ideal. Letztlich sind auf Grund eines Bürgerentscheids die Neubauten jedoch nicht in Feldafing, sondern in Bernried entstanden, wenige Kilometer entfernt. Das neu zu Bauende löste sich dadurch stärker aus dem Kontext, in dem die Sammlung davor stand.

Vom Grundstück, aber auch von der inneren Ordnung her bot sich eine Anlage mit einem »Rückgrat« an, an dem alle Bereiche liegen sollten. Diese Art der Ordnung gibt die angelagerten Elemente frei für ihre eigene Aufgabe, Ausformung und Gestalt. So können sich die Räume für Wechselausstellungen, Gemälde und Grafiken nördlich des Rückgrats großflächig entwickeln, gut belichtbar und flexibel unterteilbar. Südlich des »Rückgrats« ist die Situation offener. Hier liegen der »Raritäten-/

That was the ideal. In the end, a local community decision determined that the new buildings would be realised not in Feldafing, but in Bernried, just a few kilometers away. The planned construction, hence, was strongly detached from the context where the collection had formerly stood.

In response to the new site, but also in terms of the internal organisation, a "spine" appeared to be the most appropriate solution, along which all the different departments were aligned. This type of organisation permitted to the various elements the freedom to develop their own tasks, arrangements and respective formal criteria. The rooms for temporary exhibitions, paintings and graphics could spread themselves

4

5

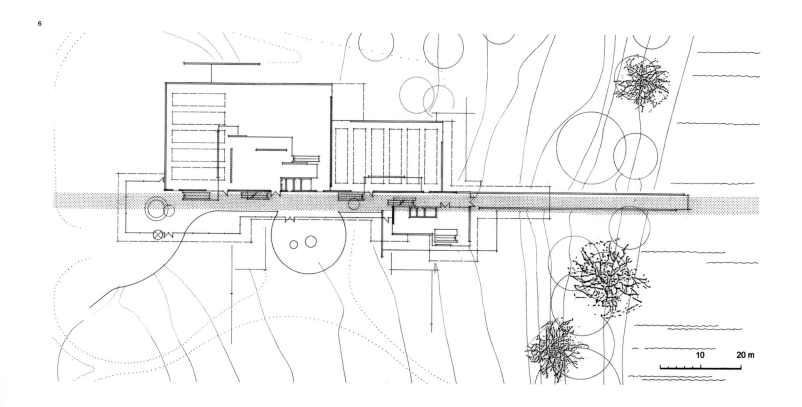

6

10   20 m

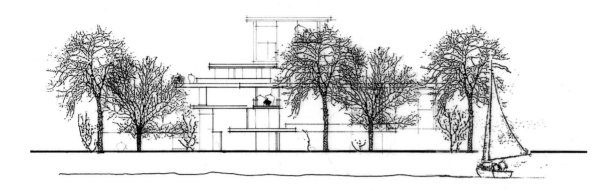

7

8

Volkskundeteil«, die »Buchheim-Welt« und im Erdgeschoss das Café. Nach oben, sozusagen aus dem Rückgrat heraus, wachsen zwei »Villen« mit kleineren, privateren Ausstellungsräumen.

Die das Museum umgebende Landschaft ist schön und eindrucksvoll, allein sie lohnt den Besuch des Ortes. Wenn in solcher Situation gebaut werden kann, dann sollte man diese Landschaft mit einbeziehen. Dies hat dazu geführt, dass sich Terrassen und Stege aus dem Inneren des Museums nach außen in die Landschaft schieben. Von vielen Situationen aus kann man die Landschaft sehen und oft auch hineingehen.

across extensive areas to the north of the "spine," well-illuminated and both flexible and easily divisible. To the south of the "spine," the arrangement is more open. Here lie the departments of "rarities and folklore," the "Buchheim World," and the café on the ground level. Above — growing, so to speak, out of the "spine" — are a pair of "villas" containing smaller, more intimate galleries.

The landscape surrounding the museum is strikingly beautiful, and alone justifies a visit to the area. When any new building form is introduced into such a setting, the landscape should be integrated into the plans. This consideration led to the decision to have terraces and footbridges emerge from the museum's interior and extend out into the landscape. At numerous points throughout the interior the landscape is clearly visible, and often accessible as well.

9

7 Ansicht vom See 8, 9 Restaurant 10 Ansicht Süd-Ost
7 Elevation to lake 8, 9 Restaurant 10 South-east elevation

MUSEUM DER PHANTASIE | MUSEUM OF FANTASY | 1996–2001

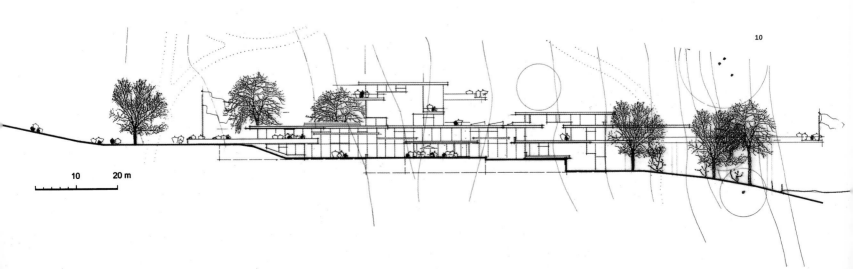

10   20 m

11

12

11, 12, 14 Steg über dem See   13 Längsschnitt   15 Starnberger See
11, 12, 14 Pier out over the lake   13 Longitudinal section   15 Lake Starnberg

MUSEUM DER PHANTASIE | MUSEUM OF FANTASY | 1996–2001

13

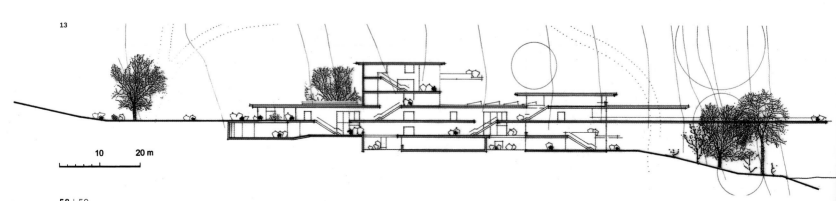

10   20 m

Die Übergänge von einem Teil des Museums zum anderen – z.B. von der Gemälde- und Grafiksammlung zum Raritätenteil – sind fließend. Man kann kurze und längere Rundgänge wählen oder sich frei und wie zufällig durch das Museum bewegen. Möglichst wenig soll vorbestimmt sein.

Der Bereich »Buchheim-Welt« wird in das Gesamtkonzept eingefügt, ist Teil der Anlage. Ziel ist, diesen auf die Person bezogenen Bereich nicht isoliert, sondern im Zusammenhang mit den anderen Teilen des »Kunst-Lebens«, den Sammlungen der Expressionisten und der Raritäten zu sehen.

Transitions from one part of the museum to the next – for example, from the collection of paintings and graphics to the one devoted to the rarities – are fluid. Both longer and shorter itineraries are possible. Visitors may simply explore the museum freely and spontaneously. As little as possible is preprogrammed.

The department "Buchheim World," to be integrated into the total concept, is one part of the complex. Here, the goal was not to isolate this department, centered around a single individual, but to show it in relationship to the other elements of the "life of art," to the Expressionist collections, and also to the rarities.

16 Eingangsebene 17 Ausstellungsbereich Volkskunst 18 Treppe Ausstellungsbereich »Buchheims Welt« | 16 Entrance level 17 Exhibition area, folk art 18 Stair, Exhibition area "Buchheims Welt"

MUSEUM DER PHANTASIE | MUSEUM OF FANTASY | 1996–2001

Das Materielle ist zurückhaltend. Licht, Raumbeziehungen, Bäume, See, individuelle Situationen für Exponate und Besucher stehen im Vordergrund.

Sicher gibt es grundsätzlich verschiedene Ansätze, sich der Entwicklung eines Museumsbaus zu nähern. Letztendlich hängt dies von vielen Faktoren ab, unter anderem von der Art der Aufgabe, den Exponaten, der Umgebung und vielem mehr. In der Vergangenheit wurden herausragende Museumsbauten

The palette of materials employed is deliberately restrained. Instead, light, the sequences of spatial relationships, the surrounding trees, the lake, individual displays and the visitors themselves are allowed to occupy the foreground.

Without doubt, there exist divergent points of departure from which to approach the design of a museum. In the end, decisions are dependent upon many factors, ranging from the nature of the tasks to be fulfilled

19

20

21

19, 23 Ausstellungsbereich Expressionisten 20, 21 Volkskunst und Raritäten 22 Grundriss Untergeschoss | 19, 23 Exhibition area, Expressionism 20, 21 Folk art and rare objects 22 Plan, basement level

MUSEUM DER PHANTASIE | MUSEUM OF FANTASY | 1996–2001

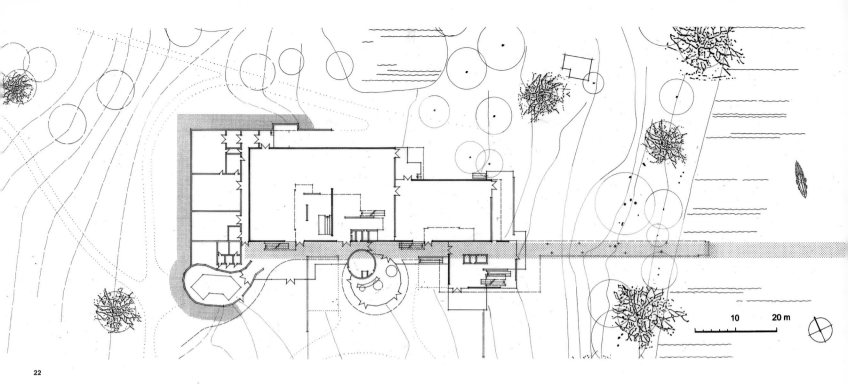

geschaffen, die, formal sehr eigenständig, allein durch ihre Architektur zur Attraktion wurden. Wir meinten, das Museum der Phantasie sollte eher sorgfältig aus seinem Inhalt heraus und aus seiner Beziehung zum Ort entwickelt werden. Es sollte kein Repräsentationstempel entstehen und keine Anlage, die ausschließlich konservatorischen und museumsdidaktischen Anforderungen genügt. Ein Museum sollte geschaffen werden, in dem Volkskunst, hohe Kunst und das Werk Buchheims gleichberechtigt nebeneinander stehen können, eingebettet in und verwoben mit der prächtigen Landschaft am Starnberger See. ◄

to the objects to be displayed, the surroundings, and many other elements. In the past, outstanding museum buildings have been produced which were formally autonomous, and which became attractions solely by virtue of their architectural qualities. We believed that the Museum of Fantasy should instead evolve slowly out of both the various contents and its relationship to its physical setting. The result was to be not an imposing temple, nor a complex serving exclusively conservation or museum-related didactic requirements. The objective was rather a museum in which folk art, high art and Buchheim's work could stand together on equal terms, embedded in and woven into the splendid landscape around Lake Starnberg. ◄

1 Wettbewerbsmodell | 1 Competition model

FREIBAD | OPEN-AIR SWIMMING POOL COMPLEX | 1997

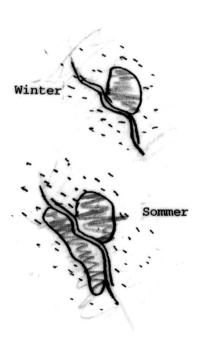

Winter

Sommer

Das Grundstück liegt in der Bachaue des Bogenbaches in einem öffentlichen Park. Das Grün der Bäume und Wiesen, die typische Topographie und die öffentlichen Wege entlang des Baches bleiben erhalten und werden dort wieder hergestellt, wo in der Vergangenheit schwächende Eingriffe stattgefunden haben. Diese Landschaft begleitet den Bach bis zur Mündung in die Donau. Das Schwimmbad bildet einen markanten Ort in der Bachlandschaft, die Aue öffnet sich dort zum Park hin.

Die freie Komposition des Schwimmbades nimmt die natürliche Ordnung des Parks auf, überlagert und bereichert sie, ohne den

The site lies in a public park, in a meadow beside a stream called "Bogenbach". The green of the trees and the meadow, the characteristic topography and the public paths along the stream were to be retained, and will moreover be restored at points that have been subject to debilitating past interventions. The landscape follows the stream right up to its confluence with the Danube. The swimming pool is an attraction within the landscape.

The freely composed design responds to the natural arrangement of the park, overlaying and enriching it without disturbing the natural setting. The pool's character is

Naturraum zu stören. Der Charakter des Bades soll leicht, heiter und offen sein, die Bäume, Wiesen und Wege bleiben erhalten. Sie bilden mit der Topographie und dem Bach die weitläufigen natürlichen Räume. Im Bereich des Freibades sind die natürlichen Räume und Wege differenzierter ausgebildet und durch architektonische Elemente, Kunst und gestaltetes Grün bereichert. Die gebauten Bereiche sind formal eher mit dem Park verbunden, als mit der gebauten Stadt. Die Elemente der Komposition liegen frei im Park, so zum Beispiel der Eingang, die Wärmehalle, der Gastraum, der Steg, die Becken etc.

one of lightness, cheerfulness and openness, trees, meadow and paths are preserved. Together with the stream and the topography, they form a series of natural open spaces. In the area of the pool, spaces and paths are formed in distinct ways, enriched by architectural elements, works of art and treatment of the landscape. Formally, the required buildings are linked to the park, rather than to the built town. They exist as elements of a composition lying freely within the park, for example, the entrance, warm-up hall, guestroom, footbridge, the pools, etc.

die Blume

Der Eingang befindet sich unweit der neuen Brücke über den Bogenbach. Der gebaute Schwerpunkt des Schwimmbades mit der Badeplatte, den Umkleideräumen und Sonnenterrassen befindet sich konzentriert an der Stelle ehemaliger Tennisplätze. Die freie Struktur fügt sich in das Grün ein, und die Funktionen stören die Umgebung wenig. Der Anteil der versiegelten Flächen bleibt gering. Die Gastterrasse liegt in der Nähe des schattigen Kinderspielplatzes, die Liegewiese schließt westlich der Badeplatte an. Sie ist durch Blumenbeete und geschnittene Hecken von dieser getrennt, liegt im Bereich der Bachwiesen und ist im Winter, wenn das Bad geschlossen ist, öffentlich zugänglich.

Ein öffentlicher Steg durchquert das im Sommer eingegrenzte Grundstück und ordnet die Bereiche des Bades in Badeplatte und Liegewiese. Der Steg lässt die Bäume, die Landschaft und das Bad von einer neuen Perspektive aus erleben. Der Steg dient bei Regen als Unterstand, darunter befinden sich die Umkleideräume und die Abgrenzung zur Liegewiese, teilweise als Schallschutzwand ausgebildet.

Die Konstruktionen und Dächer des Bades sind aus dem formbaren Material Beton hergestellt. Nicht das Material, sondern die Farben und Oberflächen, die Einbauten aus Holz und Glas, die Verkleidungen etc. stehen im Vordergrund. ◄

The entrance lies not far from the new bridge above the Bogenbach. The focal point of the swimming pool complex with its bathing platform, changing rooms and sun terraces is concentrated on the site of the former tennis courts. The free form integrates itself into the landscape, disturbing the surroundings very little. The proportion of hard-surfaced area remains small. The guest terrace is near the shaded children's playground; the sunbathing lawn borders the bathing platform to the west. The lawn, separated from the latter by flowerbeds and trimmed hedges, lies in the area of the meadow and is publicly accessible in wintertime, when the pool is closed.

A public footpath traverses the pool complex, enclosed in summertime, and formally divides the area of the pool into bathing platform and the sunbathing lawn. The footbridge allows the trees, landscape and pool to be experienced from a new perspective. It serves as a shelter against the rain, marks the boundary of the sunbathing lawn and to some degree acts as a noise barrier. Beneath it are located the changing rooms.

The pool's structures and roofs are of a malleable material, concrete. Not the material itself, but the applied colors and surfaces, the built-in features of wood and glass, the facings, etc. occupy the foreground. ◄

2

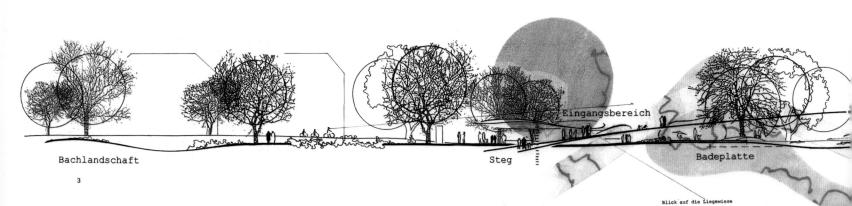

Bachlandschaft

Eingangsbereich

Steg

Badeplatte

Blick auf die Liegewiese

3

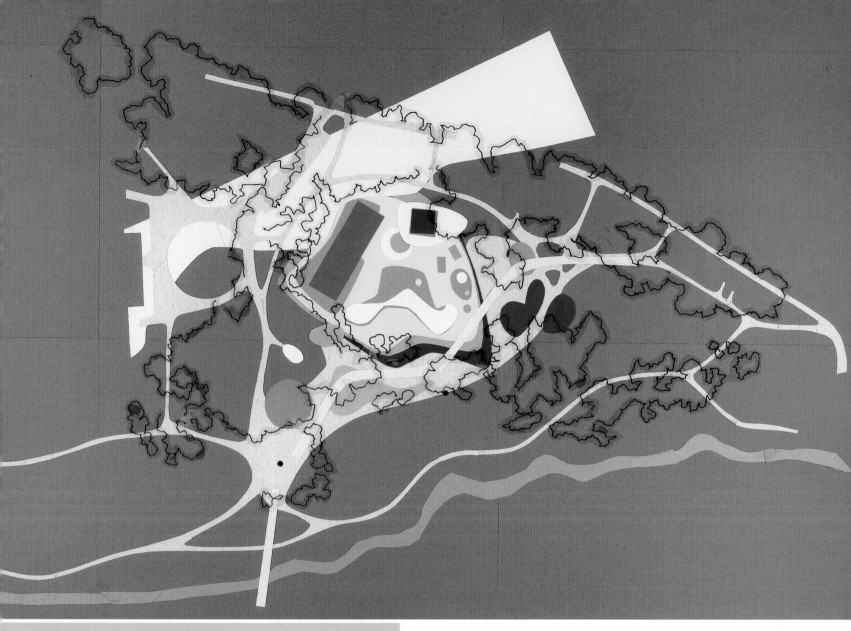

2 Wettbewerbsmodell 3 Schnitt 4 Lageplan
2 Competition model 3 Section 4 Site plan

FREIBAD | OPEN-AIR SWIMMING POOL COMPLEX | 1997

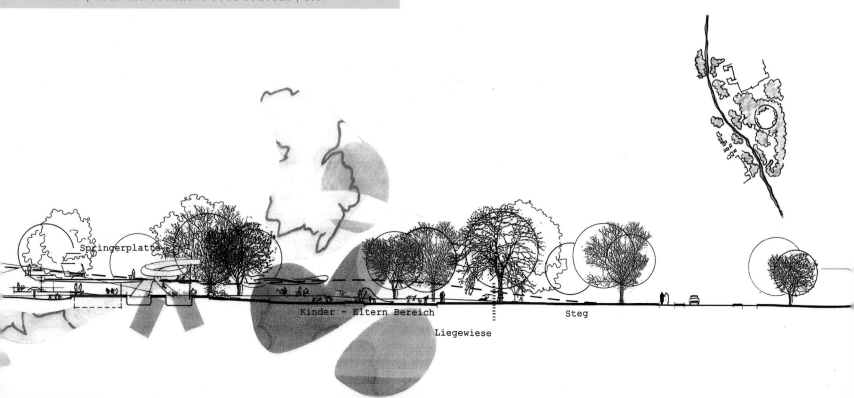

Springerplatte

Kinder – Eltern Bereich   Steg

Liegewiese

Wettbewerbe EXKURS 2

Competitions DIGRESSION 2

1

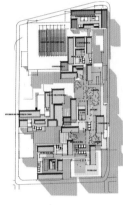

2

Wettbewerbe sind die Grundlage unserer Arbeit. Sie stehen am Beginn eines jeden Projektes, da wir nahezu alle unsere Aufträge über Architektenwettbewerbe erhalten. Wir haben die Erfahrung gemacht, dass die kontinuierliche Bearbeitung von Wettbewerben für uns und unser Büro von großer Bedeutung ist, und zwar nicht nur als Mittel zur Akquisition.

Jede Wettbewerbsaufgabe stellt in vielerlei Hinsicht eine neue Herausforderung dar. Sie zwingt einen dazu, sich mit aktuellen Themen der Architektur auseinander zusetzen und die Position immer wieder zu hinterfragen und neu zu bestimmen. Sie gibt uns aber auch die Möglichkeit, auf Entdeckungsreise zu gehen, gewissermaßen

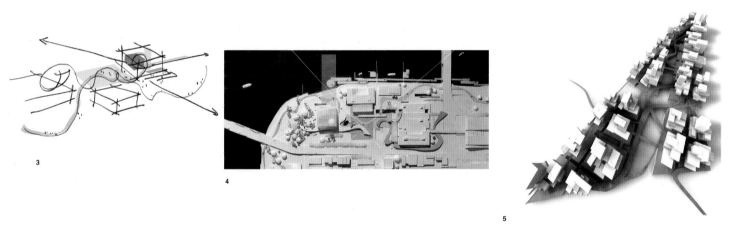

3

4

5

Competition work provides the basis of all our activities. It stands at the beginning of every project, for we receive virtually all of our commissions via competitions. In our experience, the continual preparation of competition proposals has been of great importance for the firm, and not only as a means of obtaining commissions.

In many respects, every competition contribution is a new challenge. It compels us to come to terms with contemporary themes in architecture, and to continually interrogate and redefine our own position. It also offers us an opportunity to embark on a journey of discovery, to engage in a certain amount of research, liberated

Forschung zu betreiben, noch frei von den Zwängen des praktischen Bauens. Die Arbeit in diesem frühen Stadium kann sich folglich freier entwickeln, da der Einfluss von außen noch gering ist.

Wir lernen dabei auch, unsere am Anfang eines Prozesses vielleicht noch eher vagen Gedanken und Ideen am Ende scharf und präzise zu formulieren. Die Schlüsselthemen, das Wesentliche eines Entwurfes, müssen klar und eindeutig herausgearbeitet und präsentiert werden, ähnlich einer Karikatur.

Möglichst verschiedene Konzepte werden zunächst »objektiv« entwickelt und untersucht. Die Konzepte werden diskutiert, so dass Impulse für Neues entstehen können. Das Besondere ist uns dabei näher als das Allgemeine. Konzepte werden entwickelt und wieder verworfen,

was zuerst richtig erschien, mag sich später als falsch erweisen. Neue Ideen müssen erarbeitet werden, ein kontinuierlich ablaufender Prozess setzt sich in Gang, bis zum Schluss.

Je stärker die Idee, bzw. je klarer das Konzept, desto leichter kann es sich später entwickeln, und desto eher ist es in der Lage, sich den zunehmenden praktischen Anforderungen von außen anzupassen, auf diese einzugehen oder auch ihnen zu widerstehen. Nach unserer Erfahrung sind bei dieser Arbeitsweise architektonische Konzepte aus Entwürfen, die im Wettbewerb nicht erfolgreich waren, keineswegs zwangsläufig verloren. Scheinbar zufällig kommen sie später wieder zum Vorschein, verschwinden erneut, bis irgendwann, oft zu einem späteren Zeitpunkt, eine Umsetzung in einem Projekt möglich wird, in ähnlicher oder weiterentwickelter Form.

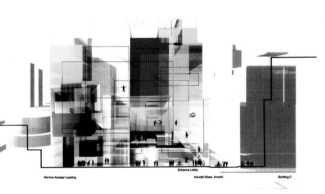

6

7

8

from the constraints of practical building. As a consequence, work in these early stages may develop more freely in the relative absence of external influences.

We also learn to clearly formulate our thoughts and ideas – often relatively vague at the beginning of the process – more sharply and precisely. Here, the key theme, the essential aspect of a design, must be explicitly and unambiguously elaborated and presented, almost in the spirit of a caricature.

To begin with, various deliberately different concepts are "objectively" developed and investigated. Concepts are discussed, so that an atmosphere promoting innovation is created. Here, the emphasis is on the particular, not the general. Concepts are developed in

parallel, and discarded when, what seemed correct at first, turned out to be false. New ideas are elaborated, a process which gathers momentum all the way to its conclusion, the submission.

The more powerful an idea, the clearer the concept, the more easily it can develop later on, and the greater its capacity to conform to the growing practical demands imposed from without, to work around them, or to resist them. Our experience with this approach to competition work demonstrates that architectural concepts related to designs that fail to win competitions are by no means necessarily futile. Apparently by happenstance, they occasionally reemerge, only to vanish again, until at some point, often only much later, their practical realisation in a project becomes possible, in a similar or subsequently developed form.

Ein gutes Beispiel dafür ist das Hochhaus, nicht als klassische, in den Himmel strebende Nadel, sondern als vielfältige vertikale Stadtlandschaft, als freie Skulptur. An diesem Thema haben wir über einen Zeitraum von gut zehn Jahren mit unterschiedlichem Erfolg während der Wettbewerbe für die Landesgirokasse am Hoppenlau-Friedhof in Stuttgart, die National- und Provinzialarchive in Kopenhagen, das Hochhaus MAX in Frankfurt und an weiteren Entwürfen experimentiert. In Hannover, beim Neubau für die Nord/LB, konnte dieses Konzept schließlich umgesetzt werden, ebenso im Genzyme Center in Cambridge in abgewandelter Form, mit einem Atrium, das sich innerhalb eines nach außen eher stringenten Kubus' frei entwickelt. In einer anderen Arbeitsform wären derartige Entwicklungen kaum möglich gewesen. ◂

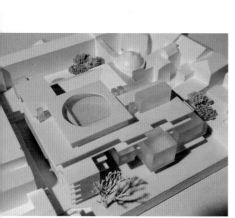

9

10

11

A good example of this is the high-rise, conceived not in classical terms, as a needle striving toward the heavens, but instead as a manifold vertical urban landscape, as a free sculpture, so to speak. We have experimented with this theme, with various degrees of success, for more than ten years, during competition work for the State Clearing Bank at Hoppenlau Cemetery in Stuttgart, the National and Provincial Archives in Copenhagen, the MAX High-rise in Frankfurt, and various other designs. In Hanover, with the new construction for the North German State Clearing Bank, this concept could finally be realised, as at the Genzyme Center in Cambridge, in modified form, with an atrium unfolding freely within a cube whose outward appearance is one of stringency. With other working methods such developments would hardly have been possible. ◂

1 Wettbewerbsmodell Detailansicht 2 Lageplan
1 Competition model, detail view 2 Site plan

INSTITUT FÜR TELEKOMMUNIKATION |
INSTITUTE OF TELECOMMUNICATIONS | 1995

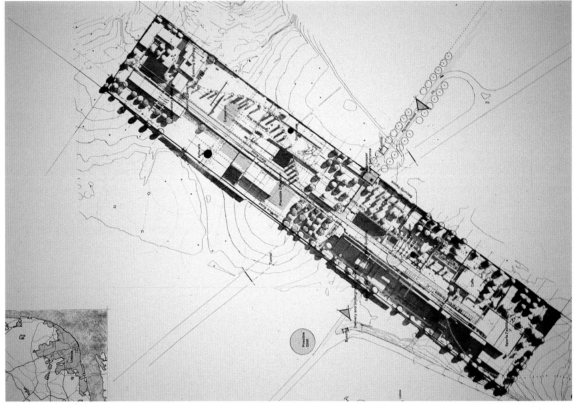

2

INSTITUT FÜR TELEKOMMUNIKATION VON PORTUGAL (ICP)

INSTITUTE OF TELECOMMUNICATIONS OF PORTUGAL (ICP)

BARCARENA, PORTUGAL; 1995

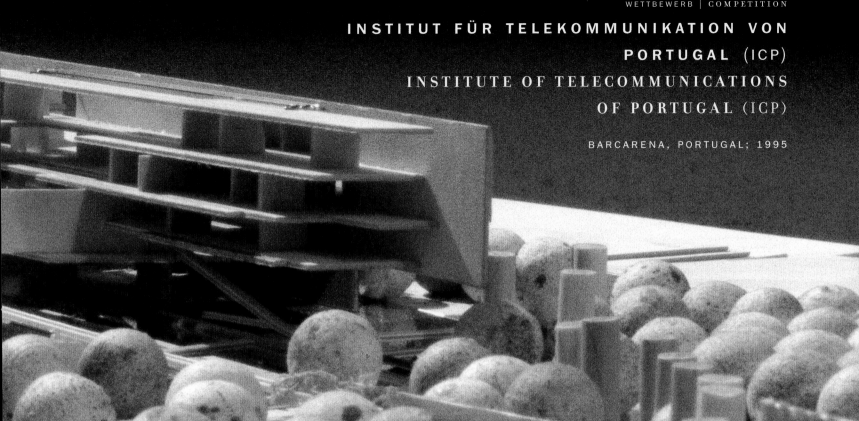

Das ICP in Portugal ist die für die Vergabe von Funkfrequenzen zuständige staatliche Behörde. Es galt, für dieses Institut neue Büro- und Laborgebäude zu planen. Zuvor war die Behörde in Lissabon angesiedelt. Die Mitarbeiter genossen die Attraktionen einer lebendigen Großstadt. Der neue Standort, sollte außerhalb der Stadt liegen. Man entschied sich für ein Areal in der Nähe von Barcarena, auf dem Lande.

Die neu zu planende Anlage sollte Attraktionen bieten, die jene des vorherigen Standortes kompensieren. Es war gewünscht, nicht nur Raum für Arbeit zur Verfügung zu stellen, vielmehr sollten auch andere Bedürfnisse des täglichen Lebens, wie Sport und Freizeitaktivitäten, Erfüllung finden.

The ICP in Portugal is the state agency responsible for awarding radio frequency licences. The task was to design a new office and laboratory building for the institute. The agency had resided before in Lisbon, where employees had enjoyed the attractions of a lively metropolis. The new location was to lie outside of town, and a rural site near Barcarena was chosen.

The complex to be planned needed to offer attractions capable of compensating for those offered by the former setting. It was the client's wish to provide more than just workspace: other demands of daily life, such as sport and leisure activities, had to be satisfied.

Der Entwurf sieht ein Gesamtkonzept vor, das der künftigen Entwicklung des ICP viel Raum lässt. Geplant wurde eine Parkanlage, gegliedert in Orte und Räume unterschiedlicher Qualitäten, die mehrdimensional angeordnet sind. Es überlagern sich verschiedene, eigenständige Ordnungen: die Ordnung der Wege, Strassen, Bäume (niedrig gehaltene Platanen oder Schirmpinien), Gärten, Räume, Bereiche der Kunst, Teiche und Wasserläufe. Diese Ordnungen bilden Interferenzen. Es entsteht eine Anlage, die vielschichtig Attraktionen bietet.

Die Gärten erstrecken sich nicht nur in der Ebene, sondern entwickeln sich auch in die Höhe. So durchdringen die Dächer die Gebäude und kippen dabei in die Vertikale. Auf diese Weise entwickelt sich z.B. ein vertikaler Garten durch die Hallen der Bürobereiche als grüne Wand.

Eine weitere Struktur des Areals bildet das Wasser im Park. Es fließt vom höchsten Punkt des Parks in einer verspringenden Rinne nach unten, überquert dabei Terrassen, füllt Becken und Teiche und spiegelt über dem Wasser schwebende Strukturen, Flächen und Kunstwerke.

The design provided a total concept that would allow the ICP room for future development. A park was planned, one divided into places and spaces of various qualities, and arranged in a multi-dimensional manner. A variety of independent arrangements overlay one another: the orders of the paths, streets, trees (low-lying plane or pine trees), gardens, rooms, art areas, ponds and waterfalls. These arrangements produce a kind of mutual interference. The result is a complex offering multi-aspected attractions.

The gardens extend not only on ground level, but also develop in the vertical. The roofs of the buildings interpenetrate, tipping up into the vertical dimension. In this way, a vertical garden, for example, develops through the halls of the office areas in the form of a green wall.

An additional structure of the site is provided by the water in the park. Water flows downward from the highest point of the park into a leaping channel, traversing terraces, filling basins and pools along the way, mirroring floating structures, surfaces and works of art that lie above the water.

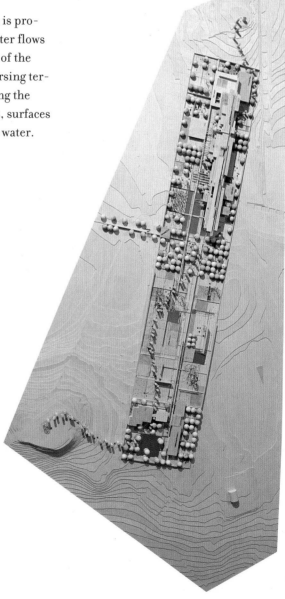

3

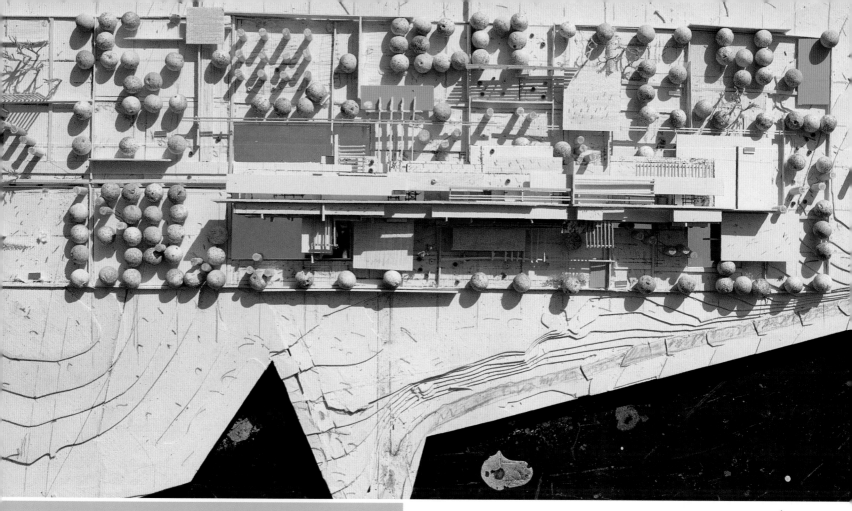

3 Wettbewerbsmodell 4 Arbeitsmodell Detailaufsicht
3 Competition model 4 Working model, detail view

INSTITUT FÜR TELEKOMMUNIKATION |
INSTITUTE OF TELECOMMUNICATIONS | 1995

Im südlichen Teil des Parks befinden sich die Sporteinrichtungen. Sie entwickeln sich aus der künstlichen Landschaft und stehen in Verbindung zum Zentrum. Östlich des Zentrums in unmittelbarer Nähe zum Haupteingang und den Sportanlagen liegt das Restaurant mit den Gartenterrassen. Umgeben ist dieses von den oben beschriebenen Gärten und Wasserbecken, erschlossen durch eine Wegestruktur.

Durch den gesamten Park zieht sich eine Struktur von Wegen, die in einer orthogonalen Ordnung von einem Ort der Anlage zum anderen führen. Sie sind gegliedert in Verbindungswege und Nebenwege. Umgeben wird die gesamte Anlage von einer Mauer, die diese Innenwelt von der umgebenden kargen Landschaft trennt. ◄

In the southern part of the park are the sports facilities. They emerge from the artificial landscape and are linked to the center. To the east of the center, in immediate proximity to the main entrance and the sports facilities, is the restaurant, with its garden terraces. It is surrounded by the above-mentioned gardens and ponds, and accessed via a system of paths.

The entire park is traversed by a system of routes which lead via an orthogonal order from one location of the complex to another. There are both connecting paths and side paths. The entire complex is surrounded by a wall, clearly separating this interior realm from the somewhat sparse landscape outside. ◄

1 Wettbewerbsmodell 2 Lageplan
1 Competition model 2 Site plan

RÖDL CAMPUS | 2002—2005

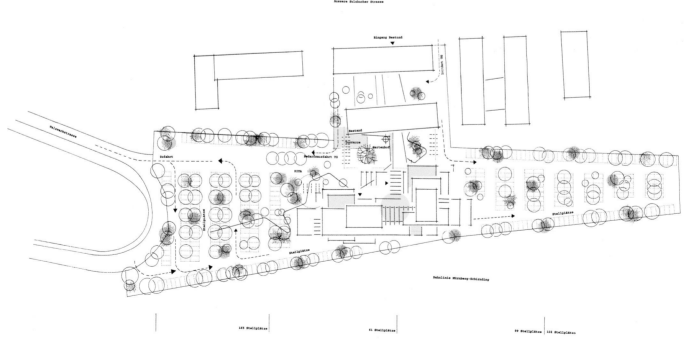

2

RÖDL CAMPUS

NÜRNBERG, DEUTSCHLAND | NUREMBERG, GERMANY; 2002–2005

Die Firma Rödl, eine international tätige Consulting-Firma, wünscht einen Erweiterungsbau, der an das jetzige Gebäude angrenzt. Das Grundstück soll über einen Realisierungsteil hinaus auf eine mögliche Bebaubarkeit unter Berücksichtigung einer bestmöglichen quantitativen und qualitativen Nutzung untersucht werden.

Gefordert ist ein Haus mit vielfältigen räumlichen Strukturen, in denen es möglich sein sollte, auf unterschiedlichste Art und Weise zusammenzuarbeiten: in offenen oder geschlossenen Strukturen – je nach Tätigkeit – in größeren Einheiten, d.h. kommunikativ im größeren Team, in kleineren Gruppen oder auch konzentriert alleine oder zu zweit. Auch für neue, derzeit noch experimentelle Formen der Zusammenarbeit (Desk Sharing etc.) soll Raum geschaffen werden.

Rödl, an internationally active consulting firm, wants to expand with a building adjacent to their existing facilities. Above and beyond the project in question, the site is to be explored with an eye toward its suitability for future development, and with attention to optimising both quantitative and qualitative uses.

Required is a building with a multitude of spatial structures, where employees can work together in the most diverse configurations: in open or closed structures – according to the activity involved – in larger units, i.e., communicatively in big teams; in small groupings; in pairs or alone in concentrated form. There is to be space as well for currently experimental forms of collective work (desk sharing, etc.).

Außerdem soll es Orte geben, an denen man sich zufällig trifft, d.h. an denen sich spontane Gespräche entwickeln, die informieren, das »Wir-Gefühl« stärken und die Integration der Mitarbeiterinnen und Mitarbeiter fördern. Der Arbeitsplatz soll vielfältig und individuell ausgestattet sein, die vielen Bereiche, aus denen sich die Anlage zusammensetzt – Eingangshalle, Vorzone, Flur, Pausenbereich, Büroraum, Terrasse etc. – sollen in ihrer Gestalt individualisiert werden.

All dies spricht gegen ein starres, formal in sich abgeschlossenes, festes Gebilde. Ein eher konventionelles Verwaltungsgebäude kann in diesem Fall keine Grundlage bilden. Auch liegt das Grundstück nicht innerhalb einer gewachsenen und festen innerstädtischen Bebauung, sondern eher in einer offenen Situation mit verschiedenen Begrenzungen, die unterschiedlich auf die Anlage einwirken.

Moreover, other spaces will encourage chance meetings where conversation occurs spontaneously, leading to exchanges which both inform and reinforce a "we"-feeling, promoting the social integration of the staff. Work stations should be diverse and designed individually. The numerous areas that comprise the office complex — entrance hall, approach area, hallways, lounges, terraces, etc. — are also to be designed in an individualised manner.

All of these criteria speak against a rigid, formally self-enclosed, fixed shape. No conventional administration building can serve here as a model. Moreover, the site does not lie within a developed or fixed urban configuration, but rather in an open area with a variety of boundary conditions, which influence the complex in a variety of ways.

3

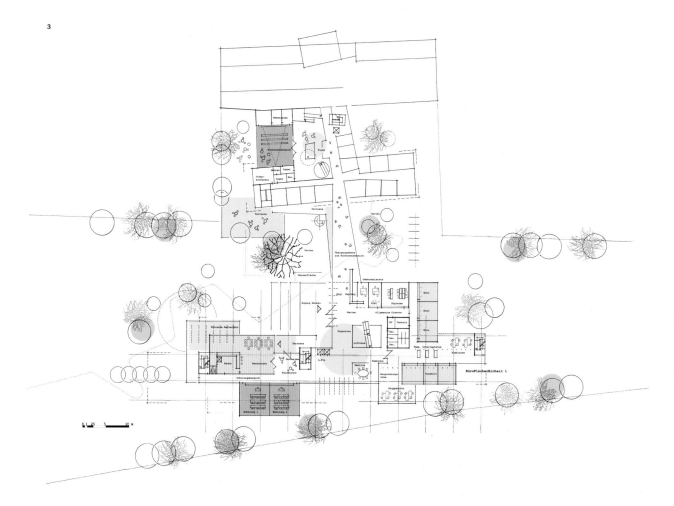

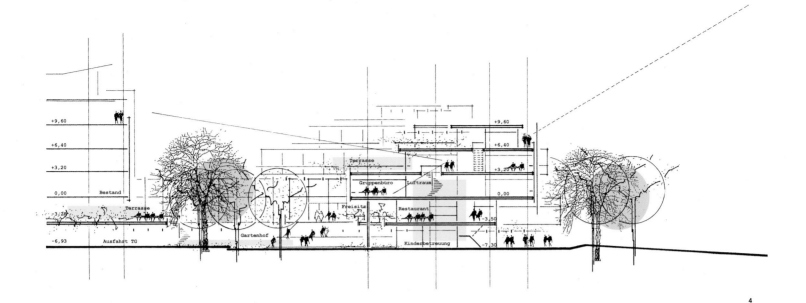

4

3 Grundriss Erdgeschoss 4 Schnitt mit Bestand
3 Plan, ground floor 4 Section with existing building

RÖDL CAMPUS | 2002–2005

Dem Entwurf liegt eine flexible Struktur zu Grunde. Diese ist nicht einem strengen Raster unterworfen, sondern schafft Raum für möglichst gleichwertige, jedoch individuell gestalt- und anpassbare Bereiche. Die Struktur bildet den Rahmen für Ausbaugewerke, die möglichst offen sind für spätere Veränderungen.

Die Räume öffnen sich zum Inneren der Anlage hin über begrünte Gärten und Dachterrassen, der Baukörper ist sensibel gegliedert und stuft sich zum Altbau hin ab. Zum bestehenden Bahndamm ist die Bebauung jedoch eher abgeschirmt. Die unterschiedlichen, individuellen Gebäudeelemente sollen ablesbar sein. Eine lange, undifferenzierte Front wäre die ungeeignete Darstellung der Firma Rödl Campus, zumal es sich um ein Unternehmen handelt, das als Ganzes durch seine Individuen geprägt ist, im Gegensatz zu einer Corporation, die als Einheit nach außen auftritt.

Hence, the design is based upon a flexible structure. It is not subordinated to a strict grid, but instead contains space for equal, yet individually adaptable areas. The structure provides a framework for finishing work which is maximally amenable to later modifications.

All rooms open onto the interior of the complex, onto landscaped gardens and terraces. The building's volume is sensitively articulated, stepping down as it approaches the preexisting building. The structure acts to screen itself from the existing railroad embankment. The various individual elements of the building are deliberately legible. A long, undifferentiated front would have presented an image inappropriate for the Rödl firm, particularly in the case of a firm whose character is expressed by individuals, in contrast to the corporation which attempts to make a unified impression.

5

Die nachfolgenden Bauabschnitte können –
der Gebäudestruktur folgend – in den erforderlichen Größen realisiert werden. Auch hier
wird auf eine architektonisch formale Unter-
gliederung in kleinere Einheiten Wert gelegt.
Diese können organisatorisch zusammengefasst als funktionale Einheit, oder getrennt
für kleinere Nutzergruppen betrieben werden.
Die gesamte Anlage ist so gegliedert, dass

Given the building's structure, future
building phases can be realised in a range
of dimensions. In response to actual requirements, here too, priority is accorded
architecturally to formal subdivision into
smaller units. These can be either combined into functional units, or else separated for use by smaller groups. The entire
complex is articulated so that smaller

kleinere einzelne »Häuser« entstehen, die über Hallen miteinander vernetzt sind. In ihnen sind, auf unterschiedlichen Ebenen, Besprechungsinseln, Sekretariate, Pausenbereiche und andere gemeinschaftliche Nutzungen untergebracht. Die Hallen bilden die pulsierenden kommunikativen Herzen der Anlage. Offene Treppen, Galerien, Stege etc. überlagern sich dort, sodass in mehrfacher Hinsicht lebendige Orte entstehen.

Die meisten Gebäude sind heute horizontal geschichtet orientiert. Gleichförmige Geschossdecken sind übereinander gestapelt und lassen eine komplexere Betriebsorganisation kaum zu. Lange Wege in der Horizontalen sind die Folge. Nach unserer Erfahrung wird der vertikale »Kurzschluss«, also die dritte Dimension, meist vernachlässigt und ist so schon bei der Programmerstellung nicht berücksichtigt. Bringt man diese vertikale Verbindung ins Spiel, entstehen zwar komplexere, aber um ein vielfaches effizientere Organisationsformen. ◄

individual "houses" result which are then linked together via hallways. In them are located, on various levels, conference islands, secretarial offices, lounges and other communal functions. The connecting halls form the throbbing communicative heart of the complex. Open staircases, galleries, footbridges, etc. overlap, bringing many lively spaces into existence.

Most commercial buildings today are conceived as a series of horizontal layers. Identical stories are stacked one upon the next, hindering a more complex operational organisation. This results in many long horizontal routes. It has been our experience that the vertical "short cuts," meaning the third dimension, is generally neglected, even during the initial definition of a building's program. By bringing this vertical connection into play, a more complex, but in many respects more efficient form of organisation can emerge. ◄

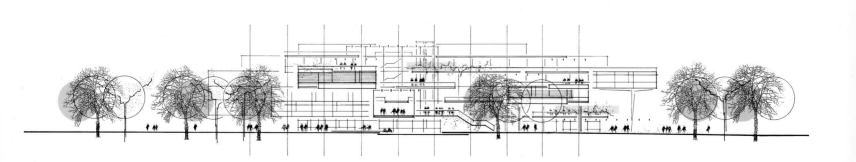

1

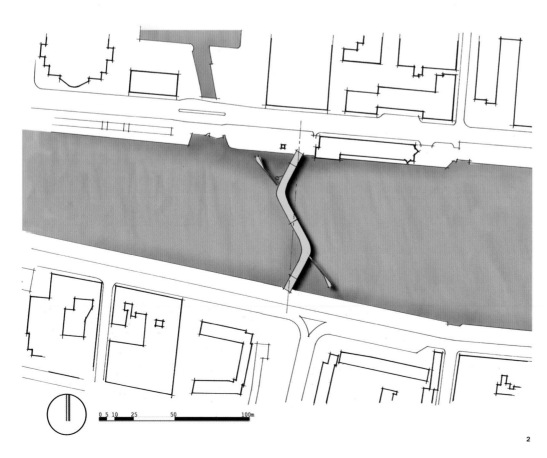

0 5 10   25   50   100m

2

FUSSGÄNGERBRÜCKE | PEDESTRIAN BRIDGE

DUBLIN, REPUBLIK IRLAND | DUBLIN, REPUBLIC OF IRELAND; 2002

1 Nachtansicht von der Uferpromenade 2 Lageplan 3 Grundriss
1 Night view from riverbank promenade 2 Site plan 3 Plan

FUSSGÄNGERBRÜCKE | PEDESTRIAN BRIDGE | 2002

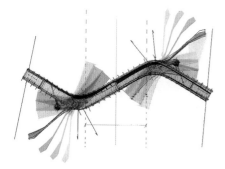

3

Mit der »Stack A«-Brücke soll eine neue Fußgängerverbindung über den Fluss Liffey in die Dubliner Innenstadt geschaffen werden. Bedingung ist, dass die Brücke sich für die Durchfahrt von Segelschiffen öffnen lässt.

Die neue Brücke soll keinesfalls in Konkurrenz zu ihrem künftigen Nachbarn, der weit größeren Martin Bridge, treten. Um zu einer Landmarke zu werden, wäre vielmehr auf Masse und Monumentalität zu verzichten. Der Reiz sollte in einer angemessenen Dimension liegen sowie in Eigenschaften, die durch eine kleinere und flexiblere Form ermöglicht werden – Filigranwirkung, Beweglichkeit und das Schauspiel von Elementen, die sich von Zeit zu Zeit oberhalb des Wassers bewegen.

The "Stack A" bridge is to provide a new pedestrian link across the River Liffey in central Dublin. The bridge is required to open to allow for the passage of sailing vessels.

The new bridge should in no way try to compete with its much larger future neighbour, the Martin Bridge. Instead, if the new bridge is to achieve the desired landmark status, it should offer qualities which are not based upon either quantity or monumentality. Such an attraction should be based rather on the appropriate scale of the pedestrian bridge and take advantage of the qualities that this smaller and freer bridge form allows for, concentrating upon the filigree, on the ability to move, the spectacle of elements travelling from time to time through the space over the river.

Die vorgeschlagene niedrige Brücke inszeniert sowohl den Akt der Flussüberquerung, als auch den Vorgang des Öffnens und Schliessens der Brücke. Ein leicht geschwungener Pfad über den Fluss bietet zwei in entgegengesetzte Richtung orientierte Kurven – flussabwärts zur Mündung des Liffey und flussaufwärts zum Stadtzentrum gerichtet. Diese Form erschließt den Passanten beim Überschreiten der Brücke neue, ungewöhnliche Perspektiven. Man bewegt sich nicht in gerader Linie auf das gegenüberliegende Flussufer zu, sondern folgt einem mäandernden Weg, so dass sich wechselnde Blickbezüge auf den Fluss selbst und die Gebäude zu beiden Seiten des Ufers ergeben und der Fußgänger diesen städtischen Raum auf bisher unbekannte Weise erleben kann. Die leichte Erweiterung der Brücke bietet Raum für Sitzbereiche, Orte zum Verweilen.

Die Brücke, die zum Scheitelpunkt in Flussmitte hin leicht ansteigt, besteht aus zwei sichelförmigen, ca. 40 m langen Elementen, jedes mit Gegengewichten ausbalanciert. Sie drehen sich über Lager in einer inszenierten Bewegung.

The proposed low-lying bridge celebrates both the act of crossing the river and the opening and closing of the bridge. A slightly meandering path across the river offers two new "promontories" facing in opposite directions – out towards the mouth of the Liffey and back upstream towards the City Center. This form offers the visitor new, rather unusual perspectives when crossing the river. Movement is not straight across to the opposite riverbank, instead the meandering offers ever-changing views of both the river itself and the buildings lining the riverbanks, allowing the pedestrian to experience this space in the city in a unique manner. The slight widening of the walkway accommodates seating areas, offering places of rest along the new pedestrian route.

Rising gently towards its apex above the center of the river, the bridge consists of two crescent-shaped walkways, each approx. 40m in length and each supported by a single counterweighted pivot.

4

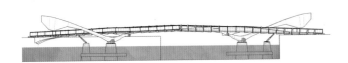

5

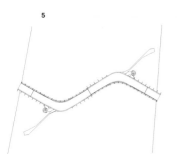

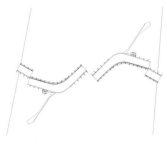

4 Öffnungssequenzen Ansicht 5 Öffnungssequenzen Grundriss 6 Perspektive
4 Opening sequences 5 Plan of opening sequences 6 Perspective

FUSSGÄNGERBRÜCKE | PEDESTRIAN BRIDGE | 2002

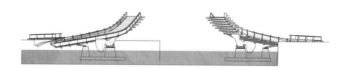

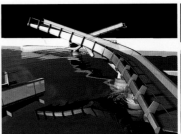

7

8

7 Öffnungssequenzen 8 Ansicht in geöffneter Position 9 Ansicht vom Fluss 10 Modellversuch
7 Opening sequences 8 Opened position 9 River elevation 10 Working model

FUSSGÄNGERBRÜCKE | PEDESTRIAN BRIDGE | 2002

0 2   5   10   20

9

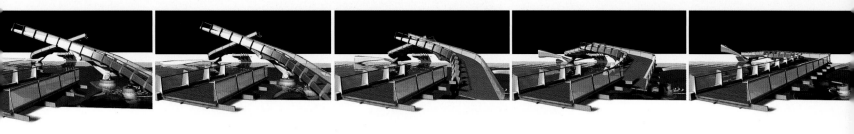

Der Betrieb dieser Brücke ist ein Schauspiel an sich. Öffnen und Schliessen sind Veranstaltungen, die in Szene zu setzen sind, Ereignisse, die von Passanten und Benutzern des Wasserweges mit Spannung erwartet würden. Der sorgfältig choreografierte Hub- und Schwenkvorgang ist mehr eine schwebende Bewegung als einfaches Drehen. Die von Elektromotoren betriebene Bewegung ist bestimmt durch die besondere Geometrie der Brücke und die Beziehung zu den rotierenden Stützarmen und ihren Gegengewichten.

Wenn sich die Brücke rotierend in die geöffnete Position bewegt, beide Gehwege hoch über dem Fluss in die Luft steigen und die Gegengewichte wie aufgestellte Ruderblätter ins Wasser tauchen, verlangsamt sich die Bewegung durch den Auftrieb der Gegengewichte. In dem Moment, wenn die zwei identischen Sichelformen sich in entgegengesetzter Richtung parallel zum Ufer ausrichten, kommt der skulpturale Charakter der Brücke zum Tragen – aus dem gewöhnlich unauffälligen Erscheinungsbild der Brücke wird ein markantes Zeichen, das auch aus der Entfernung leicht zu erkennen ist.

Nachts werden die beiden geschwungenen Formen in geöffneter wie geschlossener Stellung durch Beleuchtung hervorgehoben. Ein in die Brüstung integriertes Leuchtdiodenband wirft durch das Glas des Geländers diffuses Licht auf die Gehfläche und erzeugt auf der darunter liegenden Wasserfläche ein einmaliges Bild. ◄

The operation of such a bridge is an event in itself. The opening and closing are performances which are to be celebrated, an event which would be eagerly anticipated by both passers-by and users of water traffic. Carefully choreographed lifting and rotation describe a unique and graceful movement – a form of balanced travel, rather than simple turning. Initiated by motors the movement is determined by the distinct geometry of the bridge and the relationship with the pivoting support arms and their counterbalances.

With the bridge moving towards an open position, both walkways pitched in the air high above the river and the counterweights dipping into the waters, appearing as steadying oars, a certain buoyancy will slow its movements and allow the different tidal conditions to be reflected in its final position. Here the sculptural quality of the bridge will be fully expressed as the two similar crescent forms face in opposite directions orientated along the river – the normally subdued character of the bridge transformed to create a definite landmark easily seen from a distance.

At night, in both the open and closed positions, the curved forms will be emphasised by artificial lighting. A band of light diodes integrated into the balustrading offers diffused illumination, through the glass railings, of the walking surface and creates distinctive reflections in the water below. ◄

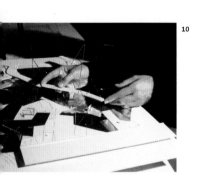

10

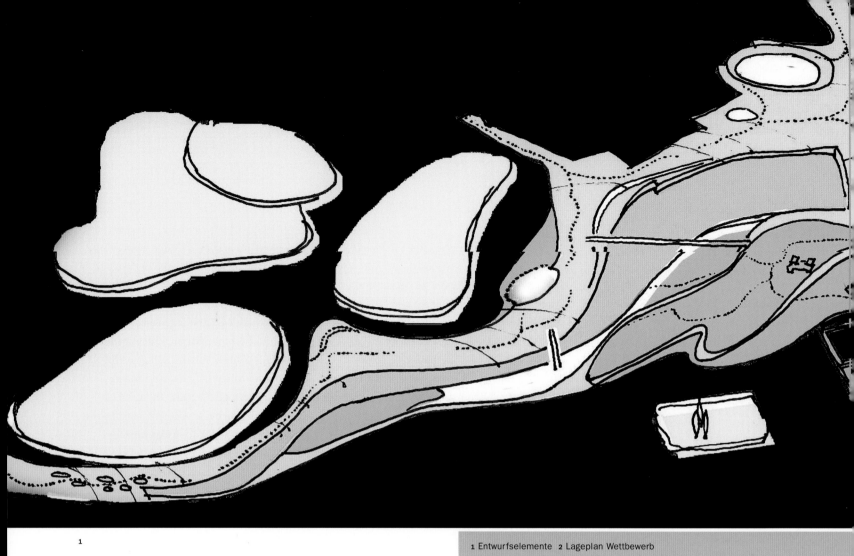

1

1 Entwurfselemente 2 Lageplan Wettbewerb
1 Design elements 2 Site plan, competition entry

SPORTS CAMPUS IRLAND | 2000–2005/6

Snugborough Road

metro station

Sports Village

courtyard

Ballycoolin Road

hotel

metro station

golf academy

sports pitches

sports bodies offices

sporting halls

Arena

tennis

Sports Facilities

velodrome

coach parking

Pool

sports science

terraces

connecting roofs

lake

neighbouring site

metro station

open playing grounds

sports pitches

lake walk

Creative Landscape

Stadium

Open Sports Facilities

field sports

green heart environment garden

entrance area

proposed green buffer

walled gardens

look-out and visitors' centre

emergency access

M50 Motorway

Abbotstown House

family and community

car parking

recreation and leisure

car parking

natural parkland

historic graveyard

to railway station

car parking overflow

Blanchardstown

emergency access

2

SPORTS CAMPUS IRLAND

DUBLIN, REPUBLIK IRLAND | DUBLIN, REPUBLIC OF IRELAND;
2000–2005/6

Im Jahr 2000 hatte die Stadt Dublin einen internationalen Wettbewerb mit vorgeschaltetem Bewerbungsverfahren für die Planung einer großen Sportanlage ausgelobt. Wir hatten diesen Wettbewerb gewonnen und wurden mit der Erarbeitung eines Masterplanes, einer Art Rahmenplan mit Gestaltungsrichtlinien und klaren architektonischen Vorgaben für Landschaft und Gebäude, beauftragt.

Der Sports Campus Irland soll in der Sportinfrastruktur des Landes eine Schlüsselposition einnehmen und Irland als Sportnation international wettbewerbsfähig machen. Gleichzeitig soll er zu einer architektonischen Landmarke werden, die den neuen Stellenwert des Sports symbolisiert.

In the year 2000, the city of Dublin announced an international competition with respective prequalification procedures for the planning of a large sports facility. We won the competition and were commissioned with the preparation of a master plan, i.e., a development plan with design guidelines, one setting clear architectonic givens for the development of both landscape and individual buildings.

The Sports Campus Ireland is intended to assume a key position in the nation's sports infrastructure and to support Ireland as an internationally competitive country of sport. At the same time, it is meant to become an architectural landmark, one symbolizing the increasingly elevated status of sports activities.

Das Problem vieler Großsportanlagen, die für einen bestimmten Zweck, aus einem einmaligen Anlass wie z. B. den Olympischen Spielen, errichtet wurden, ist die Verödung nach Wegfall des Anlasses. Es gibt weltweit viele dieser Beispiele, die, nach der Großveranstaltung weitgehend ungenutzt, langsam verfallen. Der Unterhalt ist zu teuer, das Interesse der Bevölkerung erlahmt notgedrungen. Zu speziell und zweckgebunden wurden diese Anlagen geplant, ohne einem höheren Ziel zu dienen. Es fehlt der Charakter der Landmarke, des Besonderen, der Möglichkeit einer nachhaltigen Identifikation mit dem Ort. Um von den Menschen akzeptiert zu werden, muss eine solche Anlage weitere Elemente enthalten, den Park zum Beispiel, Attraktionen, die die Sportanlage ergänzen, oder auch eine architektonische Besonderheit.

Dieses Phänomen lässt sich auch an anderen Anlagen für Großveranstaltungen erkennen. So ist z. B. das Scheitern der letzten Weltausstellungen auf dieses Phänomen zurückzuführen. Kein Atomium, keine Eiffeltürme oder ähnliche Attraktionen sind in den letzten Jahren entstanden. Oft fehlt der Mut, und es wird in sehr kurzen Zeiträumen über eine Rentabilität nachgedacht. Die Bedeutung der Attraktionen für eine Stadt, eine Region oder gar ein Land findet in der Diskussion praktisch keine Beachtung.

The problem with many large-scale sports facilities erected for a special purpose (for example the Olympic Games) is their subsequent use or indeed neglect following the conclusion of a specific occasion. There are many such examples globally of large facilities which, largely disused, slowly deteriorate. Maintenance is too expensive, and the interest of the general population diminishes as a matter of course. These facilities were planned in a too specialised and mono-functional manner, without serving any greater purpose. They lack the special features typical of landmarks, and the potential for any sustainable identification with the given location. In order to attain wider acceptance, such facilities must incorporate additional elements, a park, for example, or other attractions that supplement the sports facility, perhaps some unusual architectural element.

This phenomenon can also be observed in other facilities for large-scale events. The failure, for example, of the last World's Fairs can be traced back to the same phenomenon. No Atomium, no Eiffel Tower or comparable attraction has emerged in the past few years. Often, boldness was lacking, and short-term profitability was given high priority. The long-term significance of such attractions for a given city, a region or even nation receives but little attention in such discussions.

3 Schnitt Nord-Süd 4 Masterplan
3 Section, north-south 4 Master plan

SPORTS CAMPUS IRLAND | 2000–2005/6

3

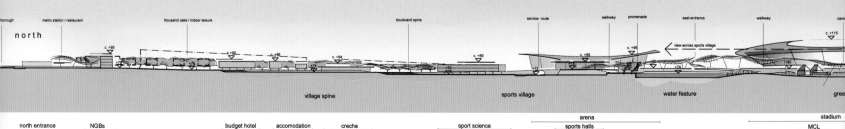

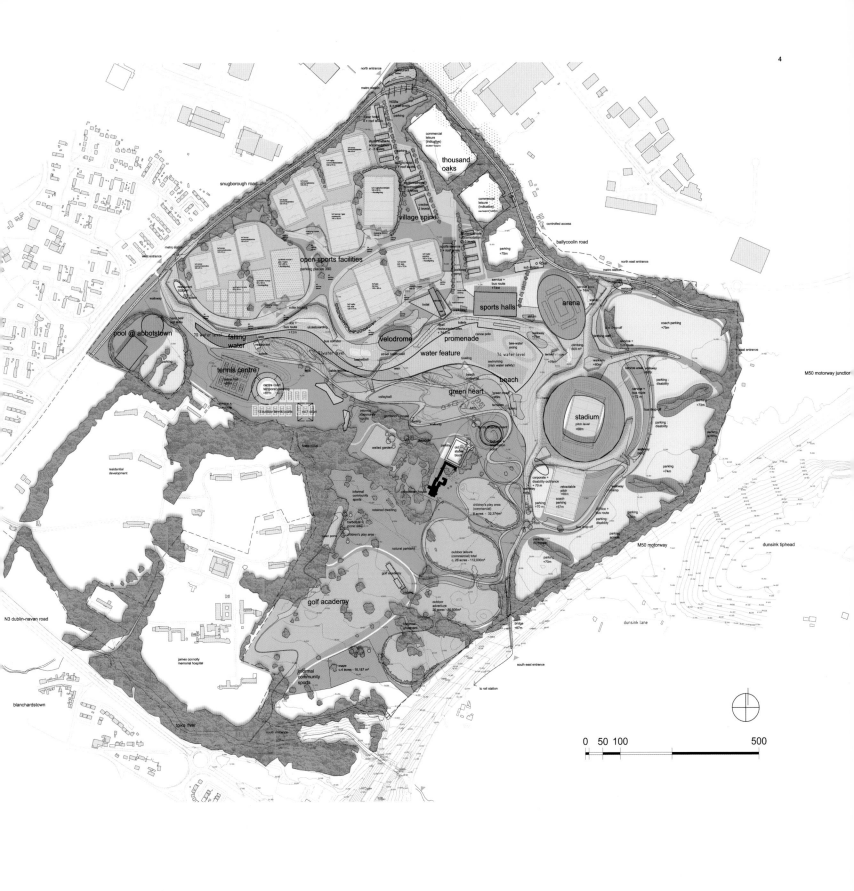

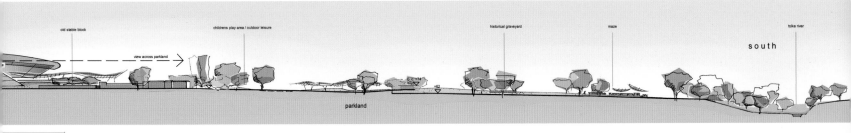

Aufgabe war es hier, eine Anlage zu schaffen, die das Besondere der Situation am Rande Dublins betont, die darüber hinaus Attraktionen bietet, die von den Bürgern Dublins angenommen werden, auch außerhalb von Großveranstaltungen. Dem Masterplan liegt ein Campuskonzept zugrunde, das neben den Einrichtungen für den Leistungssport auch für die Einwohner Dublins und der Umgebung Angebote enthält. Durch seine einladende Umgebung, in der alle Besucher gleichermaßen willkommen sind, wird das traditionelle Sportstättenkonzept neu definiert. Der die einzelnen Gebäude und Sportstätten verbindende öffentliche Raum wird mit einer Reihe von Einrichtungen für Sport- und Freizeitaktivitäten belebt, die zu allen Tageszeiten Besucher einladen.

Neben den Hallen und dem Stadion für die Hauptsportarten sind in dem Sportpark noch eine Golfakademie, ein Golfplatz, Tennisplätze mit Centercourt, eine Sportklinik und Flächen für Forschungsinstitute, Hotels, Fitness-Center und -Anlagen, Restaurants sowie ein Besucherzentrum angeordnet.

Das in Abbotstown am Rande Dublins gelegene 200 ha große leicht topografisch geformte Gelände ist nur teilweise kultiviertes Land. Der Masterplan sieht die Schaffung einer neuen, individuellen Architekturlandschaft vor – ein dreidimensionales Relief, das mit der bestehenden Umgebung verschmilzt und unterschiedliche ineinander übergehende Landschaftsbilder entstehen lässt.

In this case, the task was to create a facility that emphasised the unique character of the location on the edge of Dublin, one that moreover offers attractions appealing to Dublin's population, and not only during large-scale events. The basis of the master plan is a campus concept, which, in addition to facilities for competitive sports, incorporates a range of services for both Dublin and people from the vicinity. Via its inviting surroundings, equally welcoming to all visitors, the traditional concept of the sporting locale is redefined. The public spaces which link individual buildings and sports areas will be enlivened by a series of facilities for both sporting and leisure activities inviting a wide range of visitors at all times of day.

In the sports park, in addition to the halls and the stadium for the principal sports, are a golf academy, golf course, tennis courts with a show court, a sports clinic and areas for related research institutes, hotels, a fitness center and grounds, restaurants, and a visitors center.

The 200 ha gently undulating site in Abbotstown, on the outskirts of Dublin, consists only partially of cultivated land. The master plan provides for the creation of a new, individualised architectural landscape – a three-dimensional relief that integrates itself in the existing surroundings and permits a variety of interpenetrating landscape images to emerge.

5

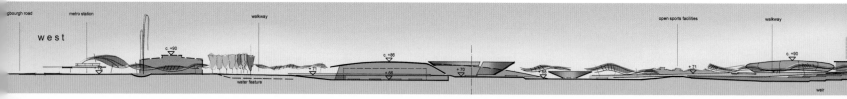

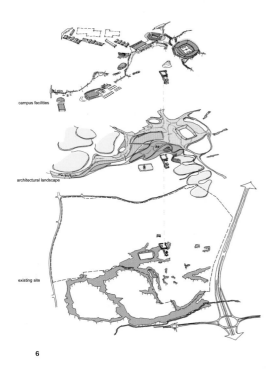

campus facilities

architectural landscape

existing site

6

Die größeren Sportstätten sind wie die Perlen einer Kette entlang eines künstlichen Wasserlaufs aufgereiht. Dieser markiert einen breiten und intensiv landschaftlich gestalteten, teilweise überdachten »Walkway«, der den Ausgangspunkt für die Freizeitangebote im Park bildet. Die größte der Sportstätten, das Stadium Ireland, ist die erste dieser Attraktionen. Es liegt mitten im Herzen der Anlage, dort, wo die von Ost nach West und von Nord nach Süd verlaufenden Wegverbindungen zusammentreffen. Die Unterkünfte für die Sportler sind im nördlichen Bereich des Geländes vorgesehen.

Behnisch, Behnisch & Partner sind mit dem Gesamtgestaltungskonzept für den Sports Campus beauftragt. Die Aufträge für die einzelnen Bauten – das Stadion, die Arena, das Sports Science Center, die Verwaltungsgebäude etc. – werden gesondert an verschiedene Architekten vergeben, unter der Federführung von B, B & P.

Freizeit, Spiel, Unterhaltung, Besuche der Sportveranstaltung, Training, Lernen, Üben oder einfach nur Verweilen, dies alles soll nicht nur möglich sein, der Campus soll vielmehr dazu animieren. ◄

The larger sports facilities are arrayed, like the pearls of a necklace, along an artificial watercourse. This is bordered by a broad and intensively designed, partially roofed "walkway," which provides the point of departure for leisure time activities in the park. The largest of the sports facilities, the Stadium Ireland, is preeminent among these attractions. It is set at the heart of the complex, where the perpendicular axes running east-to-west and north-to-south intersect. Accommodation for athletes is planned for the northern zone of the complex.

Behnisch, Behnisch & Partner are entrusted with the preparation of the total design concept for the sports campus. The commissions for the individual buildings – the stadium, the arena, the Sports Science Center, the administration building, etc. are to be awarded individually to a variety of architects, with Behnisch, Behnisch & Partner in a coordinating role as design leader.

Leisure, play, entertainment, visits to sporting events, training, learning, practice or simply passing the time should not only be possible; the campus should positively encourage and foster these activities. ◄

5 Schnitt West-Ost 6 Entwurfselemente
5 Section, west-east 6 Design elements

SPORTS CAMPUS IRLAND | 2000–2005/6

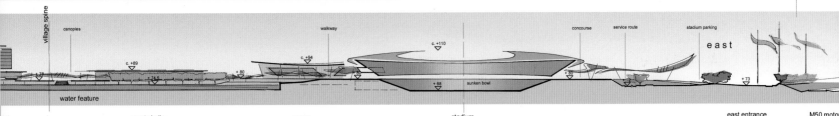

Gärten   EXKURS 3

Gardens   DIGRESSION 3

1

2

Bei der Arbeit an Wettbewerben und Projekten entwickelten wir besondere Gartenkonzepte, oft motiviert durch die vorhandene städtebauliche Situation, den Geist des Ortes oder Ähnliches. Nur zurückhaltend ergänzt durch Elemente aus Architektur und Städtebau sollte die formale Ausbildung der Landschaft im Vordergrund stehen. Intern bezeichneten wir dieses Konzept als Prinzip des »Garten Eden«, dessen friedvolle innere Welt vor der feindlichen äußeren Welt, in alten Bildern meist als von wilden und gefährlichen Tieren bevölkert dargestellt, geschützt ist.

Im Wettbewerbsbeitrag für das Institut für Telekommunikation in Barcarena, Portugal (1995) ist das Konzept sicherlich direkt umgesetzt. Hier waren die Gebäudeteile konsequent den Gärten zu- und dem Gartenkonzept

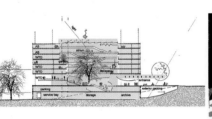  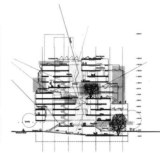 

3   4   5   6

In the course of our work on competitions and projects, we have developed certain specialised garden concepts, often motivated by the preexisting urban situation, the spirit of a place, or similar considerations. For us, the formal elaboration of a landscape should stand in the foreground, to be supplemented by built or urban planning elements only with restraint. Internally, we call this concept the "Garden of Eden" principle, where a tranquil interior world is sheltered from a hostile exterior, generally represented in old pictures as populated by untamed and dangerous creatures.

In a competition proposal for the Institute of Telecommunications in Barcarena, Portugal (1995), this concept was realised in a direct manner. Here, the different parts of the building complex were consistently oriented

untergeordnet. Sie wurden selber zu geschützten, zusammenge-
fügten und vertikal übereinander angeordneten Gärten. Die Grenzen
zwischen landschaftlichen und gebauten Elementen lösten sich
auf, die gesamte Anlage wurde geschützt von einer schönen Mauer,
die das traditionelle Bild des »Garten Eden« aufgriff.

Eine freiere Umsetzung dieses Konzeptes ist erkennbar in den Wett-
bewerbsbeiträgen für das Freibad in Deggendorf und für den Sport
Campus Irland in Dublin. Nachdem die ersten Beiträge nur Konzepte
blieben, bestand in Dublin die Chance, ein solches freies Gartenkonzept in sehr großem Maßstab (200 ha) umzusetzen. Hier wurde
erkannt, dass ein derartiger formaler Garten eine klare Identität
schaffen und eine solche große Anlage insgesamt stabilisieren kann.
Die Landschaft sollte im Vordergrund stehen, nicht das Gebaute,
und sie sollte Ausgleich bieten zu den häufig sich so ernst gebenden
Ritualen des Wettkampfsportes.

9

7

8

10

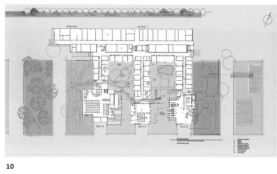

11

toward the garden, and subordinated to the garden concept. They
became themselves protected, assembled, and vertically arranged
gardens. Boundaries between landscape and built elements were
dissolved, and the entire facility was protected by a beautiful wall,
one that takes up the "Garden of Eden" image.

Freer interpretations of this concept are recognisable in our competition entry for the open-air swimming pool complex at Deggendorf and the master planning of the Sports Campus Ireland in
Dublin. Although the first contribution remained on paper, Dublin
offered an opportunity to realise such a free garden concept on a
large scale (200 ha). It was recognised that such a formal garden
is indeed capable of creating a distinct identity and can constitute
a stabilising factor in such a large-scale facility. Not built architecture, but the landscape is to occupy the foreground, where it can
offer a balance to the often so seriously regarded rituals of competitive sports.

Wir haben ähnliche Konzepte – in abgewandelter Form – in verschiedenen Projekten umgesetzt. Zum ersten Mal sowohl im Inneren als auch in der äußeren Konzeption des Instituts für Forst- und Naturforschung in Wageningen, Niederlande. Derzeit probieren wir es in einem städtischen Umfeld aus, bei der Genzyme Hauptverwaltung in Cambridge, USA. Hier bilden ca. 15 verschiedene Innengärten nicht nur horizontal, sondern auch vertikal ein grünes Netz. Zu diesen Gärten haben alle Nutzer des Hauses Zugang.

Der Entwurf für das Zentrum für Zell- und Biomolekularforschung der Universität Toronto basiert auf einem ähnlichen Konzept. Der öffentlich zugängliche Vorplatz und das gesamte Erdgeschoss sind als Architekturlandschaft ausgebildet. Nach oben hin setzt sich diese Landschaft in kleineren, mehrgeschossigen Wintergärten fort. ◄

1 Liegewiese 2 Kombibad, Nürtingen, Deutschland 3 World Trade Organisation (WTO), Genf, Schweiz 4 Verwaltungsgebäude mit Konferenzzentrum der World Intellectual Property Organization (WIPO), Genf, Schweiz 5 Neubau einer Hauptverwaltung, Genzyme Center, Cambridge, USA 6 Thüringer Ministerium für Landwirtschaft, Naturschutz und Umwelt, Deutschland 7 Umgestaltung und Erweiterung Gutenberggymnasium, Erfurt, Deutschland 8, 9 Kongresszentrum, Rom, Italien 10, 11 Institut für Forst- und Naturforschung (I.B.N.), Wageningen, Niederlande 12 Kompetenzzentrum Gartenbau, Thiensen, Deutschland 13 Institut für Telekommunikation von Portugal, Barcarena, Portugal 14 Sport Campus Irland, Dublin, Irland 15 Freibad, Deggendorf, Deutschland

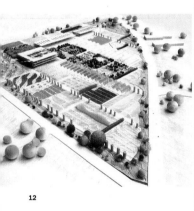
12

13

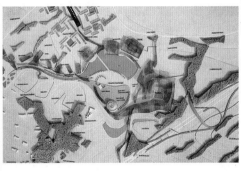
14

15

We have continued to implement similar conceptions — in altered forms — in various projects. The first time we realised such a concept was for the Institute for Forestry and Nature Research in Wageningen, Netherlands. We are currently testing it in an urban setting, at the Genzyme Head Office in Cambridge, USA. Here, approx. 15 various interior gardens compose a green network, operating both horizontally and vertically, where all staff and visitors in the building have access to the range of gardens.

The design for the CCBR building in Toronto is based on a similar concept. The publicly accessible forecourt and the entire ground floor are conceived as an architectural landscape. Above, this landscape is extended in the form of smaller, multi-story winter gardens. ◄

1 Lawn 2 Pool complex, Nürtingen, Germany 3 World Trade Organization (WTO), Geneva, Switzerland 4 Administration building with conference center for the World Intellectual Property Organization (WIPO), Geneva, Switzerland 5 New building of a head office, Genzyme Center, Cambridge, USA 6 Ministry of Agriculture and Environmental Protection, Thuringia, Germany 7 Re-modelling and extension Gutenberg Grammar School, Erfurt, Germany 8, 9 Congress center, Rome, Italy 10, 11 Institute for Forestry and Nature Research (I.B.N.), Wageningen, Netherlands 12 Horticultural center, Thiensen, Germany 13 Institute of Telecommunications of Portugal, Barcarena, Portugal 14 Sports Campus Ireland, Dublin 15 Open-air swimming pool complex, Deggendorf, Germany

Der Entwurf für den Neubau des I.B.N. (Institut voor Bos en Natuur Onderzoek – Institut für Forst- und Naturforschung) geht auf einen beschränkten Wettbewerb zurück, an dem sich drei eingeladene Architektenbüros beteiligt hatten. Dieser Wettbewerb war von der Staatsbaubehörde der Niederlande ausgeschrieben worden.

The design of the new building for the I.B.N. (Instituut voor Bos en Natuur Onderzoek – Institute for Forestry and Nature Research) goes back to a restricted competition in which three invited architectural offices participated. This competition was announced by the state building agency of the Netherlands.

INSTITUT FÜR FORST- UND NATURFORSCHUNG (I.B.N.), HEUTE ALTERRA
INSTITUTE FOR FORESTRY AND NATURE RESEARCH (I.B.N.), NOW ALTERRA

WAGENINGEN, NIEDERLANDE | WAGENINGEN, THE NETHERLANDS; 1993–1998

Der Wettbewerbsbeitrag war auf konzeptionelle Ideen ausgerichtet, um den künftigen Nutzern, den Institutsmitarbeitern und auch dem Bauherrn, die Möglichkeit zu geben, im Planungsprozess noch eigene Vorstellungen zu formulieren. Auch sollten die Nutzer des Instituts ihren Teil dazu beitragen, ihre Identität in diesem Haus der Experten zum Ausdruck zu bringen.

Nicht nur ein Pilotprojekt in ökologischer Hinsicht und in Bezug auf menschenfreundliches Bauen sollte entstehen, es galt auch die Planungs- und Entstehungsprozesse zu analysieren und eventuell als Referenz weiterzuentwickeln. Also nicht nur das Ergebnis, sondern auch Prozess und Verfahren sollten Teil dieses Pilotprojektes sein.

Das zur Verfügung gestellte Grundstück schien zunächst ungeeignet und unattraktiv als Standort für ein ökologisches Pilotprojekt. Das Grundstück liegt inmitten einer kommerziell genutzten Landwirtschaftsfläche. Das Erdreich ist überdüngt und die Gegend in ein orthogonales Raster von Wegen und Kanälen gezwungen. Ausgehend von den wenigen noch bestehenden, landschaftlich attraktiven Elementen erarbeiteten wir ein Landschaftskonzept, das keine Renaturierung im Sinne von wilder oder pseudonatürlicher Landschaftsgestaltung vorsah, sondern die Möglichkeit für die Natur bot, sich im Laufe der kommenden Jahre und Jahrzehnte von selbst neu zu entfalten und die landwirtschaftlich ausgenutzten Flächen zu überwuchern. In den verglasten Innenhöfen liegen Gärten, deren Bepflanzung und Ausgestaltung eine Nutzung über das ganze Jahr möglich macht. Darüber hinaus unterstützen die Pflanzen das Klimakonzept. Bei der Konzeption der Freianlagen und der geschützten Gärten (Innenhöfe) war es das Ziel, den Nutzern jene Elemente einer natürlichen Umgebung zurückzugeben, die der Mensch braucht, um sich in der Natur zu Hause zu fühlen: eher ein Kultur- als ein Wildgarten, mit den Möglichkeiten einer fast ungesteuerten Weiterentwicklung hin zu einer wilderen Natur.

Our competition proposal gave priority to the conceptual, in order to offer future users (the institute staff) and the client an opportunity to formulate their own ideas and contribute towards the planning process, expressing their own identity within this house of expertise.

The goal was not just to produce a pilot project with regard to ecological concerns and within the context of humanistic construction, but also to analyse the planning and production processes, and to develop this analysis as a future reference. Not only the final product, but process and method as well, were crucial aspects of this pilot project.

At first, the site made available seemed ill-suited and unattractive as the location for an ecological pilot project. It lays in the middle of a commercially used agricultural zone. The soil was over-fertilised and the vicinity forced into an orthogonal grid composed of routes and canals. Starting from the few attractive landscape elements still in existence, we developed a landscape concept that did not envision returning to a pristine state in the form of either a wild or pseudo-natural landscape design, but instead offered nature the opportunity to evolve over the course of coming years and decades, to reoccupy the agriculturally exploited areas. In the glazed interior courtyard are gardens, whose extensive plantings contribute towards making use possible throughout the year. Moreover, the vegetation supports the climatic concept. Concerning both the outdoor areas and the sheltered interior gardens (the inner courtyards), the goal was to offer users those elements of the natural environment they need in order to feel at home: more a cultural than a wild garden, harboring possibilities of an almost indeterminate future development.

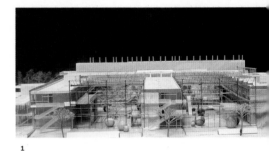

1

1 Präsentationsmodell 2 Nordansicht 3 Umgebungsplan

1 Presentation model 2 North elevation 3 Location plan

INSTITUT FÜR FORST- UND NATURFORSCHUNG |
INSTITUTE FOR FORESTRY AND NATURE RESEARCH | 1993–1998

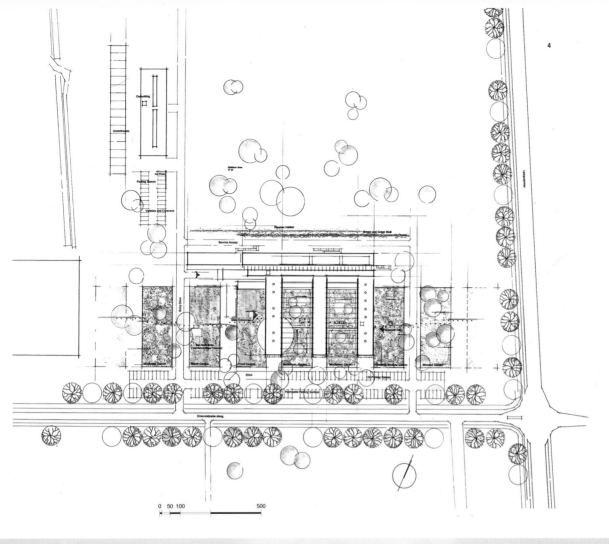

0 50 100   500

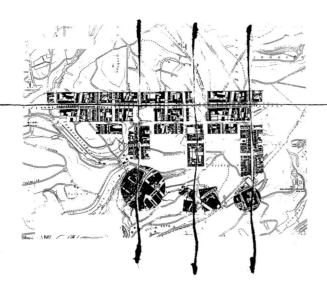

6

8

4 Lageplan Wettbewerb 5 Blick von Süden 6 Konzeptskizze 7 Galerie 8 Blick von Westen
4 Site plan, competition entry 5 View from the south 6 Conceptual sketch 7 Gallery
8 View from the west

INSTITUT FÜR FORST- UND NATURFORSCHUNG |
INSTITUTE FOR FORESTRY AND NATURE RESEARCH | 1993–1998

7

Das Gebaute selbst sollte eine weniger dominierende Rolle spielen. Geplant wurde daher eine einfache aber offene Baustruktur, die das erforderliche Programm aufnimmt. Sie ist so in die Gärten eingefügt, dass diese – dreiseitig umschlossen und überdacht – wie Innenbereiche genutzt werden können. Die Glashäuser sind ein zentrales Element des Klimakonzeptes. Sie sind Wärmepuffer und Schattenspender, die Pflanzen verbessern das Mikroklima. Das Haus fügt sich in die Gartenstruktur ein und wird so beinah zu einem Element eben dieser Struktur. Die Wärmeausstrahlung der Fassaden wird in diesen

The building itself plays a less dominant role. A somewhat simple yet open structure was therefore planned, taking up the necessary program. It is set into the gardens in such a way that the protected spaces, the courtyards – enclosed on three sides and roofed – could be used as interiors. These roofed gardens are central to the climatic concept. They act as buffer zones and provide shading, whilst the vegetation improves the microclimate. The house fits into the garden structure, almost becoming a component of it. Heat escaping through the facades is trapped by the glass houses. The

Glashäusern abgefangen. Das große Luftvolumen der überdachten Gärten gleicht Temperaturunterschiede zwischen Innen und Außen aus. Durch die diffuse winterliche Sonne erwärmen sich diese großen Volumina der Glashäuser im Winter sehr schnell und sind daher besonders gut zu nutzen. Im Sommer wirken sie wie ein Sonnenkollektor, der wiederum, durch Verdunstung des Wassers aus Blättern und Teichen und der sich daraus ergebenden Absenkung der Lufttemperatur, zur Kühlung beiträgt. Die Höfe sind nicht versiegelt, sondern reichhaltig bepflanzt. Sie können verschattet werden und liefern so kühlere Luft in die angrenzenden Bereiche.

large volumes of air contained in the roofed gardens moderate temperature differences between inside and outside. In wintertime, maximum use is made of heat gains, making the glass houses especially usable. In summer, they function like a solar collector and contribute towards evaporating moisture from leaves and ponds, lowering air temperatures. The courtyards are not paved, but instead richly planted. Extensive shading helps provide cooler air to adjoining areas.

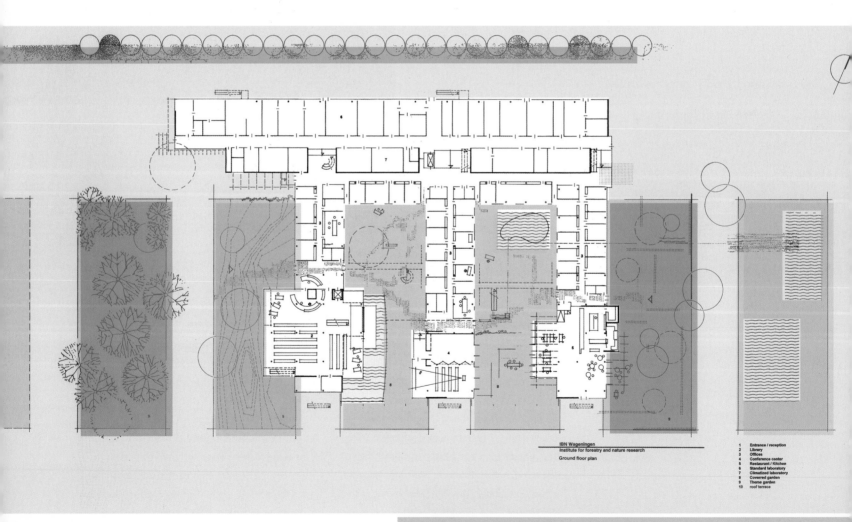

IBN Wageningen
Institute for forestry and nature research
Ground floor plan

1 Entrance / reception
2 Library
3 Offices
4 Conference center
5 Restaurant / Kitchen
6 Standard laboratory
7 Climatized laboratory
8 Covered garden
9 Theme garden
10 roof terrace

9

9 Grundriss Erdgeschoss 10 Südfassade 11 Schnitt Ost-West
9 Plan, ground floor 10 South facade 11 Section, east-west

INSTITUT FÜR FORST- UND NATURFORSCHUNG |
INSTITUTE FOR FORESTRY AND NATURE RESEARCH | 1993–1998

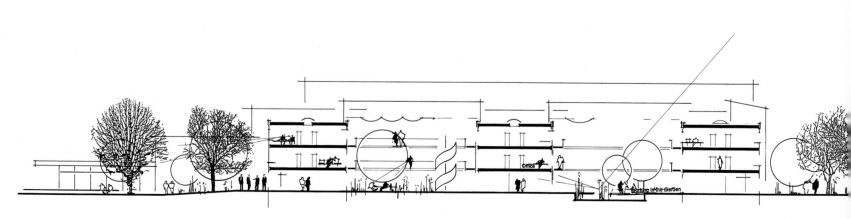

Die Innengärten sind kein Teil der geforderten Programmfläche, haben also keine Funktionen innerhalb des Nutzungsprogramms zu erfüllen. Sie bieten vielfältige, nicht definierte oder zweckbestimmte Orte und schaffen so Freiräume für die Mitarbeiter. Hier befinden sich die Pausenbereiche und Orte für Besprechungen. Wichtig erscheint, dass es eben jene nicht definierten Orte sind, die das Gebäude für die Menschen besonders interessant und attraktiv machen. Da das Innere der überdachten Gärten weder Regen noch Windlasten ausgesetzt ist, konnten hier einfacher konstruierte Holzfassaden verwendet werden. So entsteht eine Differenzierung zwischen den bewitterten Außenfassaden und diesen inneren geschützten Fassaden.

The areas of the inner gardens are themselves not included in the required program, and hence perform no defined functions within it. Instead, they offer multifarious, functionally undefined free spaces for all staff. Here are lounge areas and places for informal consultations. It is precisely such undefined spaces that make the building especially intriguing. Since the interiors of the roofed gardens are exposed to neither rain nor wind, simply-constructed wooden facades could be used here. Thus emerges a differentiation between the weather-exposed outer facades and the interior, sheltered ones.

12

12 Mitarbeiterrestaurant 13 Innengarten
12 Staff restaurant 13 Interior garden

INSTITUT FÜR FORST- UND NATURFORSCHUNG |
INSTITUTE FOR FORESTRY AND NATURE RESEARCH | 1993–1998

Die formale Zurückhaltung des Gebäudes, seiner Materialien und Details implizierte, neben der Betonung der Natur- und Gartenkonzepte, auch ökonomische und ökologische Vorteile. So wurde die Gewichtung der verschiedenen Elemente zu einem Balanceakt. Da der Rohbau auch als thermische Masse funktioniert, waren keine abgehängten Decken möglich, ausgenommen von jenen Bereichen, in denen akustische oder Brandschutzaspekte diese erforderten. Für die Gebäudehülle wurde ein besonders wirksamer Wärmeschutz realisiert. Diese Investitionen mussten an anderer Stelle eingespart werden.

Die fehlende Methodik zur Berechnung und Wertung von ökologischen Aspekten wurde durch aufwendige Untersuchungen der Grundlagen ersetzt. Dies galt nicht nur für die verschiedenen Materialien und Bauelemente im Betrieb, sondern auch für die Ressourcen und den Energiebedarf vom Transport über die Herstellung, die Verarbeitung, die Lebensdauer, die Flexibilität und die Recycling- oder Entsorgungsmöglichkeiten der Materialien bis hin zu deren energetischem Verhalten. Auch ergonomische und soziale Aspekte, sowie die Frage der Annehmlichkeit für die Benutzer flossen in die Überlegungen mit ein.

Es stellte sich heraus, dass Halbzeuge, also Großserienprodukte, auch ökologisch günstig sind. Nicht nur die Fertigungsprozesse sind optimiert, sondern auch der Materialverbrauch ist bei solchen Produkten auf ein Minimum reduziert. So bestehen viele Elemente des Gebäudes aus Produkten dieser Art, z. B. Balkone, Glasdächer, Fassaden etc.

Alongside the emphasis on nature and garden concepts, the building's formal restraint, its materials and detailing also imply both economic and ecological advantages. The weighting of the respective elements became a balancing act. Since the shell construction also performs as a thermal mass, suspended ceilings were not possible, except where required in specific areas for either acoustic or fire protection purposes. For the building's envelope, an especially effective thermal protection was realised. Such investments had to be compensated by equivalent reductions at other locations.

In lieu of a recognised standard method for calculating and evaluating ecological parameters, a painstaking investigation of the fundamentals was undertaken. This was true not only for the various materials and construction elements employed in the operation, but also for the resources and energy used, from transport to production, manufacture, service life, flexibility, and recycling/disposal possibilities of the materials, all the way to their energetic behavior. Ergonomic and social aspects, such as the question of user comfort, also found a place in such considerations.

Generally it turned out that the use of semi-finished products, i.e. large-scale serial production, is also ecologically advantageous. Not only are manufacturing processes optimised, but with such products, use of materials is reduced to a minimum. Many elements of the building, hence, consist of products of this type, for example, balconies, glass roofs, facades, etc.

14 Atrium 15 Innenfassade | 14 Atrium 15 Inner facade

**INSTITUT FÜR FORST- UND NATURFORSCHUNG |
INSTITUTE FOR FORESTRY AND NATURE RESEARCH | 1993–1998**

Bis auf Sonderbereiche, wie Küche und Bibliothek, wurde auf eine lufttechnische Behandlung oder gar Klimatisierung völlig verzichtet. Die sogenannte Behaglichkeit wird erreicht durch ein sorgfältig erarbeitetes natürliches Klimakonzept: durch das Zusammenspiel der Gewächshäuser – als Klimapuffer zwischen Innen- und Außenraum –, der Grün- und Wasserflächen – als Schattenspender und zur Luftverbesserung – sowie durch die Aktivierung der internen Speichermassen zur Nachtauskühlung.

With the exception of specific areas such as kitchen and library, it was decided not to install a ventilation or climate control system. The desired "comfort levels" are attained via the appropriate arrangement of a natural climatisation concept. This is accomplished by the interplay of greenhouses (acting as climate buffers between inner and outer space), the planted and water surfaces (which provide shadow and improve air quality), as well as by the activation of the internal storage masses and the related nocturnal cooling.

16 Atrium **17** Mitarbeiterrestaurant **18** Innengarten
16 Atrium **17** Staff restaurant **18** Interior garden

INSTITUT FÜR FORST- UND NATURFORSCHUNG |
INSTITUTE FOR FORESTRY AND NATURE RESEARCH | 1993–1998

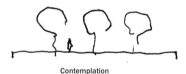

Contemplation

Ambient sound

Von staatlich beauftragten Gutachtern wurde eine Energie- bzw. Ökobilanz über die gesamte Lebensdauer des Gebäudes von der Erstellung über die Nutzungszeit bis hin zu seiner Entsorgung erstellt. Danach ergaben sich äußerst günstige Werte für dieses Projekt. Das Gutachten stellte die Umweltbelastungen und Entsorgungskosten durch eine Ermittlung der Massen sowie der verwendeten Materialien und Systeme fest. Diese wurden mit den besten bisher erforschten und quantifizierbaren Referenzmaterialien verglichen.

Es stellte eine Herausforderung dar, all diese Strategien in die Entwürfe und Planungen mit einzubeziehen, ohne dass der ökologische Aspekt alle anderen zu sehr dominiert. Es war für die Architekten interessant darzustellen, dass Ökologie und Architektur nicht

Consulting experts contracted by the state prepared an energy and ecological balance which covered the entire life-span of the building, from erection, through occupancy and use, and finally to eventual disposal. The results showed extremely favorable values for the project. The expert report determined the environmental burden and disposal costs by investigating the masses as well as the materials and systems employed. These were then compared with the most reliably researched and quantifiable reference materials.

The challenge presented itself of incorporating all such strategies in the designs and planning, without allowing the ecological aspect to dominate the others. For the architects, it was interesting to demonstrate that ecology and architecture, within

19

20

Tune your own environment

Encourage self-expression

20, 22 Büroarbeitsplätze am Innengarten **21** In der Bibliothek
20, 22 Workstations facing onto interior garden **21** Interior, library

INSTITUT FÜR FORST- UND NATURFORSCHUNG |
INSTITUTE FOR FORESTRY AND NATURE RESEARCH | 1993–1998

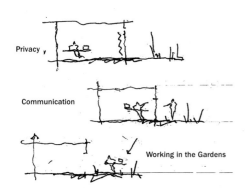

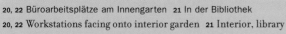

Privacy

Communication

Working in the Gardens

zwangsläufig in einem Widerspruch stehen müssen, auch wenn die Ökologie ernsthaft betrieben wird und nicht – wie oft – ein Lippenbekenntnis bleibt. Darüber hinaus schien es spannend, ein Werk zu schaffen, das sich stärker als üblich aus sich selbst heraus weiterentwickeln soll. Es galt, ein Gebäude zu planen, dass sich an die immer neuen Gegebenheiten, nach den gesteuerten Gesetzmäßigkeiten der größtenteils organisierten Strukturen der Nutzer anpasst, jedoch überlagert von den chaotischen Entwicklungen der Natur.

the standard financial constraints, are not necessarily incompatible, even when the ecological dimension is pursued seriously and not merely given lip-service, as is so often the case. Moreover, it was exciting to create a work that develops out of itself more markedly than is typical. It was a question of planning a building that would adapt to its constantly evolving circumstances, in keeping with the regulated rules of the highly organised structures of the users, and yet be overlaid by the apparently chaotic processes of nature.

23 Ostansicht | **23** East elevation

Hedge
Dry Stone Wall
Life

GEBÄUDEKONZEPT Das Institut für Forst- und Naturforschung soll sich als ein zukunftsorientiertes Gebäude darstellen, in dem der effiziente Umgang mit Energie einen Planungsgrundsatz bildet. So ist das Gebäude schon durch sein kompaktes Volumen ein Beispiel energiesparender Architektur. Durch die großen geschützten Gärten wurde das Verhältnis Volumen zu Hüllfläche optimiert, d.h., die bewitterte Außenfläche ist hier im Verhältnis zu anderen Gebäuden dieser Größe sehr gering.

Darüber hinaus erlaubt die Ost/West-Ausrichtung der Gebäudefassaden eine effiziente Solarenergienutzung im Winter. Die verglasten Atrien bieten einfache Möglichkeiten zur Minderung der Heizenergie und zur Begrenzung von sommerlichen Überhitzungssituationen. Der energiegerechte Gebäudeentwurf wird für den Gebäudenutzer unter anderem auch in der weitreichenden Tageslichtnutzung zur Raumbeleuchtung erkennbar.

ENERGIEKONZEPT Optimierungsrechnungen zur Begrenzung des Heizenergiebedarfs haben gezeigt, dass aus energieökonomischen Gründen nur die Nutzflächen des Gebäudes, d.h. nicht die Atrien, beheizt werden sollten. Die Atrien stellen eine Hauptkomponente des Energiekonzeptes dar. Der Gebäudeentwurf erlaubt eine ganzjährige multifunktionale Nutzung des Atriums, während bei nur geringfügig verändertem Heizenergiebedarf die Fassade zwischen dem Atrium und den Bürotrakten sehr viel kostengünstiger ausgeführt werden kann.

Das Wärmeschutzkonzept des Gebäudes ist so angelegt, dass es sowohl der notwendigen Umweltentlastung durch reduzierte Verbrennungsschadstoffe Rechnung trägt, als auch künftigen möglichen Energiepreissteigerungen. Es empfahl sich daher, das Bürohaus als Niedrigenergiegebäude mit einem exzellenten Wärmeschutz auszuführen. Hierdurch stellt sich das Gebäude neben anderen Gestaltungsansätzen als wegweisendes Objekt dar. Die Berechnungen ergaben, dass an das Verglasungssystem besonders hohe Ansprüche zu stellen waren. Während die Bürofassade in hochwertiger Wärmeschutzverglasung ausgeführt wurde, empfahlen sich für die Nord-Orientierungen sog. Superglazingsysteme. Der Dachbereich des Atriums ist als einfachverglaste Konstruktion mit temporärem Wärmeschutz ausgeführt. Die opaken wärmedämmenden Bauteile sind mit zukunftsorientierten Dämmstärken versehen.

Hinsichtlich des Heizsystems gab es keine begrenzenden Anforderungen. Das System ist einfach zu bedienen und kostengünstig, um der gewählten Gebäudekonzeption gerecht zu werden. Zwar ist jeder Nutzbereich getrennt regelbar, doch wurde aufgrund der durchschnittlichen solaren Belastung der Büroräume kein besonders schnelles Heizsystem erforderlich. Zur Begrenzung der Anlagengröße wurde auf die Nachtabsenkung verzichtet.

THE BUILDING CONCEPT The Institute for Forestry and Nature Research is accommodated in a future-oriented building whose design embodies the efficient use of energy as a planning principle. In its compactness, too, the building provides an example of energy-saving architecture. The large shielded gardens are designed to optimise the volume/envelope ratio, making the weathered exterior very small in comparison with other buildings of this size.

Furthermore, the east-west alignment of the facade permits the efficient use of solar energy during the winter. With their simple design, the atriums provide facile building solutions that reduce heating-energy consumption and diminish the likelihood of overheating during the summer months. The building's energy-friendly concept makes extensive use of daylight to illuminate the interiors.

THE ENERGY CONCEPT Optimisation calculations performed with the aim of reducing energy consumption showed that heating was only required in the main functional areas, i.e. excluding the atriums. The atriums are one of the main pillars of the energy concept. The building design allows for all-year-round use of the multifunctional atrium. Only a slight change in the energy requirement permits a far more economical execution of the facade between the atrium and the adjoining offices.

The heat-insulation concept takes into account the need to minimise environmental damage by reducing exhaust gas emissions, as well as the possibility of energy prices rising in the future. Proceeding from these considerations, the building was planned as a low-energy structure with excellent heat insulation. Consequently, the building provides a trend-setting example. The calculations showed that very high demands would be placed on the glazing system. Therefore, whilst high-grade heat-insulating glass offered the best solution for the office facade, super-glazing systems were used on the north side. The atrium roof zone was executed as a single-glazed structure with temporary heat insulation. The insulation thicknesses of the opaque heat-exchanging elements anticipate future developments in this area.

The heating system is not subject to any restrictive requirements. Hence, an economical, easy-to-operate system was chosen for the institute that did justice to the overall building concept. Although the heating can be regulated separately in each functional area, a particularly fast-operating heating system was not considered necessary in view of the average solar load for the office rooms. The desire to minimise the size of the heating system gave rise to the idea of dispensing with a system that would lower convector temperatures at night.

Der zu erwartende Heizenergiebedarf liegt bei jährlich ca. 40 kWh/m³, womit das Gebäude den Anspruch an ein Niedrigenergiegebäude erfüllt. Im Folgenden soll etwas ausführlicher auf die Schwerpunkte des Energiekonzeptes eingegangen werden.

LABORTRAKT Der Energieverbrauch der Laboratorien wird stark von der Lüftungstechnik beeinflusst. Ziel war es, die Anlagetechnik im Entwurf und in der Dimensionierung zu optimieren. Der Entwurf sieht die komplette Versorgung von Zu- und Abluft vom Dach der nach Norden orientierten Laboratorien vor. Eine direkte Wärmerückgewinnung ist – mit Ausnahme der Digestorien – möglich. Jeder Raum erhält einen separaten Vertikalschacht in der Flurzone (keine Brandschutzklappe) und ist von dort aus nachinstallierbar (Flexibilität). Die Installation des Klimasystems im Labor erfolgt offen sichtbar an den Decken, um so eine sommerliche Nachtabkühlung zu ermöglichen. Dieses einfache System spart Raumhöhe. Die Anlagengröße wurde nicht für ein absolutes Maximum konzipiert, sondern für einen angemessenen, tatsächlich erwarteten Bedarf. Eine Einsparung an Heizenergie durch die gewählte Anlagentechnik um ca. 60% ist realistisch. Die natürliche Lüftung der Labors wird so weit als möglich genutzt. Die Steuerung der Lüftungsanlage wird von den Mitarbeitern am Arbeitsplatz geregelt, der im Labor arbeitende Wissenschaftler wählt die notwendige Luftrate selbst. Der bewusste Umgang mit der Technik spart viel Energie: Auf eine Kühlung der Labors kann verzichtet werden. Die nächtliche Abkühlung der Speichermassen gewährleistet ein akzeptables Klima im Sommer.

ATRIEN Die Atrien dienen in besonderer Weise dem energiesparenden Konzept. Im Winter minimieren sie durch ihren doppelten Puffereffekt – Wärmeverluste durch die Fassade werden reduziert und Frischluft für Büros etc. wird vorgewärmt – die benötigte Heizenergie. Die Atrien dienen als reiner Wetterschutz und werden daher nicht beheizt. Das Dach ist einfachverglast und erhielt zum Schutz gegen nächtliche Auskühlung einen einfachen Wärmeschutz in Form eines Folienrollos. Hierdurch wird sichergestellt, dass die Temperatur in den Atrien bei durchschnittlicher Nutzung nicht unter 0°C und an weniger als 100 Stunden unter 5°C absinkt. Da die Atrien einen Windschutz darstellen, ist dort zu fast jeder Jahreszeit mit angenehmen Verhältnissen zu rechnen.

Im Sommer können die Atrien intensiv belüftet werden. Dies gilt auch, bzw. besonders, für die Nacht. Hierdurch lässt sich die Gebäudemasse aktivieren und ein ausgeglichenes Raumklima schaffen. Der temporäre Wärmeschutz wird so ausgeführt, dass er auch als Sonnenschutz dient. Hier wird auf im Gewächshausbau bewährte Systeme zurückgegriffen. Durch diese Konzeption lässt sich die Temperatur im Sommer auf maximal 28°C begrenzen.

With an anticipated heating-energy requirement of approximately 40 kWh/m³ per annum, the structure meets the requirements of a low-energy building. In the following passages, the key points of the energy concept are presented in greater detail.

THE LABORATORY WING The energy consumption of the laboratories is highly influenced by the ventilation system. The aim here has been to optimise both the design and the dimensioning of the system. All the supply and extract air is regulated via the roof of the north-facing laboratories. Direct heat recovery is used here (but not in the smoke hoods and point extracts). Each room has its own vertical shaft in the corridor zone (hence no requirement for fireproof shutters); further installations can be added later (affording flexibility). The laboratory air-conditioning units are installed exposed on the ceilings, permitting night cooling during the summer. This simple system allows a reduction of the room height. The system was not designed for an absolute maximum requirement, but for one that was considered adequate and based on realistic expectations. Proceeding from these assumptions, a system was designed that would reduce heating-energy consumption by approximately 60%. The laboratories are ventilated naturally wherever possible. The ventilation units are operated by the laboratory staff, who can regulate the air flow to suit their needs. Conscious use of the system not only brings about a considerable saving in energy, but also does away with the need to cool the laboratories. The nightly cooling of the storage masses ensures an acceptable room climate during the summer months.

THE ATRIUMS The atriums play a very important role in the energy-saving concept. During the winter, their double-buffer effect minimises energy use: the loss of heat through the facade is reduced, and fresh air destined for the offices, etc. is prewarmed. Serving to provide weather protection only, the atriums are not heated. The single-glazed roof has a series of impregnated blinds to provide protection against excessive night cooling. As a result, the temperature in the atriums never drops below 0°C during average use, and never falls below 5°C for more than 100 hours. As the atriums provide wind protection, pleasant conditions can be expected there almost all year round.

The atriums can be intensively ventilated during the summer months, especially at night, thus activating the building mass and generating a balanced room climate. The temporary heat insulation is designed to provide solar protection, too, utilizing systems tried and tested in standard greenhouses. This concept makes it possible to maintain a maximum temperature of 28°C during the summer months.

Die Atrien tragen durch eine helle Gestaltung des Bodens, der Stützen sowie der Fensterbrüstungen dazu bei, dass auch kritische Räume im Erdgeschoss zu den Atrien hin ausreichend mit Tageslicht versorgt werden. Der kritischste an die Atrien angrenzende Büroraum im Erdgeschoss besitzt einen Tageslichtquotienten von im Mittel ca. 9 % nach DIN 5034, in der Raummitte von ca. 1 %.

BÜROTRAKTE Die Fassaden des Bürotraktes sind zu zwei Dritteln mit dem Atrium überdeckt. Die Versorgung der Räume mit Frischluft erfolgt über Fensterbelüftung. Da die Fassaden im Atrium nicht mehr dem Winddruck ausgesetzt sind, wurde in der Mitte des jeweiligen Bürotraktes eine Abluftanlage installiert, die mittels Unterdruck für ein Nachströmen der Luft über die Büroräume sorgt. Aus der Abluft lässt sich über Wärmerückgewinnung ein Großteil der dem Gebäude entzogenen Energie wieder dem Heizsystem zuführen.

Der Heizenergiebedarf dieser Zonen sinkt deutlich unter 30 kWh/m³ ab. Gleichzeitig lassen sich auch durch das vorgelagerte Atrium für diese Zone Kosten einsparen. So war etwa eine einfach ausgeführte Verglasung möglich, da die Fassade keinen Wetterschutz benötigt. Auch der Sonnenschutz konnte einfach ausgeführt werden, da er keinem Wind ausgesetzt ist. Die Leistung der Heizanlage kann auf die Hälfte reduziert werden, wobei sich die hierdurch zu erwartenden Kosteneinsparungen auf 15–20 % der Konstruktionskosten für die Atrien belaufen. Darüber hinaus lässt sich der Heizenergiebedarf und damit die Heizkosten um über 23000 Euro jährlich reduzieren.

Die sommerlichen Temperaturverhältnisse in den Büroräumen stellen sich bei Nutzung intensiver Nachtlüftung und des Sonnenschutzes als sehr komfortabel mit maximal 28°C ein. Auf Klimatisierung kann verzichtet werden.

With their light-colored flooring, columns and parapets, the atriums have been designed to ensure that the critical rooms on the ground floor receive sufficient light. The most critical ground-floor room adjacent to the atriums has an average daylight quotient of approximately 9 % (1 % at the center of the room) in accordance with DIN 5034.

THE OFFICE WINGS Two thirds of the facade area of the office wings are taken up by the atrium. The rooms are supplied with fresh air through the windows. As the facades facing the atrium are not exposed to wind pressure, an exhaust-air extractor, which operates on sub-atmospheric pressure to ensure a flow of air through the office rooms, is installed in the middle of each office wing. Further saving is achieved by the use of heat recovery, whereby the exhaust air feeds much of the energy expelled from the building back into the heating system.

The heating-energy requirement of these areas is well below 30 kWh/m³. Costs can also be reduced in these wings through the design of the adjacent atrium spaces. Not requiring weather protection, technical demands on the facade were considerably reduced. Furthermore, only simple sun shading is required as there is no wind pressure. The scale and performance of the heating system can be halved, thus saving 15–20 % of the cost of constructing the atriums. Lastly, by lowering the heating-energy requirement heating costs can be reduced by more than 23,000 euros per annum.

During the summer months, the office temperatures can be kept to a comfortable maximum of 28°C using intensive night ventilation and sun shading. Air-conditioning is not necessary.

24 Dachansicht innen 25 Dachbegrünung
24 Roof, view from interior 25 Roof plantings

INSTITUT FÜR FORST- UND NATURFORSCHUNG |
INSTITUTE FOR FORESTRY AND NATURE RESEARCH | 1993–1998

24

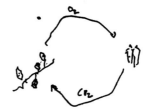

26 Innengarten | **26** Interior garden

INSTITUT FÜR FORST- UND NATURFORSCHUNG |
INSTITUTE FOR FORESTRY AND NATURE RESEARCH | 1993–1998

26

Zusammenfassend lässt sich sagen, dass das Institutsgebäude sich als Niedrigenergiegebäude auszeichnet durch

· optimierte Kompaktheit des Baukörpers
· passive Solarenergienutzung (verglastes Atrium als Klimapuffer)
· hochwärmegedämmte Gebäudehülle
· minimierte Anlagentechnik (u.a. Verzicht auf mechanische Kälteerzeugung)
· Niedertemperatur-Heizsystem, z.B. als Fußbodenheizung ohne zusätzliche statische Heizflächen
· Erdgas als Heizmedium und Brennwerttechnik zur Reduzierung des CO_2-Ausstoßes (Fernwärme nicht verfügbar; Eingriffe in das Grundwasser nicht gewollt)
· unterstützende, nutzergesteuerte Entlüftungsanlage mit Wärmerückgewinnung.

To summarise, the institute building can be characterised as a low-energy building

· displaying optimal compactness
· using passive solar energy (glazed atriums as climate buffers)
· with a highly efficient thermally insulated envelope
· with a minimised technical plant (dispensing with a mechanical cooling system)
· using a low-temperature heating system, e.g. underfloor heating without additional static heating surfaces
· using natural gas as a heating medium and useful output technology to reduce CO_2 emissions (long-distance heating not available; the ground water has been left untouched)
· with a supporting decentralised occupant-controlled ventilation system with heat recovery.

KÜHLKONZEPT Ähnlich wie bei der Lösung zur effizienten Nutzung der Heizenergie wurde für den sommerlichen Wärmeschutz ein Konzept umgesetzt, das einen möglichst geringen Einsatz von Energie bei vertretbaren Investitionsaufwendungen sicherstellt. Aus den Optimierungsrechnungen ergab sich, dass der Einsatz von Nachtluft zur Abkühlung der Gebäudemasse den Verzicht auf mechanische Kühlung erlaubt. Bei der Aufstellung örtlicher Sonnenschutzvorrichtungen (Segel) zur Vermeidung direkter Blendung im Atrium und einer ausreichend großen Querlüftungsmöglichkeit im Dachbereich des Atriums lassen sich die Temperaturverhältnisse in der Aufenthaltszone auf thermisch zumutbare Größenordnungen begrenzen. Die Bürofenster in der Fassadenebene innerhalb und außerhalb der Atrien wurden mit

THE COOLING CONCEPT To provide heat-protection during the summer months, a solution was found similar to that allowing for the efficient use of heating energy, which ensures the minimum consumption of energy at a reasonable cost. Optimisation calculations showed that cooling the building mass with night air obviated the need for mechanical cooling. Using local sun shading (horizontal blinds) to prevent glare in the atriums and by providing adequate lateral ventilation in the atrium roof zone, the temperature in these areas can be kept to a thermally acceptable level. The office windows both inside and outside the atriums require suitable sun shading. During the summer an air-channeling system and additional ventilation openings cool the building mass by providing two

geeigneten Sonnenschutzvorrichtungen ausgestattet. Durch geeignete Luftführung und zusätzliche Lüftungsöffnungen wird für den Sommer ein zweifacher Außenluftwechsel zur Abkühlung der Gebäudemasse ermöglicht. Die zusätzlichen Lüftungsöffnungen wurden regensicher angeordnet und sind im geschlossenen Zustand luftdicht. Um den Effekt der Nachtkühlung sicherzustellen, darf die Gebäudemasse thermisch nicht entkoppelt sein und muss von der Luft umströmt werden können.

TAGESLICHTKONZEPT Alle Arbeitsräume werden entweder über Lichtöffnungen nach außen oder zum zentralen Atrium belichtet. Der Lichttransmissionsgrad der verwendeten Verglasungen liegt bei der Wärmeschutzverglasung bei 70% (Gesamtenergiedurchlassgrad 62%), beim Superglazing bei 66% (Gesamtenergiedurchlassgrad 51%). Um eine gute Tageslichtbeleuchtung zu gewährleisten, wurden im Gebäudekonzept großflächige Verglasungen der Büroräume zum Atrium vorgesehen. Die Nordfassade wurde zur Verbesserung der Energiebilanz teilweise als transparentes Wärmedämmsystem ausgeführt. Hierdurch wird eine Tageslichtbeleuchtung bis in eine Raumtiefe von ca. 7 m sichergestellt.

BLEND- UND SONNENSCHUTZ Die Verglasungen sind mit einem Blend- bzw. Sonnenschutz ausgestattet, um visuellen Komfort zu gewährleisten und um übermäßige Solargewinne bei Überhitzungsgefahr der Büroräume zu reduzieren. Aus Sicht der Tageslichttechnik kann der Blendschutz bzw. Sonnenschutz außen (Verschmutzungsgefahr; Windbeanspruchung) oder innen (Solargewinne im Raum; Überhitzungsrisiko im Sommer) angebracht werden. Während der Blendschutz individuell am Arbeitsplatz einstellbar ist, wird ein optimierter Sonnenschutz, der Kühllasten oder Überhitzungsgefahr mindert, in Abhängigkeit vom Strahlungsangebot im Freien und vom zur Verfügung stehenden Tageslicht im Raum gesteuert.

TAGESLICHTSTEUERUNG Optimierte Tageslichtnutzung, um elektrische Beleuchtung teilweise zu substituieren, sollte sich an dem Grundsatz »Im Winter soviel Tageslichtnutzung – und damit Solarenergienutzung – wie möglich, im Sommer nicht mehr Tageslichtnutzung als nötig« orientieren. Da eine sinnvolle Tageslichtnutzung durch Büronutzung manuell nicht sichergestellt werden kann, empfahl sich hierzu sowohl eine tageslichtabhängige Steuerung der Allgemeinbeleuchtung in den einzelnen Büroräumen, als auch eine tageslichtabhängige Steuerung des Sonnenschutzes. ◄

air changes per hour. The additional ventilation openings are resistant to rain penetration and airtight when closed. To ensure effective night cooling, the building mass is exposed to air that flows unhindered round the building.

THE DAYLIGHT CONCEPT All workrooms have window openings providing illumination from the outside or from the central atrium. The light transmission of the glass used in these rooms is as follows: heat-protection glass: 70% (total energy transmission: 62%) and super-glazing: 66% (total energy transmission: 51%). The building has large expanses of glazing in the office rooms to the atrium to ensure an abundant supply of daylight. To improve the energy balance, the north facade has been partially executed as a transparent heat-insulation system, ensuring that daylight penetrates the rooms to a depth of approx. 7 m.

GLARE PROTECTION AND SUN SHADING The windows are equipped with glare protection and solar-shading to ensure visual comfort and reduce excessive solar gain which might otherwise overheat the office rooms. Applying the principles of daylight technology, glare protection and solar shading can be installed either outside (with the risk of soiling and adverse effects of wind pressure) or inside (risking solar gain in the room and overheating in the summer). The glare protection system can be regulated individually at the workplace. The sun shading system, which is optimally designed to reduce cooling loads and minimise the danger of overheating, operates in relation to the exposure to solar radiation on the outside and the quantity of daylight inside the rooms.

THE CONTROL OF DAYLIGHT The use of daylight as a partial substitute for electrical lighting is optimised in accordance with the principle: "As much daylight – and hence solar energy – as possible, but no more daylight than is absolutely necessary during the summer." Since a reasonable supply of daylight in the offices cannot be ensured manually, the general lighting of the individual office rooms and the sun shading are controlled in relation to the amount of daylight. ◄

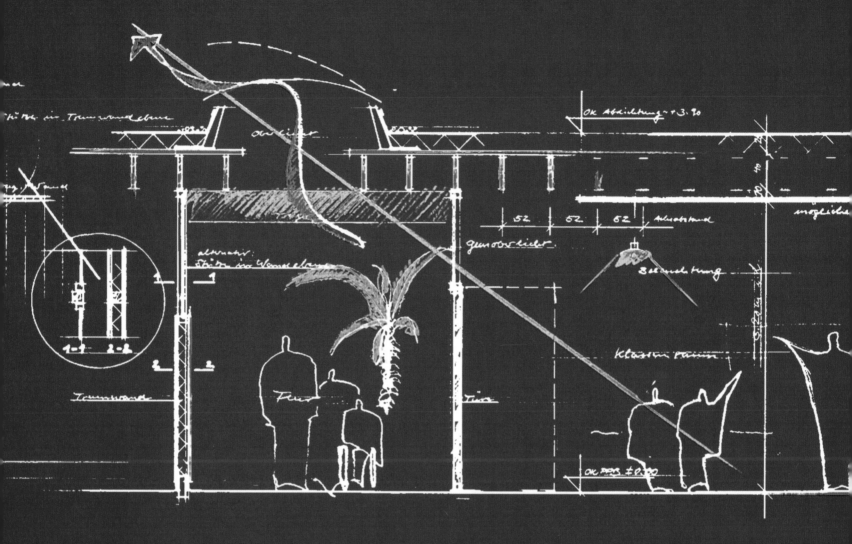

Herbrechtingen liegt im Osten der Schwäbischen Alb, etwa 20 km nordöstlich von Ulm. Das Grundstück befindet sich in einer landschaftlich reizvollen Situation, dem Naturpark »In den Badstubenwiesen«.

Der Ort scheint für diese besondere Schule gut geeignet. Die Anlage folgt einer freien Ordnung und gliedert sich in kleine Teile. Der Bau erinnert weniger an ein Haus, es handelt sich vielmehr um eine offene räumliche Struktur, in der sich jeder Bereich seinen eigenen Gesetzmäßigkeiten und jeder Schüler seinem eigenen Wesen und Vermögen entsprechend entwickeln kann.

Herbrechtingen lies in the eastern part of the Swabian Alb, approx. 20 km northeast of Ulm. The building lot sits within a charming landscape, the Nature Park "In den Badstubenwiesen".

The site seems well-suited to this special school. The complex is laid out freely and divided into small parts. The building recalls less a house than an open spatial configuration, in which each area follows its own laws, and within which each pupil can develop his or her own nature and capacities accordingly.

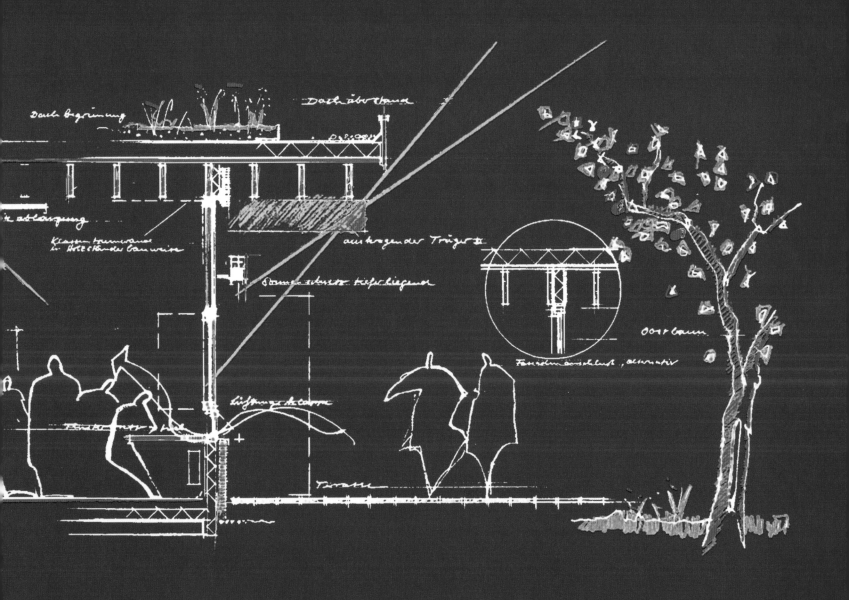

SCHULE FÜR GEISTIG- UND KÖRPERBEHINDERTE KINDER
SCHOOL FOR DISABLED CHILDREN

HERBRECHTINGEN, DEUTSCHLAND | HERBRECHTINGEN, GERMANY; 2001–2004

Vorplatz, Halle, Schulgarten, Klassenraum, Terrasse, Baum, Blumenbeet, Sitzbank etc. – jeder Bereich erhält sein eigenes Vorfeld, nach außen und nach innen, und folgt einer eigenen Ordnung. Jeder Schüler sollte seine eigenen Orte finden können, Lieblingsplätze, an die man sich erinnert, die Beziehungen und Bindungen entstehen lassen.

Die Anlage ist eingeschossig. Flache Bauten beanspruchen zwar mehr Grundstücksfläche, jedoch ermöglichen sie den direkten Weg nach außen von jedem Bereich und Klassenraum aus und bieten somit für jeden die Möglichkeit, ohne fremde Hilfe alle Orte im Gebäude zu erreichen.

Die Gesamtanlage gliedert sich in Teilbereiche, eigene »Häuser«, kleine geschützte Welten, um einen Innenhof gruppiert. Jede Klassenstufe erlebt so ihre eigene kleine Schule als Teil eines Ganzen.

Forecourt, hall, school garden, classroom, terrace, tree, flower bed, bench, etc.: each area has its own realm, extending both outward and inward following its inherent order. Each pupil is able to find his or her own place, favorite spots that will remain in memory, allowing relationships and connections to evolve.

It is a single-story complex. Such horizontal organisation entails a greater surface area, but offers direct routes to the outside from each area or classroom, and makes it possible for each pupil to reach any location in the building without any form of special assistance.

The overall complex is divided into separate zones; its individual "houses" are small, protected worlds grouped around a shared inner courtyard. Each class level, hence, will perceive its own grade level as a little school within the whole.

2

1

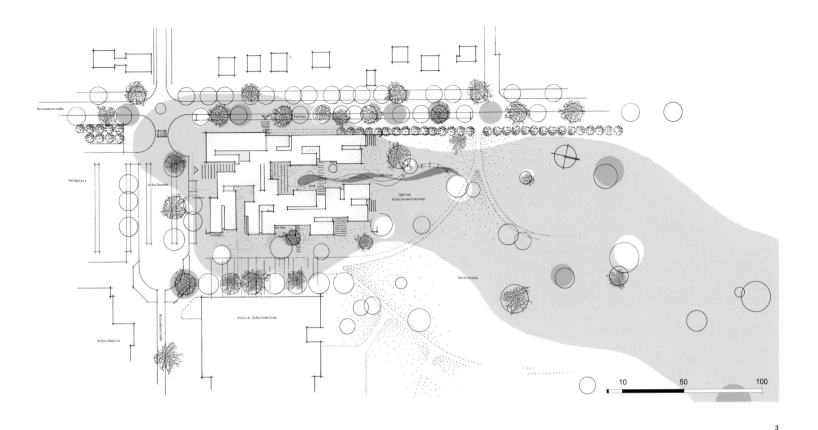

1 Umgebungsplan 2 Spatenstich 3 Lageplan 4 Fassadenstudie 5 Arbeitsmodell
1 Location plan 2 Ground-breaking ceremony 3 Site plan 4 Facade study 5 Working model

SCHULE FÜR GEISTIG- UND KÖRPERBEHINDERTE KINDER |
SCHOOL FOR DISABLED CHILDREN | 2001-2004

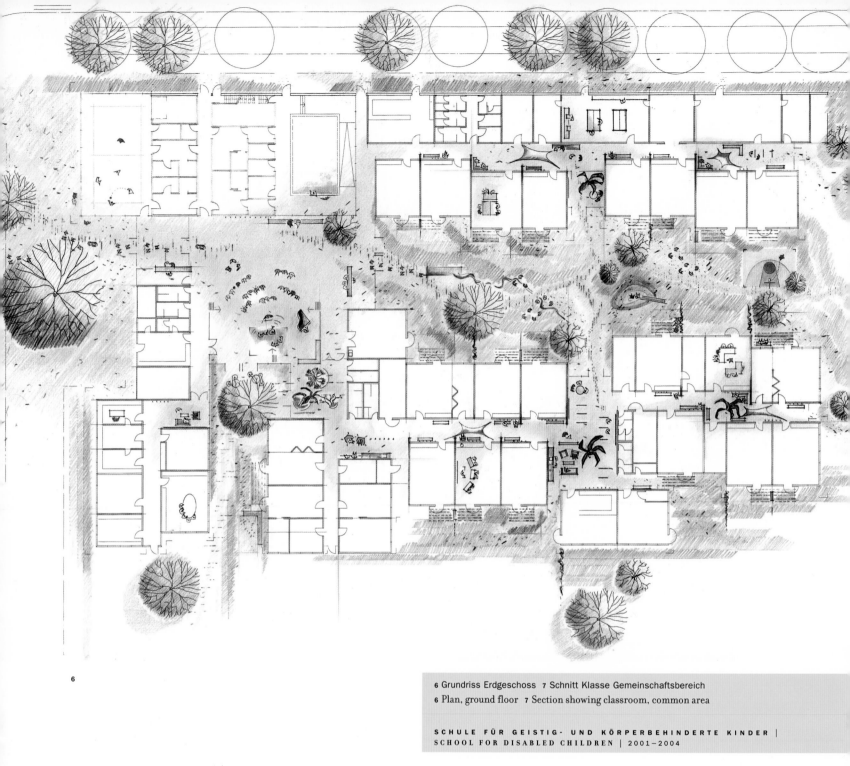

6

6 Grundriss Erdgeschoss 7 Schnitt Klasse Gemeinschaftsbereich
6 Plan, ground floor 7 Section showing classroom, common area

SCHULE FÜR GEISTIG- UND KÖRPERBEHINDERTE KINDER |
SCHOOL FOR DISABLED CHILDREN | 2001–2004

Schüler, Lehrer und Besucher betreten die
Schule von Süden. Eine Wartemöglichkeit für
Kleinbusse direkt am Vorplatz ermöglicht auch
Rollstuhlfahrern den geschützten Zugang zum
Gebäude. Durch die Lage der Sporthalle und
Nebenräume wurde Raum für die Unterrichtsräume im Grünen geschaffen, sie liegen hier
geschützt. Die Sporthalle kann auch außerhalb der schulischen Öffnungszeiten von Dritten genutzt werden, ohne dass die Schule
betreten werden muss.

Pupils, teachers and visitors enter the
school from the south. A waiting area for
small buses directly in front of the forecourt
affords wheelchair-bound pupils sheltered
access to the building. The locations of the
sports building and subsidiary spaces allow
adjoining classrooms to be set in sheltered
landscaped areas. The sports building can
also be used by third parties outside school
hours, without entering the school itself.

Aus der Eingangshalle, die teilweise nach oben verglast ist und in der auch Veranstaltungen und Feiern stattfinden können, öffnet sich der Blick in den Innenhof, den Schulgarten der Anlage. Auf einer Terrasse sitzend, kann man im Sommer die Pause im Freien genießen. Der Musiksaal mit seinen zur Halle öffenbaren Wänden verwandelt sich von einem einfachen Unterrichtsraum zu einer Bühne für Veranstaltungen.

Ein Zugang von Osten verbindet die neue Schule mit dem Bibris-Schulzentrum. Direkt an der Halle liegen die Klassenräume der Unterstufe. Hier lernen die Kleinsten, nicht weit entfernt vom Lehrerhaus.

Die flachen Bauten sind einfach konstruiert, sie bestehen aus natürlichen Materialien und nachwachsenden Baustoffen, einer Mischkonstruktion aus Holz, ausgesteift durch Stahlbetonwände. Freie Grundrisse mit nicht tragenden Wänden ermöglichen eine gute Anpassungsfähigkeit an unterschiedliche Nutzungsformen. Die Anlage kann nach Norden hin erweitert werden, die Struktur verträgt solche Erweiterungen, da sie kein in sich geschlossenes, sondern ein offenes Gebilde ist. ◄

The entrance hall, which is partly glazed above, can also be used for events and celebrations, and offers views toward an interior courtyard where the school garden is found. In summer, breaks can be enjoyed out in the open on the terrace. The music room, whose movable walls lie toward the main hall, can be transformed from a simple classroom into a stage for larger events.

An eastern entrance links the new school with the Bibris School Center. Classrooms for the lower grades lie directly around the hall. Here, the smallest children study, not far removed from the staff accommodation.

The horizontal structures are constructed simply, and consist of natural and renewable building materials, a mixed construction of wood, braced with reinforced concrete. Free floor plans with non-load-bearing walls ensure good adaptability to a variety of functions. The complex can be expanded to the north; its open articulation, as opposed to a self-enclosed one, will enable the structure to accommodate such modifications. ◄

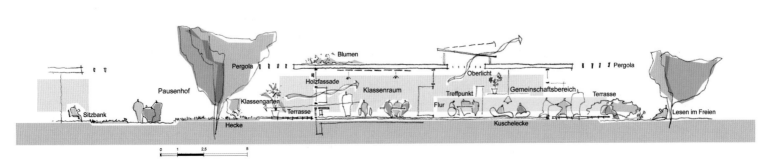

School House

WATER

H_2O

1

WETTBEWERB | COMPETITION

SCHULZENTRUM CHICAGO
SCHOOL COMPLEX CHICAGO

ILLINOIS, USA; 2001

In einem Vorort Chicagos hatte die Stadtverwaltung einen Wettbewerb zum Bau zweier Schulen in sehr unterschiedlicher Lage ausgeschrieben. Grundlage war jeweils ein Programm, das darauf ausgerichtet war, Behinderte in die Schulgemeinschaft zu integrieren. Die Teilnehmer konnten sich für eines der beiden Gelände entscheiden. Behnisch, Behnisch & Partner wählten den Bauplatz in einem der typischen parzellierten Einfamilienhaus-Quartiere.

In dem Gebäude, das die Stufen Vorschule bis achte Klasse beherbergt, werden 800 Kinder ihre ersten Schuljahre erleben. Die in der Schule verbrachte Zeit umfasst einen grossen Teil ihres Alltags. Die gebaute Umgebung der Kinder ist für ihre Entwicklung gerade in diesen entscheidenden Jahren

In the middle of an undistinguished city suburb the school authorities of Chicago ran a competition calling for the design of two different schools on two quite different sites. The program for each school was characterised by the requirement to illustrate how the disabled, the disadvantaged could be fully integrated into the school community. The entrants were free to choose either of the sites. Behnisch, Behnisch & Partner chose to address the demands of the site in the typical single-family-dwelling, lot-structured neighborhood.

800 pupils will spend the first years of their school life in the new Pre K – 8th Grade School. The time spent in school accounts for a major proportion of their

von großer Bedeutung und es stellt sich die Frage, welche Einflüsse für Mädchen und Jungen, für körperlich und geistig Benachteiligte, für Behinderte und Unbehinderte sinnvoll sind. Was ist eine geeignete Umgebung?

daily lives. The child's built environment will naturally have an influence upon their development, particularly in these formative years. We ask ourselves, just which influences are befitting for both girls and boys, the physically or mentally disadvantaged, the disabled or able bodied. What is an appropriate environment?

2

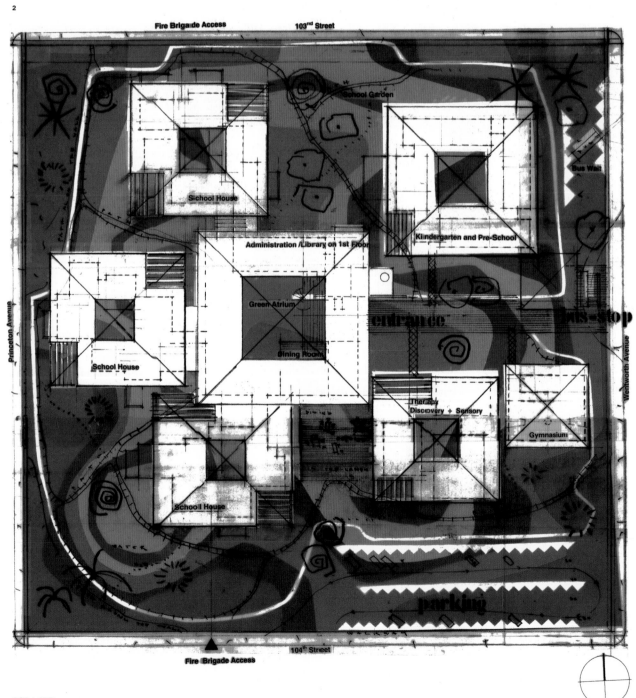

3

4

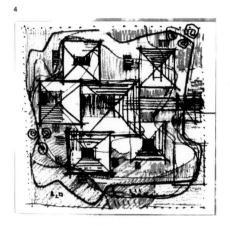

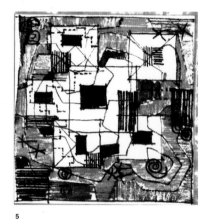

5

Man könnte versuchen, hohe, rigide Bauvolumen zu vermeiden, deren Bild sich so häufig mit der Vorstellung der typischen Schule verknüpft – wir glauben nicht, dass sie als Lebensraum für diese Kinder geeignet sind. Die Durchsetzung bestimmter Ideale, ökonomische Rücksichten, Methoden des standardisierten Bauens, Elemente der Massenfabrikation, Fragen der Rentabilität, Geschossflächenzahlen etc. liessen sich durchaus als Kriterien verwenden, sind für die Kinder und ihre Entwicklung jedoch die falschen Kriterien. Niedrige, zweigeschossige Flachbauten beanspruchen zwar unbestreitbar mehr Grundfläche, der Schulgemeinschaft bieten sie aber offenkundig Vorteile.

Der weite Schulkomplex könnte in mehrere prägnante, überschaubare Segmente aufgeteilt werden – vielleicht nicht in rein technischer Hinsicht, zweifellos aber was den Charakter betrifft. Es könnten so genannte Provinzen entstehen, die sich dem Anschein nach unabhängig voneinander entwickeln und durch die Verbindung von Texturen, Materialien, Farben und individuell gestalteter Umgebung ihre unverwechselbare Identität erhalten. Diese »Provinzen« bilden in ihrer Gesamtheit wiederum ein geschlossenes Ensemble, das Verbindende ist die klare Individualität der Einzelnen.

One could try to avoid the tall, rigid building masses often associated with the school typology, as we consider them not suitable as a habitat for these children. Ideals, economic restraints, standard building construction methods, elements of mass production, issues of profitability, of floor area ratios etc. may well be applicable but are of little interest to the children. In this context it follows that whilst it is certainly true that low-lying, single-story structures require more ground space, this building form has obvious advantages for the school community as a whole.

The rather large school complex could be split up into various identifiable, physically manageable segments – perhaps not purely in technical terms, but certainly in terms of character. So called "Provinces" could emerge, developing seemingly independent of one another, where a combination of textures, materials, colors and individually landscaped environments combine to provide each with a distinct identity. These "Provinces" united, produce a cohesive ensemble.

6

Die Organisation eines solchen Ensembles erlaubt es, auf das Umfeld zu reagieren. Dies bedeutet hier, entweder vom System der rechteckigen geometrischen Muster des urbanen Kontextes auszugehen und diese dann differenzierend aufzulösen oder etwas völlig anderes zu schaffen – etwas Freies, Fließendes, das zu diesem Muster in direktem Gegensatz steht. Wir entschieden uns für eine Überlagerung dieser zwei formalen Konzepte: Die vorgeschlagenen Gebäude entsprechen dem urbanen Raster und bilden einen Kontrast zu den Gärten, einer betont freien, ja extravaganten Landschaft mit farbigen, geschwungenen Formen, der eine nicht der orthogonalen Struktur folgende Mauer, die das Grundstück umschliesst, ein gewisses Maß an Schutz verleiht. Den Mittelpunkt der Anlage bildet ein grünes Zentrum – ein Wintergarten, ein Raum, der seine Eigenart durch die Farben und Düfte der Landschaft erhält, ein Gemeinschaftsraum, der für Meetings, Erholungspausen und Veranstal-

The organisation of such an ensemble offers the opportunity to respond to the surroundings, here it is either possible to start out from the regimented rectangular geometric patterns as defined by the existing urban context, then to dissolve and differentiate them further, or to create something totally different, formally free and fluid in direct contrast to this pattern. We chose to superimpose these two very formal concepts. The proposed buildings follow the urban pattern that forms a contrast to the gardens – a deliberately free, even extravagant landscape, distinguished by colorful, curved forms with a degree of protection offered by a free-flowing wall surrounding the property. At the heart of the ensemble lies a green center, a winter garden, a space characterised by the colors and scents of the landscape, a common space to be used for meetings, to relax during the breaks, or to hold community events. The classrooms are to be flooded

NATURAL VENTILATION

Administration

Entrance

tungen genutzt werden kann. Die Klassenzimmer sind von Tageslicht durchflutet, da sie sich zu den Gärten hin orientieren; Fensterbänder in den Korridoren lassen zusätzliches Tageslicht in die Gebäude.

Die Konstruktion der Flachbauten sollte einfach sein und wo immer möglich sind natürliche, erneuerbare Werkstoffe zu verwenden. Als gesonderte Häuser sind der Kindergarten mit seinem eigenen überdachten Hof und das Gesundheitszentrum zu betrachten – kleine Welten darstellend –, die auf einem ruhigen Teil des Grundstücks liegen.

In einem so weitläufigen, mannigfaltigen Komplex brauchen weder das Material noch die baulichen und formalen Aspekte im Voraus eindeutig festgelegt zu werden; alles sollte vielmehr offen und frei gestaltbar bleiben, um dann gemeinsam mit den Nutzern in den Planungsphasen präzisiert zu werden. ◄

with daylight as each faces into the gardens beyond; strip windows in the corridor walls ensure further penetration of daylight.

The series of low-lying buildings should be of simple construction, and where possible made of natural, regenerative materials. The kindergarten with its own sheltered courtyard and the Health Center are to be considered as individual houses – defining small worlds – located in a quiet part of the site.

In such a large, diverse complex neither the materials, nor the constructional or formal aspects need to be clearly predetermined, instead everything should remain open and free: our goal is the appropriate solution for each specific task. ◄

Die World Intellectual Property Organization (WIPO), eine internationale Organisation, deren Aufgabe der Schutz des geistigen Eigentums ist, hat ihren Hauptsitz in Genf. Sie ist zur Zeit auf mehrere Standorte in der Stadt verteilt. Diese Büroflächen sollen an einen Ort zusammengefasst und konzentriert werden. Ein neues Projekt soll in unmittelbarer Nähe zum Hauptgebäude der WIPO entstehen, ein Verwaltungsgebäude mit Konferenzzentrum.

The World International Property Organization (WIPO), an international organisation responsible for the protection of intellectual property, has its headquarters in Geneva. Its facilities are currently distributed throughout several locations in the city. All of these offices are to be consolidated and concentrated in one place. A new project, an administration building with conference center, is to rise in the immediate vicinity of the main WIPO building.

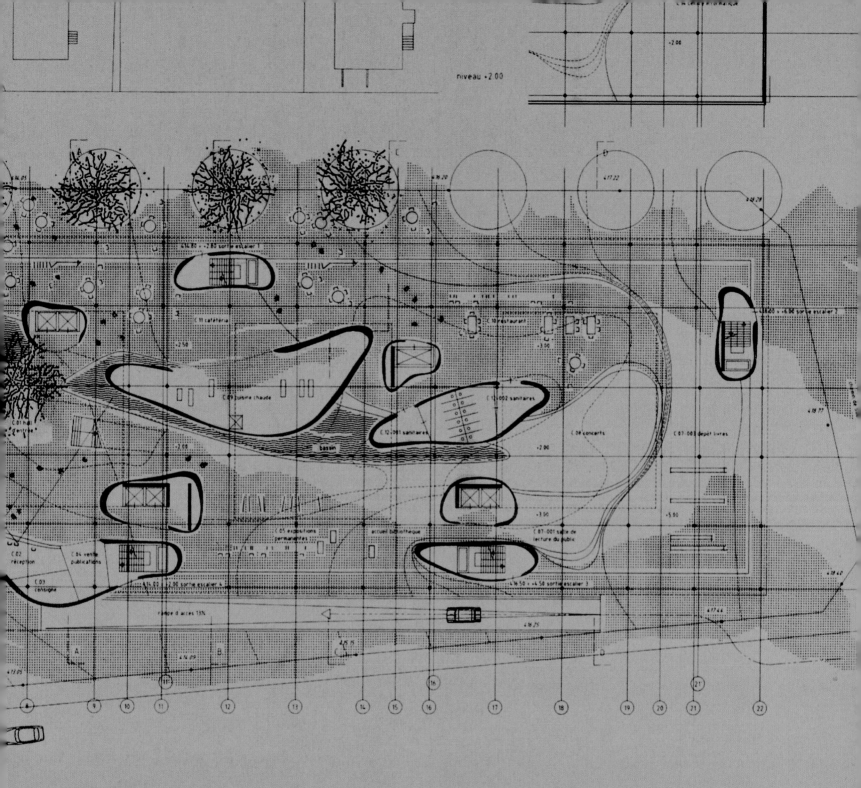

WORLD INTELLECTUAL PROPERTY ORGANIZATION (WIPO)

VERWALTUNGSGEBÄUDE MIT KONFERENZZENTRUM | ADMINISTRATION BUILDING WITH CONFERENCE CENTER

GENF, SCHWEIZ | GENEVA, SWITZERLAND; 2000–2005

1

2

1 Präsentationsmodell 2 Lageplan 3 Umgebungsplan
1 Presentation model 2 Site plan 3 Location plan

WORLD INTELLECTUAL PROPERTY ORGANIZATION | 2000–2005

Ende 1999 wurde ein international offener Realisierungswettbewerb mit vorgeschaltetem Qualifizierungsverfahren ausgeschrieben. Der Wettbewerbsbeitrag von Behnisch, Behnisch & Partner wurde im März 2000 mit dem ersten Preis ausgezeichnet und sollte nach einstimmigem Urteil der Jury realisiert werden.

Das Grundstück liegt auf einer leichten Anhöhe zwischen Stadtzentrum und dem Flughafen im Nordwesten, im internationalen Distrikt von Genf. Der Blick von dort aus reicht über den Genfer See bis hin zu den Alpen mit dem Mont-Blanc, der, ganzjährig schneebedeckt, ein eindrucksvolles Panorama bietet. Die Lage direkt am Place des Nations, mit den Gebäuden anderer internationaler Organisationen wie der UNHCR, der WMO und der UNO in der näheren Umgebung, verleiht dem Ort ein besonderes Ambiente.

In late 1999, an open international design competition with respective pre-qualification procedures was advertised. The submission by Behnisch, Behnisch & Partner was awarded 1st prize in March of 2000 and, following unanimous approval by the jury, was to be carried forward through to realisation.

The site lies on a slight rise in Geneva's international district, between the city center and the airport to the north-west. The view from here reaches past Lake Geneva all the way to the Alps, where Mont Blanc, covered with snow year round, offers a striking panorama. The site, lying directly on the Place des Nations, with buildings belonging to other international agencies such as the UNHCR, the WMO and the UNO in the immediate vicinity, offers a special ambience.

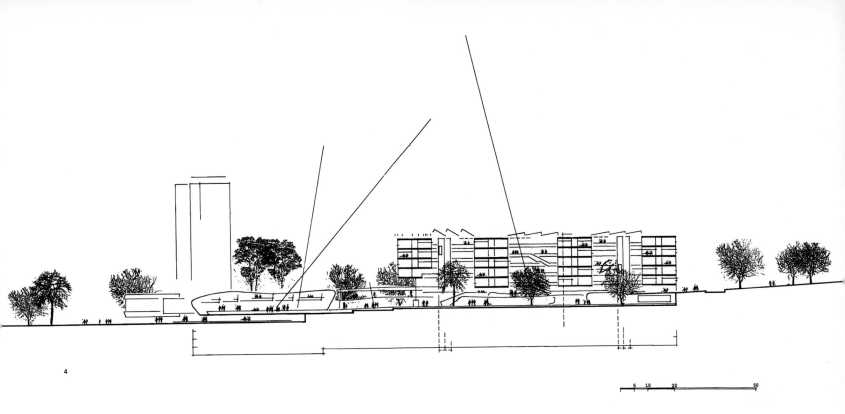

4

Das gewünschte Raumprogramm zum Wettbewerb und die spezifischen Anforderungen an die Nutzungen waren detailliert beschrieben. Die Vorgaben und die Einhaltung der maximalen Abmessungen des Baukörpers in Länge, Breite und Höhe sind wichtige Kriterien. Für die Gestaltung der Freianlagen waren aufgrund der sehr begrenzten Grundstücksverhältnisse, mit teilweise direkter Anbindung an den öffentlichen Straßenraum, bereits im Auslobungstext klare Vorstellungen formuliert.

Gefordert sind Arbeitsplätze für insgesamt 560 Mitarbeiter, ein Konferenzbereich für 650 Delegierte sowie öffentlich nutzbare Flächen für Ausstellungen, Veranstaltungen und eine Bibliothek für WIPO-Mitarbeiter. Ein Restaurant mit Cafeteria liegt im Erdgeschoss. Tiefgaragenstellplätze sowie Lager- und Anlieferungsflächen, die übergreifend auch für die anderen WIPO-Gebäude nutzbar sein sollen, werden im Zuge des Neubaus mit realisiert.

The desired spatial program and the specific user requirements were prescribed in the competition brief in some detail. Observance of these preconditions and of the maximum dimensions of the building's envelope are important criteria. Given the unusually constrained location with its direct adjacency in places to public thoroughfares, the design brief already formulated explicit prerequisites for the design of outdoor spaces.

Required were work stations for altogether 560 employees, a conference area for 650 delegates, as well as publicly usable areas for exhibitions, events and a library for WIPO employees. A restaurant with cafeteria was to be located on the ground floor. Underground garage parking, as well as storage and delivery areas, meant to be accessible to the other WIPO buildings as well, will be realised in the course of the new construction.

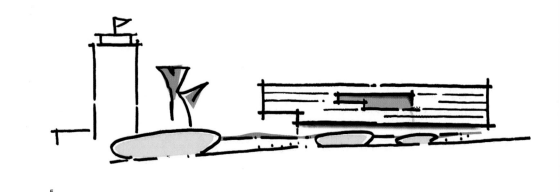

5

WORLD INTELLECTUAL PROPERTY ORGANIZATION | 2000–2005

6

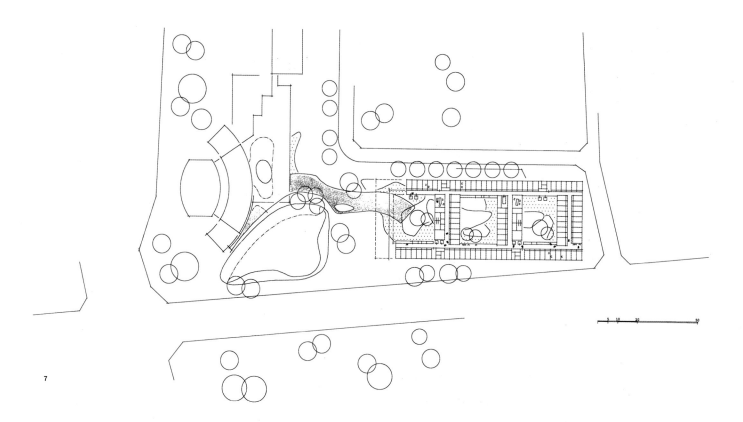

7

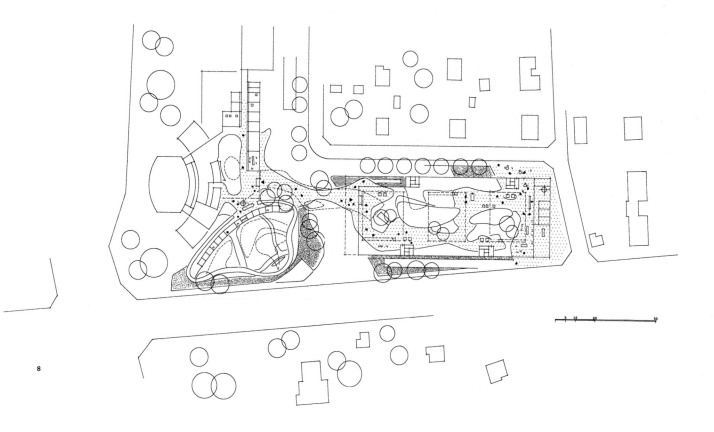

8

Die relativ eng gefassten Rahmenbedingungen, aber auch das umfangreiche, sehr differenzierte Raumprogramm hätten Voraussetzungen für einen großen, starren Apparat sein können. Verschiedene Aspekte sprachen jedoch gegen eine solche Lösung.

Allzu leicht werden Teile großer Anlagen den praktischen und pragmatischen Aspekten unterworfen. Die Kraft der Beteiligten ist begrenzt und die Eigendynamik solcher großen Projekte bindet viel Energien. Wir werden den Ort, an dem gearbeitet wird, individualisieren: Arbeitsplatz, Arbeitsraum, Flure, Treppenhäuser, sowie alle anderen Bereiche, aus denen sich solch eine große Anlage zusammensetzt, sollten ein eigenes Gesicht erhalten. Der Wettbewerbsentwurf hat sich im weiteren Verlauf der Bearbeitung weiterentwickelt und verändert. Die Auslagerung und Anbindung des Konferenzsaals an das bestehende Hauptgebäude wurde auf Wunsch des Bauherrn geplant, das großzügige, bestehende Foyer des Hauptgebäudes sollte angebunden sein. Die konzeptionelle Grundidee des Wettbewerbsentwurfs wurde beibehalten. Der ausgelagerte Saal ist in die konzeptionelle Idee des Erdgeschosses integriert.

These relatively challenging preconditions, combined with the comprehensive and highly differentiated spatial program, could have resulted in a large, stiff apparatus. Various considerations, however, spoke against such a solution.

Sections of large complexes are all too readily subordinated to practical and pragmatic aspects. The capacities of the parties involved are constrained, and such extensive projects bind much energy with their own dynamics. We wanted to individualise the areas that would be utilised for work: work stations, workspaces, hallways, stairways, as well as all other areas making up this large complex, each was to retain a certain individual profile. Over the course of subsequent preparations, the competition design was developed further and eventually transformed. The external relocation of the conference chamber and its connection to the existing main building was planned at the client's request; the generous existing foyer of the main building was to abut the chamber. However, the basic conceptual idea of the competition brief was retained. The relocated chamber has been integrated into the idea of the open ground floor.

9

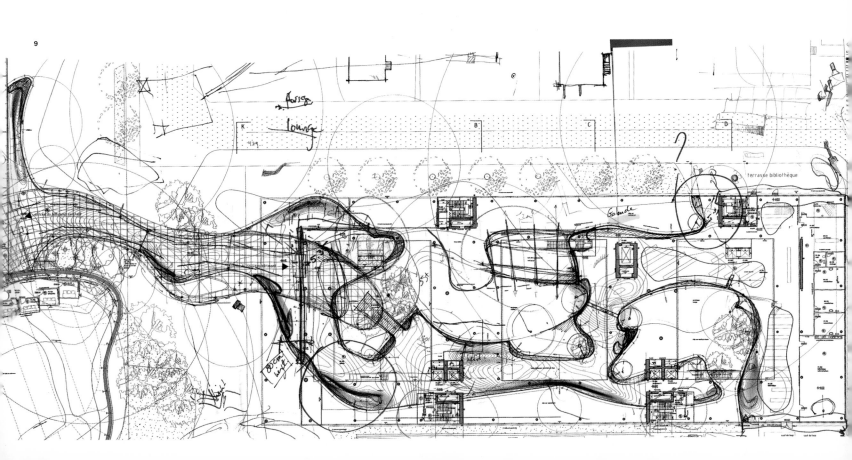

Die öffentlichen und vor allem gemeinschaftlich genutzten Bereiche liegen im Erdgeschoss. Sie entwickeln sich formal nach anderen Gesetzmäßigkeiten als die Bürobereiche: Sie werden formal überhöht zu einer weichen, gerundeten architektonischen Landschaft, im Gegensatz stehend zu den darüber schwebenden, rational angeordneten Büroflächen der öffentlichen Ebenen.

Der Konferenzsaal sowie die Sondernutzungen im Inneren des Gebäudes werden Teil einer artifiziellen Landschaft; als frei geformte Volumen sind sie hier wie Findlinge eingebettet. Sie werden von den öffentlichen Nutzungen im Erdgeschoss und 1. Obergeschoss umspült. Die Landschaft durchdringt die Anlage, fließt durch sie hindurch und wieder heraus, sie verbindet Vorhandenes und Neues. Auf dieser Ebene betritt man das Gebäude über die zweigeschossige Eingangshalle, von der aus sich alle weiteren Nutzungen erschließen. Die Halle stellt einen Ort zum Verweilen dar, zugänglich für die Öffentlichkeit.

Public and especially commonly used areas are located in the ground level. They are designed formally according to standards different from those governing the office levels: they will be formally elevated to a soft, rounded architectural landscape, in contrast to the rationally configured office levels floating above the public levels.

The conference chamber, as well as other special areas of the building's interior, will become components of an artificial landscape, freely shaped volumes embedded like stranded boulders. They will be surrounded playfully by the public facilities on the ground level and first story. The landscape will penetrate into the complex, flowing through it and out again, connecting new with preexisting elements. The building is entered via the double-story-height entrance hall, which gives access to all further facilities. The hall is a place to linger, and is publicly accessible.

10 Modellstudien zur Konstruktion des Konferenzsaales **11** Grundriss Konferenzsaal **12** Perspektivische Darstellung **13** Schnitt | **10** Model studies for construction of conference hall **11** Plan, conference hall **12** Rendering **13** Section

WORLD INTELLECTUAL PROPERTY ORGANIZATION | 2000–2005

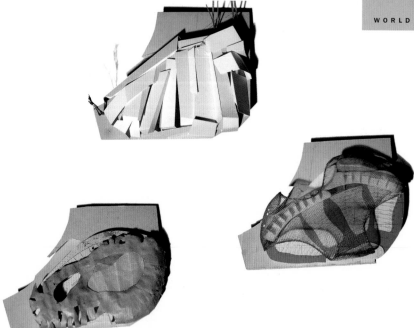

10

11

12

13

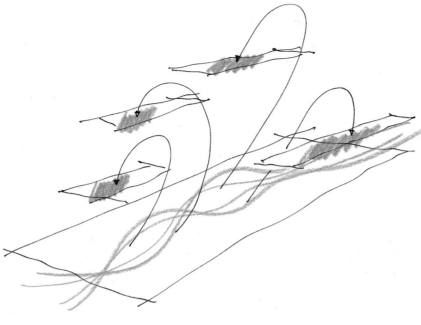

14

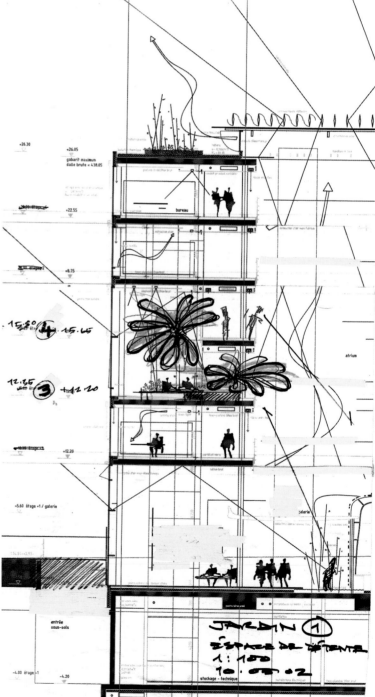

15

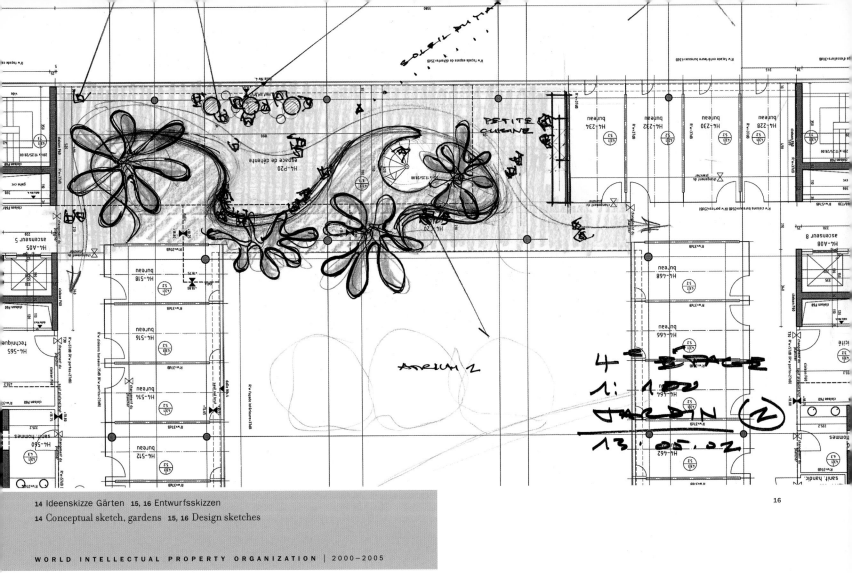

14 Ideenskizze Gärten 15, 16 Entwurfsskizzen
14 Conceptual sketch, gardens 15, 16 Design sketches

16

Vom Foyer gelangt man über eine großzügige Treppe auf die offene, frei geschwungene Galerie, einer Art Transferebene zwischen Erdgeschoss und den darüber liegenden Büroebenen. Das bestehende Hauptgebäude wird von hier aus über einen wettergeschützten Steg angebunden.

Die Büroräume für die Mitarbeiter »schweben« über dieser Landschaft, sie liegen in den fünf Obergeschossen. Die Räume sind sachlich geordnet, gliedern sich über eine orthogonale Struktur. Die Nutzungsbereiche organisieren sich um drei Innenatrien, die durch großzügige Oberlichtverglasungen ihren thermischen Abschluss erhalten. Intensiv begrünte, teilweise zweigeschossige Gärten mit direktem Außenbezug über Loggien werden in die strenge Ordnung integriert und lockern diese auf. Lange und dunkle Flurzonen werden durch diese vielschichtige Struktur vermieden. ◂

From the foyer, a generous staircase leads to the open, freely formed gallery, a kind of transitional zone between the ground floor and the office levels above. The existing main building will be linked to this part of the new complex via a footbridge that is sheltered from the elements.

The offices for employees "float" above this landscape, set in the five upper stories. The spaces are pragmatically ordered, and are divided within an orthogonal structure. Areas of use are organised around three inner atriums, which receive their thermal closures through generous glazed roof lights. Intensively planted, partially two-story gardens with direct access to the outside via loggias are integrated into the strict order, punctuating and enlivening it. By means of this many-layered structure, long, dark hallways are avoided. ◂

Am Rande Cambridges, nahe der Longfellow Bridge, entwickelt eine Investorengesellschaft ein neues Areal auf einer ehemaligen, 42.000 m² großen Industriebrache. In zweiter Reihe, zurückgesetzt vom Charles River, in fußläufiger Entfernung zum bekannten Kendall Square, wird dieses Gebiet eine interessante Ergänzung und ein neues Subzentrum für Cambridge sein. Nur wenige Gehminuten entfernt liegen die berühmten Universitäten Massachusetts Institute of Technology und Harvard.

On the edge of Cambridge, Massachusetts, near Longfellow Bridge, an investment company is developing a new site, one lying within a disused industrial zone covering 42,000 m². Set back from the Charles River, just a short walk from well-known Kendall Square, this district will be a valuable supplement to it and a new sub-center for Cambridge. Only a few minutes walk away are both the renowned Massachusetts Institute of Technology and Harvard University.

WETTBEWERB UND REALISIERUNG | COMPETITION AND REALISATION

GENZYME CENTER

NEUBAU EINER HAUPTVERWALTUNG | NEW HEAD OFFICE BUILDING
CAMBRIDGE, USA; 2000—2003

1 Blick von Westen (vor Fertigstellung, November 2002) 2 Blick von Süden (vor Fertigstellung, August 2003) 3 Lageplan | 1 View from west (under construction, November 2002) 2 View from south (under construction, August 2003) 3 Site plan

GENZYME CENTER | 2000–2003

Es werden sieben neue Gebäude entstehen, vier sind schon im Bau, weitere in Planung, ein Wohn- und Geschäftshaus (geplant von der Architects Alliance aus Toronto), je ein Laborgebäude, von Steven Ehrlich und Anshen & Allen, beide Los Angeles, und das Genzyme Center, Behnisch, Behnisch & Partner Inc. (Venice, Kalifornien). Den Masterplan für die Gesamtanlage, eine Art städtebaulichen Rahmenplan, hatten Urban Strategies aus Toronto entwickelt.

Der Bauherr, Lyme Properties LLC, hatte für alle Bauvorhaben Wettbewerbe ausgelobt. International arbeitende Büros wurden eingeladen und stellten in einem nicht-anonymen Verfahren ihre Entwürfe vor.

Seven new buildings are planned in all, and four are already under construction. Still in planning are a residential and commercial building (planned by Toronto-based architects Alliance); a laboratory building designed by Steven Ehrlich and one by Anshen & Allen, both of Los Angeles; and the Genzyme Center by Behnisch, Behnisch & Partner Inc. (Venice, California). The master plan for the overall complex, a kind of urban-planning site plan, was prepared by Urban Strategies of Toronto.

The client, Lyme Properties LLC, announced design competitions for all planned projects. Internationally active firms were invited and presented designs in a non-anonymous procedure.

2

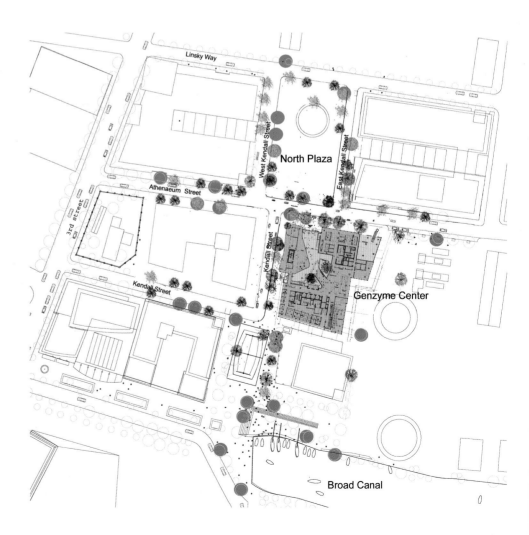

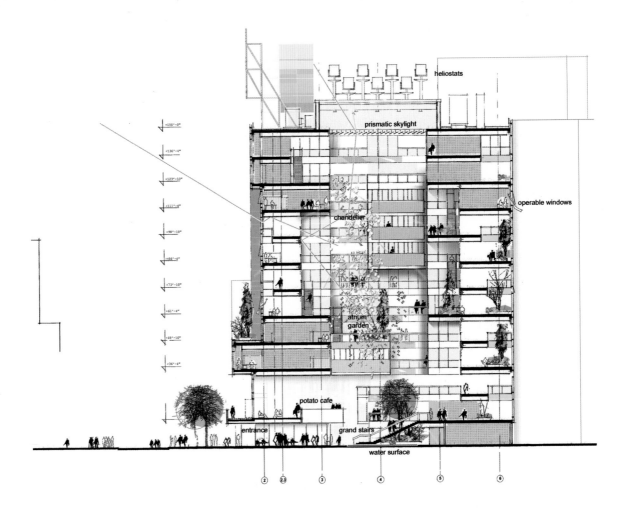

heliostats

prismatic skylight

+150'-0"
+136'-4"
+123'-10"
+111'-4"
+98'-10"
+86'-4"
+73'-10"
+61'-4"
+48'-10"
+36'-4"

operable windows

chandelier

atrium
garden

potato cafe

entrance

grand stairs

water surface

② ㉓ ③ ④ ⑤ ⑥

4

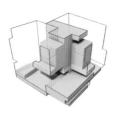

5

Beim künftigen Genzyme Center waren neben Architekten, Vertretern der Stadt Cambridge und dem Bauherrn auch die Nutzer in der Jury vertreten. Der CEO (Chief Executive Officer) der Genzyme Corporation hatte Einfluss im Preisgericht. Sein Augenmerk war auf die Nachhaltigkeit, die Qualität der Arbeitsplätze und innovative Ideen gerichtet.

Im April 2000 gewannen wir den Wettbewerb, wenig später begann die Planung. Unser Büro in Kalifornien steuert das Projekt und ist Auftraggeber für Ingenieure, ausführende Architekten, Bauleitung etc. Die Entwurfs-Arbeit wurde weitgehend von unserem Stuttgarter Büro geleistet.

In the case of the future Genzyme Center, the jury included – besides architects, representatives of the city of Cambridge and the client – also the future users. The CEO of Genzyme Corporation also had significant influence in the jury. He was attentive to the project's sustainability and the qualities of the work stations, and welcomed innovation.

In April of 2000, we won the competition, and soon began the planning process. Our office in California continues to direct the project, awarding the contracts for engineers, executing architects, construction work, etc. Design work has been performed principally by the Stuttgart office.

4 Schnitt 5 Massenstudien 6 Blick von Norden 7 Grundriss 1. Obergeschoss Empfang
4 Section 5 Massing studies 6 View from the north 7 Plan, 2nd floor reception

GENZYME CENTER | 2000–2003

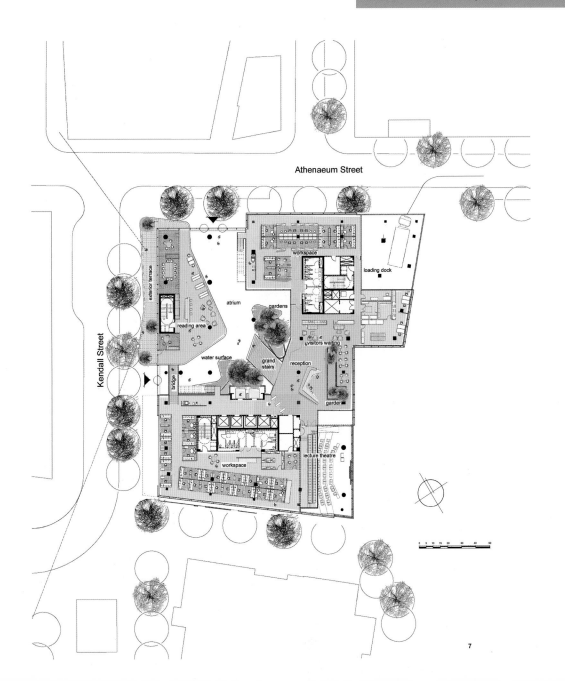

Athenaeum Street

Kendall Street

exterior terrace

reading area

atrium

gardens

workspace

loading dock

visitors waiting

water surface

grand stairs

reception

bridge

garden

workspace

lecture theatre

0 5 10 15 20   30   40   50

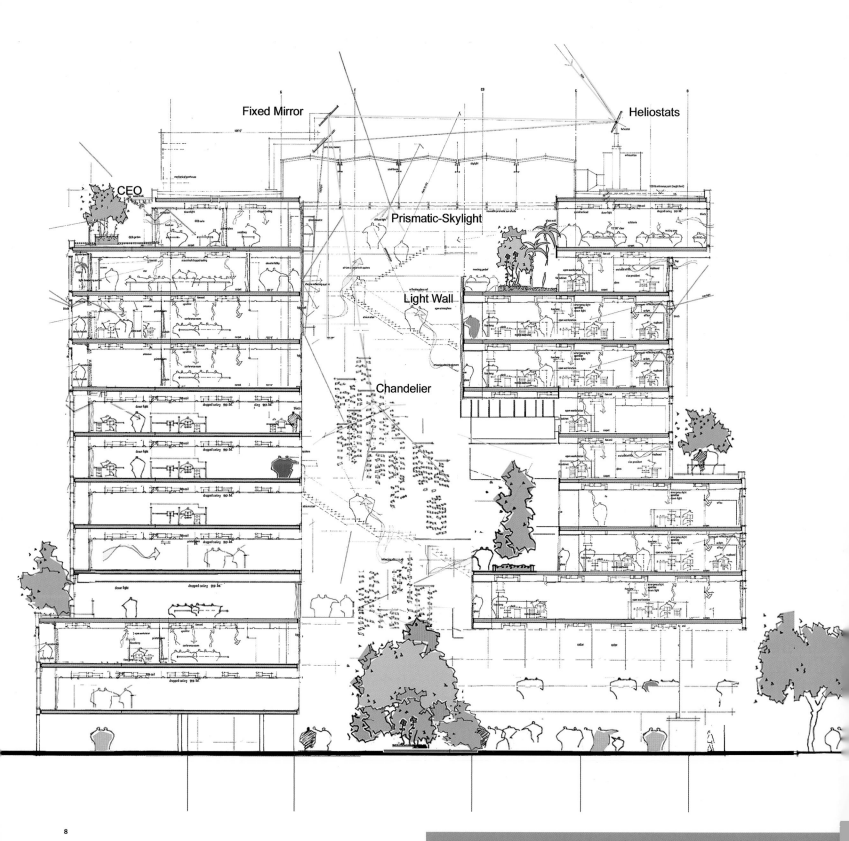

Fixed Mirror

Heliostats

CEO

Prismatic-Skylight

Light Wall

Chandelier

8 Schnitt durch Atrium 9, 10, 11 Erläuterungsskizzen des Wettbewerbs
8 Section showing atrium 9, 10, 11 Sketches competition entry

GENZYME CENTER | 2000–2003

Dieses Verwaltungsgebäude mit einer Brutto-geschossfläche von 28.000 m² sollte in einem von dynamischen Forschungsunternehmen dominierten Umfeld auf besondere Weise für Fortschritt stehen und einen Identifikationspunkt für die 920 Mitarbeiter und die Besucher bilden. Hohe Funktionalität und Flexibilität, aber auch Rücksicht auf Natur und Umwelt waren gewünscht.

Die strikten städtebaulichen Vorgaben begrenzten die Möglichkeiten der Gestaltung des Baukörpers. Aus diesem Grund entschieden wir uns für eine zurückhaltende, entsprechend den städtebaulichen Richtlinien geformte Gebäudehülle. Diese ist geprägt durch das Zusammenspiel von Einzelelementen wie Doppelfassaden, öffenbaren Fenstern, beweglichem Sonnenschutz und farbigen Vorhängen. Die Gestaltungselemente helfen, die Energieverluste des Gebäudes zu senken. Der einzelne Nutzer reguliert dabei bewusst seine eigene »Umwelt« und beeinflusst so auch indirekt die äußere Erschei-

This administration building, with a gross floor area of 28,000 m², and sited in a zone dominated by dynamic research enterprises, is meant to symbolise progress in an appropriate fashion, while providing a sense of corporate identity to the 920 employees, as well as to visitors. Desired were a high degree of functionality and flexibility, but also attentiveness to nature and the environment.

In designing the overall architectural volume, our options were limited by strict urban planning criteria. For this reason, we decided for a restrained envelope consistent with the relevant planning guidelines. The building's appearance is marked by the interplay of individual elements such as the double facades, openable windows, adjustable sun protection, and colored curtains. Such elements have been used to reduce energy loss from the building further. The individual user consciously regulates his own "environment" and thus also

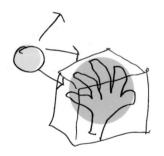

Boston-Oasis

9

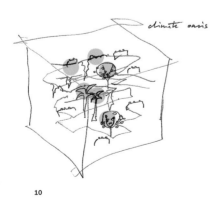

climate oasis

10

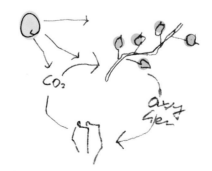

CO_2

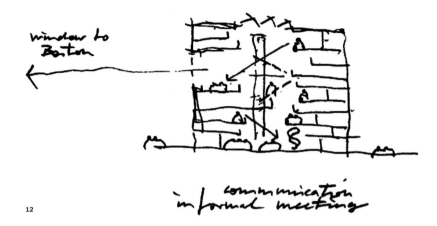

window to Boston

communication informal meeting

nung des Gebäudes. Die verschiedenen Elemente der Hülle stehen gemeinsam mit den räumlichen Strukturen des Inneren in einem Wechselspiel. Hier entwickelt sich frei von den Zwängen des Außenklimas die Architektur: Ein komplex geformtes Atrium mit großzügigen Flächen, offenen Gärten und einem öffentlich zugänglichen Erdgeschoss bildet die Grundlage der räumlichen Entwicklung.

Es entsteht eine Klima-Oase, die sich über zwölf Geschosse ausbreitet, sich wie ein Baum in Äste und Zweige gabelt. Sie entwickelt sich aus der Mitte des Grundrisses bis an die Fassade und schafft über dieses Atrium räumliche Situationen mit unterschiedlichen privaten und öffentlichen Identitäten. Gleichzeitig wird das Gebäude natürlich entlüftet.

indirectly influences the building's exterior appearance. The various elements of the envelope engage in an interplay with the spatial articulation of the interior. Here, the architecture develops free from the constraints of both the outer climate and urban guidelines. An atrium of complex form, with spacious areas, open gardens and an openly accessible ground level provides the basis for spatial development.

The result is a climate oasis extending over all twelve levels, spreading like a tree with its limbs and branches. It develops from the center of the building through to the facades, creating distinct spatial arrangements throughout the atrium with different private and public atmospheres. At the same time, the atrium is integral to the natural ventilation of the building.

12 Skizze Wettbewerb 13 Halle und Prismendecke, Baustellenfoto 14 Ausschnittsfoto des
Arbeitsmodells Atrium | 12 Sketch competition entry 13 Atrium and prismceiling, construction
photograph 14 Photograph of large-scale atrium model

GENZYME CENTER | 2000–2003

14

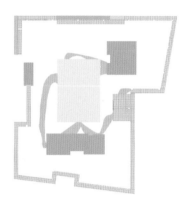

15

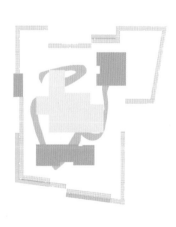

16

15 Deckenbild, exemplarische Abwicklung ausgewählter Geschosse 16 Atrium, Baustellenfoto, Mai 2003
15 Ceiling paintings of selected stories 16 Atrium, construction photograph, May 2003

GENZYME CENTER | 2000–2003

Das Atrium verbindet die verschiedenen Bereiche des Gebäudes. Treppen zwischen den Geschossen bilden Verbindungen und Orte, führen durch Gärten, die, auf Terrassen gelegen, am Atrium entlanglaufen. Sie sind Teil eines Boulevards, der in der Lobby des Erdgeschosses zwischen Bäumen und Wasserflächen beginnt und sich ähnlich einer Stadt mit Gassen und Plätzen, Engen und Weiten, Ausblicken und Einblicken in die Höhe entwickelt.

Es entstehen horizontale und vertikale Nachbarschaften, verbunden durch Wege und das Atrium selbst. Die Arbeitsplätze erhalten ihre Identität durch ihre Lage in unterschiedlichen Raumsituationen: Konzentrierte, private Arbeitsbereiche stehen den öffentlichen und freien Räumen der Gärten und des Atriums gegenüber, offene Arbeitsplätze und geschlossene Büros wechseln sich hierbei entsprechend den Anforderungen und Situationen ab. Eine vielfältige und flexible Bürolandschaft entsteht.

The atrium acts to link together the various departments. Stairs between levels create connections and places, leading through gardens which, laid out on terraces, run around the atrium. These are parts of a route which begins in the lobby on the ground level between trees and expanses of water, and proliferates like a city with narrow streets and squares, with spaces both narrow and broad, composing vistas and views into the height.

This results in horizontal and vertical neighborhoods, linked by paths and by the atrium itself. Work stations are identified via their locations in various spatial settings: concentrated, private work areas lie across from the public and open spaces of the gardens and atrium, open work stations and closed offices alternate according to the relevant requirements and situations. The result is an office landscape characterised by multiplicity and flexibility.

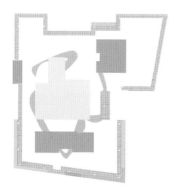

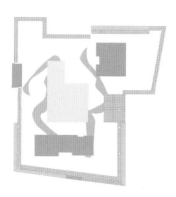

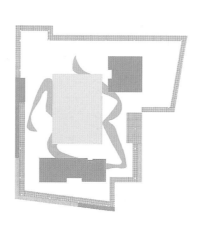

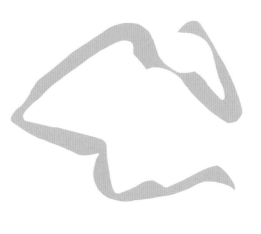

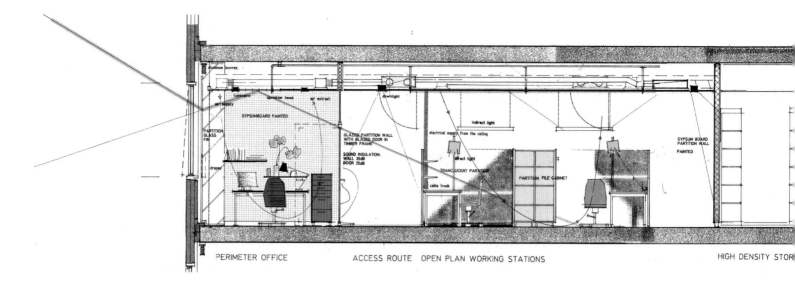

PERIMETER OFFICE   ACCESS ROUTE   OPEN PLAN WORKING STATIONS   HIGH DENSITY STOR

17

17, 18, 19, 20 Einzelarbeitsplatz 21 Grundriss 4. Obergeschoss 22 Grundriss 11. Obergeschoss
17, 18, 19, 20 Cubicle 21 Plan, 5th floor 22 Plan, 12th floor

GENZYME CENTER | 2000–2003

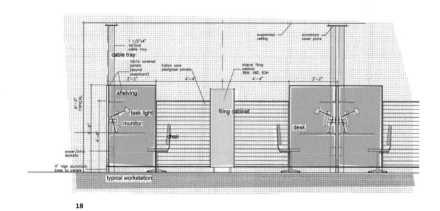

18

19

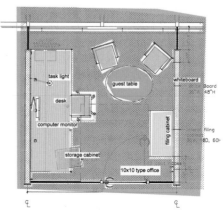

20

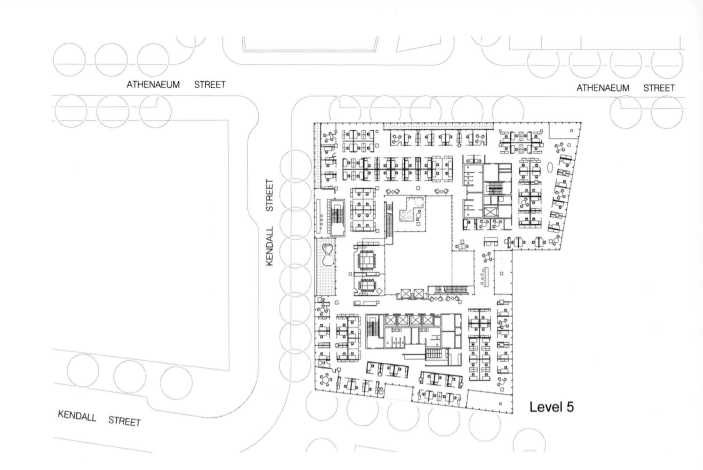

ATHENAEUM STREET

ATHENAEUM STREET

KENDALL STREET

KENDALL STREET

Level 5

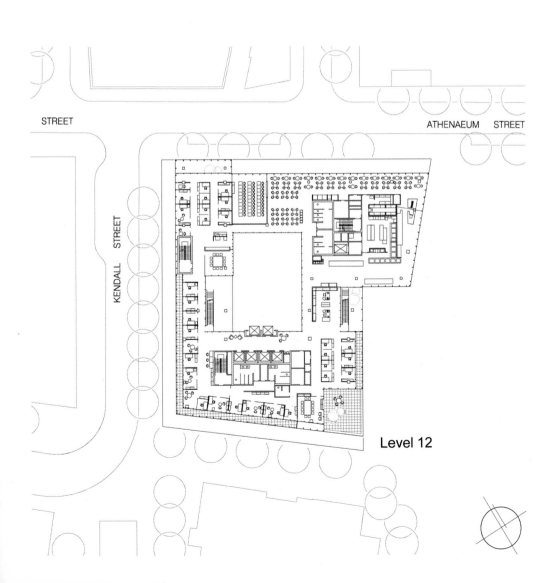

STREET

ATHENAEUM STREET

KENDALL STREET

Level 12

Die Arbeitsplätze werden weitgehend natürlich belichtet, unterstützt durch die im Sonnenschutz integrierten Umlenklamellen an der Fassade. Das Atrium ist durch den Einsatz von Heliostaten mit Tageslicht ausgeleuchtet. Die Prismendecke unter dem Glasoberlicht filtert dabei das Licht nach unten und dient als Sonnenschutz und Blendschutz, ohne die Lichtmenge zu reduzieren. Das so eingespiegelte Sonnenlicht wird im Inneren des Gebäudes über Lichtobjekte verteilt, durch artifizielle »Kronleuchter« und mittels einer »Lichtwand« – vertikalen, verspiegelten, sich bewegenden Lamellen – in die Tiefe des Raums reflektiert.

Ein Gebäude soll entstehen, das neben der Förderung interner Kommunikation unsere natürlichen Ressourcen schützen helfen soll. Darüber hinaus soll es für die Mitarbeiterinnen und Mitarbeiter von Genzyme einen identitätsstiftenden Ort, ein Zuhause bilden.

Work stations will be mostly naturally lit, supported by light-redirecting blinds at the facade. Via the introduction of heliostats, the atrium will be fully illuminated by daylight. The prismatic skylight below the glazed top-lighting filters light passing downward and provides both sun and glare protection without reducing the quantity of available light. The sunlight thus reflected is distributed throughout the interior via light objects, and reflected deep into the spaces by means of a series of "chandeliers," and a "light wall" composed of vertical, mirrored, moveable blinds.

The result is to be a building which, beyond fulfilling the requirements of internal communication, will also contribute towards the protection of our natural resources. Moreover, it should provide Genzyme employees with a setting that offers a sense of identity, and of home.

23

23 Präsentationsmodell 24 Ansicht Ost 25 Bemusterung der Vorhangfarben

23 Presentation model 24 East elevation 25 Mockup curtains

GENZYME CENTER | 2000–2003

25

Die ökologische Planung der Genzyme Firmenzentrale erstreckt sich über alle Teile des Gebäudes: die Fassade, das Atrium, die Gebäudetechnik, die Beleuchtungsanlage und das Regenentwässerungssystem. Das Entwurfsteam, der Auftraggeber und der Bauunternehmer suchten nach dem optimalen Zusammenspiel von Architektur, Baukosten, Ausführung und Funktionssicherheit, um aus dem Investorengebäude einen ökologisch sinnvollen Firmenhauptsitz zu machen. Und sie waren bestrebt, das Beste zu erreichen: einen Bau mit der LEED-Platinum-Auszeichnung.

Die Fassade ist eine elementierte Vorhangfassade mit öffenbaren Fenstern über alle zwölf Geschosse. Die Fenster sind so platziert, dass sie während der kühlen Sommernächte zur Gebäudekühlung geöffnet werden können. Sie sind mit der zentralen Gebäudetechnik vernetzt, so dass die Klimaanlagen im Bereich geöffneter Fenster automatisch abschalten. Außerdem bestehen mehr als 40% der Außenhülle aus einer belüfteten Doppelfassade mit einem nutzbaren Zwischenraum von 1,20 m Breite. Diese Klimafassade dient als Wärmepuffer: Im Sommer bildet sie einen Sonnenschutz und dient als Wärmeentlüftung bevor die Luft ins Gebäude eintritt, im Winter hält der Fassadenzwischenraum die solaren Wärmegewinne zurück und verringert damit den Wärmeverlust über die Fassade.

The environmental design features of the Genzyme Headquarters touch all parts of the building: the building envelope, the atrium void, the central mechanical plant, the office lighting systems, and the stormwater discharge systems. The design team, the client and the construction team balanced aesthetics, cost, constructability and reliability to make this developer building an environmentally responsible corporate headquarters. And they strived for the best, a LEED Platinum rated building.

The building envelope is a high performance curtain-wall glazing system with operable windows through all twelve stories. These operable windows afford the user the opportunity to take advantage of the cooler summer nights, with fresh air venting out the building and cooling down the available thermal mass. Also, over 40% of the exterior envelope is a ventilated double-facade with a four foot interstitial space that can be occupied. These double-facade areas act as a buffer zone: in the summer they block solar gains and ventilate the heat away before it enters the space, and in the winter they capture the solar gains heating the interstitial space and reducing the heat loss from the facade.

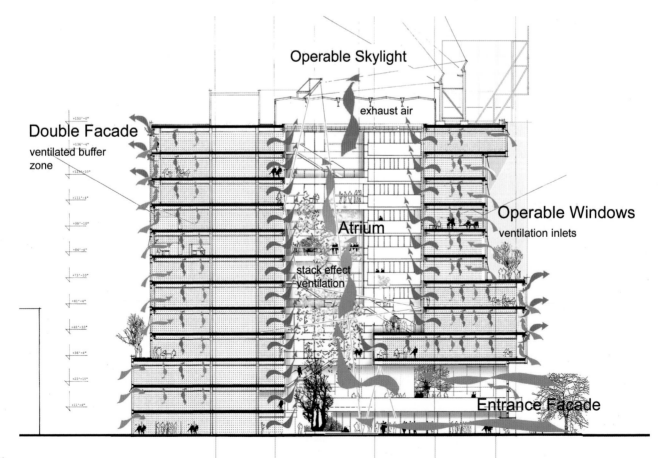

Das Atrium wird als großer Entlüftungs- und Lichtraum genutzt. Frisch-luft wird den Büroflächen über Lüftungsauslässe in der Decke und über die Fenster zugeführt. Anschließend wird die Luft durch den Luftdruck-unterschied in das Atrium geführt und verlässt den Raum über die Entlüftungsventilatoren im Glasdach.

Das Beleuchtungssystem wird durch das im Überfluss vorhandene Sonnenlicht, das durch die Glasfassade und das Atrium einfällt, unter-stützt. Dem Sonnenverlauf folgende Spiegel über dem Glasdach des Atriums leiten die Sonnenstrahlen weit in das Gebäude hinein. Wenn die Lichtsensoren genügend Licht fangen, wird das künstliche Licht automatisch gedimmt und somit Energie gespart.

Die zentrale Heiz- und Kühlanlage für das Gebäude nutzt Dampf von einem benachbarten Kraftwerk. Dieses Kraftwerk hatte zuvor keinen Dampf produziert, wurde aber vor kurzer Zeit mit gasgefeuerten Turbinen ausgebaut, so dass nun eine der Maschinen als Blockheiz-kraftwerk eingesetzt werden kann. Der Dampf kühlt im Sommer über so genannte Absorptionskühlgeräte das Gebäude und wird im Winter direkt in Heizleistung umgesetzt. Dieser Energieumlauf produziert keinerlei Verlust und nutzt eines der effizientesten Kühlsysteme. Das Kraftwerk liefert je nach Bedarf Dampf und hat wirkkräftige Emissions-filter. Energie, die als Beiprodukt der Stromerzeugung sowieso an die Atmosphäre abgegeben wird, ist hier direkt zur Kälteerzeugung genutzt.

Das Regenentwässerungssystem fängt das Wasser zunächst in zwei Wassertanks auf, bevor es in die Kanalisation weitergeleitet wird. Der eine Tank dient dem Wasserbedarf der Kühltürme. Obwohl dieses Regenwasser nicht den gesamten Kühlwasserbedarf decken kann, wer-den damit doch jedes Jahr tausende Liter von Trinkwasser gespart. Der zweite Tank wird von der Dachentwässerung des Atriums gespeist und versorgt das Grasdach, sobald Feuchtigkeitssensoren in der Erde Trockenheit anzeigen.

All diese ökologischen Planungsdetails – Energie- und Wasserspar-maßnahmen, Materialwahl, Bauplatzwahl und das ökologisch optimier-te Arbeitsklima im Inneren – tragen zur LEED-Platinum-Auszeichnung bei, wenn der Bau voraussichtlich nächstes Jahr zur Abnahme fertig sein wird. LEED ist ein System des US-amerikanischen Green Building Councils zur Erfassung und Bewertung der Nachhaltigkeit von Gebäuden.

The atrium void is utilised as a huge return air duct and as a light shaft. Fresh air is introduced to the occupied space by ceiling grilles throughout the floor plates or through the operable facade openings. It then moves, through pressure differentials, into the atrium and up and out exhaust fans near the skylight.

The lighting systems are aided by the abundance of natural light from both the fully glazed facade and the atrium, where solar-track-ing mirrors above the skylight bounce sunlight down deep into the building. When lighting sensors detect sufficient natural light in the area, the overhead lights slowly dim to off and energy is saved. Low energy task lights on all desktops reduce the overhead lighting out-put even more and give focused light to computer related work.

The central heating and cooling for the building use steam from a power plant two blocks away. The plant has not distributed steam in the past, but it has recently upgraded to gas fired jet turbines and now has the ability to distribute district steam from one of its power generation cycles. This steam drives absorption chillers for summer cooling and is exchanged directly into heat for winter heating. This local energy cycle has no distribution losses, uses one of the most efficient cooling methods, has economies of scale from the power plant, and has emission filters to remove particulates and sulfur.

The stormwater drainage system flows into two collection tanks before being discharged into local sewers. The first tank collects water to supplement the water demand for the evaporative cooling towers. Although this collected rainwater cannot supply all the water needed for the cooling towers, it will save thousands of gallons of potable water every year. The second collection tank is fed from the skylight runoff and waters the landscaped roof when soil sensors indicate the grass is dry.

All of these environmental design strategies – energy conservation, water conservation, material selection, urban site selection and indoor environmental quality – contribute to the Platinum LEED rating this building expects to achieve next year upon completion. The team has worked hard to incorporate these design strategies.

KONZEPT FÜR DIE TAGESLICHT-NUTZUNG UND FÜR DAS SYSTEM DER LICHTVERSTÄRKUNG

ROBERT MÜLLER | BARTENBACH LICHTLABOR GMBH, ALDRANS/INNSBRUCK, ÖSTERREICH

NATURAL LIGHTING CONCEPT AND ENHANCEMENT SYSTEMS ROBERT MÜLLER | BARTENBACH LICHTLABOR GMBH, ALDRANS/INNSBRUCK, AUSTRIA

Jede einzelne Komponente des natürlichen Beleuchtungssystems wurde im Hinblick auf eine bestmögliche Nutzung des Tageslichts sowie hinsichtlich eines optimalen Verhältnisses von Tageslicht zu Kunstlicht im Gebäude entworfen. Die Lichtleitsysteme wurden so gestaltet, dass sich mit ihnen die Sonneneinstrahlung regeln lässt.

Das Glasdach über dem Atrium ist mit einem Sonnenschutzsytem aus prismenförmigen Elementen ausgestattet, das die Menge des in den Raum einfallenden Sonnenlichts genauestens regulieren kann. Auf der Nordseite reflektieren sieben Heliostaten, auf der Südseite eine Reihe von fest montierten Spiegeln das Tageslicht in das Atrium. Direkte Sonneneinstrahlung wird in die Tiefe des Atriums gelenkt, wo sie sich in einer spiegelnden Wasseroberfläche bricht.

Im Atrium hängen Kronleuchter mit beweglichen prismenförmigen Flächen, die in einem bestimmten Winkel das Licht durchlassen und in anderen Winkeln die Sonnenstrahlen reflektieren. So können diese Flächen nicht nur das in das Atrium einstrahlende Sonnenlicht über die Arbeitsbereiche verteilen, sondern auch den Einfallswinkel steuern und damit ein Blenden verhindern, das durch den direkten Einfall von Sonnenlicht auf vertikale Flächen entstehen könnte.

Each individual component of the natural lighting system has been designed to ensure that the maximum amount of daylight is obtained in the building, and that the proportion of natural lighting is optimised. The apertures are also designed to control the effects of solar radiation.

The atrium roof incorporates a sun shading device of prism elements that can tightly control the amount of sunlight being reflected or diffused into the space. Daylight is reflected into the atrium area by means of seven heliostats to the north of the atrium and a series of fixed mirrors arranged on the south side. Direct sunlight is deflected down into the ground floor area of the atrium, where a reflecting water surface redistributes it.

Inside the atrium, chandeliers are hung with moving prism plate elements, that are designed to allow light hitting the plates at a certain angle to pass through, but also reflecting the sunlight at other angles. Thus, these prism plates not only act to redistribute the sunlight entering the atrium into the surrounding workspaces, but can also control the range of angles at which sunlight is reflected into these spaces, avoiding problems of glare caused by sunlight directly hitting vertical surfaces.

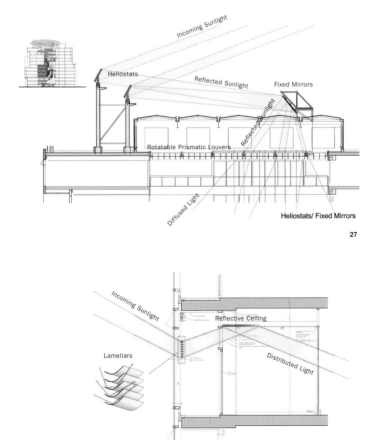

27

28

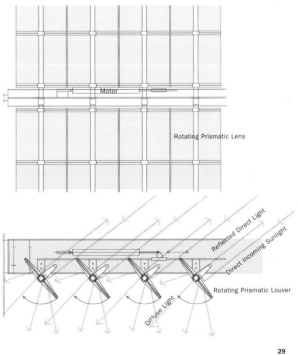

29

30

27, 28, 29 Komponenten des natürlichen Beleuchtungssystems 30 Modell Atrium
27, 28, 29 Components of natural lighting system 30 Model, atrium

GENZYME CENTER | 2000–2003

Reflektierende Brüstungen und eine Lamellenwand an der Südseite verstärken das Sonnenlicht und leiten es in die angrenzenden Geschosse weiter. Die Lamellenwand hat verstellbare vertikale Elemente, die in bestimmten Winkeln das Licht reflektieren. Sie können den Eintritt der Lichtmenge kontrollieren, abhängig von dem Grad der Öffnung der Lamellen. Diese verstellbare Wand mit unterschiedlichem Lichtdurchlass hat auch Einfluss auf die Wahrnehmung der Größe und Geschlossenheit des Raumes.

An allen Außenfassaden des Gebäudes filtern Lamellen das direkte Sonnenlicht und lassen indirektes Licht in die dahinter liegenden Arbeitsbereiche einfallen. Dies wird durch eine äußerst präzise Steuerung der Lamellen möglich, die dem jeweiligen Stand der Sonne folgen kann. Das Licht wird damit sehr effektiv verteilt, denn ohne Filterung wäre es in den an die Fassade angrenzenden Arbeitsbereichen zu stark. Diese einzigartige Kombination von Lichtsteuerungssystemen trägt dazu bei, dass das natürliche Tageslicht in dem Gebäude optimal genutzt wird. ◄

The enhancement of the amount and distribution of daylight in the atrium and surrounding spaces is also aided by reflective balustrades and by a lamellar wall to the south side of the atrium. This lamellar wall has movable vertical elements which reflect the light at different angles depending on their position, and can control the amount of light entering the space beyond by the degree by which they are opened or closed. This controllable reflective wall, as well as having daylighting control uses, can manipulate our perception of the volume and permeability of the atrium space.

At the perimeter facade areas, lamellar stores are used to deflect the direct sunlight while allowing diffuse daylight into the adjacent office spaces. This can be done to a high degree of accuracy due to the control system which repositions these lamellar plates in response to the position of the sun. This allows a more effective redistribution of the daylight, the levels of which under normal conditions would be too high at the areas adjacent to the facades. It adds to the overall increase in the use of natural lighting within the building achieved through this unique combination of light enhancement systems. ◄

Am nördlichen Stadtrand von Ettlingen, auf einem 15.000 m² großen ehemaligen Gelände der Rheinlandkaserne, liegt die neue Hauptverwaltung der entory AG für etwa 350 Mitarbeiter. Weite Streuobstwiesen im Norden, die Nähe zu den weichen Hängen des Schwarzwaldes im Osten, sowie die repräsentative Lage direkt am Stadteingang von Ettlingen, auf dem Weg zur nahe gelegenen Autobahn, bestimmen den Ort.

On the northern edge of the town of Ettlingen, on the 15,000m² former grounds of the Rhineland Barracks, lies the new headquarters of the firm entory AG, with facilities for approx. 350 employees. The area is characterised by broad fruit orchards to the north, proximity to the gentle slopes of the Black Forest to the east, as well as its impressive location directly at the gateway to the town of Ettlingen, en route to the nearby motorway.

NEUBAU DER ENTORY AG
NEW ADMINISTRATION BUILDING OF ENTORY AG

ETTLINGEN, DEUTSCHLAND | ETTLINGEN, GERMANY; 1999–2002

Karlsruher Strasse

1

1 Lageplan 2, 3 Haupteingang | 1 Site plan 2, 3 Main entrance

ENTORY AG | 1999–2002

2

Die entory AG wünschte sich ein Haus mit vielfältigen räumlichen Strukturen. Zellen-, Gruppen-, Großraumbüros sowie Kombizonen, in denen es möglich sein sollte, auf unterschiedlichste Art und Weise, in wechselnden Konstellationen zusammenzuarbeiten: in offenen oder geschlossenen Räumen – je nach Tätigkeit – kommunikativ im größeren Team oder in kleineren Gruppen bzw. konzentriert alleine oder zu zweit. Außerdem sollte es zentrale Orte geben, an denen man sich trifft und die die Integration der Mitarbeiter fördern.

An diesem Ort, am Übergang von fester Stadtbebauung zu ländlicher Region, konnte man die landschaftlichen Qualitäten der Umgebung aufgreifen und stärken. So sollte keine in sich geschlossene Großform entstehen, sondern

The firm entory AG wanted a building with a multiplicity of spatial structures including individual, group and open-plan offices, as well as multi-purpose zones, where it would be possible to work together in a variety of ways and in flexible configurations: in open spaces or closed ones – according to the task at hand –, communicatively in big teams or in smaller groupings, alone in concentrated form or in pairs. The building also required a central place where people could meet, and which would promote the social integration of the staff.

On this site, marked by the transition from dense urban settlement to rural areas, it was possible to respond to and enhance the landscape qualities of the surroundings. This meant avoiding a large, self-enclosed

4

4 Gartenfassaden 5 Detail Westfassade 6 Perspektive
4 Facades to the garden 5 Detail of the western facade 6 Perspective

ENTORY AG | 1999–2002

ein Gebäude, das sich auflöst, gliedert in einzelne Gebäudeflügel, die aus dem Zentrum der Anlage sozusagen in die Landschaft wachsen und von Landschaft umspült werden.

Das erhöht liegende Eingangsniveau erreicht man über eine einladende, flache Freitreppe (»spanische Treppe«). Von dort gelangt man weiter in die mehrgeschossige, nach oben verglaste Halle. Der Blick öffnet sich in den Garten auf der anderen Seite des Gebäudes, Restaurant und Konferenzsaal sind ebenso zum Garten ausgerichtet. Bei größeren Veranstaltungen können diese Bereiche durch verschiebbare Wände zur Halle hin geöffnet werden.

architectural form, opting instead for a structure that opened outwards, divided into individual wings which would, in a manner of speaking, grow from the center of the complex and reach outward into the landscape.

The raised entry level is attained via an inviting shallow (or "Spanish") stair. From there, the way leads into a multi-story entrance hall, which is glazed above. The view opens toward the garden on the other side of the building; both restaurant and conference hall are also oriented toward the garden. For larger events, these zones can be opened onto the main hall via moveable walls.

5

6

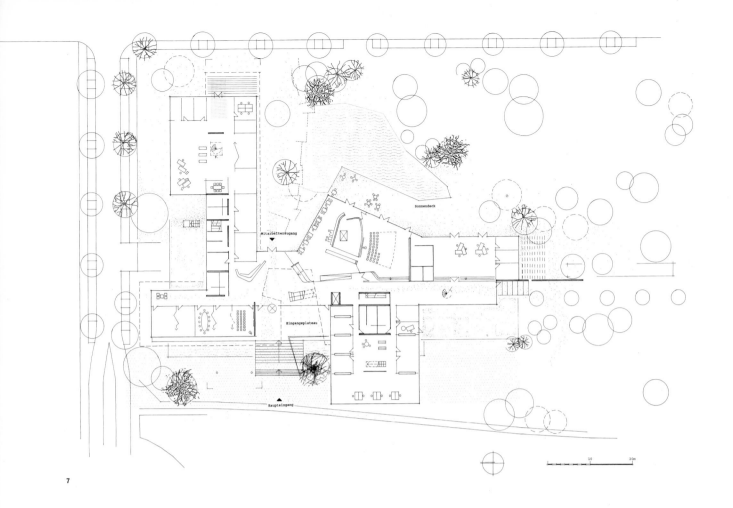

7

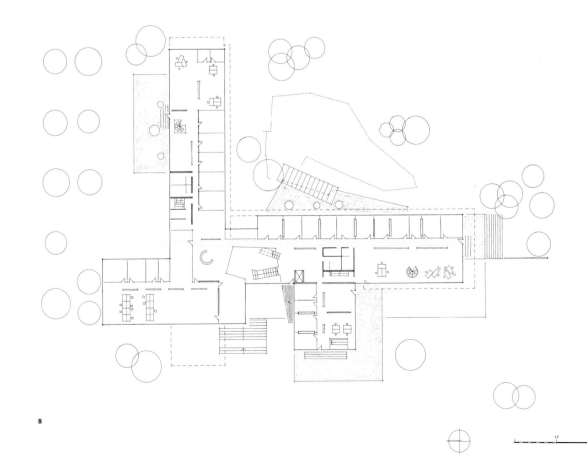

8

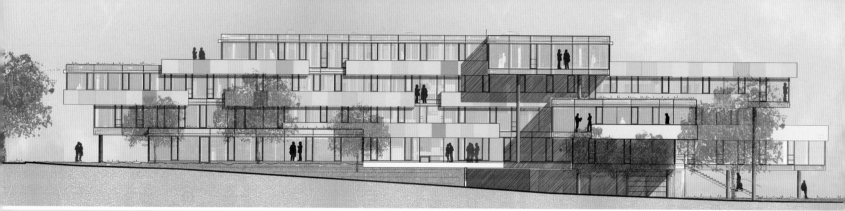

7 Grundriss Erdgeschoss 8 Grundriss 1. Obergeschoss 9, 10 Ansicht Nord
7 Plan, ground floor 8 Plan, 2nd floor 9, 10 North elevation

ENTORY AG | 1999–2002

Die einzelnen Flügel der Anlage sind über die Halle miteinander vernetzt. Am Hallenbereich liegen auf unterschiedlichen Ebenen Besprechungsinseln, Sekretariate, Pausenbereiche und andere gemeinschaftliche Nutzungen. Die Halle ist das pulsierende kommunikative Herz der Anlage, offene Treppen, Galerien, Stege usw. überlagern sich dort. Zusätzliche interne, offene Treppen in den peripheren Bereichen schaffen funktionale, aber auch räumliche Bezüge zwischen den Geschossen der einzelnen Flügel.

The individual wings of the complex are interconnected across the hall. In the hall area, conference islands, offices, break areas and other common areas lie on various levels. The hall constitutes the communicative heart of the facility, open stairs, galleries, footbridges, etc. are overlaid there. Additional internal, open stairs in peripheral areas provide functional as well as spatial relationships between the stories of the respective wings.

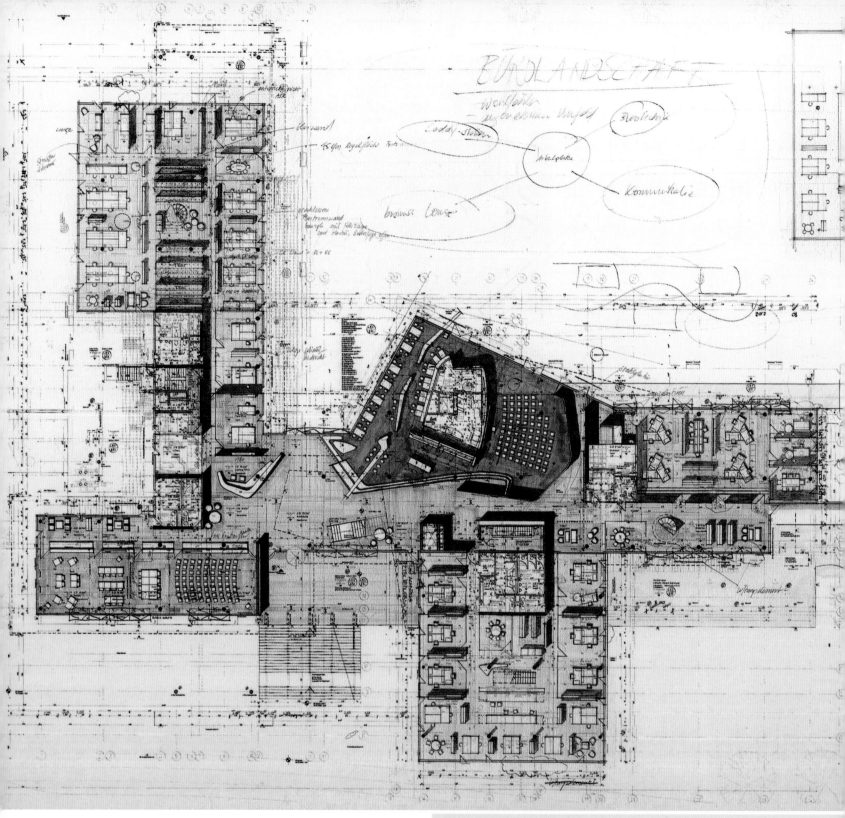

11 Werkplan 12, 13, 14 Situationen
11 Construction document 12, 13, 14 Situations

ENTORY AG | 1999–2002

Das Gebäude ruht auf 150 thermisch genutzten, bis zu 8 m langen Stahlbeton-Erdpfählen. In den Pfählen verlegte Rohrschlangen fördern während der Winterzeit durch Erdwärme temperiertes Wasser zu Heizzwecken in die mit Rohrregistern versehenen Betondecken. Eine Wärmepumpe bringt die Temperaturen auf ein nutzbares Niveau. In der Sommerzeit sorgt die in den Decken vorhandene Bauteilkühlung für ein angenehmes Raumklima. Alle Räume haben öffenbare Fenster zur freien Lüftung. ◂

The building rests on 150 thermally functional, sunken reinforced concrete piles measuring up to 8 m in length. During the winter months water, circulated through coiled piping laid within the piles and warmed by the earth, is used for heating purposes, in conjunction with the pipework laid in the concrete ceilings. A heat pump elevates temperatures to functional levels. In the summer months, component cooling elements in the ceilings provide a pleasant indoor climate. Windows in all rooms can be opened for natural ventilation. ◂

12

13

14

1 Fassadenausschnitt 2 Grundriss Erdgeschoss 3, 4 Perspektivische Skizzen
1 Facade detail 2 Plan, ground floor 3, 4 Perspectival sketches

WOHN- UND GESCHÄFTSHAUS | APARTMENTS, SHOPS AND OFFICES | 2001

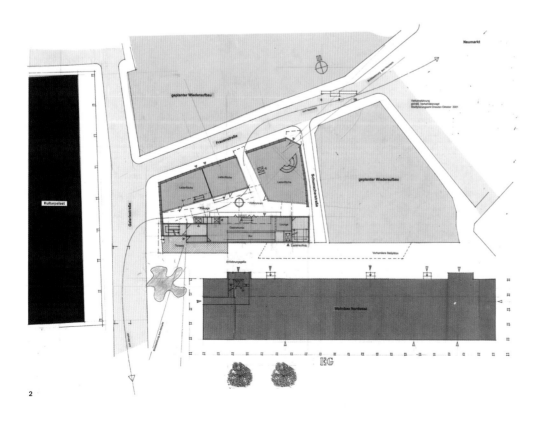

WOHN- UND GESCHÄFTSHAUS NEUMARKT
APARTMENTS, SHOPS AND OFFICES AT NEUMARKT

DRESDEN, DEUTSCHLAND | DRESDEN, GERMANY; 2001

Die Dresdner Innenstadt war gegen Ende des Zweiten Weltkriegs vollständig zerstört worden. Das Umfeld der Frauenkirche in Dresden, der Neumarkt, soll nun wiederaufgebaut werden. Ob Rekonstruktion, kritische Rekonstruktion in Anlehnung an historische Bauten, oder zeitgenössische Architektur ist noch weitgehend ungeklärt. Heftige, kontroverse Diskussionen begleiten die stadtplanerischen Überlegungen.

Toward the end of World War II, Dresden's city center was completely destroyed. Now the surroundings of the Frauenkirche (Church of Our Lady) in Dresden, called Neumarkt, are to be rebuilt. Whether this will take the form of reconstruction, critical reconstruction with reference to historical structures, or contemporary architecture remains substantially unresolved. Urban planning discussions have been vigorous and accompanied by controversy.

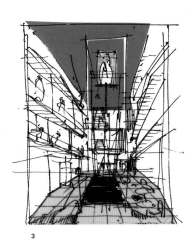

3

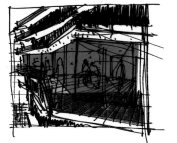

4

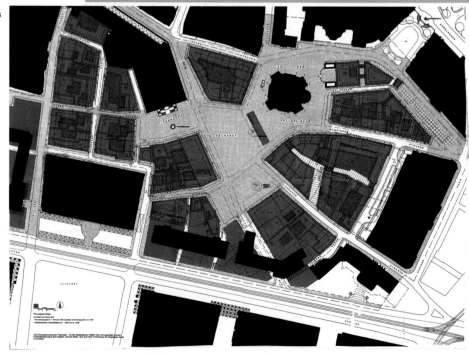

Die historische Situation spiegelte die alte geschlossene, evangelische Bürgergemeinde um die Frauenkirche in der Residenzstadt Dresden wider. Die Kraft dieser im Barock entstandenen Situation war noch im 20. Jahrhundert erkennbar, allerdings nur an den historischen Gebäuden selbst. Die ursprünglichen Funktionen waren entfallen, andere Funktionen jedoch, die auch in diese alte Situation passten, hatten sich neu angesiedelt.

Vieles davon existiert heute nicht mehr in seiner ursprünglichen Gestalt und man kann die alte Situation, vor allem deren Geist, nicht durch neue Bauwerke wiedererwecken, auch wenn man sie in der alten Form wieder aufbauen würde.

Es gibt eine Tendenz, im Blick auf die Vergangenheit vieles verklärt zu betrachten. Man sieht die alten Hüllen, aber selten deren Inhalte und schon gar nicht die damit für die damaligen Bewohner verbundenen Probleme. Man sollte die teils unmenschlichen Gesellschaftssysteme, die Grundlage der damaligen Architektur waren und die wir in der heutigen Zeit keinesfalls akzeptieren würden, in diesem Zusammenhang nicht ignorieren. Die Architektur sollte in der Retrospektive nicht losgelöst von geschichtlichen Zusammenhängen betrachtet werden.

The historical situation reflected the old, exclusive Protestant community around the Frauenkirche in Dresden, the residence of Saxon dukes and kings. The forcefulness of this situation, dating from the Baroque, was still detectable in the 20th century, if only in the historical buildings themselves. If their original functions had been forgotten, then new ones, also well-suited to the old situation, had established themselves.

Many such structures no longer exist in their original forms, and it would be impossible to recreate the old arrangement, especially its spirit, even if they were to be precisely reconstructed.

There exists a tendency to transfigure the past retrospectively. We perceive only the old shells, more seldom their content, and tend to disregard the problems they presented to their historical inhabitants. In this connection, we ought not to ignore the somewhat inhuman social order that formed the basis of architecture at that time, an order we would hardly find acceptable today. It follows that when being examined in retrospect, architecture should never be dissociated from its historical context.

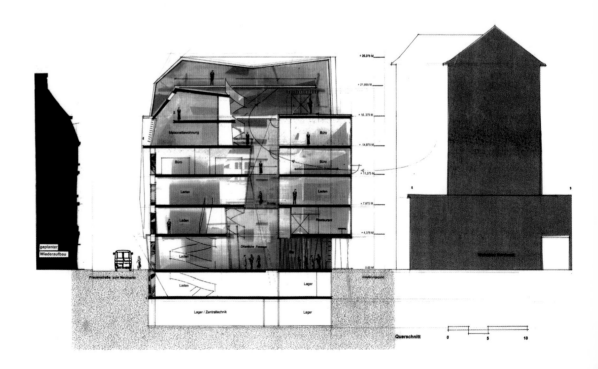

Einzelne Aspekte des Früheren könnte man jedoch neu schaffen, zum Beispiel das Spielerische, den »schönen Schein« und die dadurch erzeugte Leichtigkeit der barocken Bauten. In der Barockarchitektur wurde versucht, das zwangsläufig Notwendige mit dem frei Gewollten zu überspielen. Die Schwere der Konstruktion, d.h. die Zwänge der Realität, wurden aufgelöst durch das Spiel mit Formen und Farben. Auch waren Materialgerechtigkeit und konstruktive Ehrlichkeit gewiss keine Tugenden des Barock. Vieles war erlaubt, um jenem »schönen Schein« zu folgen.

Unsere Konstruktionen heute sind nicht mehr schwer, jedoch häufig streng und rigide, aus der Funktion oder den Fertigungsprozessen heraus entwickelt. Dieses streng »Sittliche« unserer heutigen technischen Bauweise könnte man überspielen. Das Rationale der modernen Architektur, ihr manchmal fast pietistischer Ansatz, ist häufig Anlass zur Kritik und führt im Ergebnis oft in die Vergangenheit, zur Flucht in historisierende Baustile. Dies konnte nicht Ziel unserer Arbeit am Dresdner Neumarkt sein.

Aus diesen Überlegungen hat sich das Konzept für den Neubau in dieser ehemals durch den Barock geprägten Umgebung entwickelt. Nach außen, zu den historischen Straßenräumen, soll sich eine vom Innenraum tendenziell freie und unabhängige »Maske« zeigen, die sich in ihrer Höhe, ihren Proportionen und ihrer Grundstruktur am historischen Bild orientiert. Die Vielfalt, der Reichtum, der Schmuck der Barockfassade sollen mit den Mitteln unserer heutigen Zeit erzeugt werden. Im Inneren der Anlage, hinter der die Straßenräume definierenden »Maske«, kann sich somit ein den Anforderungen an unsere Zeit entsprechendes Raumgefüge entwickeln. ◄

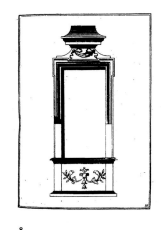

8

That is not to say, individual aspects of an earlier structure cannot be reproduced, for example its playfulness, its "beautiful appearance," and the resulting effect of lightness so characteristic of Baroque buildings. Baroque architecture sought to surpass the compulsions of necessity with freely willed forms. The heaviness of the construction, i.e., the dictates of reality, were dissolved via the play of shapes and colors. The imperatives of doing justice to the material and of constructive authenticity: these hardly counted as virtues of the Baroque era. Much was permitted for the sake of attaining the desired "beautiful appearance."

If contemporary construction is no longer heavy, it is still often strict and rigid, growing out of function or the manufacturing process. But it is possible to outmaneuver the severe "moralism" of today's technological building practices. The rationality of modern architecture, its sometimes almost pietistic beginnings, has often prompted criticism whose result has been a flight into the past, toward historicist building styles. But that could hardly be the objective of our work at Dresden's Neumarkt.

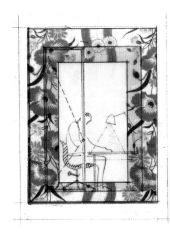

9

Our concept for new construction in this district, formerly stamped by the Baroque style, developed out of such considerations. Facing the historical street zone, and tending to be free, independent of the interior spaces, will be a "mask," which in terms of height, proportions and basic structure will be oriented towards such historical appearance. The diversity, wealth, and decorative character of the Baroque facade will be recreated via contemporary methods. Behind the "mask" that defines the street zone, the interior exists as a decidedly different spatial framework which responds to the demands of our own time. ◄

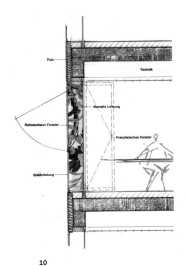

10

8, 9, 10 Fassadenstudien 11 Ansicht West Galeriestraße 12 Fassadendetail
13 Fassadenausschnitt zur Frauenstraße 14 Historische Fassade
8, 9, 10 Studies, facade 11 West elevation, Galeriestrasse 12 Detail of facade
13 Detail of facade, looking onto Frauenstrasse 14 Historical facade

WOHN- UND GESCHÄFTSHAUS | APARTMENTS, SHOPS AND OFFICES | 2001

14

DIENSTLEISTUNGSZENTRUM DER LANDESGIROKASSE, HEUTE LBBW
CENTRAL ADMINISTRATION BUILDING FOR THE
STATE CLEARING BANK, NOW LBBW

STUTTGART, DEUTSCHLAND | STUTTGART, GERMANY; 1997

Der Standort am Bollwerk, in unmittelbarer Nähe zum Berliner Platz mit der angrenzenden Liederhalle von Rolf Gutbrod und Adolf Arndt, ist der höchstgelegene Ort in der Stuttgarter City. Er liegt am Übergang der Geschäftsstadt zum Gründerzeitwohnquartier des sogenannten Stuttgarter Westens, das durch Blockrandstrukturen geprägt ist.

The location near the "Bollwerk," in the immediate vicinity of Berliner Platz, adjacent to Rolf Gutbrod and Adolf Arndt's "Liederhalle" (song hall), is the most elevated spot in the city, and marks the transition from the commercial district to the Gründerzeit residential quarter of so-called Stuttgart West, characterised by

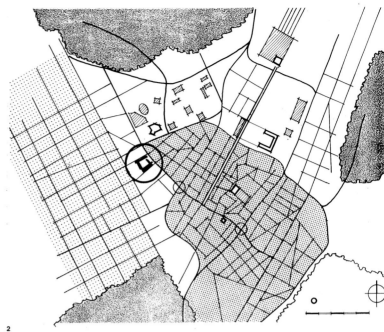

1 Blick auf die Hügel Stuttgarts 2 Lageplan 3 Blick von Nord-Osten
1 View of the hills of Stuttgart 2 Site plan 3 View from the north-east

DIENSTLEISTUNGSZENTRUM DER LANDESGIROKASSE | CENTRAL
ADMINISTRATION BUILDING FOR THE STATE CLEARING BANK | 1997

1

Wenn alte Stadtquartiere neu bebaut werden sollen, entsteht in der Regel mehr Nutzfläche als zuvor. Heute beansprucht ein Mitarbeiter in einer Verwaltung ein Vielfaches von dem, was ihm früher zugestanden wurde. Es entstehen größere Baumassen und diese führen zu größerer Dichte und zu höheren Gebäuden. Unter stadtplanerischen Aspekten wünscht man sich jedoch Häuser in vertrauter Dimension. Diese in der Regel schwer zu vereinbarenden Gegensätze führen oft zu problematischen Erscheinungen: versteckte Geschosse, vertiefte, zu enge Innenhöfe etc.

In dieser Situation erschien es sinnvoll, mit fünfgeschossigen Baukörpern, die die Traufhöhen der umgebenden Bebauung aufnehmen und den Grundstücksgrenzen folgen, die Straßenräume zu stabilisieren. Weitere Büroflächen wurden in darüber angeordneten Staffeldachgeschossen untergebracht, die somit den Straßenraum wenig tangieren. Die

When old urban districts are redeveloped, the process generally yields increased usable area. Administrative staff today require many times the area previously provided. The result are larger architectural volumes, and these lead to higher densities and building heights. From an urban-planning perspective, however, structures with more customary dimensions are desirable. These dictates are difficult to reconcile, and often lead to problematical appearances: concealed stories, excessively deep or narrow interior courtyards, etc.

Given this situation, it appeared appropriate to adhere to the eaves heights of the surrounding structures with a five-story building which stabilised the boundaries of the city block. Higher office levels were set into staggered attic stories, so that they do not impinge on surrounding streets. The five-storied sections of the buildings

3

4

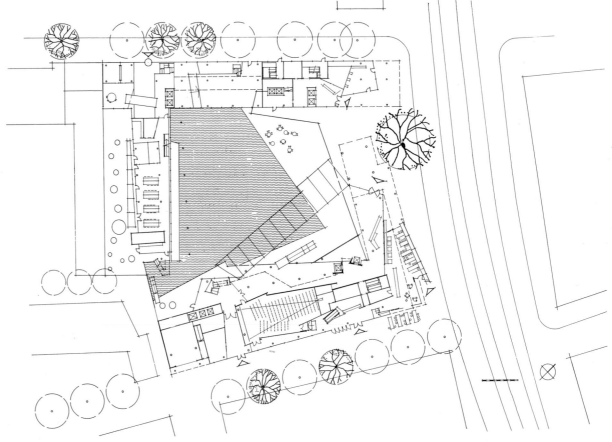

5

4 Haupteingang 5 Grundriss Erdgeschoss 6 Hofgeschoss 7 Eingangsebene Erdgeschoss
4 Main entrance 5 Plan, ground floor 6 Courtyard level 7 Entry level, ground floor

DIENSTLEISTUNGSZENTRUM DER LANDESGIROKASSE | CENTRAL
ADMINISTRATION BUILDING FOR THE STATE CLEARING BANK | 1997

fünfgeschossigen Bauteile formulieren das Straßencarré. Die höheren Bauteile im Innenbereich des Grundstücks nehmen Beziehungen auf größere Distanzen hin auf. Die mehrschichtige Orientierung antwortet den Bedingungen dieses Stadtbereichs. Es handelt sich um eine städtische Übergangszone, die weder der geometrisch geordneten Geschäftsstadt im Osten, noch der freier strukturierten Wohnstadt im Westen zuzuordnen ist. Auch schien der für den Neubau vorgesehene Platz von seiner Umgebung her nicht ohne weiteres geeignet, einen neuen Schwerpunkt im Stadtgefüge zu bilden. Zur City hin ist das Vorfeld für die neue Anlage durch die Breite der Straße, den starken Verkehr und die Rampe der Bahn beeinträchtigt.

form the square perimeter block structure. The taller sections of the building located around the inner court contribute towards the city skyline. The multi-layered orientation responds to the specific conditions in an area of urban transition which can be assigned neither to the geometrically ordered shopping district to the east, nor to the more freely structured residential district to the west. The site envisioned for the new building does not immediately appear suitable as a new focal point within the urban texture. Toward the city, the approach to the new complex is impaired by the breadth of the street, the heavy traffic, and the tram platform.

Diese Überlegungen bildeten den Hintergrund für die Entwicklung der neuen Anlage. Den Prinzipien einer klassischen Blockrandbebauung folgend, definiert sie nach außen die Straßenräume, in ihrem Inneren entsteht ein Hof. Eine Wasserfläche, die Innen- und Außenraum miteinander verbindet, spiegelt das Sonnenlicht und die Farben des Gebäudes wider. Durch das Spiel von Licht, Farbe und Wasser soll ein lebendiger Ort für Mitarbeiter, aber auch für die Bürger der Stadt entstehen. Aus einer Stütze wird eine Bahn, die sich im Wasser spiegelt, und aus einem farbigen Brüstungspaneel wird ein Blatt, das im Wasser treibt. Die Elemente treten in eine andere, scheinbar zufällige Ordnung zueinander.

These considerations formed the background for the development of the new complex. The principles of a classical block perimeter structure define the surrounding street patterns, while within, they demarcate a courtyard. An expanse of water, which ties interior and exterior space together, mirrors the sunlight and the colors of the building. The play of light, color and water creates an animated locale for employees and citizens alike. From a column emerges a path, which is mirrored in the water, and from a colored balustrade panel emerges a leaf that sprouts into the water; elements interpenetrate, seemingly organised by happenstance.

8 Treppe zum Hofgeschoss 9, 10 Innenhof 11 Schnitt
8 Stairs to courtyard level 9, 10 Interior courtyard 11 Section

DIENSTLEISTUNGSZENTRUM DER LANDESGIROKASSE | CENTRAL
ADMINISTRATION BUILDING FOR THE STATE CLEARING BANK | 1997

8

9

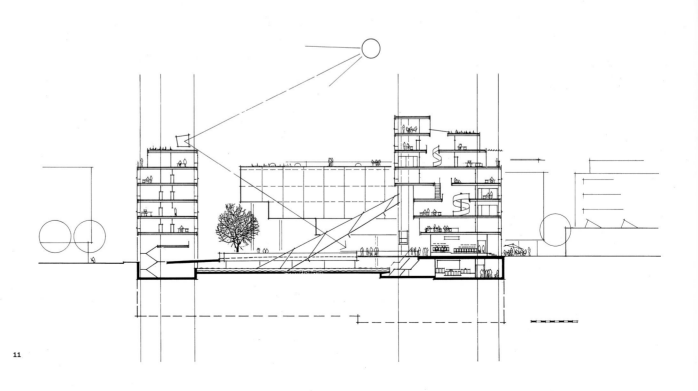

12

13

14

15

Mit dem Bauherrn bestand von Anfang an Konsens, dass man von dem großen Areal, welches man okkupiert, einen Teil an die Stadt, d.h. die Bürger, zurückgeben sollte. Diesem Gedanken folgend, wurden die Erdgeschossbereiche als Teil des öffentlichen Stadtraums behandelt, sowohl im Architektonisch-Formalen, als auch in ihrer Nutzung. Dieser Charakter ist nun mit Läden, den im Erdgeschoss untergebrachten Kinos und dem Restaurant Fellini, vor allem aber mit dem offenen Innenhofraum gegeben. Ursprünglich sollte der Hof durch eine Großplastik von Frank Stella bereichert werden – leider scheiterte dieses Vorhaben.

Die Eingangshalle liegt, an die öffentlichen Räume angrenzend, geschützt im Innenhof der Anlage. Weitere bankinterne Sondernutzungen wie die Cafeteria oder die Schulungs- und Konferenzräume sowie das Handelszentrum liegen in einem unter Erdgeschossniveau angeordneten so genannten

Right from the beginning, a consensus with the client was reached that, given the large area under development, a certain portion should be returned to the city, i.e., to the people. Accordingly, the ground floor zone is treated, in architectural and formal as well as in functional terms, as part of the public urban realm. This character is reinforced by shops, a ground level cinema, and the restaurant Fellini, but in particular by the open interior courtyard. Originally, the courtyard was to have been enriched by a large sculpture by Frank Stella; regrettably, this was not realised.

The entrance hall, bordered by public space, is sheltered within the complex's interior courtyard. Additional internal special functions, such as the bank's cafeteria or educational facilities and conference rooms as well as a commercial center, lie below at the so-called court level, illuminated from within and at the same time protected from

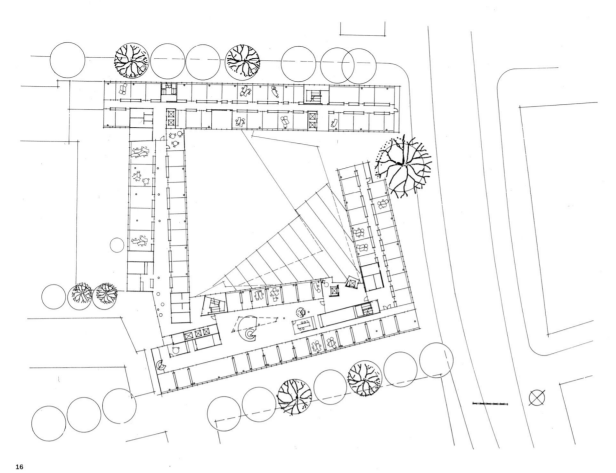

16

17

Hofgeschoss, von innen belichtet und gleichzeitig geschützt vor Straßenlärm. Somit treten auch diese Flächen im Gebäudevolumen nach außen nahezu nicht in Erscheinung. Die Bereiche im Erd- und Hofgeschoss entwickeln sich formal freier, ihren eigenen Gesetzmäßigkeiten entsprechend. Hier soll man an Landschaft und Außenraum erinnert werden. Die darüber angeordneten Bürobereiche hingegen sind ihrer Funktion entsprechend sachlich und klar strukturiert. Offene Treppenverbindungen und Lufträume zwischen den Geschossen sowie für alle Mitarbeiter zugängliche begrünte Dachterrassen fördern die Kommunikation im Haus.

street noise. Hence these areas hardly influence the appearance of the building volume. The areas of the ground and court levels develop more freely, according to their own dictates. The character of these spaces is meant to recall landscapes and outdoor areas. The office areas lying above, by contrast, are clearly structured, as befits their purpose. Open stair linkages and generous voids between levels as well as planted roof terraces that are accessible to all employees promote communication within the building.

16 Grundriss 3. Obergeschoss 17 Kombibüro 3. Obergeschoss 18 Kombizone 19, 20 Flurbereiche
16 Plan, 4th floor 17 Multi-use office, 4th floor 18 Multi-use zone 19, 20 Hallway area

DIENSTLEISTUNGSZENTRUM DER LANDESGIROKASSE | CENTRAL
ADMINISTRATION BUILDING FOR THE STATE CLEARING BANK | 1997

19

20

21

Linien und Flächen in unterschiedlichen Farben überziehen das Äußere des Hauses in einem freien Spiel, tendenziell unabhängig von Bindungen der Konstruktionen und Funktionen, in einer Ordnung, die sich in erster Linie an formalen und ästhetischen Gesichtspunkten orientiert. So können sich die Fassaden von den Zwängen der technischen Anforderungen befreien. Die Straßenfassaden sind etwas formeller und geschlossener: Sie sind mit vorgehängten Glasbrüstungen aus Verbundgläsern in transparenten Farben unterschiedlicher Dichte beschichtet. Die Farbwirkung verändert sich je nach Lichteinfall.

Lines and surfaces of various colors freely overlay the building's exterior, relatively independent of construction or function, in an arrangement conceived primarily in formal and aesthetic terms. The appearance of the building is thus freed from the constraints of technical requirements. The street facades are somewhat more formal and closed: they are clad with balustrades of laminated glass in transparent colors of varying thickness. The chromatic effects vary according to changing illumination.

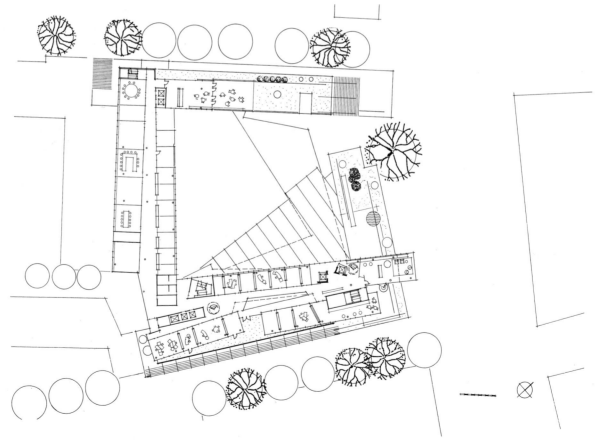

Der Hof, vor der Hektik der Außenwelt schützend, sollte mehr an einen Innenraum erinnern. Die Wahl der Materialien unterstützt diesen etwas privateren Eindruck: Holzfassaden in den Erdgeschosszonen sowie farbig beschichtete Faserzementtafeln im Brüstungsbereich. Die Fassaden zum ruhigen Hof sind offener und einige Büroräume haben so genannte französische Fenster. Ziel war es, eine offene, heiter und einladend wirkende Anlage entstehen zu lassen. ◄

The courtyard, sheltered from the hectic activity of the outer world, feels decidedly softer, reminding us of an interior. The choice of materials reinforces this intimate impression: wooden facades over the lower stories and colored layered fiber cement panels in the area of the balustrades. The facades near the tranquil courtyard are more open, affording several offices to have so-called French windows. The goal was a transparent, cheerful facility. ◄

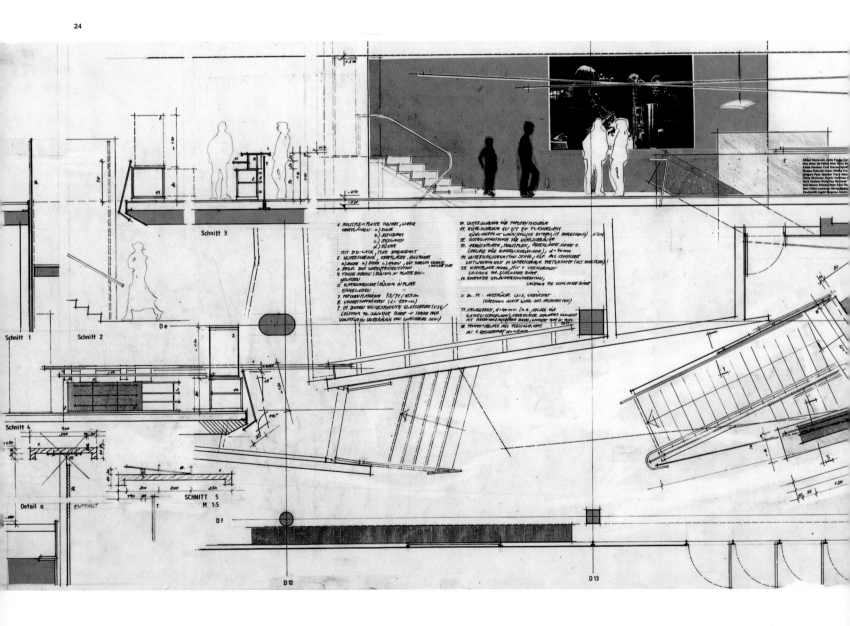

24 Werkplan Kinofoyer **25, 28** Kino Foyer **26, 27** Restaurant
24 Construction document, cinema foyer **25, 28** Cinema foyer **26, 27** Restaurant

**DIENSTLEISTUNGSZENTRUM DER LANDESGIROKASSE | CENTRAL
ADMINISTRATION BUILDING FOR THE STATE CLEARING BANK | 1997**

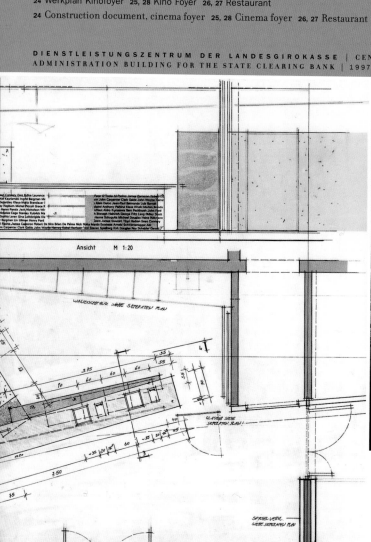

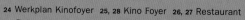

Ansicht M 1:20

Hochhäuser EXKURS 4

High-rises DIGRESSION 4

1

2

Hochhäuser sind weitgehend durch technische und organisatorische Anforderungen geprägt: Statik, vertikale Erschließung, Brandschutz und Gebäudetechnik mit aufwendigen Schächten lassen wenig Raum für eine freie Grundrissentwicklung oder formale architektonische Aspekte. Zumeist bewegen sich die freieren architektonischen Elemente im rein Dekorativen, Ornamentalen. Tiefe Grundrisse mit einem eher geringen tagesbelichteten Nutzflächenangebot an der Fassade sind die Regel. Gut nutzbare Grundrisse, tagesbelichtet, nach Möglichkeit natürlich be- und entlüftet, sind in Hochhäusern bisher kaum zu finden.

3

4

5

6

7

High-rises are conditioned to a significant degree by technical and organisational demands: statics, vertical circulation, fire safety and building technology with extensive shafts leave but little room for a freer development of the floor plans and of the more formal aspects of architecture. For the most part, freer architectonic elements tend toward the purely decorative, the ornamental. Deep floor plans affording only minimal sunlit functional surfaces, located near the facade, are the rule. Well-functioning daylit plans with natural ventilation, where possible, are extremely rare among high-rises.

Ende der 80er Jahre entwickelte unser Büro einen Hochhaustypus, der, weitgehend unabhängig von technischen Einschränkungen, bestimmte Aspekte der Architektur zum Ausdruck bringen sollte.

Unsere Hochhauskonzepte sehen eine vertikale Entwicklung gut nutzbarer, aber unterschiedlicher Grundrisse vor, architektonisch freier gegliedert – auch nach formalen Aspekten. Ziel ist es, sowohl in der Horizontalen, als auch in der Vertikalen, vielfältige und eng miteinander verwobene innenräumliche Strukturen zu schaffen. Ein hohes Haus sollte doch mehr bieten können als die monotone Stapelung immer gleicher Grundrisse und die Dekoration der Fassaden in Zuckerbäckermanier.

Inhaltliche Aspekte sollten sich auch im Architektonisch-Formalen darstellen, im Inneren, wie im Äußeren eines Gebäudes. Die vielen unterschiedlichen Bereiche, aus denen sich jedes Gebäude zusammensetzt, sollten, ihrer unterschiedlichen Funktion entsprechend, in Form, Gestalt, Farbe etc. individualisiert werden. Das Technisch-Konstruktive zu ästhetisieren und architektonisch in den Vordergrund zu stellen, erscheint wenig sinnvoll, es sollte sich in der Gestalt der Gebäude zurückhalten. Die Erscheinung wiederum sollte durch andere Themen geprägt sein.

Erstrebenswert ist außerdem, dass Hochhäuser nicht in den vom Passanten erlebbaren Stadtraum zu stark hineinreichen, diesen beset-

8

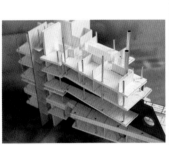

9

10

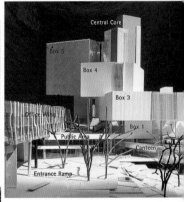

11

In the late 1980s, our office developed a new high-rise type, one meant to give expression to certain aspects of architecture, while remaining largely independent of technical constraints.

Our high-rise concept is meant to foster the vertical development of well-functioning yet diverse floor plans, ones architectonically freely articulated – in formal terms as well. The goal is to create – in the horizontal dimension as well in the vertical – a multiplicity of tightly interwoven, well-integrated interior spatial structures. A tall house should offer more than the monotonous stacking of identical floor plans, with the facade decorated like a layer cake.

Content-related aspects should also find expression in the architectonically formal aspects, and in the interior as well as on the exterior of a building. The various different areas composing a building should be individualised in terms of form, shape, color, etc., in a way consistent with their various functions. We consider it not necessarily appropriate to merely aestheticise technical and constructive dimensions and set them in the foreground architectonically. Instead, these should be restrained from appearing too noticeably in the shape of a building. Indeed, the appearance ought to be conditioned by other aspects.

zen und mit ihren aus der Höhe abgeleiteten Zwängen dominieren. Öffentliche Räume, Straßenfluchten, Plätze, Hallen, also Attraktionen für den Fußgänger, sollten im Vordergrund stehen, weniger die mächtige Basis eines Hochhauses. Aus diesen Gedanken heraus wurden in unserem Büro Konzepte entwickelt, wie sie am Beispiel der Norddeutschen Landesbank in Hannover zu sehen sind. ◄

1 Pressehaus Dumont Schauberg, Köln, Deutschland 2 Hauptverwaltungsgebäude Landesgirokasse, Stuttgart, Deutschland 3 Norddeutsche Landesbank am Friedrichswall Nord/LB, Hannover, Deutschland 4 Studie Hochhausspitze Nord/LB, Hannover, Deutschland 5 Modellstudien Technisches Zentrum der Landeszentralbank Bayern (LZB), München, Deutschland 6 Hochhaus MAX, Frankfurt, Deutschland 7 LZB, München, Deutschland 8 Landesbausparkasse, Potsdam, Deutschland 9 LZB, München, Deutschland 10 Bürogebäude und Hotel, Hamburg, Deutschland 11 National- und Provinzialarchive, Kopenhagen, Dänemark 12 Modell Nord/LB, Hannover, Deutschland 13 Nord/LB, Hannover, Deutschland 14 LZB, München, Deutschland 15 U2 Studios, Dublin, Irland 16 Studie Hochhausspitze Nord/LB, Hannover, Deutschland

12

13

14

15

16

Moreover, it is worth attempting to prevent high-rises from too aggressively invading the realm of the passers-by, and with their height-conditioned imperatives, from dominating the public domain. The quality of the public spaces, streetscape, squares, passages, and other pedestrian attractions should take prominence, not the massive base of a high-rise. Starting from such considerations, our office has continued to develop various concepts, an example of which can be seen in the North German State Clearing Bank in Hanover. ◄

1 Publishing house Dumont Schauberg, Cologne, Germany 2 Central administration building for the State Clearing Bank, Stuttgart, Germany 3 North German State Clearing Bank on Friedrichswall (Nord/LB), Hanover, Germany 4 Study, high-rise apex, Nord/LB, Hanover, Germany 5 Model studies, Technical Center of the Bavarian State Clearing Bank (LZB), Munich, Germany 6 MAX High-rise, Frankfurt, Germany 7 LZB, Munich, Germany 8 State Savings Bank, Potsdam, Germany 9 LZB, Munich, Germany 10 Commercial development, Hamburg, Germany 11 National and Provincial Archives, Copenhagen, Denmark 12 Model, Nord/LB, Hanover, Germany 13 Nord/LB, Hanover, Germany 14 LZB, Munich, Germany 15 Landmark tower and U2 Studios, Dublin, Ireland 16 Study, high-rise apex, Nord/LB, Hanover, Germany

1

2

HAUPTVERWALTUNGSGEBÄUDE DER
LANDESGIROKASSE AM HOPPENLAU-FRIEDHOF
STATE CLEARING BANK HEAD OFFICE BUILDING
AT HOPPENLAU CEMETERY

STUTTGART, DEUTSCHLAND | STUTTGART, GERMANY; 1989

1 Modellausschnitt 2 Lageplan | 1 Model, detail 2 Site plan

HAUPTVERWALTUNGSGEBÄUDE DER LANDESGIROKASSE |
STATE CLEARING BANK HEAD OFFICE BUILDING | 1989

Im Planungsgebiet überschneiden sich zwei Bereiche der Stadt Stuttgart: Stuttgart-Mitte und Stuttgart-West. Dieser Situation sollte die neu zu planende Anlage der Landesgirokasse (LG) gerecht werden. An einem solchen Schnittpunkt wäre Platz für eine Landmarke gewesen und man hätte den Wünschen der LG nach einem signifikanten Gebäude gut entsprechen können.

Die Seidenstraße, an der der Neubau geplant war, bildete einen einigermaßen intakten Straßenraum, der durch eine Randbebauung stabilisiert werden sollte. Allerdings war die gegenüberliegende sowie die im Süden angrenzende Bebauung tendenziell orientierungslos und in unterschiedlichen

Two distinctly different sections of the city of Stuttgart overlap within the planning area: Stuttgart Mitte and Stuttgart West. Plans for a new complex for the State Clearing Bank (Landesgirokasse, or LG) responded to this particular situation. Such a convergence point would have been a suitable location for a landmark, and would certainly have satisfied the wishes of the LG for a prominent and striking building.

Seidenstraße, where the new building would have been located, is structurally intact; it would have been stabilised by a perimeter block building. The buildings lying on the opposite side of the street, as well as those adjoining to the south, lacked

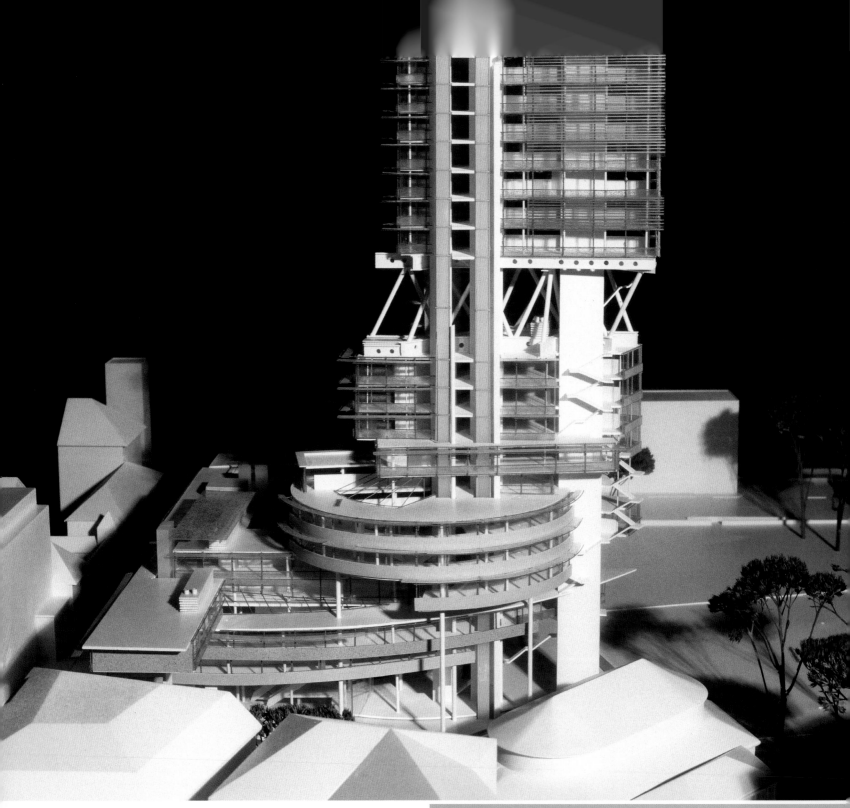

3 Präsentationsmodell 4 Ansicht Süd
3 Presentation model 4 South elevation

HAUPTVERWALTUNGSGEBÄUDE DER LANDESGIROKASSE |
STATE CLEARING BANK HEAD OFFICE BUILDING | 1989

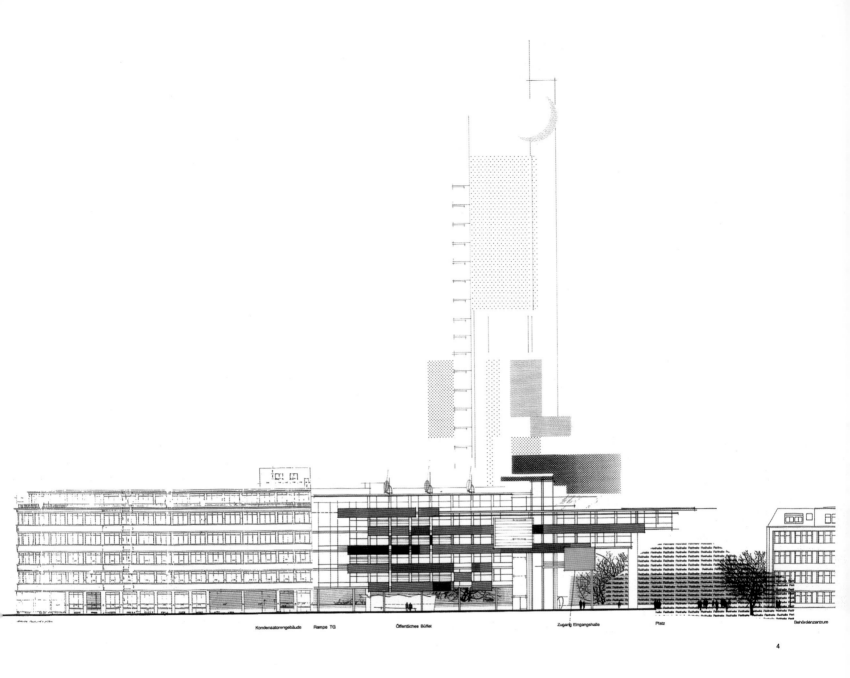

Kondensatorengebäude   Rampe TG   Öffentliches Büffet   Zugang Eingangshalle   Platz   Behördenzentrum

4

Maßen gegliedert (Länge, Höhe, Größe). Die Fassade des Neubaus an der Seidenstraße folgte dieser Vorgabe aus der Umgebung.

Quer zur Straßenrandbebauung wurden zwei senkrecht zur Seidenstraße stehende Baukörper angeordnet. Der südliche sollte sich zu einem höheren, von weitem sichtbaren Gebäude in der Achse der Kriegsbergstraße entwickeln. Um den Hoppenlau-Friedhof herum war ein städtebauliches Ensemble vorgesehen, dass die dort vorhandenen

any common orientation nor indeed shared any common proportions (i.e., length, height, or scale). The Seidenstraße facade of the new building respected these givens.

Two building volumes were arranged perpendicular to Seidenstraße perimeter block. The southernmost of the two was planned as a higher structure, running along the axis of Kriegsbergstraße and clearly visible from afar. A distinct ensemble

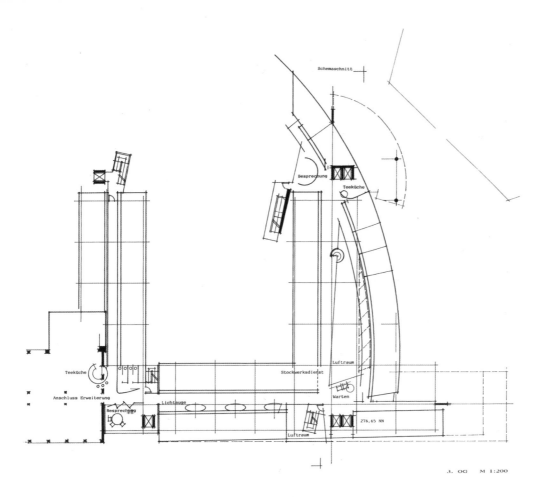

Schemaschnitt

Besprechung

Teeküche

Teeküche

Anschluss Erweiterung

Besprechung

Stockwerksdienst

Lichtauge

Luftraum

Warten

276,65 NN

Luftraum

J. OG   M 1:200

5

unterschiedlichen Elemente wie Friedhof, Max-Kade-Heim, Kongresszentrum, LG-Gebäude, Reithalle etc. integrieren sollte.

Die äußere Erscheinung wirkt offen, hell und freundlich. Leichtmetall, Glas und – in der Seidenstraße – auch Natursteinverkleidungen bestimmen das Bild. Das Gebäude wird mit zunehmender Höhe immer lichter, keinesfalls soll der Eindruck einer unangemessenen Baumasse entstehen. ◄

was envisioned for the area surrounding Hoppenlau Cemetery, one capable of integrating the various heterogeneous elements, such as the cemetery itself, the Max Kade Heim, the Congress Center, the State Clearing Bank Building, the Indoor Riding Arena, etc.

The building's external appearance makes an open impression, both bright and friendly. Light metal, glass and – to Seidenstraße – natural stone cladding define its appearance. The building, gradually becoming lighter as it climbs into the heights should under no circumstances give the impression of a disproportionate building volume. ◄

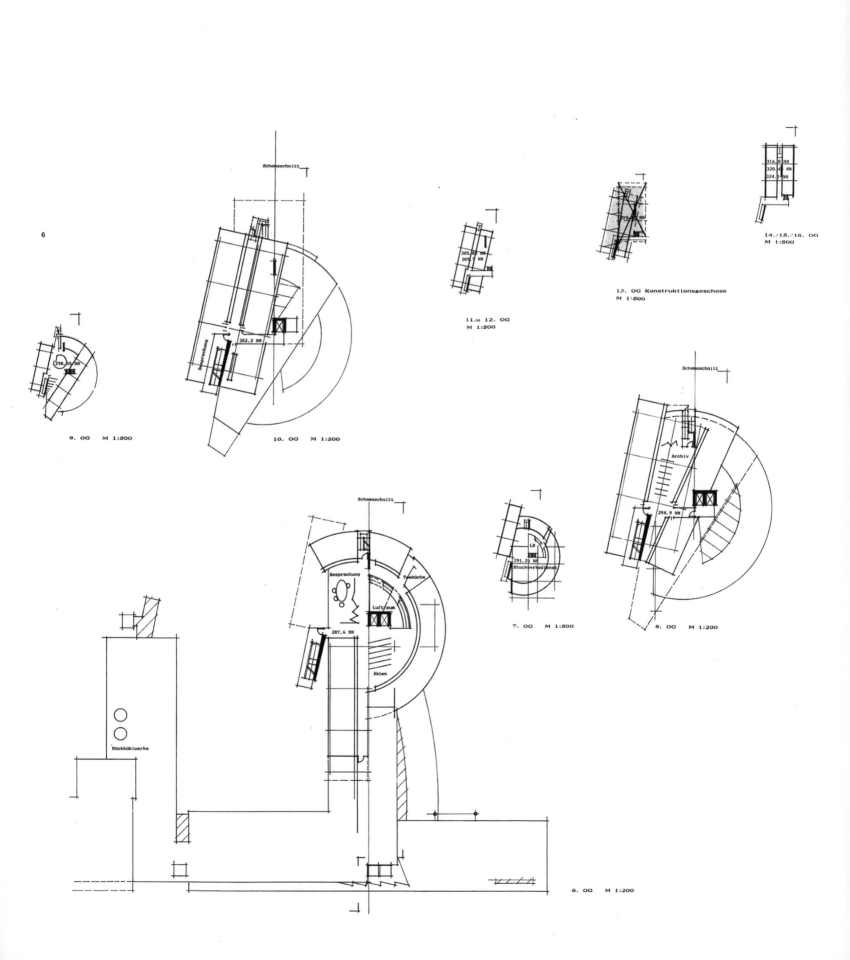

6

9. OG   M 1:500

10. OG   M 1:200

11.u 12. OG
M 1:500

13. OG Konstruktionsgeschoss
M 1:500

14./15./16. OG
M 1:500

Schemaschnitt

305,8 NN
30?,9 NN

302,2 NN

Besprechung

?12,? NN

316,8 NN
320,4? NN
324,0? NN

298,55 NN

Schemaschnitt

Archiv

294,9 NN

7. OG   M 1:500

8. OG   M 1:200

LR

291,25 NN
Stockwerksdienst

Schemaschnitt

Besprechung   Teeküche

Luftraum

287,6 NN

Akten

Rückkühlwerke

6. OG   M 1:200

1

1 Skyline Frankfurt 2 Lageplan | 1 Skyline, Frankfurt 2 Site plan

HOCHHAUS MAX | MAX HIGH-RISE | 1999

2

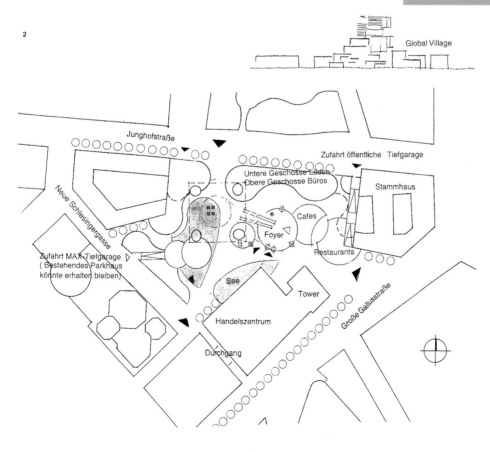

Global Village

Junghofstraße

Zufahrt öffentliche Tiefgarage

Neue Schlesingergasse

Untere Geschosse Laden
Obere Geschosse Büros

Stammhaus

Cafes

Foyer

Restaurants

Zufahrt MAX-Tiefgarage
(Bestehendes Parkhaus
könnte erhalten bleiben)

See

Tower

Große Gallusstraße

Handelszentrum

Durchgang

HOCHHAUS MAX | MAX HIGH-RISE

FRANKFURT, DEUTSCHLAND | FRANKFURT, GERMANY; 1999

In einem zweistufigen Wettbewerbsverfahren sollte ein neuer Hochhaustypus, in dem viele verschiedene Nutzungen wie Läden, Arbeiten, Wohnen und Kongresszentrum angeordnet sind, entwickelt werden. Ein Haus von 200 m Höhe bietet heute keine ernsthaften technischen Probleme mehr. Standfestigkeit, Tragwerk, Fluchttreppen, Klimahüllen etc. müssen funktionieren, in ihrer Gestalt aber könnten sie eher zurücktreten. Andere Momente von Architektur könnten sich dagegen entwickeln und auch sichtbar werden.

Eine interessante Landmarke sollte entstehen. Allein Volumen und Höhe können das in diesem Umfeld kaum leisten. Viele Hochhäuser unterschiedlichster Qualität stehen hier im Zentrum Frankfurts. Die Vielfalt der Nutzungen im Inneren sollte auch in der äußeren Gestalt sichtbar werden, der Idee einer vertikalen Stadt folgend, nicht nur im Technisch-Konstruktiven, sondern im Ideellen.

A two-stage competition process called for the development of a new high-rise type, one capable of accommodating various functions such as shops, offices, residences and a congress center. Today, a building rising to 200m no longer offers any serious technical difficulties. Stability, structure, emergency staircases, climate envelope, etc. must function, but may appear very restrained in design terms. By contrast, other architectural aspects can evolve, assuming greater prominence.

In this case, the task was to create an interesting landmark. In such surroundings, however, volume and height alone could hardly impress. Many high-rises of differing quality already stand in Frankfurt's downtown. The multiplicity of uses are also meant to be clearly readable on the exterior form, in keeping with the idea of a vertical city, not only in technical-constructive but

Mannigfaltige vertikale Strukturen bieten größere Möglichkeiten als die Addition immer gleicher Elemente oder Ebenen.

Man sollte an der Gestalt und am ästhetischen Wert dieses Gebäudes erkennen können, dass hier andere Kräfte als bei Hochhäusern üblich wirksam waren. Dieses Gebäude wird im Stadtbild und im Ensemble der anderen Hochhäuser sofort erkennbar sein, und man sollte sich gern daran erinnern.

Der Entwurf sieht vor, dass die geschlossene Blockrandstruktur teilweise zu den Straßenräumen hin geöffnet wird. Im Inneren wird ein für die Bürger offener und lebendiger städtischer Raum geschaffen. Dieser Innenhof entwickelt sich nach anderen Gesetzmäßigkeiten als die Bereiche des Hochhauses – auch im Formalen. Freiere Formen, begrünte Terrassen, Wasserflächen, verglaste Pavillons, Fußwege, kleinere Plätze und Baumhaine schaffen ein differenziertes Bild. Hier stehen eher die Landschaft, frische Luft, Freizeit und Erholung im Vordergrund als die hektische Stadt.

Aus diesem Blockrand entwickelt sich im Inneren der Anlage das Hochhaus. Bei dem Entwurf sind Entwicklungen der 70er Jahre aufgegriffen worden. In diesen Konzepten, die leider durch die Postmoderne aus dem Bewusstsein und der öffentlichen Diskussion vertrieben wurden, steckt unserer Meinung nach viel Potenzial. Man sollte an diesem Punkt wieder anknüpfen und die Konzepte mit unseren heutigen Erkenntnissen bereichern und weiterentwickeln. ◂

also in ideal terms. Multifarious vertical structures contain more potential than the addition of identical levels.

Through both the tower's aesthetic value and characteristic form, it should become readily evident that other forces are at play here than those usually expected with highrises. The building is meant to be immediately recognisable as an individual within the city's skyline and within the ensemble of other high-rises, and people should carry away positive images of it.

At street level the design ensures that the closed urban block structure of the site is partially opened. For the interior of the site, a more open and lively urban space is created. An inner courtyard develops according to other demands than those conditioning the tower itself. Freer forms, landscaped terraces, expanses of water, glazed pavilions, footpaths, intimate spots and small groves create a differentiated world. Here, in place of the hectic city, the landscape, fresh air, leisure activities and relaxation come to the fore.

Out of this block perimeter, in the middle of the complex, evolves the high-rise. Its design revives memories of certain developments of the 1970s. These concepts – regrettably driven from consciousness and public discussions by Postmodernism – still harbor, in our opinion, great potential. Now is the time to reengage such ideas, enriching them with contemporary knowledge and developing them further. ◂

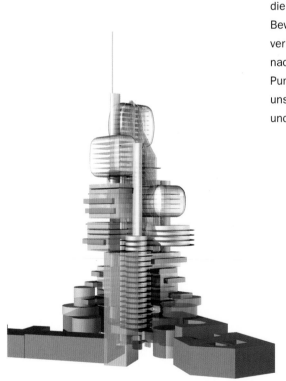

3

5

6

7

8

4

3–4 Perspektivische Darstellung 5–8 Entwurfsstudien
3–4 Rendering 5–8 Design studies

HOCHHAUS MAX | MAX HIGH-RISE | 1999

Das Grundstück liegt an der Schnittstelle
zwischen der eigentlichen City und den
Wohngebieten der Südstadt, am Friedrichswall. Westlich des Grundstücks befindet sich
in unmittelbarer Nachbarschaft das Rathaus
mit dem angrenzenden Sport- und Naherho-
lungsgebiet – dem Maschpark. Der Aegidientorplatz an der nordöstlichen Ecke des
Grundstücks ist als ein Hauptverkehrskno-
tenpunkt der Stadt Hannover durch den
Verkehr stark belastet.

The site lies on Friedrichswall, at the intersection between the city itself and residential districts to the south. To the west, lying
in the immediate vicinity of the town hall,
is the Maschpark with its adjoining sports
and recreational facilities. Aegidientorplatz,
lying at the north-eastern corner of the
site, is one of Hanover's overburdened
central traffic junctures.

NORDDEUTSCHE LANDESBANK AM FRIEDRICHSWALL (NORD/LB)
NORTH GERMAN STATE CLEARING BANK ON FRIEDRICHSWALL (NORD/LB)

HANNOVER, DEUTSCHLAND | HANOVER, GERMANY; 1996–2002

1 Blick von Nord-Osten 2 Lageplan 3 Blick vom Maschpark
1 View from north-east 2 Site plan 3 View from Maschpark

NORDDEUTSCHE LANDESBANK |
NORTH GERMAN STATE CLEARING BANK | 1996–2002

2

3

Das Erdgeschoss des Hauses ist von ent-
scheidender Bedeutung als Bindeglied
zwischen Wohn- und Geschäftsstadt. Es ist
durchlässig für Bürger und Passanten, ohne
den Verwaltungsbetrieb zu stören. So öffnet
sich der Innenhof an verschiedenen Stellen
und schafft Bezüge zum Maschpark, zur City
an der Gebäudeecke Maschpark/Friedrichs-
wall und zum Aegidientorplatz. Dieser Ort
wird belebt durch Restaurants, Läden, Cafés
und eine Galerie. Der Innenhof ist mit großzügigen Wasserflächen, begrünten Dächern,
Terrassen und Wegen tendenziell landschaftlich gestaltet. Er gleicht einer eher artifiziellen Landschaft am Übergang von fester
Stadtbebauung zum grünen Naherholungs-
bereich Maschpark.

The building's ground floor is an important
link between the residential and commercial districts. It permits access to the public,
yet without interfering with administrative
activities. The inner courtyard opens at
various points, establishing relations to
Maschpark, to the city on the corner where
Am Maschpark and Friedrichswall con-
verge, and to Aegidientorplatz. This location is enlivened by restaurants, shops,
cafés and a gallery. The inner courtyard
with its spacious expanses of water, landscaped roofs, terraces and paths, resembles
an artificial landscape marking the transition from dense urban settlement to the
green recreation areas of Maschpark.

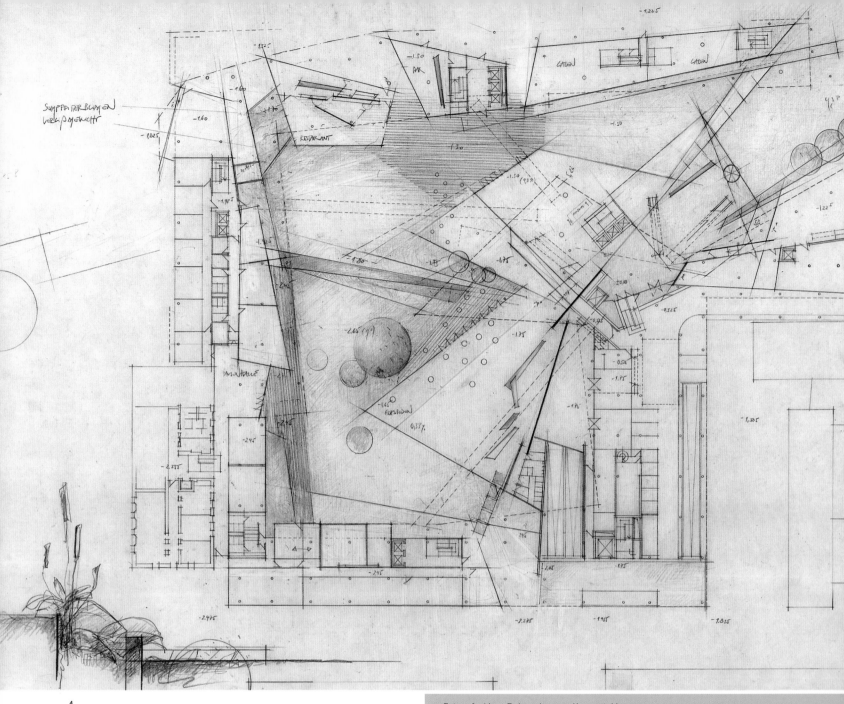

4

4 Entwurfsskizze Erdgeschoss 5 Konzeptskizzen
4 Design sketch, ground floor 5 Concept sketches

NORDDEUTSCHE LANDESBANK |
NORTH GERMAN STATE CLEARING BANK | 1996–2002

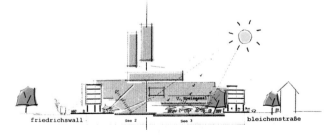

5

Konzept | Concept

Wasserkaskade | Water cascade

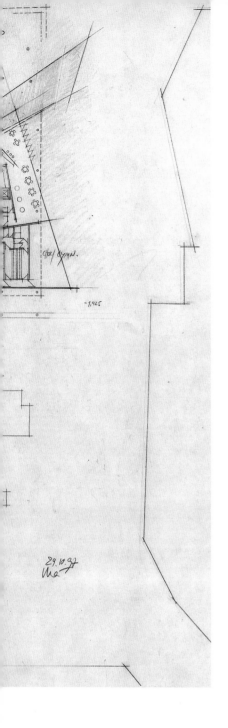

Die mehrgeschossige Eingangshalle der Nord/LB liegt im ruhigeren Innenhof im Zentrum der Anlage und ist durch ein großzügiges »Tor zum Aegi« über einen eher privat wirkenden Vorplatz zu erreichen. So erhält das Gebäude trotz der belasteten Verkehrssituation ein angemessenes Entrée. In unmittelbarer Verbindung zur Halle mit direktem Bezug zum Garten liegen das Mitarbeiterrestaurant, Bereiche für weitere Sondernutzungen, sowie ein Forum, das für Ausstellungen und Veranstaltungen verschiedenster Art geeignet ist.

Der Straßenraum ist in der vertrauten Höhe begrenzt, der moderne Blockrand ist erhalten. Hiervon zurückgesetzt entwickelt sich der höhere Gebäudeteil, nach anderen Aspekten geformt, als nach denen des orthogonalen Rasters des Straßenraums. Den Bezug bilden hier vielmehr die verschränkten Raster der älteren Innenstadtstrukturen. Auch die freie Geometrie des inneren Gartens spiegelt sich in der Entwicklung dieses Teils der Anlage wider. Zu den Straßenräumen zeigt sich der Bau dagegen sachlich und zurückhaltend.

The multi-story entrance hall of the Nord/LB lies within the tranquil interior courtyard at the complex's center, and is accessed via a generous "Gate to Aegi" across a forecourt, which is rather private in character. In spite of the burdensome traffic situation, the building thus acquires an appropriate entrée. Immediately linked to the hall, and with direct access to the garden, lies the staff restaurant, areas for further special functions, as well as a forum, suitable for exhibitions and events of various kinds.

Toward the street, the building restricts itself to the heights prevailing in the district, and the modern block perimeter structure is retained. From here, set back, rises the taller part of the complex, shaped by considerations other than those governing the orthogonal grid of the surrounding streets. Instead, the point of reference here is the interlocking structure of the older inner-city. Even the free geometry of the inner garden is reflected in this part of the complex. Toward the street, however, the building displays a clear and restrained front.

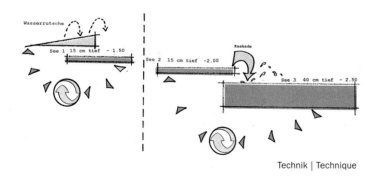

Technik | Technique

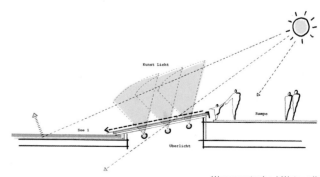

Wasserrutsche | Water slide

6

7

Nach unterschiedlichen Richtungen orientierte Terrassen in vielen Geschossen des Gebäudes sind den Aufenthaltsräumen, Großraumbüros oder Teeküchen vorgelagert. Sie können von den Mitarbeitern in Pausen genutzt werden, strukturieren das Gebäude, bieten Aussichtspunkte. Ferner wird eine Beziehung zum Innenhof des Erdgeschosses hergestellt.

In many stories, oriented in various directions, are terraces set before lounges, group offices and kitchenettes, oriented in various directions. These areas, which can be used by employees during breaks, structure the building, offering vantage points. They also create a connection to the interior courtyard on the ground floor.

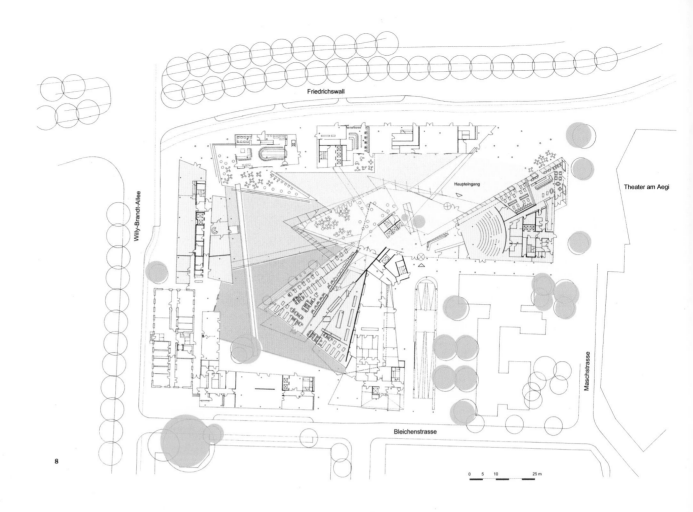

Friedrichswall

Willy-Brandt-Allee

Haupteingang

Theater am Aegi

Maschstrasse

Bleichenstrasse

8

0 5 10   25 m

6 Haupteingang 7 Restaurant 8 Grundriss Erdgeschoss 9 Grundriss 1. Obergeschoss
6 Main entrance 7 Restaurant 8 Plan, ground floor 9 Plan, 2nd floor

NORDDEUTSCHE LANDESBANK |
NORTH GERMAN STATE CLEARING BANK | 1996–2002

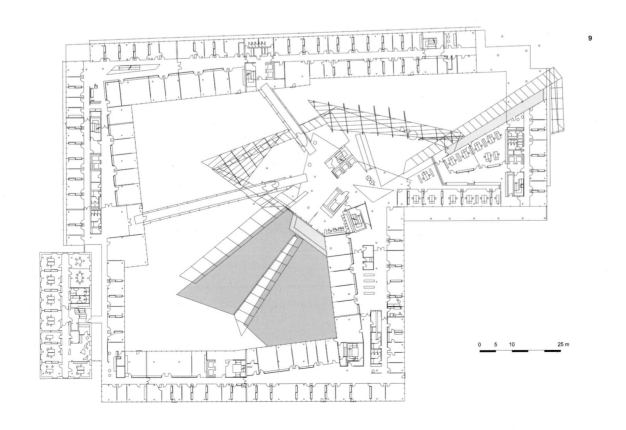

9

0 5 10   25 m

Je nach Himmelsrichtung und Anforderungen aus der Umgebung sind die Bürofassaden unterschiedlich entwickelt. Zum Friedrichswall, zur Willy-Brandt-Allee sowie zum Theater am Aegi ist eine Doppelfassade ausgeführt, die sowohl klimatechnisch arbeitet, als auch dem Schallschutz dient. Sie führt die unbelastete Außenluft des ruhigeren Innenhofs über die – durchgängig vorhandenen – öffenbaren Fenster in die Räume. Die Innenhoffassaden sind gestalterisch leichter, weniger repräsentativ, vielleicht etwas privater. Hier sind die hohen Anforderungen an den Schallschutz nicht gegeben. Die Fassaden zur umgebenden Wohnbebauung haben ebenfalls nicht die hohen Anforderungen, wie sie zur Willy-Brandt-Allee und zum Friedrichswall hin bestehen, zu erfüllen. Die Fassaden des höheren Gebäudeteils (Hochhausbereich) müssen anderen Ansprüchen gerecht werden: Sie sind höheren Windlasten, mehr Sonneneinstrahlung und dem Regen ungeschützt ausgesetzt. Hier schützt eine Doppelfassade auf der Südseite des Hochhauses den vor der inneren Fassade montierten effektiven Sonnenschutz.

The office facades vary according to orientation and to requirements related to the immediate surroundings. Toward Friedrichswall, toward Willy-Brandt-Allee, and toward the Theater am Aegi, there is a double facade, which serves both climate control and sound-insulation purposes. It carries the unpolluted outer air of the tranquil inner courtyard into the rooms through operable windows. The facades of the inner courtyard are lighter in design terms, certainly less representative in appearance, and perhaps more intimate. There are no high demands here for sound protection. Likewise, the facades facing the surrounding residential buildings need not fulfill the kinds of requirements of those oriented toward Willy-Brandt-Allee and Friedrichswall. The facades of the higher parts of the building (the high-rise) must meet different demands: increased wind loads, greater solar radiation and immediate exposure to rainfall. Here a double facade on the south side of the tower shields the effective sun protection mounted before the inner facade.

10

10, 11 Innenhof mit Verbindungsstegen

10, 11 Interior courtyard with connecting footbridges

NORDDEUTSCHE LANDESBANK |
NORTH GERMAN STATE CLEARING BANK | 1996–2002

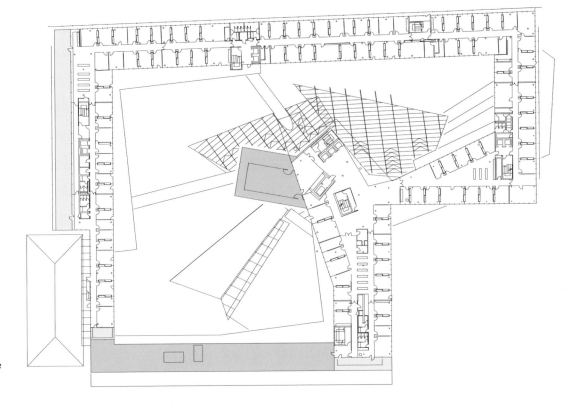

12

13

Die Spitze des Hochhauses ist eine Stahl-Glas-Konstruktion. Die Glasscheiben führen die Geometrie des oberen Gebäudeteils zu einem materiell weniger bestimmten Abschluss. So genannte Interferenzgläser, metallbedampfte Glasscheiben, reflektieren das Licht in den Tönen Gelb und Blau, und je nach Sonnenstand entsteht ein abwechslungsreiches Licht- und Farbenspiel. Für die Nachtwirkung sind in der Konstruktion Leuchtdioden eingelassen.

Sich überlagernde Wellen von verschiedenen Gelb- und Blautönen gliedern in den Bürobereichen die längeren Flurzonen. In den Büros sind die Schiebetüren der Schrankwände farbig. Es wurde darauf geachtet, diese Farben der Büronutzung entsprechend zurückhaltend auszuführen. Die farbintensiven Flächen sind in besonderen, allgemein zugänglichen Flurzonen, Treppenhäusern oder Kombizonen ausgeführt. Hier unterstützen sie den hellen, freundlichen Charakter des Hauses. Eigenständige, für sich selbst stehende Farbflächen sind an den durch Künstler gewählten Orten, wie einem Treppenhaus, dem Betriebsrestaurant und am Altbau, ausgeführt.

The top of the high-rise is marked by a steel-glass construction. The glass sheets develop the geometry of the upper part of the building to a terminus that is, in material terms, less defined. So-called interference glazing — consisting of panes with vapor-applied metallic coatings — reflect the light in tones of yellow and blue, and, according to the position of the sun, produce a rich play of light and color. Light diodes set into the construction create a further dance of effects at night.

Overlapping ripples of various yellow and blue tones structure the longer hallways in the office areas. The sliding doors of the office cabinets are also colored. Generally, an effort was made to insure that the colors used in the offices were correspondingly restrained. Color-intensive surfaces are introduced in generally accessible hallways, staircases and multi-purpose areas. Here, bright, friendly tones reinforce the character of the building. Self-sufficient colored surfaces are set in particular places selected by artists, such as a staircase, the restaurant, and the facade of an existing listed building integrated into the complex.

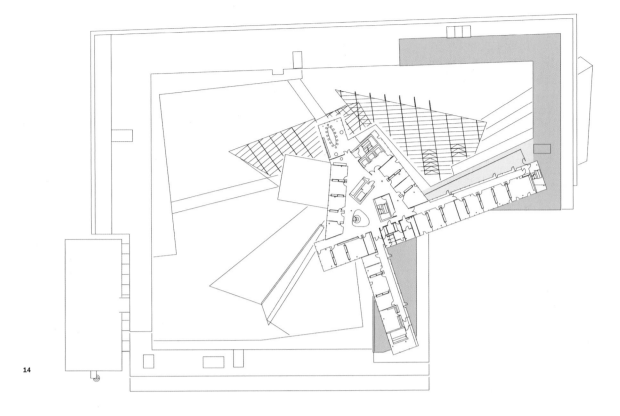

14

NORDDEUTSCHE LANDESBANK |
NORTH GERMAN STATE CLEARING BANK | 1996–2002

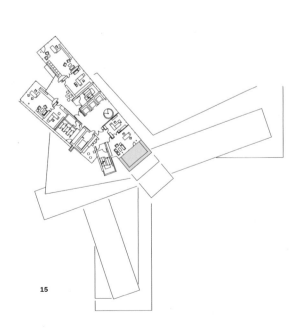

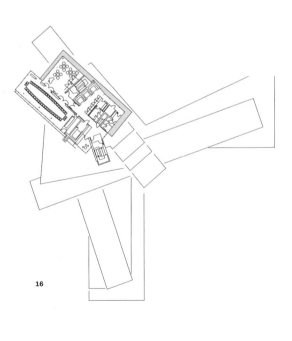

16

15

17

18

NORDDEUTSCHE LANDESBANK |
NORTH GERMAN STATE CLEARING BANK | 1996–2002

19

KLIMATECHNIK Durch die Ausnutzung natürlicher Ressourcen wie Sonne, Wind, Außenluft und Erdreichkühle konnte bei der Nord/LB auf Klimaanlagen weitgehend verzichtet werden. Tageslichtoptimierte Büros reduzieren den Einsatz von Kunstlicht, alle Räume besitzen die Möglichkeit der Fensterlüftung. Dadurch ist auf einfache Weise das große Kühlpotenzial der Außenluft erschlossen, die in Hannover in nur knapp 5% der Jahreszeit über 22°C liegt. In die Doppelfassade am Friedrichswall wird die sauberere Luft des Innenhofs über einen Zuluftkanal geleitet, so dass auch an den stark verkehrsbelasteten Straßenseiten Fensterlüftung möglich ist. Im Innenhof befinden sich mehrere Seeflächen, die sich günstig auf das Mikroklima auswirken und ein Überhitzen der Bodenflächen im Hochsommer verhindern. Die natürliche Lüftung ist ergänzt durch einen definierten Luftdurchlass im Bereich der Flurtrennwand, der auch schallschutztechnische Anforderungen erfüllt. Hier wird die verbrauchte Raumluft mit Hilfe des Kamineffekts über Schächte zum Dach abgeführt.

CLIMATE CONTROL TECHNOLOGY Via the exploitation of natural resources such as sun, wind, exterior air and earth cooling, the Nord/LB can essentially dispense with traditional air-conditioning technology. Optimal use of daylight in the offices reduces the necessity for artificial light, and all rooms can be ventilated via operable windows. This enables convenient access to the enormous cooling potential of the external air; in Hanover this reaches temperatures of over 22°C for only 5% of the year. In the double facade facing Friedrichswall, the clean air of the inner courtyard passes through an intake channel, making window ventilation possible on the heavily trafficked street side as well. In the inner courtyard are several ponds which have a beneficial effect on the microclimate and help to prevent overheating of floor surfaces in summertime. Natural ventilation is supplemented by a specified air channel through the separating walls to the hallways, which also fulfill sound-insulating demands. Assisted by this chimney effect, stale air is led through shafts up to the roof.

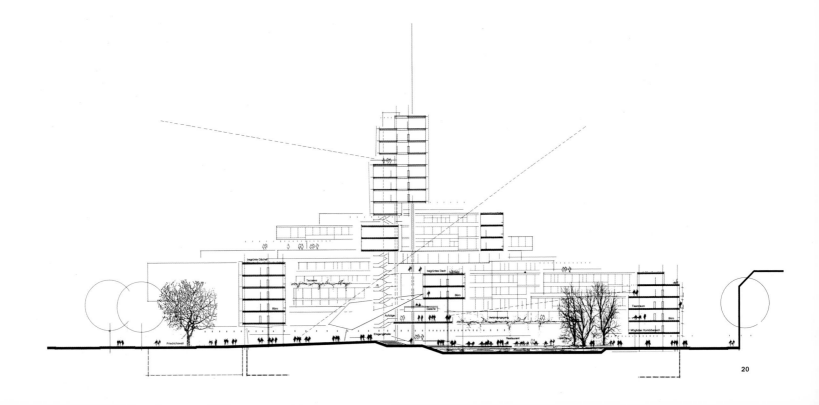

21

23

21 Vorplatz Haupteingang **22** Eingangshalle **23** Empfangstresen
21 Forecourt, main entrance **22** Entrance hall **23** Reception desk

NORDDEUTSCHE LANDESBANK |
NORTH GERMAN STATE CLEARING BANK | 1996–2002

Zur Festlegung der Qualitäten des Sonnenschutzes und der Verglasung wurden compu-
tergestützte Verschattungsstudien durchgeführt. Der Sonnenschutz ist so gestaltet,
dass bei optimaler Sonnenschutzwirkung
eine zu starke Abdunkelung der Räume ver-
hindert wird. Die obersten Lamellen sind ver-
setzt zum restlichen Behang einjustiert und
spiegeln das Tageslicht an die reflektierende
Decke.

Computer-assisted studies helped to
determine the required qualities of sun
protection measures and glazing typology.
The sun protection is designed so that
even with maximal utilisation, excessive
darkening of the rooms is prevented. The
uppermost louver blinds are reversed and
can be adjusted independently of the other
hangings to redirect daylight toward the
reflective ceilings.

24

25

24 Wandbild Michael Craig-Martin **25, 26** Mitarbeiterrestaurant
24 Mural by Michael Craig-Martin **25, 26** Staff restaurant

NORDDEUTSCHE LANDESBANK |
NORTH GERMAN STATE CLEARING BANK | 1996–2002

In den Sommermonaten reicht das Kühlpotenzial der Außenluft für ein angenehmes Raumklima oft nicht mehr aus. Für die aktive Kühlung der Büroräume sorgt dann die so genannte Bauteilkühlung. Dabei wird heruntergekühltes Wasser durch ein System in der Rohdecke eingegossener Polyethylenrohre geführt. An normalen Sommertagen genügt es, wenn das Rohrsystem nachts durchspült wird, die massive Betondecke die eingebrachte Kälte zwischenspeichert und langsam am Tag wieder in den Raum abgibt.

In the summer months, the cooling potential of the outer air is often insufficient for pleasant room temperatures. Active cooling of the offices is provided by component cooling. Here, cooled water flows through a system of polyethylene piping set into the exposed concrete ceiling. On normal summer days it suffices to flush the piping system at night, so the massive concrete ceilings hold the cold temporarily until it can be released gradually again into the space during the daytime.

27, 28 Büros 6. Obergeschoss 29 Verbindung zwischen Alt- und Neubau, Wandbild Heimo Zobanek
30 Planausschnitt 31 Skulptur Heiner Blum | 27, 28 Offices, 7th floor 29 Connection between
old and new construction, mural by Heimo Zobanek 30 Plan, detail 31 Sculpture by Heiner Blum

NORDDEUTSCHE LANDESBANK |
NORTH GERMAN STATE CLEARING BANK | 1996–2002

28

Für die Bereitstellung des Kühlwassers sorgen Rückkühlwerke. Der Einsatz von Kältemaschinen ist nicht notwendig. An extremen Sommertagen wird die Decke auch tagsüber aktiv mit kaltem Wasser gekühlt. Die Kaltwasser-Erzeugung erfolgt dann über einen Erdreichwärmetauscher, der unter dem Hochhaus in den Gründungspfählen angeordnet ist. Die geothermische Energie wird dabei zweifach genutzt: Die im Sommer an das Erdreich abgegebene Wärme wird gespeichert und im Winter wieder entzogen, um die Bauteilkühlung als Niedertemperatur-Flächenheizung einzusetzen. Das Wasser in den

Re-cooling units provide for cool water. The introduction of a cooling plant proved superfluous. On extreme summer days, the ceilings are actively cooled by cold water also during the day. Cold water is then provided via a ground heat exchanger, set into the foundation piles under the high-rise. The geothermal energy produced is utilised in two ways: the warmth flowing into the ground in summertime is stored and accessed again in wintertime in order to employ component cooling in the form of low-temperature plate heaters. The water in the heat exchanger has a temperature

29

30

31

32 Cafeteria 33 Verbindungssteg 34 Flurbereich 35 Vorstandsbüro
32 Cafeteria 33 Connecting footbridge 34 Circulation area 35 Executive offices

NORDDEUTSCHE LANDESBANK |
NORTH GERMAN STATE CLEARING BANK | 1996–2002

Wärmetauschern hat eine Temperatur von ca. 6 °C. Das Wasser im Heizkreis wird mittels einer Wärmepumpe auf ein Temperaturniveau von ca. 30°C gebracht. Aufgrund des geringen Temperaturhubes arbeitet die Wärmepumpe sehr effizient. Im Sommer wird der Prozess umgekehrt: Die Wärme fließt von den Büroräumen über die Geschossdecke in das ausgekühlte Erdreich. Dabei wird das Umlaufwasser mit ca. 25°C aus den Geschossdecken im Erdreichwärmetauscher abgekühlt und steht dann wieder für Kühlzwecke zur Verfügung. Für diesen Prozess ist Antriebsenergie nur für den Betrieb der Umwälzpumpe erforderlich. Die Jahresbilanz von zugeführter und abgeführter Wärmemenge ist für das Erdreich ausgeglichen.

of approx. 6°C. The water in the heating cycle is then raised by a heat pump to approx. 30°C. Given the minimal temperature differences, the heat pump is highly efficient. In summer, the process is reversed: warmth flows from the offices across the ceilings into the cooled ground. Hence, the circulated water from the ceilings, at approx. 25°C, is cooled in the ground heat exchanger, and is made available again for cooling purposes. For this process, energy is required solely for operating the circulation pump. For the earth, the annual balance of introduced and exhausted warmth is held at an equilibrium.

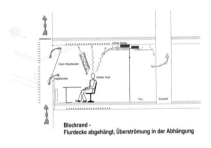

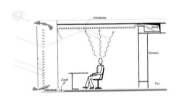

36 Verlegen der Bauteilkühlung 37 Montage der Kühldecken im Hochhaus 38 Sonnenschutz geschlossen 39 Klimakonzept Büro 40 Diagramm Bauteilkühlung 41 Diagramm Klimakonzeption
36 Installation of component cooling system 37 Montage of cooling ceiling in the high-rise 38 Sun protection, closed position 39 Climate control concept, offices 40 Diagram, component cooling system 41 Diagram, climate control concept

NORDDEUTSCHE LANDESBANK |
NORTH GERMAN STATE CLEARING BANK | 1996–2002

Blockrand -
Flurdecke abgehängt,
Überströmung durch Klappe über der Tür

Blockrand -
Flurdecke abgehängt, Überströmung in der Abhängung

Auf den Einsatz von Fotovoltaik hat man aufgrund des geringen Einsparpotenzials verzichtet. Lediglich das Warmwasser der Küche des Betriebsrestaurants wird über Kollektoren auf dem Flachdach des Blockrandes erzeugt.

Im Gegensatz zur Blockrandbebauung wird in den Räumen des Hochhauses, ab dem 9. Obergeschoss, keine Bauteilkühlung eingesetzt, vielmehr finden aufgeputzte Kühldecken und lufttechnische Anlagen Anwendung. ◄

Given the minimal potential for savings, it was decided not to introduce photovoltaic cells. Only in the kitchen serving the restaurant, warm water is supplied by solar collectors mounted on the flat roof of the perimeter block.

In contrast to the perimeter block development, in the rooms of the high-rise, beginning on the 9th floor, no component cooling is used; instead, preference is given to plastered cooling ceilings and air circulation technology. ◄

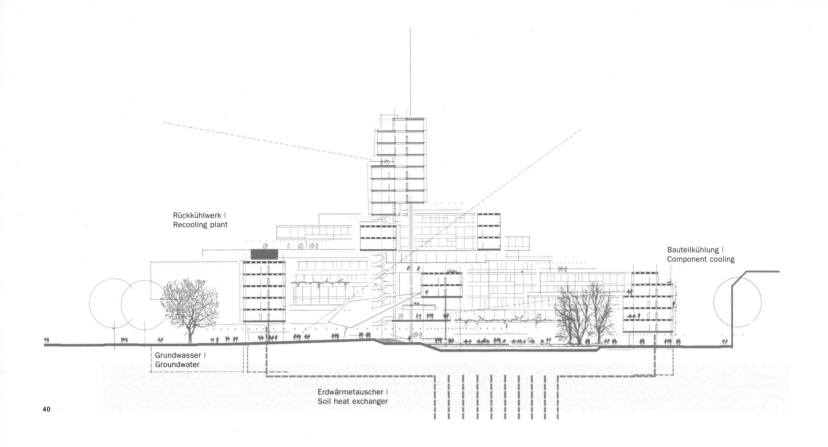

Rückkühlwerk |
Recooling plant

Bauteilkühlung |
Component cooling

Grundwasser |
Groundwater

Erdwärmetauscher |
Soil heat exchanger

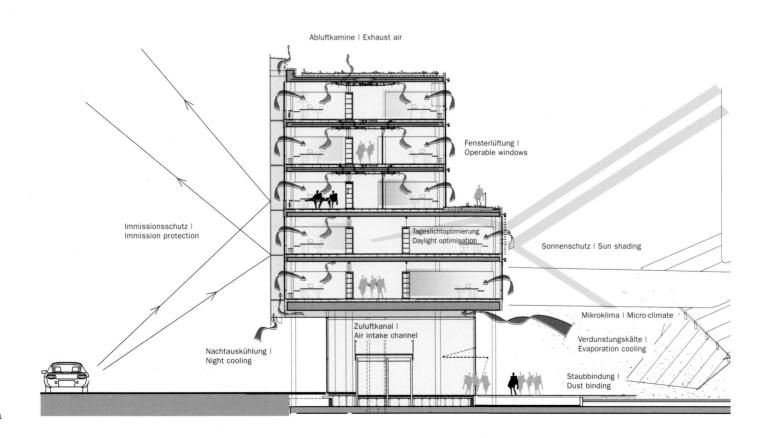

Abluftkamine | Exhaust air

Fensterlüftung |
Operable windows

Immissionsschutz |
Immission protection

Tageslichtoptimierung |
Daylight optimisation

Sonnenschutz | Sun shading

Mikroklima | Micro-climate

Nachtauskühlung |
Night cooling

Zuluftkanal |
Air intake channel

Verdunstungskälte |
Evaporation cooling

Staubbindung |
Dust binding

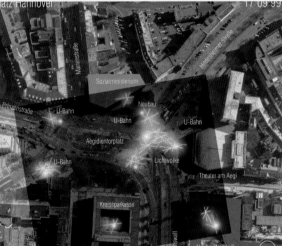

1 Lageplan 2 Präsentationsmodell | 1 Site plan 2 Presentation model

ARCHITEKTUR-/KUNSTOBJEKTE |
ARCHITECTURAL/ARTISTIC OBJECTS | 1999–2001

1

Die Stadt Hannover hatte für den Aegidientorplatz einen internationalen Wettbewerb ausgelobt. Eingeladen waren sowohl Architekten, als auch Künstler aus dem In- und Ausland. Der Aegidientorplatz sollte mehr Gewicht im Stadtgefüge erhalten, um seiner Lage und Bedeutung auch formal gerecht zu werden. Die meisten Elemente wie Bepflanzung, Beleuchtung, Pflasterung, Straßenführung etc. lagen jedoch leider schon fest und sollten nicht verändert werden. So blieb nur der Luftraum zur Gestaltung.

Gemeinsam mit Heinz Mack entwickelten wir eine Skulptur, die den Platz markieren, den Ort belegen, aber nicht verstellen oder auf-

The city of Hanover had announced a competition for Aegidientorplatz; architects, as well as artists from both Germany and abroad, were invited to participate. In order to do justice to its position and significance, Aegidientorplatz was to receive increased formal emphasis within the urban fabric. Unfortunately, the majority of elements, such as plantings, lighting, paving, street alignments, etc., had already been decided upon and were not subject to revision. This left only the air space itself.

In collaboration with the artist Heinz Mack, we designed a sculpture to mark the square, occupying the space above without obstructing or crowding it. The result was

ARCHITEKTUR-/KUNSTOBJEKTE
ARCHITECTURAL/ARTISTIC OBJECTS

AEGIDIENTORPLATZ
HANNOVER, DEUTSCHLAND | HANOVER, GERMANY; 1999–2001

füllen sollte. Es entstand die so genannte Lichtwolke, ein Raumgebilde aus verspannten Edelstahlstäben, mit dem wir in vielen Varianten experimentiert haben. Die hoch reflektierenden Stäbe sollten die Umgebung, das Licht, den Himmel widerspiegeln, den Raum verfremden, Teile wegspiegeln, dafür fremde Elemente der Umgebung an diesen Ort einspiegeln. Auch von Witterung und Tageszeit abhängig, sollte sich die Erscheinung der Lichtgestalt ändern.

Der Beitrag wurde mit dem 1. Preis ausgezeichnet. Leider konnte das Projekt aus Kostengründen nicht realisiert werden. ◂

the so-called Light Cloud, a spatial structure of braced steel beams, developed via a series of experiments involving numerous variants. The highly reflective beams were intended to reflect the vicinity, the light, the sky, subjecting the space to an alienation effect, rendering some elements invisible, while bringing unfamiliar ones into the field of vision via reflections. Depending too on weather conditions and on time of day, the appearance of the light configuration was to change constantly.

Our contribution was awarded first prize. Unfortunately, due to financial restrictions the project was not realised. ◂

2

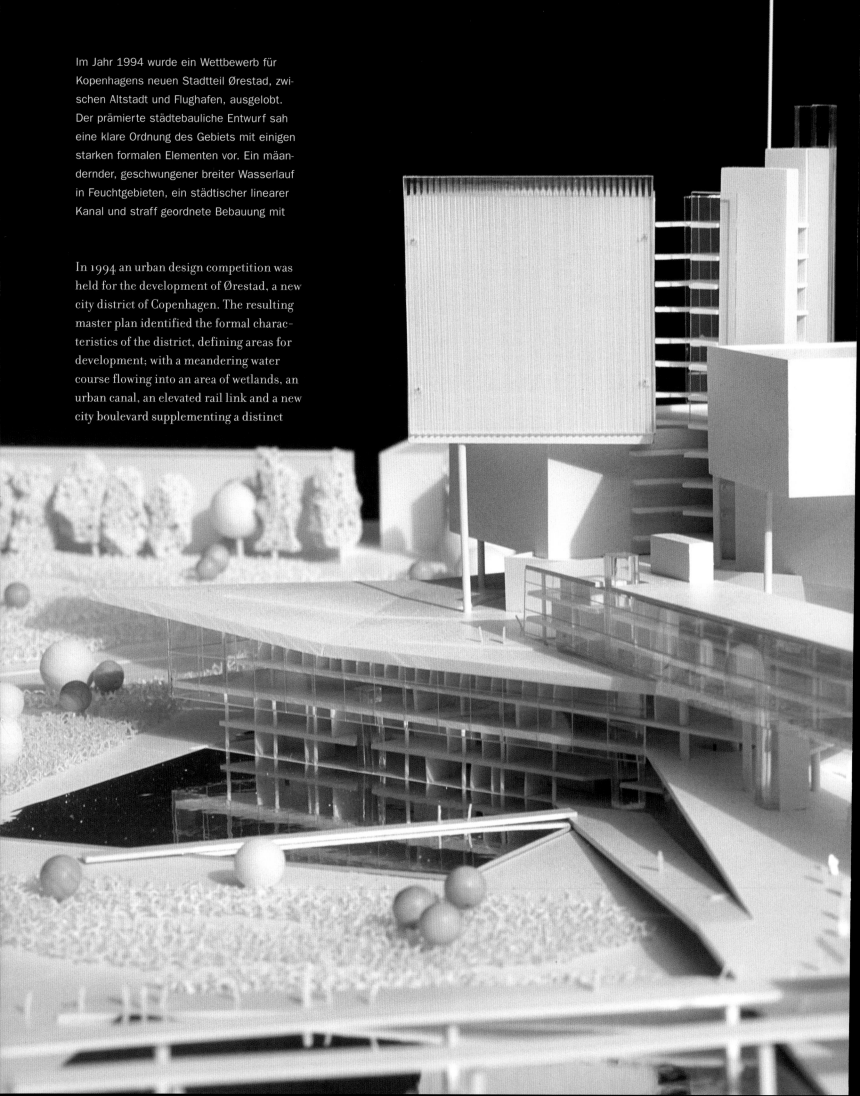

Im Jahr 1994 wurde ein Wettbewerb für
Kopenhagens neuen Stadtteil Ørestad, zwischen Altstadt und Flughafen, ausgelobt.
Der prämierte städtebauliche Entwurf sah
eine klare Ordnung des Gebiets mit einigen
starken formalen Elementen vor. Ein mäan-
dernder, geschwungener breiter Wasserlauf
in Feuchtgebieten, ein städtischer linearer
Kanal und straff geordnete Bebauung mit

In 1994 an urban design competition was
held for the development of Ørestad, a new
city district of Copenhagen. The resulting
master plan identified the formal characteristics of the district, defining areas for
development; with a meandering water
course flowing into an area of wetlands, an
urban canal, an elevated rail link and a new
city boulevard supplementing a distinct

einigen freien Plätzen für wichtige Solitär-
bauten waren zentrale Elemente. Eine erhöhte
Stadtbahnlinie und neue Boulevards sollten
das Gebiet erschließen. Am südöstlichen
Rande dieses neuen Stadtteils sollten die
neuen National- und Provinzialarchive entstehen. Maßstab und Volumen dieses zentralen Gebäudes wurden im Masterplan schon
festgeschrieben.

In der 1996 formulierten Wettbewerbsaus-
lobung für die Nationalarchive wurde deutlich
auf die kulturelle Bedeutung des Projekts
hingewiesen. Gefordert wurde, dass das Gebäude zu einem neuen Wahrzeichen der Stadt
Kopenhagen werden solle. Das staatlich
finanzierte Projekt galt als Initialprojekt für
die künftige Entwicklung von Ørestad.

Aus den Vorgaben und der Größe des zur
Verfügung stehenden Grundstücks sowie
einem hohen Grundwasserspiegel und funktionellen Anforderungen ergab sich zwangsläufig
ein Hochhaus. Der Entwurf berücksichtigt
die Bedeutung der Aufgabe – unersetzbare,
jahrhundertealte Originaldokumente werden
hier gelagert –, reagiert aber auch auf den
Kontext: die Nähe zum Stadtzentrum und die
besondere Lage auf der Grünfläche Amager
Fælled unmittelbar südlich des Zentrums.
Auch dass Kopenhagen eine Anzahl signifikan-
ter Türme hat, spielte bei der Entwicklung
des Konzepts eine Rolle.

treatment of the landscape and providing
the main structuring elements. The master
plan identified the site of the National
Archives in the southern part of this new
district and anticipated both the scale and
massing of the building complex.

The 1996 competition brief for the National
Archives clearly pointed out the cultural
importance of the project and identified the
need for the building to establish itself as
a new landmark in the city. This state-
financed project was seen as a key element
in the future development of Ørestad.

The demands of program in relation to the
actual size of the available site together with
a high ground water table and functional
requirements, such as the favored vertical
transport system, resulted in the development of a high-rise proposal. The design
responds to the importance of the contents
of the building – irreplaceable original
documents, several centuries old – whilst
also acknowledging the context: the actual
proximity to the city center and the specific
location on Amager Fælled, directly to the
south of the city center.

1

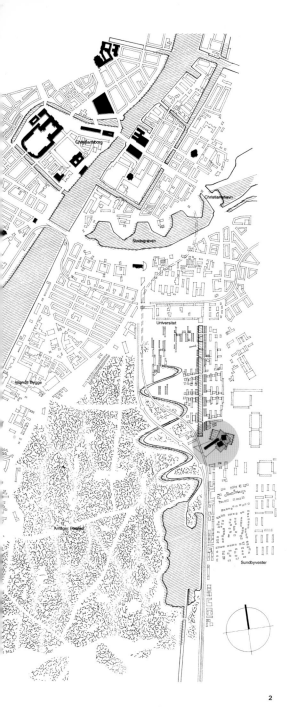

1 Fotomontage Stadtteilsilhouette 2 Umgebungsplan 3 Lageplanmodell
1 Photomontage cityscape 2 Location plan 3 Site model

NATIONAL- UND PROVINZIALARCHIVE |
NATIONAL AND PROVINCIAL ARCHIVES | 1996–2002

2

4 Modell 1:500 5 Lageplan | 4 Presentation model 1:500 5 Site plan

NATIONAL- UND PROVINZIALARCHIVE |
NATIONAL AND PROVINCIAL ARCHIVES | 1996–2002

Die Struktur des ca. 54.000 m² großen Gebäudes ist, gemäß den vier Hauptfunktionen
des Programms, klar und kompakt: Werkstätten, Sortierräume und Lagerräume sind
auf den zwei unteren Geschossen um die
Anlieferung angeordnet und bilden im Wesentlichen ein Sockelgeschoss. Die Zufahrt zu
einem überdeckten Anlieferungshof wie auch
zum Personal- und Besucherparkplatz erfolgt
über den Grønjordsvej. Foyer, Restaurant,
Bibliothek und Leseräume bilden zusammen
mit Seminar- und Konferenzräumen den
öffentlichen Bereich. Besucher betreten das
Gebäude von Südwesten über eine großzügige, ansteigende Eingangsplaza. Geometrie
und Bodenbelag des vom Hochbahn-Bahnhof

The organisation of this large building
(approx. 54,000 m²) is clear, simple and
compact, respecting the four main elements
of the program: workshops, sorting rooms
and depots are organised over the two lower
levels around the document reception, these
form what is essentially a plinth. Vehicular
access to both a covered delivery yard and
staff and visitor parking is via Grønjordsvej
to the south. Foyer, restaurant, library and
reading rooms together with seminar and
conference facilities constitute the public
areas. Visitors are to enter the building from
the south-west via a generous ramped
entrance plaza. Rising from Ørestad Boulevard past the new elevated railway station

und vom Ørestad Boulevard her ansteigenden Platzes sind formal bearbeitet. Die öffentlichen Bereiche bieten in ihrer erhöhten Lage Sichtbezüge auf die Naturlandschaft von Amager Fælled und die dahinter liegende Stadt. Die Verwaltung ist in den drei Geschossen des Büroflügels untergebracht, der weit in die Plaza greift und als liegender Kubus das vierte Element, den Archivturm, ergänzt.

Der weit überwiegende Teil des Programms umfasst den eigentlichen Archivbereich mit etwa 330.000 Lfm Regalfläche. Hier müssen stabile klimatische Bedingungen gewährleistet sein. Die Dokumente sind in den Ebenen des Hochhauskomplexes in geschlossenen Archivräumen gelagert. Sechs große, einfache Kuben unterschiedlicher Größe stapeln sich scheinbar frei bis zu einer Höhe von 75 m um einen zentralen Erschließungsturm. Entsprechend den Anforderungen stellen sie jeweils isolierte Einheiten dar, die zur Transparenz der öffentlichen Bereiche in deutlichem Kontrast stehen. Die formale Gliederung des Hochhauses schafft ein deutliches Bild und sucht den Bezug zu den übrigen Türmen der

both the geometry and surface finish of this plaza ensure that it shares the same formal characteristics as the public areas. Sitting on a plinth above the reflecting pool, the public areas are raised to a height affording views out over the natural landscape of Amager Fælled and the city beyond. The administration is housed in the three floors of the office wing, which floats out over the entrance plaza and whose rectilinear form complements that of the fourth element, the archival tower.

A vast extent of the program is pure archival storage, housing some 330,000 running meters of shelving, where stable environmental conditions are required. Situated on the upper floors of the complex the documents are stored in strongrooms, a series of six large, simple boxes of differing proportions stacked around a central circulation tower to a total height of 75 m. Performing a naturally protective role they tend to isolate themselves, providing a distinct contrast to the openness of the lower levels, and therefore playing a quite different part in the life

5

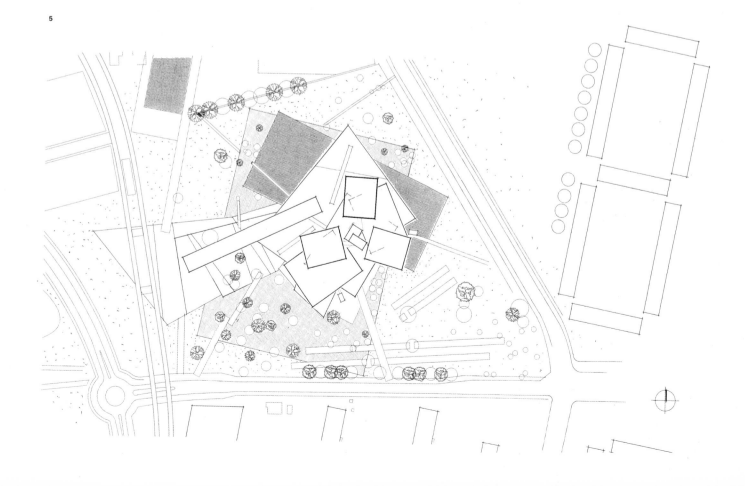

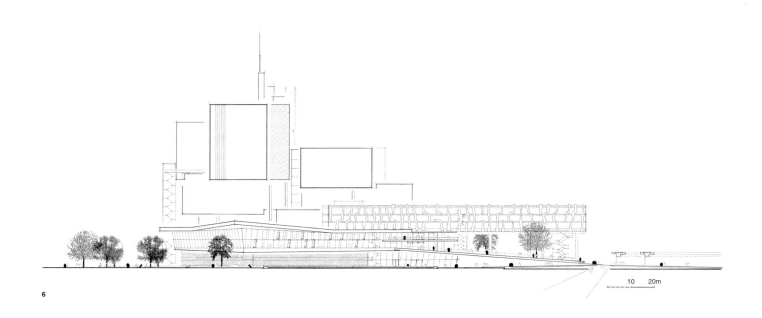

6

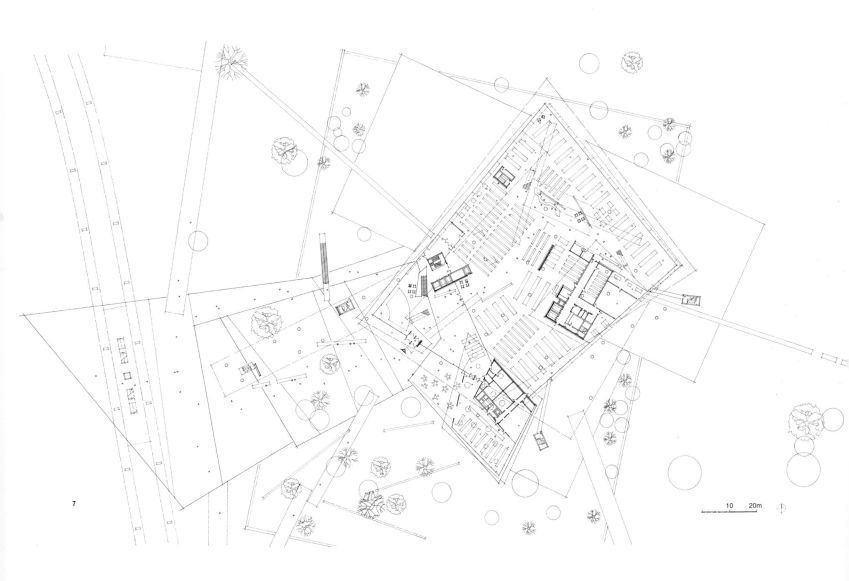

7

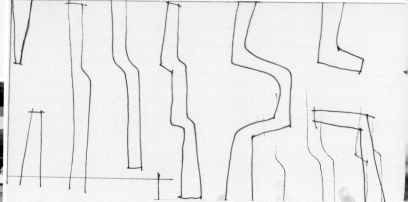

6 Ansicht Nord-Osten 7 Grundriss öffentlicher Bereich 8, 9 Eingangsplaza 10 Skizze Bürofassade
6 North-east elevation 7 Plan of public area 8, 9 Entrance plaza 10 Sketch of office facade

NATIONAL- UND PROVINZIALARCHIVE |
NATIONAL AND PROVINCIAL ARCHIVES | 1996–2002

8

9
10

Kopenhagener Skyline. Die skulpturale An-
ordnung der Archivkuben, im Wesentlichen
Monolithen, wird weiter artikuliert durch die
Wahl des Materials und seine absehbare
Wirkung bei wechselnden Lichtverhältnissen.

Die Planung eines Bauwerks dieser Art und
Größe folgt eigenen Gesetzen und unterliegt
gewissen Einschränkungen. Die Verbindung
von Bereichen so unterschiedlichen Maß-
stabes, die interne Organisation unter Berücksichtigung einer komplexen Reihe klar
definierter funktionaler Anforderungen sowie
die Tatsache, dass ein großer Teil des Bau-
volumens von der Außenwelt praktisch abge-
schottet ist, ließen ein sehr charakteristi-
sches Ensemble entstehen: ein Ensemble,
das in der geometrischen Gestaltung der

of the city. The form of the high-rise is
articulated to create a clearly recognisable
image and establish a relationship with
the other towers of the Copenhagen skyline.
The sculptural arrangement of the archive
boxes, essentially blind monoliths, is further emphasised through the choice of
materials and their anticipated play in the
quite different lighting conditions offered
by the changing seasons.

The planning of a building complex of
this size and type is subject to its own inherent rules and certain unique constraints.
The combining of areas of such different
scale, an internal organisation respecting
a complex series of clearly defined functional requirements and the fact that a

landschaftlichen Elemente seine Ergänzung findet, wo ein großes Wasserbecken und eine rechteckige Rasenfläche bewusst mit dem Charakter der bestehenden Landschaft kontrastieren. Mit der Anlage des »Rasenteppichs« bot sich darüber hinaus die Möglichkeit, ein klar definiertes Gelände zu schaffen – eine Korrektur der Grundstücksform, die sich durch laufende Anpassungen an die städtebaulichen Bedürfnisse von Ørestad ausgesprochen pittoresk entwickelte.

Die Flexibilität, die sich aus der freien Form besonders des Turms ergibt, ermöglicht auch die für die Zukunft geforderte bauliche Erweiterung; ergänzende Elemente ergeben sich aus der natürlichen Weiterentwicklung der plastischen Form. Weitere Kuben können dem Turm bei laufendem Betrieb angegliedert werden, ohne den Charakter des Gebäudes zu beeinträchtigen. Die Bauherrschaft erwartete einen Erweiterungsbedarf auf bis zu 90.000 m².

major proportion of the building volume is practically cut-off from the outside world has resulted in a rather distinct ensemble: an ensemble complemented by the geometrical designs of the surrounding landscape, where a large reflecting pool and rectilinear-shaped lawn deliberately set off the qualities of the existing landscape. The lawn also provides the possibility to create a clearly defined site, as the actual boundaries of the site, changing in relation to the developing demands of Ørestad, have resulted in a rather odd shape.

Given the flexibility afforded by the free formal nature of the designs, in particular the tower, a range of required future extensions can be accommodated as additive elements, in a natural development of the sculptural form. Boxes can be strategically added to the tower, to be literally plugged into the existing infrastructure without compromising either operations or the character of the building. The client expected extensions of up to a total of 90,000 m² in the near future.

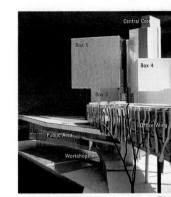

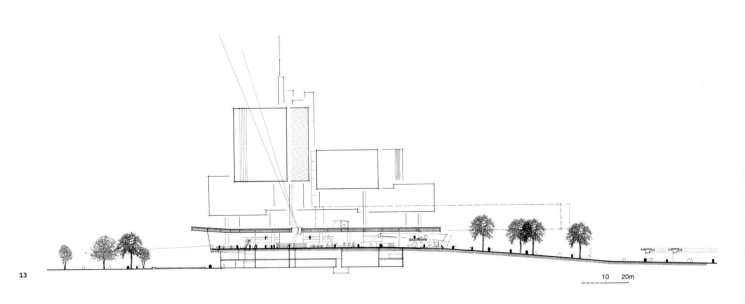

10   20m

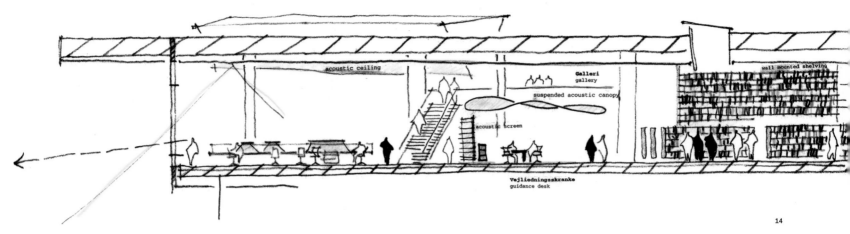

acoustic ceiling

Galleri
gallery

suspended acoustic canopy

wall mounted shelving

acoustic screen

Vejliedningsskranke
guidance desk

14

11 Arbeitsmodell 12 Modellstudien Archivtürme 13 Längsschnitt 14 Schnitt Lesesaal
11 Working model 12 Model studies, archive towers 13 Section 14 Section, reading room

Die Komponenten des Gebäudes sind von sehr unterschiedlicher Größe und von daher besteht eine gewisse Gefahr, dass die dem Anschein nach weniger attraktiven Elemente, die Archivkuben, die kleineren, doch äußerst wichtigen öffentlichen Räume dominieren könnten. Verschiedene Maßnahmen helfen hier: die Betonung der kleineren, scheinbar schwächeren Bereiche – zum Beispiel durch die Verwendung einer nachdrücklicheren, kontrastierenden, zugleich aber ergänzenden architektonischen Sprache –, ein Bezug zur bebauten Landschaft oder die formale Überhöhung. Es erschien also nur konsequent, Leseräume und Bibliothek in Bodennähe unterzubringen, in einem der Bereiche, die sich leichter öffnen – dem Besucher ebenso wie der Landschaft. Diese Lage erlaubt eine freiere Entwicklung und eine differenziertere Formgebung: die prägnante Charakterisierung durch den Landschaftsbezug und eine formale architektonische Sprache.

The various elements of the building are of very different scales, as such there is the risk that the seemingly less attractive elements, the archive boxes themselves, will dominate the smaller but highly important public spaces. This risk is countered by "promoting" the smaller, seemingly weaker elements and placing deliberate emphasis on aspects such as the use of a stronger, contrasting yet complementary architectural language, by strengthening the relationship to the landscape, or by finer detailing etc. Given these circumstances it seems logical to accommodate the reading room and library close to the ground, in one of the areas which are capable of more easily "opening up," both towards the landscape and to receive its visitors. In this location they are able to develop more freely, and to adopt an architecturally more sophisticated form, assuming a distinct character clearly associated with the natural landscape yet respecting the complex series of daily operations of the building.

ANMERKUNG Nach dem Regierungswechsel in Dänemark wurde das Projekt im Frühling 2002 überraschend beendet. Bis zu diesem Zeitpunkt hatten Behnisch, Behnisch & Partner fast fünf Jahre lang an dem Projekt gearbeitet. Die Planungsarbeit war abgeschlossen, auf dem Gelände wurden die ersten Bauvorbereitungen getroffen. Der Generalunternehmer wartete darauf, mit den Bauarbeiten beginnen zu können.

Wie sich diese Entscheidung auf Ørestad auswirken wird, ist noch unklar; die Stadt Kopenhagen jedoch hat nach eigener Aussage einen neuen Identifikationspunkt und ein bedeutendes Wahrzeichen für Ørestad verloren.

Dass angesichts der Größenordnung des Projekts kreatives und finanzielles Potential verschwendet wurde, liegt auf der Hand. Ein enormer Aufwand an Zeit und Mühe ist vertan. Ein Gewinn allerdings bleibt, denn für uns als Architekten ist jedes Projekt, unabhängig davon, ob es realisiert wurde oder nicht, eine wertvolle Erfahrung, die neue Einsichten ermöglicht und uns weiter voranbringt. ◄

NOTE In spring 2002 the project was surprisingly cancelled after a change in the Danish Government. Up until this date Behnisch, Behnisch & Partner had spent almost five years working on this project. Planning works had been completed and works had actually started on site with a general contractor ready to commence construction.

For the public, the impact this decision will have upon the development of Ørestad is not yet clear, but the city of Copenhagen has lost, according to its own estimation, a new landmark and an important cultural asset.

Given the scale of this project the waste of artistic and financial resources is obvious. A vast amount of time and effort has been unnecessarily wasted. On the other hand, all is not lost, as for us as architects, each project, whether realised or not, is indeed a valuable experience providing us with new insights and contributing towards a further development of our practice. ◄

15

15, 16 Arbeitsmodelle Lesesaal 17 Grundriss Bibliothek
15, 16 Working models, reading room 17 Plan, library

NATIONAL- UND PROVINZIALARCHIVE |
NATIONAL AND PROVINCIAL ARCHIVES | 1996–2002

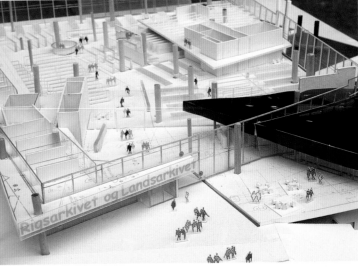

16

main foyer

seating area

info desk

reading room

sideboard

library

guidance area

coloured carpet

sideboard

Seminarraums
seminar rooms

reservation desk

Die Universität Toronto und ihr angeschlossene Institute sind weltweit führend bei der Erforschung des Zusammenhangs von Genen und Krankheit, der Schnittstelle von Genetik und Medizin. Das neue Forschungsgebäude wird die hoch spezialisierten Labors und Instrumentarien beherbergen, die es der Universität ermöglichen sollen, ihre Stärke in der biomolekularen Forschung auszubauen. Der Entwurf nimmt unmittelbaren Bezug auf das interdisziplinäre Konzept der Fakultät, das eine spezielle Arbeitsumgebung verlangt. So soll z.B. die Zusammenarbeit der etwa 400 verschiedenen Forscher gefördert werden – darunter Computerwissenschaftler, Ärzte, Pharmazeuten und Ingenieure. Sie werden in einer funktionellen, hoch flexiblen und mit den modernsten technischen Mitteln ausgerüsteten Forschungsanlage arbeiten.

The University of Toronto and its affiliated institutions are world leaders in the quest to link genes to disease. The new CCBR building will provide the sophisticated laboratories and tools to enable the university to build on its strengths in biomolecular research. The design proposal responds directly to the faculty's interdisciplinary concept, which calls for a distinct working environment encouraging interaction among some 400 diverse research specialists, including computer scientists, physicians, pharmacists and engineers, all are to be accommodated in a functional, highly flexible and technically advanced research facility.

ZENTRUM FÜR ZELL- UND BIOMOLEKULARFORSCHUNG
DER UNIVERSITÄT TORONTO (CCBR)
CENTRE FOR CELLULAR AND BIOMOLECULAR
RESEARCH (CCBR), UNIVERSITY OF TORONTO

ONTARIO, KANADA | ONTARIO, CANADA; 2001–2005

1

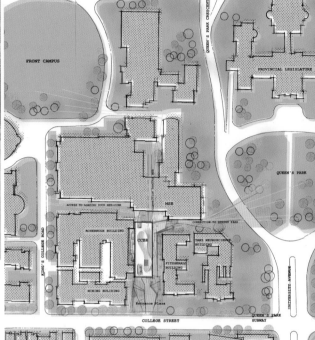

1 Präsentationsmodell Ansicht Süd 2 Haupteingang 3 Lageplan
1 Presentation model, southern facade 2 Main entrance 3 Location plan

ZENTRUM FÜR ZELL- UND BIOMOLEKULARFORSCHUNG |
CENTRE FOR CELLULAR AND BIOMOLECULAR RESEARCH | 2001–2005

Mit dem Gebäude, das einen Schwerpunkt im bestehenden, zwischen Kings College Circus und Queens Park zentral gelegenen Campus bildet, wird die Universität an einer belebten Durchgangsstraße, der College Street, neu in Erscheinung treten. Der ca. 20.000 m² große Bau ist als zwölfgeschossiger transparenter Kubus konzipiert, der sich über einem öffentlichen Bereich erhebt. In diesem sind Büros, Seminarräume und eine Fakultätscafeteria untergebracht. Er erstreckt sich von der College Street bis zum nördlich gelegenen bestehenden Gebäude der Medizinischen Fakultät und ist in der Gestaltung bewusst vom darüber schwebenden streng kubischen Baukörper abgesetzt.

Situated at the heart of the existing downtown campus, between Kings College Circus and Queens Park, the building creates a new University presence on a busy city thoroughfare, College Street. The 20,000 m² building is conceived as an eleven-story-high transparent rectangular volume, elevated above a public concourse. This concourse, housing offices, seminar facilities and a faculty cafeteria, stretches from College Street through to forge new connections to the existing Medical Sciences Building to the north, with the architectural language deliberately contrasting that of the overlying building volume.

Dieser als nuancenreiche architektonische Landschaft gestaltete öffentliche Bereich spielt eine wichtige Rolle für die bereits vorhandenen Verkehrswege und schafft Verbindungen zwischen den bestehenden Nachbargebäuden. Die Situation des Grundstücks – eine Lücke zwischen bestehenden Altbauten – wird genutzt, um für die Universität ein neues öffentliches Forum zu schaffen. Durch Überdachung des Hofes zwischen dem Rosebrugh-Gebäude und dem neuen CCBR-Gebäude entsteht ein großzügiges Atrium; zwei- und dreigeschossige Grünräume in den Obergeschossen charakterisieren das Gesamtbild und bilden zusätzlich zu den einzelnen Arbeitsbereichen spezifische Orte. Die relativ geringe Geschosstiefe ermöglicht eine gute Nutzung des Tageslichts und, soweit die Laborbedingungen es gestatten, natürliche Belüftung. Die Schichtung der Fassaden erlaubt einen effizienten Sonnen- und Blendschutz. Farbige Elemente in Höhe der Fassadenbrüstung schaffen einen individuellen Charakter.

Der Wintergarten, den die charakteristischen Elemente des neuen und der bestehenden Gebäude prägen, liegt im Zentrum des öffentlichen Erdgeschosses. Vom Tageslicht durchflutet, stellt das natürlich belüftete Atrium einen zentralen Ort dar, an dem sich Mitarbeiter, Studierende und Besucher gern aufhalten. Über die mehrgeschossig angelegten großzügigen Innengärten überträgt sich der formale Charakter des Vorbereichs bis ins Gebäudeinnere; Sitz- und Wartezonen sind willkommene Ergänzungen für die Eingangshalle und auch die angrenzenden Konferenzbereiche.

Verschiedene Treppenanlagen, die vom Westkorridor her, der die Laborgeschosse erschließt, eine direkte Verbindung zwischen den Geschossen und Abteilungen herstellen, machen den Garten aus ganz unterschiedlicher Perspektive sicht- und erlebbar.

The concourse, taking the form of a modulated landscape, plays an important role in maintaining existing public thoroughfares and establishes links between each of the neighboring existing buildings. The constraints of the site have been used to create a new public forum for the University. The court between the Rosebrugh Building and the CCBR is to be roofed over to create a large atrium space, whilst single and double-story garden spaces in the upper levels characterise the layout, providing alternative workstations to the individual workspaces. The relatively shallow floor plans enable good use of daylight and – laboratory demands permitting – allow for natural ventilation. The layering of the facades will provide shading and glare protection, colored elements at balustrade level of the facades contribute towards a distinct individual expression.

Characterised by the different attributes of the new and existing buildings, the new interior garden court lies at the heart of the concourse. Flooded with natural light, the naturally ventilated atrium will become a focus, the gardens drawing staff, students and visitors into the center of the complex. Spreading over several levels, the generous internal gardens will extend the character of the forecourt into the building, providing seating/waiting areas and enriching both the entrance lobby and the adjoining meeting spaces.

Various stairs – projecting from the western corridor serving the laboratory floors – provide direct interdepartmental connections between floor levels and allow the garden to be viewed or experienced from quite different perspectives.

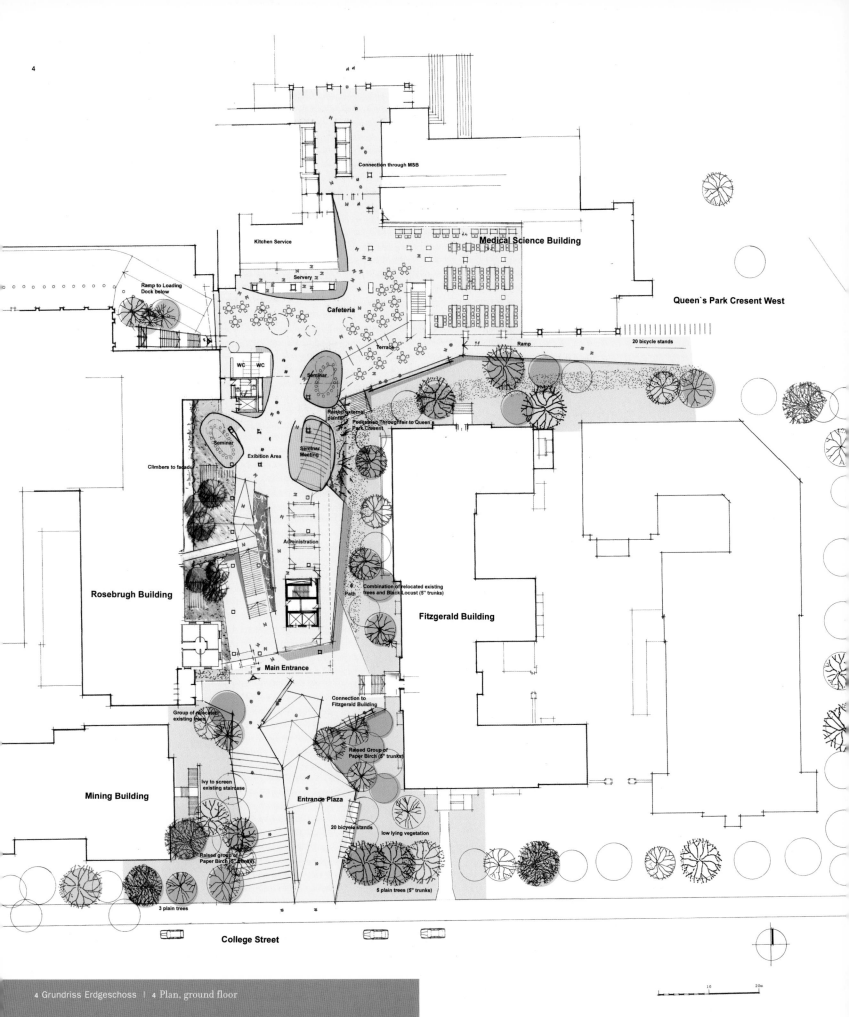

4

Connection through MSB

Kitchen Service

Servery

Cafeteria

Medical Science Building

Queen`s Park Cresent West

Ramp to Loading Dock below

Terrace

Ramp

20 bicycle stands

WC   WC

Seminar

Raised external planter

Pedestrian Throughfair to Queen's Park Cresent

Seminar

Exibition Area

Seminar Meeting

Climbers to façade

Rosebrugh Building

Administration

Path

Combination of relocated existing trees and Black Locust (5" trunks)

Fitzgerald Building

Main Entrance

Connection to Fitzgerald Building

Group of relocated existing trees

Raised Group of Paper Birch (5" trunks)

Ivy to screen existing staircase

Mining Building

Entrance Plaza

20 bicycle stands

low lying vegetation

Raised group of Paper Birch (5" trunks)

5 plain trees (5" trunks)

3 plain trees

College Street

10   20m

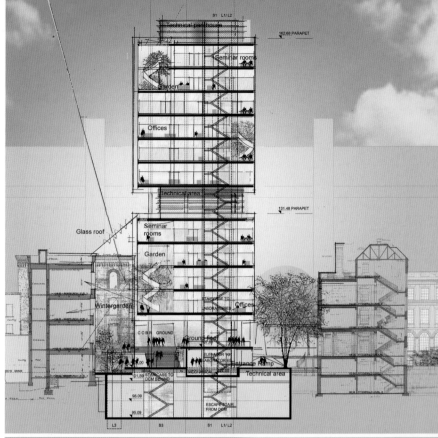

5 Schnitt West-Ost 6 Schnitt Südfassade 7 Laborgeschoss 8 Detail Garten
5 Section, west-east 6 Section, southern facade 7 Laboratory level 8 Detail of garden

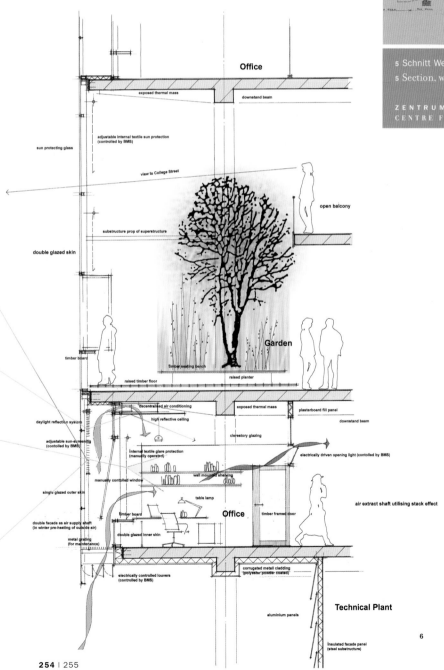

Office

exposed thermal mass

downstand beam

adjustable internal textile sun protection
(controlled by BMS)

sun protecting glass

view to College Street

open balcony

substructure prop of superstructure

double glazed skin

timber board

Garden

timber seating bench

raised planter

raised timber floor

decentralised air conditioning

exposed thermal mass

plasterboard fill panel

daylight reflection system

high reflective ceiling

downstand beam

clerestory glazing

adjustable sun-screening
(controled by BMS)

Internal textile glare protection
(manually operated)

electrically driven opening light (contolled by BMS)

wall mounted shelving

manually controlled window

table lamp

single glazed outer skin

air extract shaft utilising stack effect

double facade as air supply shaft
(in winter pre-heating of outside air)

timber board

Office

timber framed door

double glazed inner skin

metal grating
(for maintenance)

electrically controlled louvers
(controlled by BMS)

corrugated metall cladding
(polyester powder coated)

Technical Plant

aluminium panels

insulated facade panel
(steel substructure)

6

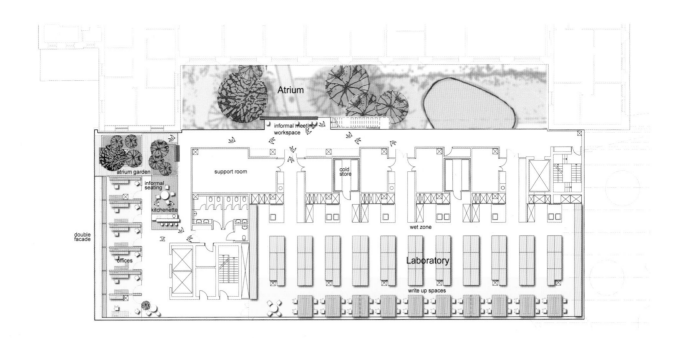

Die einzelnen Laborgeschosse sind ähnlich strukturiert, um möglichst flexibel zu sein. Sie haben alle das gleiche Grundlayout. Jedes Geschoss nimmt die Büros der sechs Forschungsleiter sowie Laborräume für 36 bis 38 weitere Wissenschaftler oder Praktikanten auf.

Ein Schlüsselelement bei der Gestaltung der Labors und angeschlossener Räume ist die mögliche Anpassung an vielfältige Nutzungen. Nasslabors sollten flexibel genug sein, um Biologen, Chemikern und Bioinformatikern als Arbeitsplatz zu dienen. Computerlabors sollten sich mit geringem Aufwand in Nasslabors verwandeln lassen. Form und Anordnung der Installationen sind so geplant, dass sie eine relativ leichte Umnutzung ermöglichen. Ein stringentes Planungsraster berücksichtigt die Gestaltung der Arbeitsplätze und ermöglicht weitere Unterteilungen. Die relativ geringe Geschosstiefe, die großflächige Verglasung sowie Art und Farbe der Materialien erlauben ein hohes Maß an Transparenz durch alle genutzten Bereiche. Bei relativ niedriger Deckenhöhe wird durch den Verzicht auf eine abgehängte Decke in Verbindung mit unverkleideter Installationstechnik und Tragkonstruktion sowie der Wahl einfacher und widerstandsfähiger Materialien dennoch eine leichte, loftartige Atmosphäre geschaffen.

The laboratory floors are repetitive to provide a maximum practical level of flexibility. Each floor supports six principal investigators, each with their own separate office and 36 to 38 trainees or research associates are accommodated in the laboratory itself.

A key element in the design of the laboratory and respective support spaces is the ability to adapt the spaces to accommodate a variety of different uses. Wet laboratory spaces should be able to change from biology to chemistry to bio-informatics. Dry laboratory spaces should be able to change to wet laboratory with the addition of fume hoods and laboratory casework. Utilities are to be provided in a form and arrangement that will allow relatively easy conversion from one use to another. Repetitive structural bays respect workbench layouts and ensure provision for future subdivision. The relatively shallow floor plate, the extent of glazing and the nature and colors of proposed materials and fittings ensures high levels of transparency throughout all occupied areas. Although the floor-to-floor heights are relatively low, the omission of suspended ceilings will contribute, together with exposed services and superstructure, the choice of simple and robust materials, to a light, airy loft-type atmosphere.

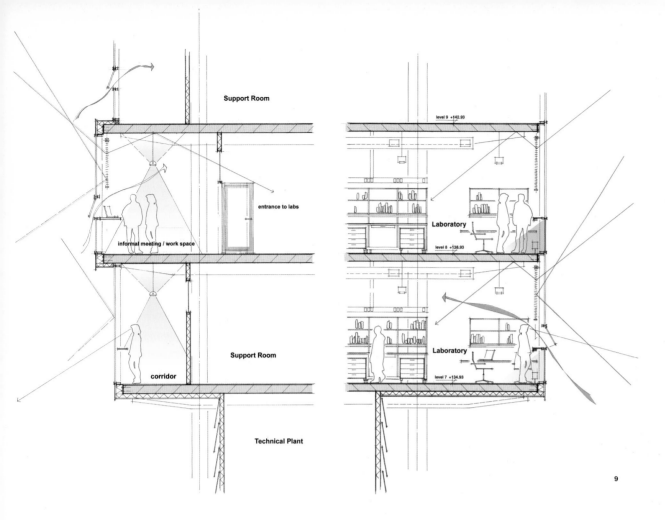

Support Room

entrance to labs

informal meeting / work space

Support Room

corridor

Technical Plant

level 9 +142.93

Laboratory

level 8 +138.93

Laboratory

level 7 +134.93

9

In den relativ hohen Büros der Forschungsleiter an der Südseite des Geschosses,
ist die Atmosphäre eine ähnliche wie in den
Labors. Die Fenster sind an allen Arbeitsplätzen manuell zu bedienen; die doppelte
Fassade schützt vor dem Wetter und gewährleistet ein gewisses Maß an Lärmschutz. Die
oberen Gärten, die angrenzend an die Büros
der Forschungsleiter direkt hinter der vollver-
glasten Südfassade liegen, spielen eine ent-
scheidende Rolle für die äußere Erscheinung
des Gebäudes. Eine Kombination von zwei-
und dreistöckigen Volumen wird als Lounges
genutzt und schafft mit Erholungsbereichen
und improvisierten Arbeitsplätzen eine Auf-
wertung des allgemeinen Arbeitsumfelds. Die
Gärten werden temperiert, be- und entwäs-
sert. Durch die Auswahl der Pflanzen erhält
jeder Garten einen individuellen Charakter.
Im Sommer spendet das Laubwerk Schatten,
während das Licht im Winter durch das zum
Teil entblätterte Buschwerk und Gehölz
tiefer in das Gebäude eindringen kann und
ein angenehmes Arbeitsumfeld schafft. ◄

At the southern end of the floor plate the
principals' offices benefit from their relatively high ceilings and share a similar
atmosphere to that of the laboratories.
Manually operable windows are provided at
each workstation, with a simple double
facade acting as a weather screen and providing a degree of acoustic protection.
Located adjacent to the principals' offices,
directly to the rear of the fully glazed south
facade, the upper gardens play a defining
role in the external appearance of the building. A combination of single/double-story
volumes, they serve as lounges enhancing
the general working environment, providing
areas for relaxation and informal workstations. The gardens will be tempered, irri-
gated and drained. The selection of plants
ensures that each garden has a distinct
character. In summer the foliage will provide shade, whilst in winter when certain
vegetation loses a proportion of its leaves
light will be allowed to penetrate deeper into
the building, increasing both warmth and
comfort levels. ◄

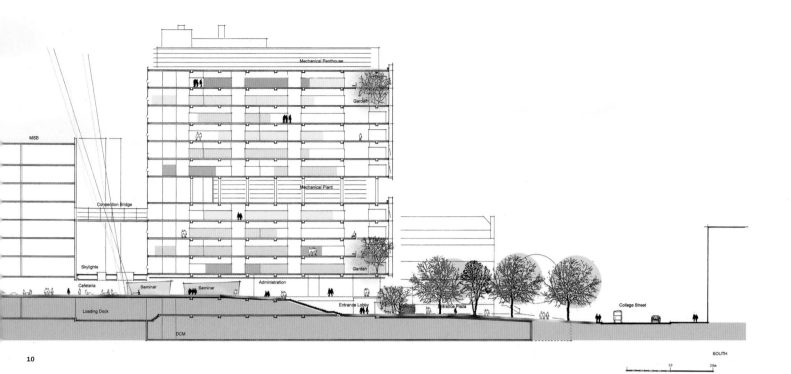

10

SOUTH

ZENTRUM FÜR ZELL- UND BIOMOLEKULARFORSCHUNG |
CENTRE FOR CELLULAR AND BIOMOLECULAR RESEARCH | 2001–2005

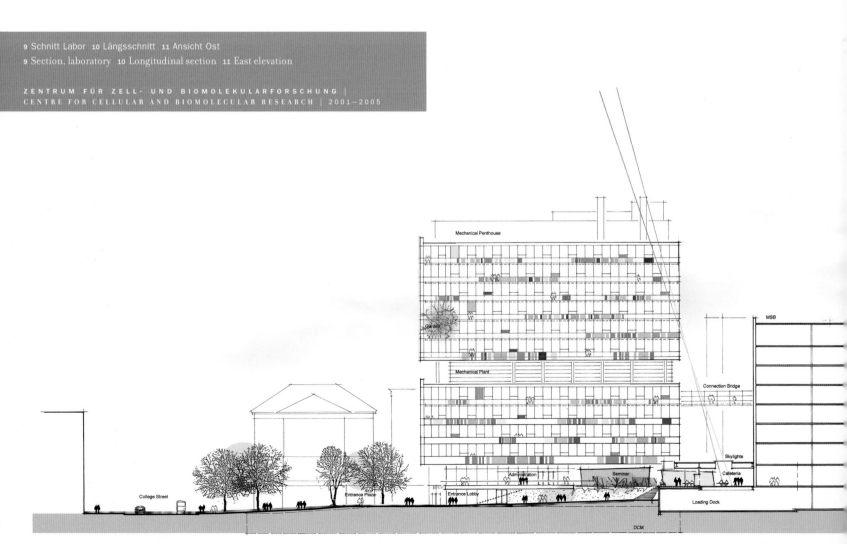

11

Das neue Technologiegebäude auf dem Campusgelände der Universität Ilmenau ist für die Grundlagen- und angewandte Forschung auf dem Gebiet der Mikroelektronik bestimmt. Ein Teil der Forschungsarbeit muss unter Reinraumbedingungen durchgeführt werden.

The new technology building on the campus of Ilmenau University is intended for basic and applied research in the field of microelectronics. A portion of the research activities must be conducted under clean room conditions.

TECHNOLOGIEGEBÄUDE DER TU ILMENAU
TECHNOLOGY BUILDING FOR THE
TECHNICAL UNIVERSITY OF ILMENAU

DEUTSCHLAND | GERMANY; 1997–2002

1 Haupteingang 2 Umgebungsplan 3 Detail Bürobereich
1 Main entrance 2 Location plan 3 Detail of office area

TECHNOLOGIEGEBÄUDE | TECHNOLOGY BUILDING | 1997–2002

Ilmenau

Großer Teich

Bahnhof

Technologiegebäude

Sportplatz

Mensa

Senatssaal

Grenzhammer

Bahn

2

3

Das Grundstück liegt am Rande des Campus der Universität Ilmenau in Thüringen. Leicht abfallend bietet die Lage einen schönen Blick über ein landschaftlich reizvolles Naturschutzgebiet mit See. Diese Lage bestimmte weitgehend die Ausrichtung des Gebäudes, die Büros und Aufenthaltsräume orientieren sich zu dieser Aussicht. Im Süden und Osten liegen weitere Labor-, Lehr- und Forschungsgebäude der Universität.

Die Anlage besteht aus zwei über eine Halle miteinander verbundenen Gebäudeteilen – dem Reinraum und dem daran angelagerten Bürobereich. In den beiden oberen Geschossen befinden sich die Büroarbeitsplätze, darunter weitere Laborräume. Der Reinraumbereich als komplexe Anlage mit Technikbereich, Arbeitsebene und Lufttechnikebene liegt hangseitig hinter dem Bürotrakt. Große »Schaufenster« in der beide Bereiche

The site lies at the edge of the campus of Ilmenau University in Thuringia. The gently sloping site enjoys views across a charming protected natural area that includes a lake. To a large degree, this locale determined the alignments of the building, since the offices and lounges are oriented toward this view. Further to the south and east lie additional laboratories, as well as the university's teaching and research buildings.

The complex consists of two parts, the clean room and the adjacent office areas, connected via a hallway. In both upper stories are the office work areas, and beneath additional laboratories. The clean room area, as a complex facility with technical area, work level and ventilation equipment, addresses the slope of the landscape lying behind the office tract. Large "picture windows" in the dividing walls separating the

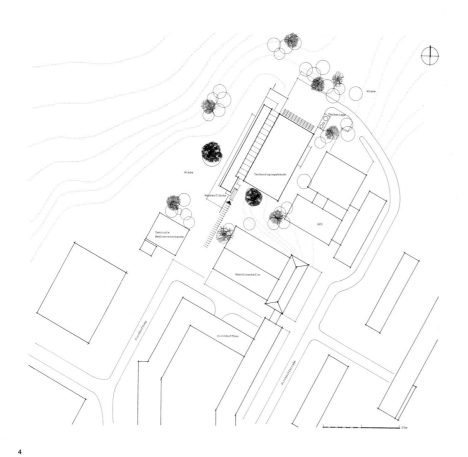

4

6

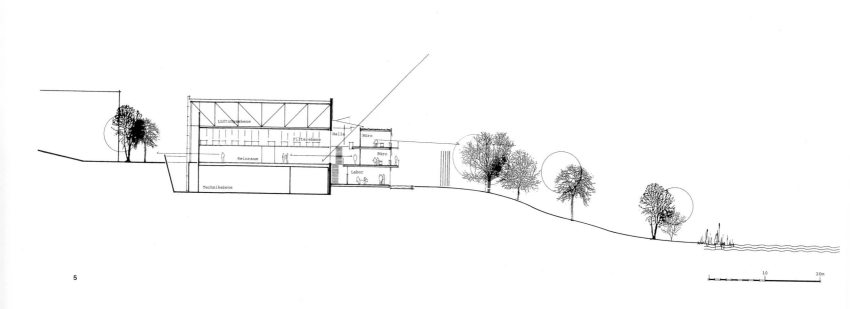

5

4 Lageplan 5 Schnitt 6 Blick von Süden 7 Ansicht West
4 Site plan 5 Section 6 View from the south 7 West elevation

TECHNOLOGIEGEBÄUDE | TECHNOLOGY BUILDING | 1997–2002

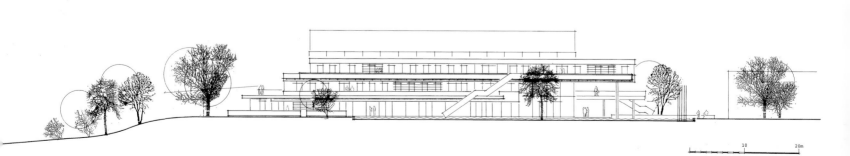

10   20m

trennenden Wand schaffen eine optische Beziehung zwischen Reinraum und Büro. Die
mehrgeschossige, verglaste Halle mit ihren
offenen Galerien, Treppenverbindungen und
Einblicken in den Reinraum ist das kommunikative Herz der gesamten Anlage. Die Halle
selbst ist von ihrer Stimmung und ihrem Licht
her eher ein geschützter Teil des Außenbe-
reiches: hell, offen, von Tageslicht durchflutet,
im Gegensatz stehend zu der introvertierteren,
sterilen Welt der Laborräume. Der Arbeitsbe-
reich wird auf drei Seiten von dem so genannten Besucherkorridor eingefasst, von dem aus
Besucher Einblick in den Reinraumbereich
und die Labors erhalten. ◄

two zones create visual links between the
clean room and the offices. The multi-story
glazed hall with its open galleries, connections via stairs, and views into the clean
room is the communicative heart of the
entire complex. The hall itself, in terms
of mood and lighting, is a somewhat sheltered part of the outside world: bright, open,
flooded with daylight, in contrast to the
introverted, sterile world of the laboratories. The work area is surrounded on three
sides by the so-called visitor's corridor,
which offers views into the clean room and
the laboratories. ◄

8 Blick von Nord-Osten, Reinraumbereich 9 Halle mit Schaufenster in die Reinräume
10 Grundriss 1. Obergeschoss | 8 View from the north-east, clean room area
9 Hall with window into the clean room 10 Plan, 2nd floor

TECHNOLOGIEGEBÄUDE | TECHNOLOGY BUILDING | 1997–2002

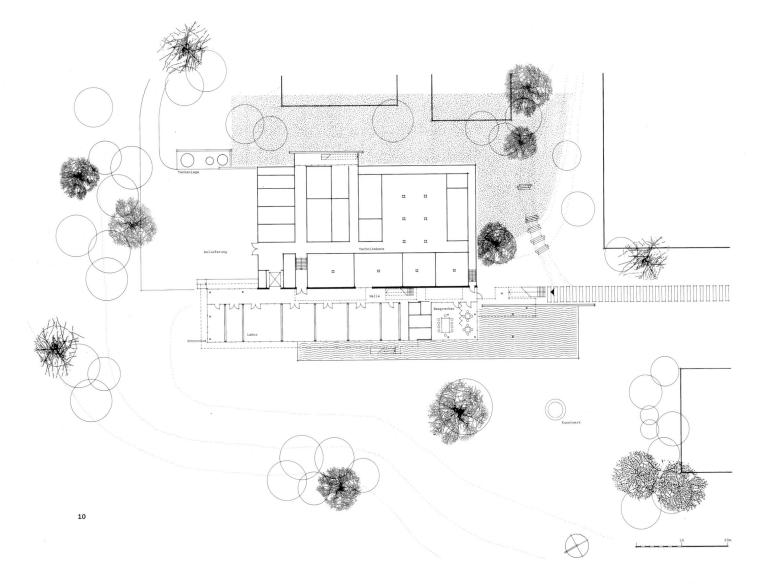

Reichstagsufer

Biotop

Terrasse

Terrasse

Fahne

Alters

1

1 Schnitt 2 Wettbewerbsabgabemodell 3 Grundriss Gartengeschoss
1 Section 2 Competition submission model 3 Plan, garden level

KINDERTAGESSTÄTTE DES DEUTSCHEN BUNDESTAGES |
CHILDREN'S DAY CARE CENTER, GERMAN PARLIAMENT | 1997

2

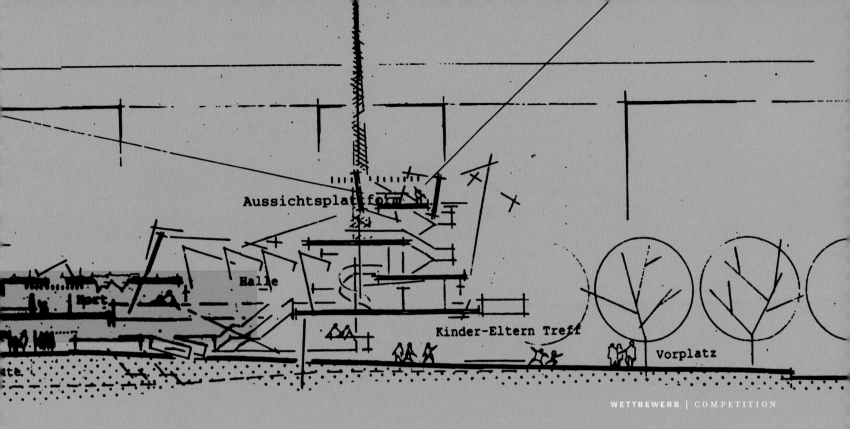

Aussichtsplattform

Halle

Kinder-Eltern Treff

Vorplatz

KINDERTAGESSTÄTTE DES DEUTSCHEN BUNDESTAGES
CHILDREN'S DAY CARE CENTER, GERMAN PARLIAMENT

BERLIN, DEUTSCHLAND | BERLIN, GERMANY; 1997

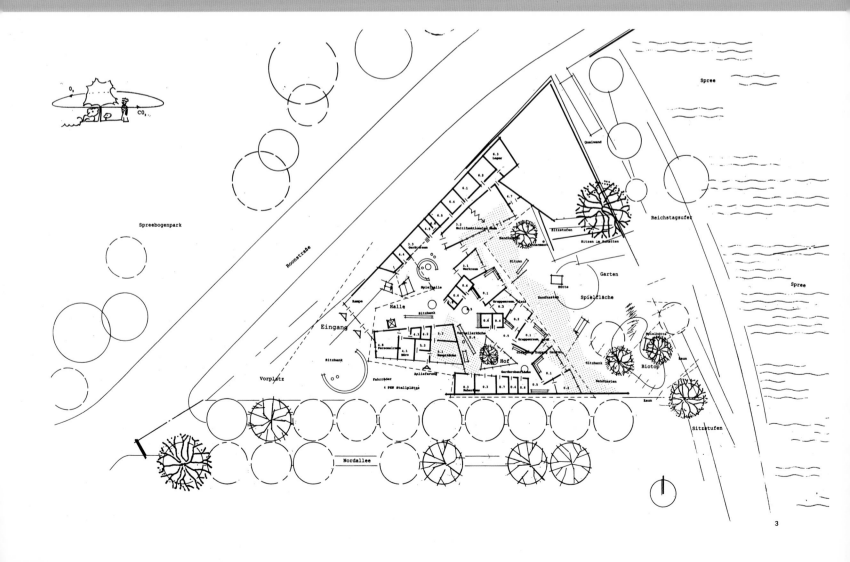

Am Rande von Leipzig war in den frühen 80er Jahren eine Satellitenstadt entstanden. Dieser Stadtteil, Leipzig-Grünau, schaffte Wohn- und Lebensraum für ca. 80.000 Menschen. Konsequent sind hier die Aspekte des Städtebaus umgesetzt worden, ein orthogonales Raster, die Serienproduktion von Wohnraum, ein hoher Grad an industrieller Fertigung sind die gestaltbestimmenden Elemente.

In the early 1980s, a satellite city arose at the edge of Leipzig. This part of the city, Leipzig-Grünau, provided residential and living space for approx. 80,000 people. In urban planning terms, the area was executed with consistency, orthogonal grid patterns, serial production of living spaces, and a high degree of industrially manufactured elements determined the design.

SCHWIMMHALLE │ SWIMMING POOL COMPLEX

LEIPZIG, DEUTSCHLAND │ LEIPZIG, GERMANY; 1996–1999

1 Haupteingang 2 Umgebungsplan, Strukturplan
1 Main entrance 2 Location, structural plan

SCHWIMMHALLE | SWIMMING POOL COMPLEX | 1996–1999

Nach der Wende sollte im Zentrum dieser Anlage ein öffentliches Stadtteilbad als erste größere Investition nach dem neuen Shopping Center geplant werden. Wir meinten, es sollte eine Anlage entstehen, die sich von der strengen Ordnung der Umgebung löst. Ein Park wurde angelegt, in dessen Landschaft sich das Gebaute einfügen sollte.

After German reunification, a public district swimming hall was planned for the center of the complex, the first large-scale investment since the construction of a new shopping center. We believed that the planned facility should disengage itself from the severe order of its surroundings. A park was laid out, within which the new building was inserted.

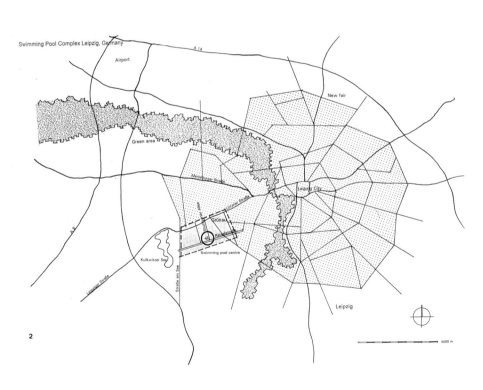

Swimming Pool Complex Leipzig, Germany

2

3

4

Das Schwimmbad liegt mit seinen öffentlichen Bereichen, dem Eingang und dem Restaurant, an der Fußgängerzone und bildet so eine städtische Adresse an diesem Ort. Es entstand ein kleiner Vorplatz, an dem zurückversetzt die Eingangshalle und leicht erhöht das Restaurant liegen. Von hier sieht man durch das Gebäude hindurch bis in den Park. Die freie Form des Gebäudes ist prägnant und schafft städtebauliche Akzente. Ziel war es, die Schwimmbecken frei in eine Parklandschaft zu legen und diese nur klimatisch zu schützen. Einige Bereiche wurden erhöht (Restaurant, Sauna), so entstand auch innerhalb des Gebäudes eine Topografie, die interessante Blickbeziehungen schafft.

The swimming hall, with its public amenities, the entrance and the restaurant, lies along the main pedestrian route, and hence constitutes an urban locale. There is a small forecourt where the entrance hall and restaurant are located, the former slightly set back, the latter elevated. From this point, there are views through the building into the park beyond. The structure's free form is highly suggestive, and provides an urban-planning accent. The goal was to set the swimming pools freely within the park landscape, sheltered only from the elements, to offer an impression of openness and transparency. Several areas were elevated (restaurant, sauna), hence, the building contains a scenic topography, one offering a diverse range of ever changing perspectives.

3, 4 Modellaufsicht 5 Lageplan 6 Detail Eingang Cafeteria
3, 4 Model from above 5 Site plan 6 Detail cafeteria entrance

SCHWIMMHALLE | SWIMMING POOL COMPLEX | 1996–1999

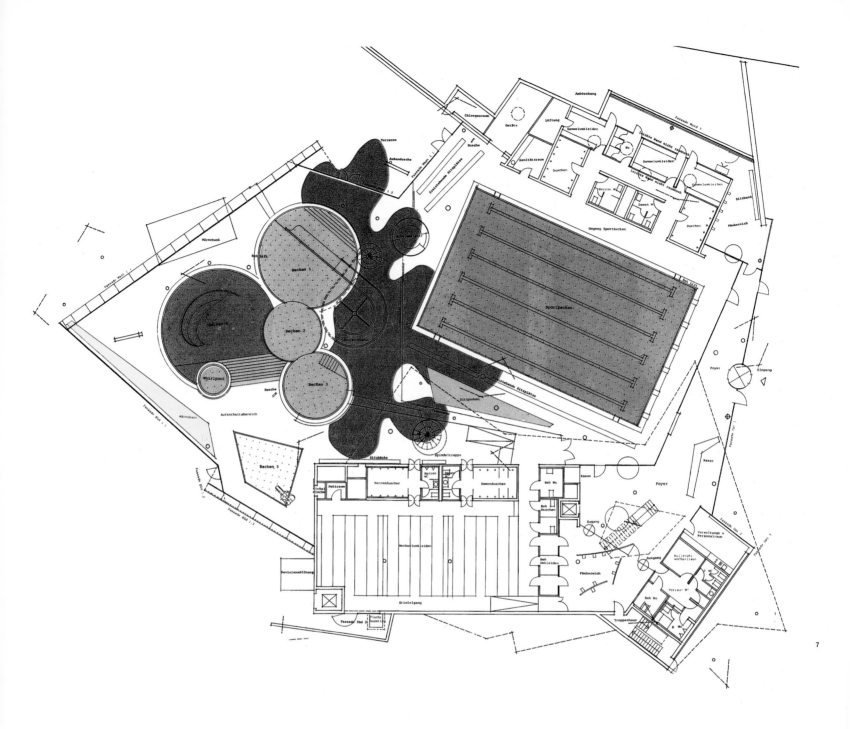

Die relativ offene Anlage wurde hinsichtlich materieller Aspekte sparsam angelegt. In warmen Farben beschichteter Sichtbeton bestimmt das Bild und verleiht dem Objekt eine besondere Stimmung. Die beiden Schwimmbereiche, die funktional getrennt werden können, unterscheiden sich ebenso formal. Das Sportbecken ist seinem Zweck und den Anforderungen entsprechend orthogonal ausgeformt. Die Freizeitbecken entwickeln sich eher verspielt und frei. Diese orientieren sich zum Park und den möglichen Liegewiesen.

With regard to material aspects, the relatively open layout was executed frugally. Exposed concrete washed in warm colors determines the look and lends the facility a special mood. Both swimming areas, which can be functionally separated, are distinguished from one another in formal terms. The competition pool, in conformity with its purpose and requirements, assumes an orthogonal form. The leisure pools are instead free and playful in form. They are oriented toward the park and the potential sunbathing lawns.

7 Grundriss Erdgeschoss 8 Sportbecken
7 Plan, ground floor 8 Sports pool

SCHWIMMHALLE | SWIMMING POOL COMPLEX | 1996–1999

9 Blick von Nord-Westen 10 Ansicht Haupteingang 11 Beckenrand
9 View from north-west 10 Elevation, main entrance 11 Around the basin

SCHWIMMHALLE | SWIMMING POOL COMPLEX | 1996–1999

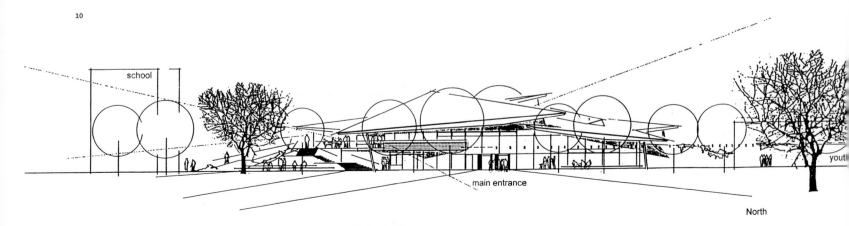

10

school

main entrance

North

Stuttgarter Allee

11

Das Tragwerk für die Halle ist eine Stahl-
betonkonstruktion. Die Funktionsbereiche
sind in Ortbeton und Mauerwerk, die Fassaden bestehen in thermisch getrennten Pfos-
ten-Riegel-Konstruktionen. Auf Aluminium
wurde aus ökologischen Gründen verzichtet.
Generell wurde bei der Wahl der Materialien
auf deren baubiologische und ökologische
Verträglichkeit geachtet.

Das Schwimmbad liegt in einer topografisch
bearbeiteten Grünanlage. Für die Erhebungen
wurde der Aushub der Schwimmhalle verwendet. Es entstanden leichte Hügel, die von den
Besuchern der Sportanlagen als Liegewiesen
genutzt werden können. ◄

The hall is a reinforced concrete construction. The functional areas are of in-situ
concrete and brickwork, the facades consist
of thermally insulated transom-mullion
structures. Aluminum was ruled out on ecological grounds. In general, materials were
selected with attention to their biological
and ecological tolerability.

The swimming hall lies within a topographi-
cally treated landscape. For the elevations,
excavated earth from the swimming pool
was used. The result was a landscape of gently rolling hills, which can be used by visitors to the sports facilities as sunbathing
lawns. ◄

Expressive Elemente   EXKURS 5

Expressive Elements   DIGRESSION 5

1

In unseren Büros gab es seit jeher Strömungen, Entwicklungen und Tendenzen, die immer wieder eigenständige, vom Gängigen scheinbar unabhängige Lösungen hervorgebracht haben. Solche eigenwilligen Entwicklungen verlaufen über Jahre hinweg. Sie treten manchmal deutlich in Erscheinung, hin und wieder ganz konkret am Wettbewerb oder Projekt getestet und verfeinert, oft jedoch nur in Skizzen und Arbeitsmodellen, nahezu unbewusst, scheinbar zufällig und schnell wieder zur Seite gelegt.

Vieles bleibt im Theoretisch-Konzeptionellen, wird wieder von uns verworfen oder kann nicht in reale Architektur umgesetzt werden. Alle an einem Projekt Beteiligten spielen hier eine Rolle – Berater, Fachplaner, Behörden etc.

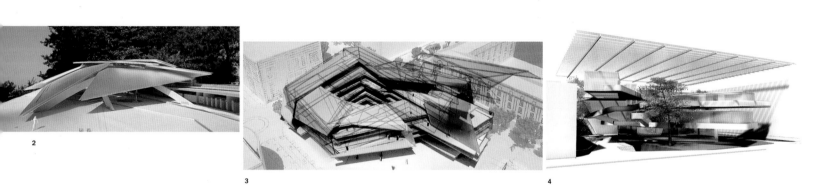

2

3   4

For some time now, trends, developments and tendencies have made their presence known in our offices, trends which have continually produced autonomous solutions, independently of convention. Such self-willed developments have been dispersed throughout the years. Sometimes they emerge clearly into view, at times tested or refined in highly concrete form via work on competitions or projects, but often surfacing only in sketches and working models, almost unconsciously, arising seemingly by chance, only to be quickly laid aside once again.

Much remains at the theoretical-conceptual level, only to be discarded by us, or is simply not amenable to architectural realisation. All individuals involved in a given project play a role in this context: consultants,

und nicht zuletzt die Bauherrn. Erwartungen und Hoffnungen gehören dazu, aber auch Sorgen und Ängste.

Jedoch oft, plötzlich und unerwartet, tauchen manche Gedanken wieder auf, kommen an anderer Stelle zum Vorschein, oft Jahre später, werden weiter entwickelt und verfeinert. So liegen die Wurzeln von Projekten, die wir heute realisieren können, zum Beispiel die der Nord/LB in Hannover, auch in der Vergangenheit, in diesem Fall in der Arbeit am Hochhaus der Landesgirokasse in Stuttgart (1989) und dem Harbourside Centre in Bristol (1996), die beide nicht gebaut wurden.

Für uns sind solche Strömungen im Büro spannend, oft auch erstaunlich, da eine klare Kontinuität nicht immer erkennbar scheint. Diese Strömungen können praktische oder ideologische Themen – wie zum Beispiel die Nachhaltigkeit von Gebäuden – beinhalten. Es kann jedoch

auch um eine architektonisch-formale Formensprache, bis hin zu dekonstruktivistischen oder fraktalen Elementen gehen. Auch das architektonisch sich frei, nach anderen als den bekannten Gesetzmäßigkeiten entwickelnde Hochhaus war ein solches oft wiederkehrendes Thema.

Seit den frühen 80er Jahren gab es im Büro Behnisch & Partner Entwicklungen, die, von der Kritik oft weniger beachtet, zu Projekten führten, die von Dritten später unter dem architektonischen Begriff des Dekonstruktivismus oder der fraktalen Architektur diskutiert wurden. Wir selber diskutieren selten unsere Architektur in Relation zu solchen Begriffen. Zum einen meinen wir, dass dies eher eine Aufgabe der Kritik sei, zum anderen fühlen wir uns natürlich weniger an Zeitströmungen gebunden. Auch sollten sich unsere Architekten nicht verpflichtet oder versucht fühlen, den Erwartungen der Kritiker zu entsprechen.

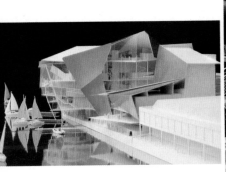

5

6

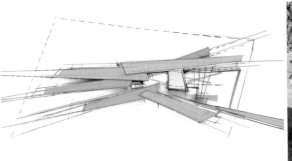

7

8

technical specialists, government agencies, etc. and not least the client. Expectations and hopes belong here, but also anxieties and fears.

Still, certain trains of thought often reappear, suddenly and unexpectedly, manifesting themselves in new contexts, occasionally years later, only to be developed further and refined. Thus the roots of projects we are able to realise today, for example those of the North German State Clearing Bank in Hanover, are to be found in part in earlier episodes, in this particular case in the context of planning a high-rise for the State Clearing Bank in Stuttgart (1989), or the Harbourside Centre in Bristol (1996), neither of them actually executed.

For us, the presence of such trends in the office is exciting, occasionally even astonishing, for often no obvious continuity between them is evident. These trends may harbor practical or ideological

themes – for example, the sustainability of buildings. They may also concern formal architectonic idioms, extending all the way to deconstructive or fractal elements. A frequently recurring topic has been the idea of a high-rise that develops freely in architectonic terms, according to standards that diverge from the familiar.

Since the early 1980s, developments present in the office of Behnisch & Partner – often little noticed by critics – have resulted in projects that others have later discussed in architectonic terms such as Deconstructivism or Fractal Architecture. We ourselves have seldom discussed our architecture in such terms. Firstly, we believe that such a task is better left to critics, and secondly, we find ourselves less bound to such momentary tendencies. In any event, our architecture is under no obligation, and we are under no temptation to conform to the expectations of critics.

Auch das Bauen mit industriell vorgefertigten Elementen hat das Büro Behnisch einige Zeit beschäftigt. Dieses Thema wird sicherlich in den kommenden Jahren noch näher untersucht werden, wenn auch auf anderem Niveau als in den 70er Jahren, als vor allem die Produktion im Vordergrund stand. Heute haben wir weit mehr Handlungsspielraum in der Architektur und sind überzeugt, dass wir jetzt vorgefertigte Teile und Systeme auf weit höherem Niveau einsetzen können.

Aus den Erfahrungen der realisierten, allzu systematisierten Bauten der 60er und 70er Jahre heraus entwickelte sich in unseren Büros die Vorstellung, dass man sich abkehren sollte von diesen stark durch die Bauwirtschaft geprägten produktionsbedingten Ordnungen in der Architektur. Etwas Neues musste gefunden werden, das diesen, durch das Technisch-Rationale geprägten Theorien, in denen sich die Form zuletzt ausschließlich den Bedingungen der Massenproduktion unter-

ordnete, etwas ebenso Starkes, jedoch Freieres entgegensetzen sollte. Das Individuelle und Vielfältige sollte unsere Arbeit bestimmen, dem facettenreichen Konzert der architektonischen Aufgaben entsprechend. Eine architektonische Sprache entwickelte sich, die dem Einzelnen als Teil des Ganzen eine eigene Identität und das Recht auf eine eigenständige Entfaltung zuspricht. ◄

1 Opernhaus, Oslo, Norwegen 2 Schönrainbad, Reutlingen, Deutschland 3 Parzelle 2, Lanyon Place, Belfast, Irland 4 San José State University Museum, San José, USA 5 Harbourside Centre, Bristol, Großbritannien 6 Hauptverwaltungsgebäude der Landesversicherungsanstalt Schleswig-Holstein, Lübeck, Deutschland 7 Gymnasium, Erding, Deutschland 8 Kindertagesstätte des Deutschen Bundestages, Berlin, Deutschland 9 Schönrainbad, Reutlingen, Deutschland 10 Schwimmhalle, Leipzig, Deutschland 11 Regionales Ausbildungszentrum, Leiden, Niederlande 12 Parzelle 2, Lanyon Place, Belfast, Irland

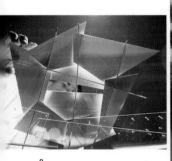

9

10

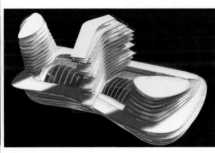

11

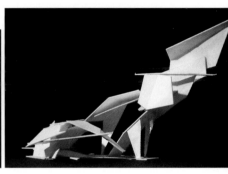

12

Construction with industrially prefabricated elements has been a preoccupation of the Behnisch firm for some time. This question will doubtlessly be investigated more closely in coming years, if on a different level than that of the 1970s, when production stood very much in the foreground. Today, we have considerably more room to maneuver in architecture, and we are convinced that we can introduce prefabricated elements and systems on a far higher level than previously.

In our offices, experiences with the excessively systematised buildings of the 1960s and 1970s strengthened our conviction that it was time to abandon such strongly production-conditioned principles of architectural order, so conditioned by the contracting industry. Something new had to be found to oppose theories so heavily oriented to technical rationality, which subordinated form exclusively to the dictates of mass-production – something equally powerful, if far

freer. We wanted our work to be characterised by the individual and the multifarious, albeit in keeping with the multi-faceted concept of a given architectonic task. An architectural language evolved which grants the particular – as an aspect of the whole – its own identity, and the right to an autonomous elaboration. ◄

1 Opera House, Oslo, Norway 2 Public swimming pool complex, Reutlingen, Germany 3 Site 2, Lanyon Place, Belfast, Ireland 4 San José State University Museum, San José, USA 5 Harbourside Centre, Bristol, UK 6 Administration building for the State Insurance Agency, Schleswig-Holstein, Lübeck, Germany 7 Grammar School, Erding, Germany 8 Children's day care center, German Parliament, Berlin, Germany 9 Public swimming pool complex, Reutlingen, Germany 10 Swimming pool complex, Leipzig, Germany 11 ROC Leiden – Regional Education Center, Leiden, Netherlands 12 Site 2, Lanyon Place, Belfast, Ireland

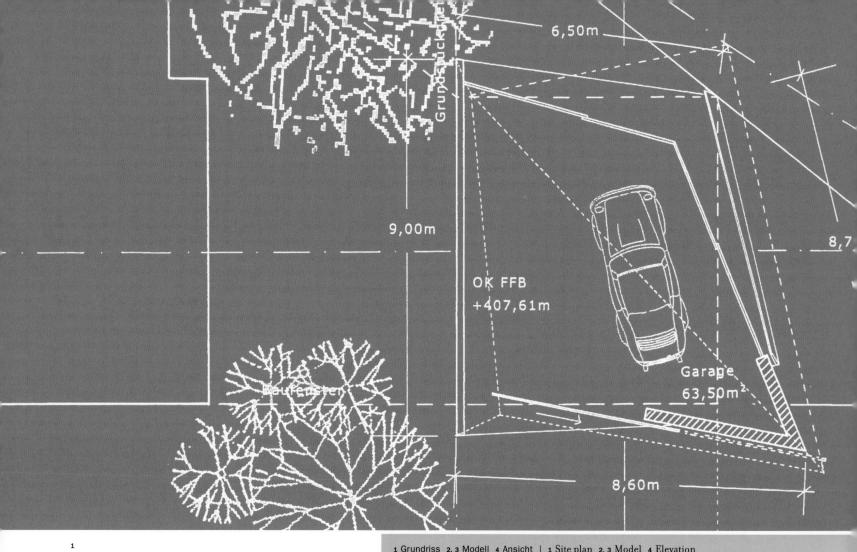

1

GARAGE SEITH | SEITH GARAGE | 2002

2

3

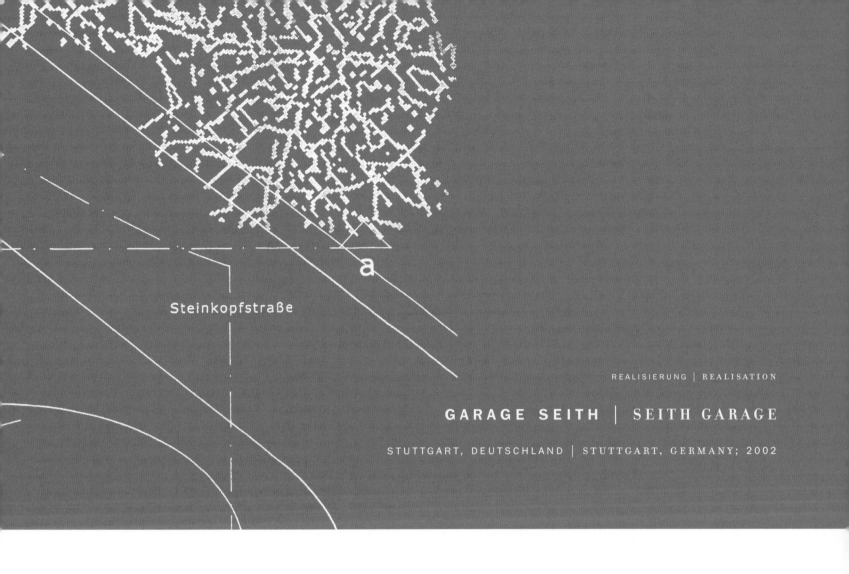

GARAGE SEITH | SEITH GARAGE

STUTTGART, DEUTSCHLAND | STUTTGART, GERMANY; 2002

Steinkopfstraße

a

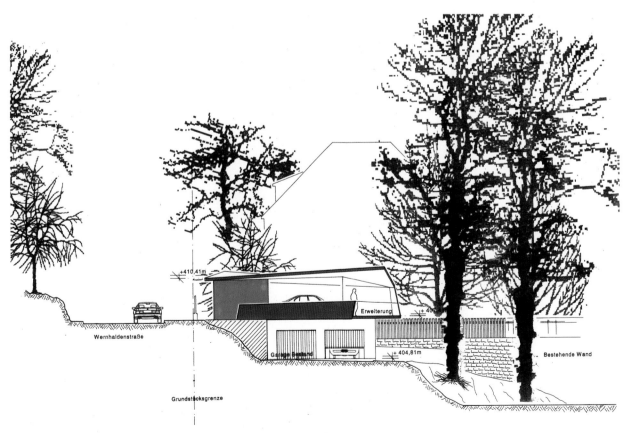

4

Die LVA wünschte sich mit ihrem neuen
Haus einen Ort, in dem ihre Beschäftigten
»Zuhause« sein und in dem auch Besucher
und Kunden der LVA sich wohlfühlen könnten. Darüber hinaus sollte das neue Haus
auch ökologische Aspekte des Bauens
berücksichtigen und schließlich die LVA
repräsentieren.

With its new building, the LVA wanted a
location where employees could feel "at
home," and where visitors and LVA clien-
tele would be at ease. Beyond that, the new
house was to be attentive to ecological
aspects of construction, and finally to publicly represent the LVA.

WETTBEWERB UND REALISIERUNG | COMPETITION AND REALISATION

HAUPTVERWALTUNGSGEBÄUDE DER

LANDESVERSICHERUNGSANSTALT SCHLESWIG-HOLSTEIN
(LVA 2000)
ADMINISTRATION BUILDING FOR THE

STATE INSURANCE AGENCY SCHLESWIG-HOLSTEIN
(LVA 2000)

LÜBECK, DEUTSCHLAND | LÜBECK, GERMANY: 1992–1997

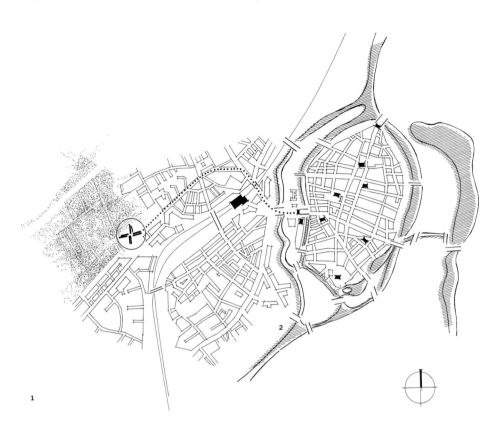

1

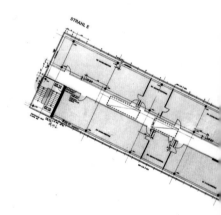

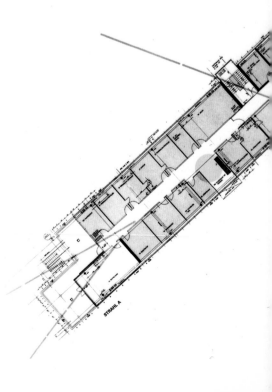

Wenn die LVA nach über 100 Jahren einen neuen Standort außerhalb der Kernstadt Lübecks wählt, der durch eine heterogene Umgebung – Kleingärten, Siedlungshäuser, Hallenbad – geprägt ist, dann gilt es, den Nutzern dort Qualitäten zu bieten, die zwar nicht die gleichen, wohl aber möglichst gleichwertig denen des alten Standorts sein sollten.

Im Neubau sind alle Mitarbeiter in einem Gebäude vereint. Die Anlage ist wesentlich weitläufiger als die ehemaligen Einzelgebäude der LVA. Diese strukturellen Veränderungen stellten eine besondere Herausforderung dar: Das Gebäude sollte, trotz der Größe, für den Einzelnen erfassbar bleiben.

After 100 years, the LVA chose a new location outside Lübeck's city center, one characterised by its heterogeneous surroundings – small gardens, residential blocks, an indoor swimming pool. The intention was to offer qualities which, albeit dissimilar, were maximally equivalent to those enjoyed by the former address.

In the new building, all employees are assembled in a single place. The complex is far more spacious than its predecessor which consisted of several single buildings. This structural change presents a special challenge, as the building is expected, despite its size, to be perceptibly graspable for individual users.

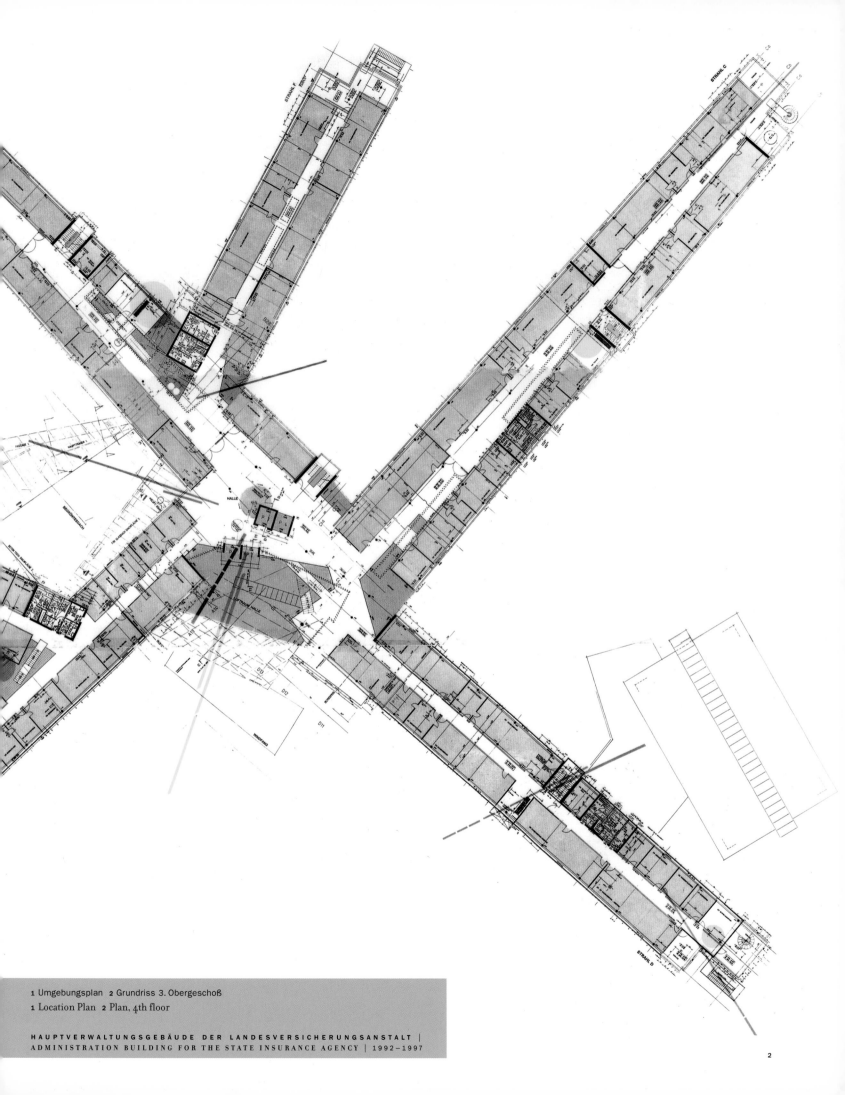

1 Umgebungsplan 2 Grundriss 3. Obergeschoß
1 Location Plan 2 Plan, 4th floor

HAUPTVERWALTUNGSGEBÄUDE DER LANDESVERSICHERUNGSANSTALT |
ADMINISTRATION BUILDING FOR THE STATE INSURANCE AGENCY | 1992–1997

2

3

3 Blick von Westen **4** Blick von Süden, Hauptzugang
3 View from west **4** View from the south, main approach

HAUPTVERWALTUNGSGEBÄUDE DER LANDESVERSICHERUNGSANSTALT |
ADMINISTRATION BUILDING FOR THE STATE INSURANCE AGENCY | 1992–1997

Alle Arbeitsplätze sind natürlich belichtet und belüftet, sie orientieren sich zur umgebenden Landschaft und den grünen Gartenhöfen. Die präzise formulierten organisatorischen Wünsche des Bauherrn konnten mit der sternförmig aus der Halle ausstrahlenden Figur konsequent umgesetzt werden. Die Einbindung des Neubaus über die Außenanlagen in einen größeren Zusammenhang konnte dazu beitragen, das Problem der Größe zu mildern. An den Grundstücksgrenzen zeigen sich die Büroflügel maßvoll mit dreigeschossigen Giebelseiten.

All work places are naturally lit and ventilated, and all are oriented toward the surrounding landscape and toward the green of the garden courts. The client's precisely formulated organisational desires could be successfully realised in terms of a star-shaped figure that radiates from the central entrance hall. The tying of the new building into the larger context of the overall site can contribute to alleviating size problems. At the boundaries of the site, the office wings — with their three-story gabled ends — make an impression of moderation.

5 Eingangshalle 6 Einweihungsfest in der Halle 7 Ansicht mit Schnitt durch Eingangshalle
5 Entrance hall 6 Inaugural ceremony in the hall 7 South elevation with section through
entrance hall

HAUPTVERWALTUNGSGEBÄUDE DER LANDESVERSICHERUNGSANSTALT |
ADMINISTRATION BUILDING FOR THE STATE INSURANCE AGENCY | 1992–1997

Das Zentrum des Neubaus der Hauptverwaltung LVA ist die große, schräg verglaste Eingangshalle. In der Halle herrscht immer ein angenehmes Klima, das mit natürlicher Lüftung, unterstützt durch minimierte Technik, erreicht wird. Über den im Grundwasser liegenden betonierten Erdkanal strömt im Sommer Außenluft aus den Grünflächen in die Halle. Sie kühlt sich im Erdreich um mehrere Grad ab und ist damit ein wesentlicher Faktor für die Temperierung der Halle im Sommer. Der Solarkamin unterstützt diese natürliche Luftströmung. Auch die Büroflügel werden so weit wie möglich mit natürlichen Mitteln klimatisiert.

The center of the new building for the headquarters of the LVA is its large, slanting glazed entrance hall. Here, a pleasant climate prevails, one attained via natural ventilation, with support from minimal technology. In summertime, fresh air flows from green areas into the hall, passing through a concrete earth channel lying in the groundwater. This air is cooled by several degrees in the earth, and is hence an essential factor for cooling the hall in summer. The solar chimney supports this natural airflow utilizing principles of stack effect. The office wings too are climatised, as far as possible, by natural means.

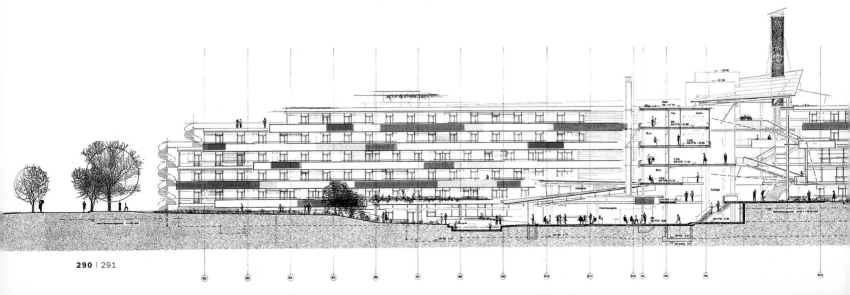

6

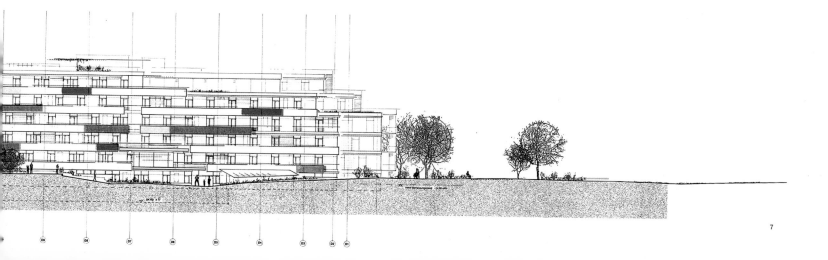

8 Teeküchen 9 Büroarbeitsplätze 10, 12 Flurbereiche 11 Dachterrasse
8 Kitchenettes 9 Offices 10, 12 Circulation areas 11 Roof terrace

HAUPTVERWALTUNGSGEBÄUDE DER LANDESVERSICHERUNGSANSTALT |
ADMINISTRATION BUILDING FOR THE STATE INSURANCE AGENCY | 1992–1997

Die Nachtauskühlung ist, bezogen auf die im Neubau konsequent aktivierten Speichermassen und den Verzicht auf abgehängte Decken, eine Möglichkeit zur Verschiebung von hohen Temperaturen am Tage in die späteren Nachmittagsstunden. Voraussetzung für ein solches Konzept ist jedoch, dass die Nutzer des Gebäudes bereit sind, diese Technik zu verstehen und aktiv zu nutzen.

Cooling by night – based on effective activation of the new building's storage mass and the consequent avoidance of suspended ceilings – makes it possible to displace higher daytime temperatures toward late afternoon. But this concept does presuppose a preparedness on the part of users to understand this technology and to actively employ it.

13

14

13 Mitarbeiterrestaurant 14 Cafeteria | 13 Staff restaurant 14 Cafeteria

HAUPTVERWALTUNGSGEBÄUDE DER LANDESVERSICHERUNGSANSTALT |
ADMINISTRATION BUILDING FOR THE STATE INSURANCE AGENCY | 1992–1997

15, 16 Sporthalle 17 Parkhaus 18 Grundriss Parkhaus 19 Modell
15, 16 Sports hall 17 Parking garage 18 Plan, parking garage 19 Model

HAUPTVERWALTUNGSGEBÄUDE DER LANDESVERSICHERUNGSANSTALT |
ADMINISTRATION BUILDING FOR THE STATE INSURANCE AGENCY | 1992–1997

17

Zeitgleich mit dem Gebäude wurden auf einem benachbarten Grundstück ein Parkhaus und die Wohnungen für Hausmeister und Gebäudetechniker erstellt. Ein Parkhaus in dieser Nachbarschaft schien problematisch. Der hohe Grundwasserstand erlaubte nur eine geringe Unterbauung im Erdreich. So wurde ein Parkhaus geplant, das sich von der strengen, scheinbar funktionalen Geometrie der üblichen Park-Stapelgeschosse löst. Die Struktur befreit sich von den scheinbaren Notwendigkeiten einer rigiden Statik und nutzt die Freiheiten, die der Ortbetonbau einräumt. Das Untergeschoss ist über großzügige Öffnungen natürlich belichtet und belüftet. ◄

Simultaneous with construction of the new building, a parking garage and apartments for the caretaker and staff in charge of technical infrastructure were completed on a neighboring site. A parking garage in this neighborhood appeared problematic. The high groundwater level permitted only minimal below-ground construction. For this reason, a parking garage was planned, one that distinguishes itself from the strict, seemingly functional geometry typical of such stacked structures. It is released from the apparent necessity of rigid statics, and exploits the freedom permitted by the use of in-situ concrete. The basement level is naturally ventilated and lit via spacious openings above. ◄

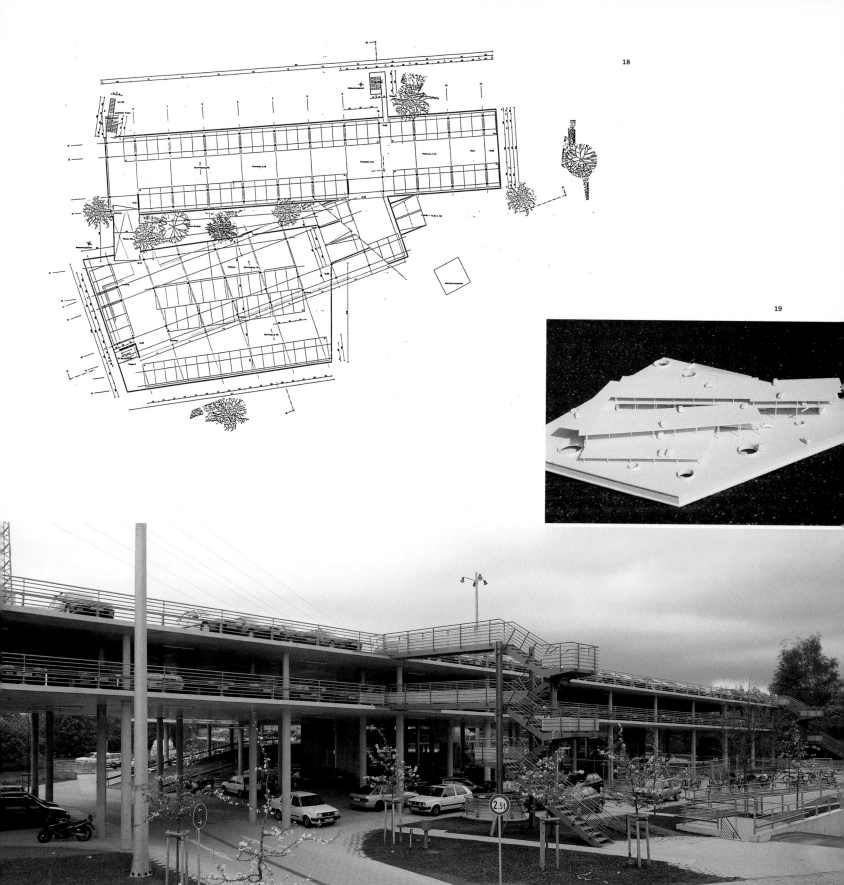

1

Das Grundstück für den geplanten Neubau der Schule ist umgeben von mehrgeschossigen Wohn- und Gewerbebauten unterschiedlichster Art und Größe. Es liegt also nicht innerhalb einer festen und homogenen Stadtbebauung mit eindeutiger Charakteristik, sondern in einem eher heterogenem Umfeld, ohne klare Schwerpunkte im Stadtgefüge.

Dieser Hintergrund sollte den Entwurf prägen. Es wird ein Gebäude vorgeschlagen, das sich von den eher sachlichen Wohn- und Gewerbebauten der Umgebung unterscheidet. Geplant ist, die Räume für die Schüler in einer ringförmigen Anlage unterzubringen. Durch die besondere Form des Gebäudes, die kreisförmige Anordnung der Räume um einen Hof, entsteht eine typische und unverwechselbare Gestalt, die den Gedanken der Schulgemeinschaft insgesamt stärken soll.

The lot for the planned new building for the school is surrounded by multi-story residential and commercial structures of various forms and dimensions. It does not lie, hence, within a dense or homogeneous city setting with a definite character, but in a somewhat heterogeneous environment, one lacking distinct foci within the urban texture.

This background is to condition the design. The proposal is for a structure that sets itself off from the somewhat neutral residential and commercial buildings of the vicinity. The plan incorporates the spaces for the pupils into a ring-shaped layout. The building's special form, the circular arrangement of the rooms around a courtyard, results in a characteristic and unmistakable shape, one intended to strengthen the capacity for thought on the part of the school community as a whole.

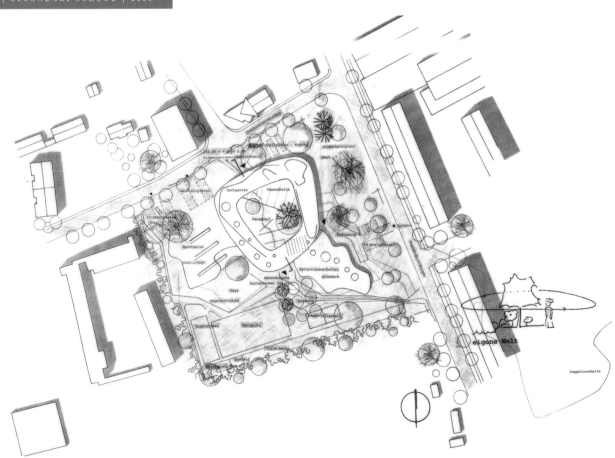

BUNDESOBERSTUFENGYMNASIUM
SECONDARY SCHOOL

GRAZ, ÖSTERREICH | GRAZ, AUSTRIA; 1999

1 Wettbewerbsmodell 2 Lageplan | 1 Competition model 2 Site plan

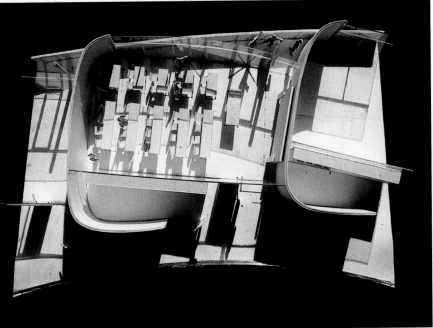

3

3 Innenmodell Klassenraum 4 Wettbewerbsmodell 5 Grundriss Gartengeschoss
6 Grundriss Erdgeschoss 7 Grundriss Obergeschoss 8 Grundriss Dachgeschoss
3 Interior model. classroom 4 Competition model 5 Plan, garden level 6 Plan,
ground floor 7 Plan, upper level 8 Plan, roof level

BUNDESOBERSTUFENGYMNASIUM | SECONDARY SCHOOL | 1999

4

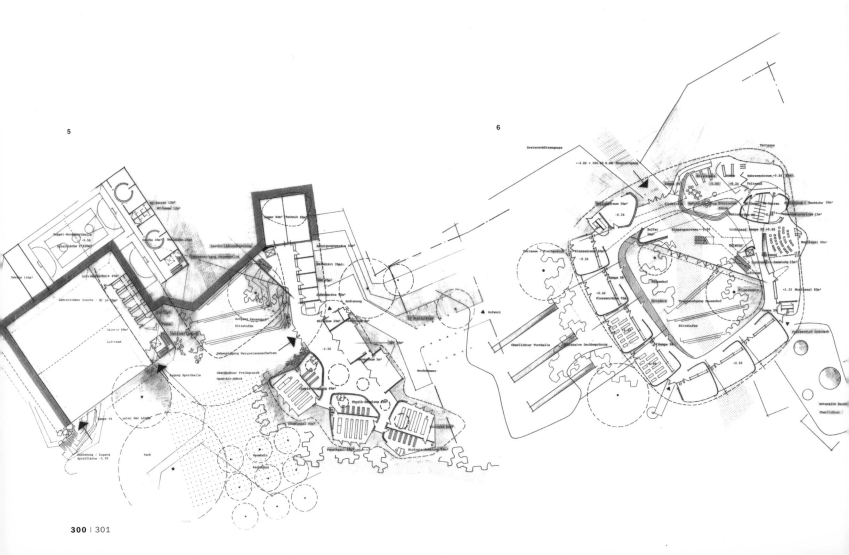

5

6

Über offene Treppen und einen Aufzug in einer teilweise verglasten Eingangshalle erreicht man die Räume für Lehrer, Schulverwaltung und die Elternsprechzimmer auf dem Galeriegeschoss, die Klassenräume im 1. Obergeschoss sowie die Räume für Kunst und Werken im Dachgeschoss. Alle Räume erhalten Terrassen oder Balkone. Die Räume für Musik liegen im Eingangsgeschoss in direktem Bezug zur Halle. Bei Veranstaltungen können diese gemeinsam mit der Halle genutzt werden. Durch das Wechselspiel transparenter, halb transparenter und geschlossener Elemente im Dach der Halle entsteht eine Stimmung im Raum, als befände man sich unter einer begrünten Laube oder im Spiel von Licht und Schatten unter einem großen Baum.

Die Fachklassen liegen außerhalb des Rings in einem Gebäudeflügel im östlichen Bereich des Grundstücks, ähnlich Pavillons im Grünen. An schönen Tagen könnte der Unterricht auf Terrassen im Freien stattfinden. Offene Stege und Rampen durchziehen die Halle, die das Herz der Anlage bildet. Somit ergeben sich vielfältige räumliche Situationen. Nach Süden, zum Park, öffnet sich der Ring und bereits von der Halle aus kann man in die Landschaft blicken. ◄

Open staircases and an elevator in a partially glazed entrance hall give access to rooms for teachers, school administration and parent consultations at the gallery level, to classrooms in the second level, as well as to rooms for art and workshops in the attic story. All rooms have terraces or balconies. The music rooms are set at the entrance level, giving directly onto the entrance hall. For events, they can be used in combination with the hall. The interplay of transparent, partially transparent, and opaque elements in the roof of the hall creates a distinct mood, reminiscent of an arbor or of the play of light and shadow beneath the canopy of a grand, spreading tree.

Special classrooms lie outside of the ring in a wing in the eastern part of the site resembling pavilions in a landscape. On fair days, lessons can be given on the terraces in the open air. Open footbridges and ramps traverse the hall, which forms the heart of the facility, resulting in a diversity of spatial situations. To the south, toward the park, the ring opens, and the landscape outside is clearly visible from the hall. ◄

7   8

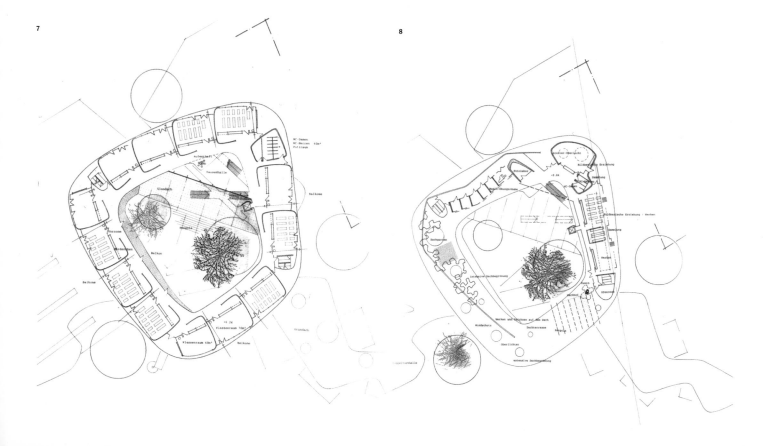

1 Ansicht West | 1 West elevation

MUSICON KONZERTHALLE | MUSICON CONCERT HALL | 1995

Der Wettbewerb wurde von einem privaten Förderverein ausgelobt. Der Verein hat sich zum Ziel gesetzt, für Bremen eine Konzerthalle von Weltrang zu bauen. Das neue Musicon-Gebäude liegt in der Nähe des Bahnhofs, zwischen Klangbogen und Gustav-Deetjen-Allee. Zusammen mit dem Bahnhofsgebäude fasst es einen Platzraum, hält Distanz zu den andersartigen Großbauten für Sport und Ausstellung, hat Anteil am Park und am Messeplatz und bezieht sich auf die Achse zum Hotel im Norden.

Der Konzertsaal selbst wurde aus seiner speziellen Aufgabe heraus entwickelt; ein Raum, in dem Musik, Musiker und Publikum leicht zueinander finden werden. Alle Plätze

The competition was announced by a private sponsoring society. The goal of the society was to erect a concert hall of international rank in Bremen. The new Musicon building lies in the vicinity of the train station, between Klangbogen and Gustav-Deetjen-Allee. Together with the station, it forms a square. It keeps its distance from the untypical, large structures for sports and exhibitions, while enjoying proximity to the park and Messeplatz, and is aligned on an axis leading to the hotel to the north.

The concert hall itself was developed with special tasks in mind; a space in which music, musicians and public could mingle

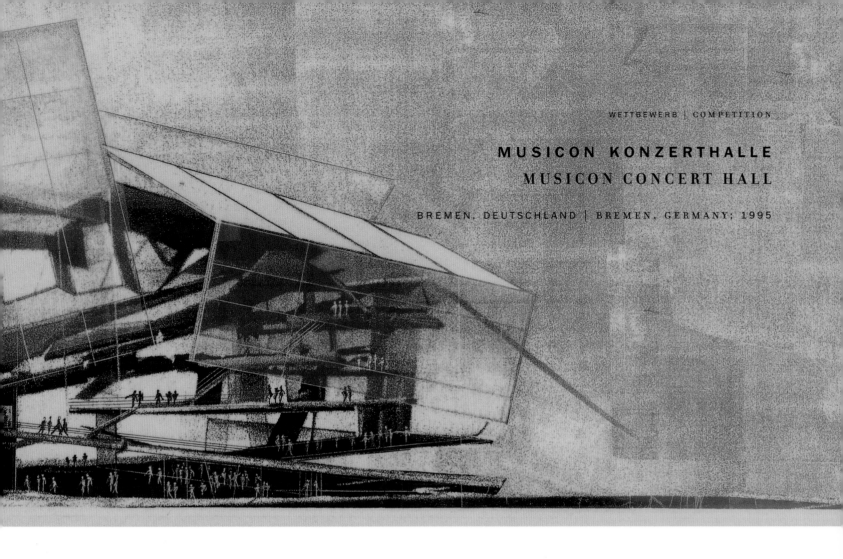

MUSICON KONZERTHALLE
MUSICON CONCERT HALL

BREMEN, DEUTSCHLAND | BREMEN, GERMANY; 1995

sind in ihrer akustischen und optischen Qualität annähernd gleichwertig. Die Gemeinschaft der Musikerlebenden steht im Vordergrund des Konzepts.

Der innere Raum entwickelt sich – losgelöst von äußeren Bedingungen (Klima, Konstruktion, städtebauliche Bindungen etc.) – aus seiner eigentlichen Aufgabe heraus. Dieser Ansatz führt letztlich dazu, dass Innen- und Außenschale getrennt werden, so dass um den von Innenraumbedingungen her geformten Konzertsaal herum eine äußere Schale liegt, es entsteht das Haus im Haus. Dieses Konzept löst die bauphysikalischen Probleme. Darüber hinaus kann sich – unabhängig von den Konditionen des Konzertsaals – ein

easily on common ground. All seats are nearly equal in terms of both acoustic and visual qualities. In the foreground of the concept stands the music-loving community.

The interior space is developed in terms of the task it has to fulfill and released from external conditions (climate control, construction, urban-planning obligations, etc.). This point of departure led to the decision to separate the inner and outer shells, so that an outer envelope would surround a concert hall shaped exclusively by interior considerations: a building within a building. This concept solves the related architectonic problems. Moreover, given

in dieser speziellen Situation interessantes Äußeres formen. Zwischen Innen- und Außenschale ist ausreichend Raum für die erforderlichen Einrichtungen der Technik (Tragwerke, Klimaanlage, raumakustische Maßnahmen, Haustechnik etc.), so dass diese Anlagen sich ebenfalls weitgehend nach ihren eigenen Bedingungen entwickeln und im Hintergrund halten können.

Die Mulde des Saales liegt über dem Platzniveau. Unter den Schrägen der Mulde entfalten sich die Foyers, Zugänge und für andere Aufgaben erforderlichen Räume. Die Räume für dienende Nutzungen sind in formal einfacheren Bauteilen angeordnet. Der Saal selbst ähnelt dem der Philharmonie von Hans Scharoun in Berlin. Allerdings wird das dort Geschlossene des Innenraums aufgelöst, indem z.B. eher immaterielle Flächen statt materieller Wände den visuellen Raum bilden. Der visuelle Raum ist getrennt vom akustischen und materiellen Raum. Das Musikerlebnis wird somit weniger vom Materiellen berührt und dadurch befreit und gestärkt.

Beabsichtigt ist eine äußere Erscheinung, die sich eher der Kunstwelt zuordnet als dem Trivialen. So sieht der Entwurf sich scheinbar durchdringende Kuben vor. Wünschenswert wäre es, wenn diese Würfelflächen aus Glas wären. Die Glasflächen könnten unterschiedlich gefärbt sein, so dass das Innenleben unterschiedlich klar oder diffus durchscheinen würde. In den verschiedenen geneigten Glasflächen würden sich Himmel, Wolken, Bäume, Umgebung, Menschen etc. spiegeln. Das eher Immaterielle soll auch hier in den Vordergrund treten. Dem »schönen Schein« soll größerer Raum und größere Bedeutung zukommen als dem materiell Vorhandenen.

this special situation, an interesting outer form could be shaped, irrespective of the requirements of the concert hall itself. Lying between the inner and outer shells is ample space to accommodate necessary technical facilities (structure, air-conditioning, acoustic measures, infrastructure, etc.), so that such facilities will also be designed essentially according to their intrinsic conditions, and can remain in the background.

The bowl form of the hall lies above the level of the square. Under the slopes of the bowl are foyers, entrances and support rooms. Spaces for services are set in formally simpler sections of the building. The hall itself resembles Hans Scharoun's Berlin Philharmonic Hall. However, the enclosure of the interior space is dissolved, so that relatively immaterial surfaces articulate the visual space, not solid elements. Visual space is distinguished from acoustic or material space. The experience of music, hence, is unencumbered by material conditions, and thereby freed and highlighted.

The objective is an external appearance belonging more to the sphere of art than to the commonplace. The design envisions apparently interpenetrating cubic volumes. Ideally, these cubic surfaces would be composed of glass. Such glass surfaces could be variously colored, so that the interior would enjoy contrasting degrees of transparency/opaqueness. The variously angled glass surfaces will reflect sky, clouds, trees, the surroundings, people, etc. Here, the immaterial is to occupy the foreground as well. The "beautiful appearance" should occupy more space and assume greater significance than the material object.

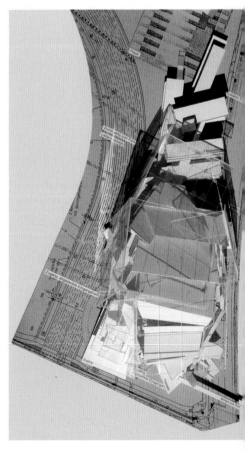

2

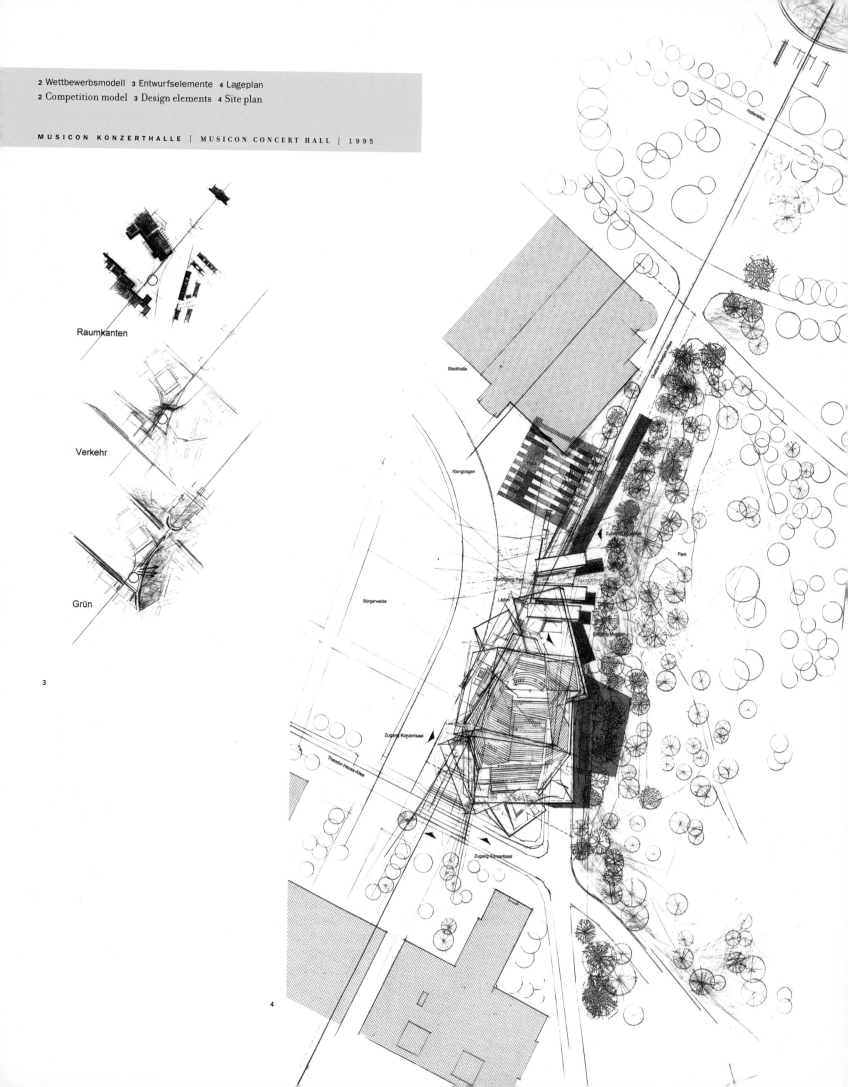

MUSICON KONZERTHALLE | MUSICON CONCERT HALL | 1995

Raumkanten

Verkehr

Grün

3

4

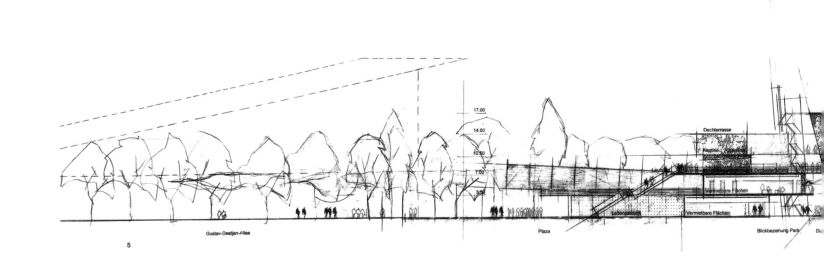

5

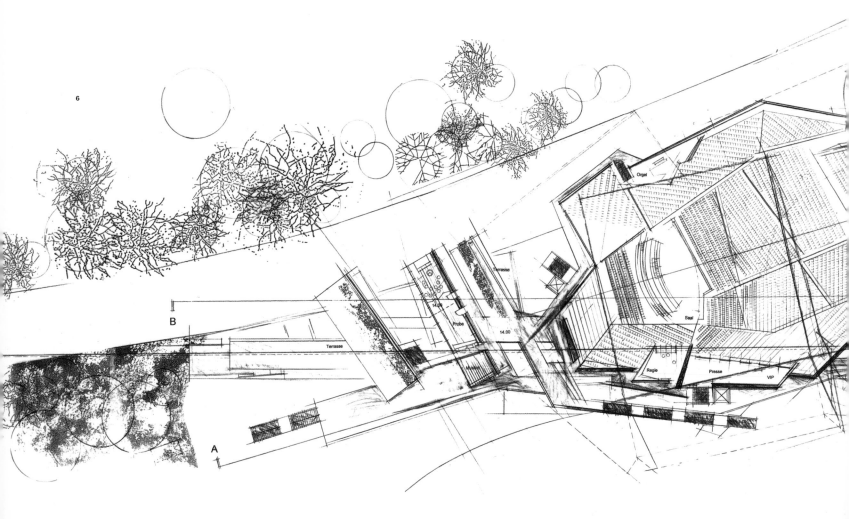

6

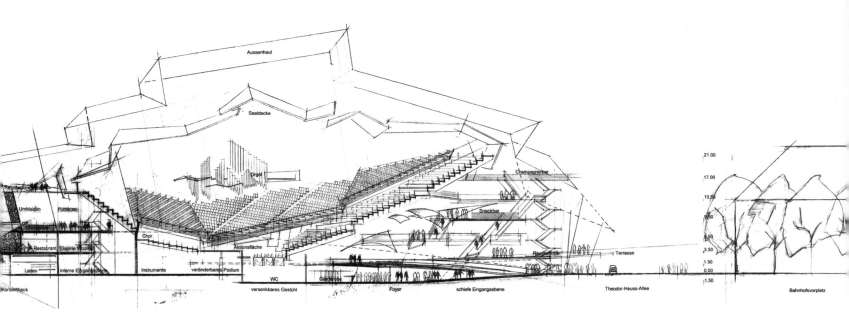

MUSICON KONZERTHALLE | MUSICON CONCERT HALL | 1995

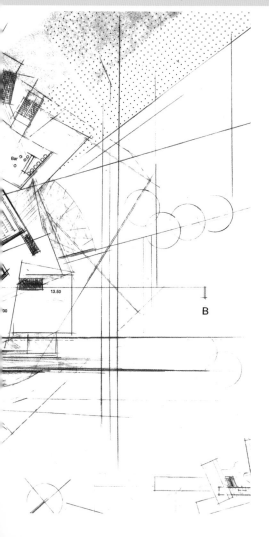

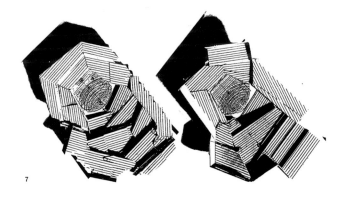

7

Dieses Immaterielle könnten eben jene Reflektionen, der Blick nach Außen, das Licht, farbige Flächen oder architektonische Elemente sein, die sich losgelöst von den Bedingungen des akustischen Raums entfalten werden. Konkret kann diese Trennung der verschiedenen Erlebnisräume durch Glas, akustische Paneele und andere materielle Maßnahmen erreicht werden. ◄

Such immateriality might consist of precisely such reflections, of the view to the outside, the light, colored surfaces, or architectural elements, which unfold severed from the conditions of the acoustic space. In concrete terms, such a separation of the various realms of experience can be achieved by using glass, acoustic panels and others materials. ◄

1

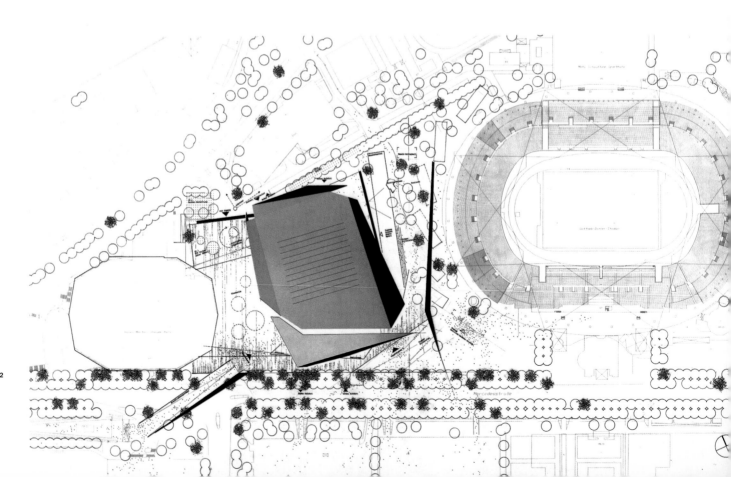

2

MULTIFUNKTIONALES
SPORT- UND VERANSTALTUNGSZENTRUM
MULTI-FUNCTIONAL CENTER FOR SPORTS
AND CULTURAL EVENTS

STUTTGART, DEUTSCHLAND |
STUTTGART, GERMANY; 1999

1 Ansicht 2 Lageplan 3 Silhouette
1 Elevation 2 Site plan 3 Silhouette

SPORT- UND VERANSTALTUNGSZENTRUM |
CENTER FOR SPORTS AND CULTURAL EVENTS | 1999

Eine neue Sport- und Veranstaltungshalle soll-te zwischen der Schleyerhalle und dem Gott-lieb-Daimler-Stadion entstehen. Die Nachbar-bauten dominieren aufgrund ihrer Bedeutung und Größe den Ort. Hier galt es für die neue Anlage, sich zu behaupten. So wurde eine Form gewählt, die sich weitgehend von den inneren Bedingungen der Halle löst. Nicht die Funktionen, z.B. der Zuschnitt des Feldes oder der Tribünen, bestimmen die Form und treten nach außen in Erscheinung, sondern eine Hülle, die nach anderen, freieren Ge-sichtspunkten entwickelt ist. Sie nimmt Bezie-hungen zur Umgebung auf und grenzt sich im Formalen von den Nachbargebäuden ab.

A new sports and event hall was planned for the site lying between Schleyerhalle and the Gottlieb Daimler Stadium. Given their importance and scale, the neighbor-ing buildings dominate the area. However, the new complex also had to assert itself. Therefore, an external form was chosen that is substantially independent of the hall's interior circumstances. Not its func-tions — for example the dimensions of the playing field or the seating distribution — determined the appearance, but instead the envelope was designed according to other, looser criteria. This outer shape establishes relationships with its sur-roundings, while limiting itself formally from the neighboring structures.

Eine eigenständige, und auch eigenwillige Anlage entsteht, die nicht nur in der Reihe der vorhandenen Bauten bestehen kann, sondern die ebenso typisch und unverwechselbar – auch an internationalen Maßstäben gemessen – in ihrer Erscheinung ist. So wird die Nähe zu Gebäuden der Umgebung oder anderen national und international bereits realisierten Sportbauten bewusst vermieden, denn nur so kann eine Anlage von internationalem Rang entstehen, wovon die Stadt Stuttgart durchaus profitiert.

Die Halle wird über eine erhöhte Ebene erschlossen, die eine Verbindung zur benachbarten Schleyerhalle herstellt. Eine gemeinsame Eingangshalle bildet die wettergeschützte Verbindung. Auf dieser modellierten Ebene sind weitere Freizeitanlagen wie Skateboardbahn, Kunsteisbahn, Kletterwand u.ä. angeordnet, um auch außerhalb der Veranstaltungszeiten Attraktionen für Besucher zu bieten. Über diese Ebene werden auch die Besucherränge erschlossen. Relativ kurze Wege führen von hier auf die oberen und unteren Tribünen.

EPILOG Der Entwurf war ein zweiter Preis mit dem Hinweis auf vermutete höhere Kosten als eine andere Lösung. Bedauerlicherweise hat die Stadt Stuttgart sich in der Folge entschlossen, keinen der Entwürfe der Preisträger zu realisieren, sondern plant, einen Investor zu beauftragen, ein typisches Kommerzzentrum für Sport in dieser bedeutenden Situation zu erstellen. ◄

As such, it is possible to create an independent and original complex, capable not just of holding its own in relation to existing buildings in the vicinity, but also characteristic and unmistakable in appearance – even measured by international standards. Any resemblance to nearby buildings, or to other existing sports facilities in Germany or abroad was deliberately avoided, for only thus can a complex of international rank arise, one from which the city of Stuttgart could profit considerably.

The hall itself is reached via an elevated surface which creates links to the neighboring Schleyerhalle. A shared entrance hall provides a direct connection, one sheltered from the weather. Set upon this modulated plane are additional leisure facilities such as a skateboard park, artificial ice rink, climbing wall, etc., in order to offer attractions for visitors when no events are scheduled. The seats are also accessed on this level. From here, relatively short distances lead to the upper and lower seating areas.

EPILOGUE The proposal was awarded second prize, with the comment that it was expected to cost more than an alternative solution. Regrettably, the city of Stuttgart decided, as a consequence, not to realise any of the prize-winning designs, but plans instead to commission an investor to produce a typical commercial center for sports on this important site. ◄

4

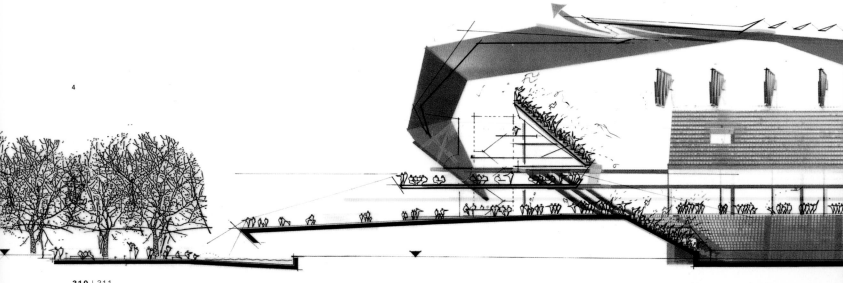

Boxen

Obere Tribüne 6,200
Untere Tribüne 7,800
Spielfeld 2,500

16,500

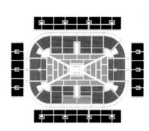

4 Schnitt 5 Wettbewerbsmodell 6 Bestuhlungsvarianten
4 Section 5 Competition model 6 Seating variants

S P O R T - U N D V E R A N S T A L T U N G S Z E N T R U M |
C E N T E R F O R S P O R T S A N D C U L T U R A L E V E N T S | 1999

Banquet

Obere Tribüne 0
Untere Tribüne 0
Spielfeld 2,000

1500-2000

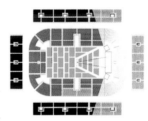

Fussball

Obere Tribüne 6,200
Untere Tribüne 7,800
Spielfeld 0

14,000

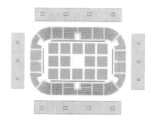
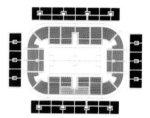

Konzerte (Kopftribüne)

Obere Tribüne 3,500
Untere Tribüne 4,000
Spielfeld 2,000

9,500

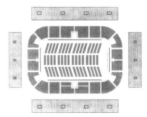

Hauptversammlungen

Obere Tribüne 0
Untere Tribüne 0-7,800
Spielfeld 2,500

2,500

1

2

Dem Beispiel zahlreicher anderer europä-
ischer Kommunen folgend, betreibt die Stadt
Oslo die Revitalisierung brachliegender
Industrieflächen und plant, das Gelände des
alten Industriehafens gegenüber Bjørkvika
neu zu erschließen. Die Lage unmittelbar im
Süden des Stadtzentrums schafft gute
Möglichkeiten für die zukünftige Stadtent-
wicklung. Als eines der ersten Gebäude
könnte das geplante Opernhaus ein wichtiges
Initialprojekt werden und zugleich den Maßstab für die Qualität weiterer Bebauungen
setzen.

Der Entwurf fasst die Mehrzahl der funktionalen Elemente – Zuschauerraum, Bühne,
ein ausgedehnter Hinterbühnenbereich,
Werkstätten und Verwaltung – in eine streng
organisierte und funktional ausgerichtete

The Municipality of Oslo has, following the
example of many of its European counter-
parts, decided to develop the old industrial
harbor area fronting onto Bjørkvika.
Located immediately to the south of the
existing city center, the waterfront offers
great potential for the future expansion of
the city. The new Opera House will be one
of the first buildings in this development
and could therefore act as an important
catalyst whilst also providing the opportunity to set a precedent for the quality of further developments.

The design proposal accommodates the
majority of the functional elements; extensive backstage facilities, workshops and
administration, into a rigidly organised
and functionally orientated rectilinear

OPERNHAUS | OPERA HOUSE

1 Wettbewerbsmodell 2 Schilf | 1 Competition model 2 Reeds

Rechteckform. Tageslichttürme setzen Akzente und ermöglichen eine natürliche Beleuchtung und Belüftung. Die Form dieses Gebäudeteils berücksichtigt so weit wie möglich das Raster sowohl der Stadt als auch der zukünftigen Erschließungsgebiete unmittelbar südlich der wichtigsten Eisenbahnlinien.

Die öffentlichen Bereiche dagegen – die verschiedenen Zugangs- und Zufahrtsmöglichkeiten, Halle, Foyers, Geschäfte, Bars sowie die allgemeine Verkehrsführung zusammen mit der Uferpromenade – sind sehr viel freier konzipiert; sie folgen anderen Kriterien als rein pragmatischen und orientieren sich an den Besonderheiten der Lage am Hafen. Hier wird die eigentliche Funktion des Opernhauses sichtbar, gespiegelt in der

form. Punctuated by various light-wells ensuring natural light and ventilation wherever possible the general form of this part of the building respects the grid pattern of both the existing city and the planned developments immediately to the south of the main railway lines.

The areas for public use, the various approaches (both vehicular and pedestrian), the concourse, foyers, shops, bars and general circulation areas together with the waterside promenade are, in contrast, arranged much more freely, responding to criteria other than the pragmatic and taking full advantage of the harbor-front location. Such elements are arranged in a manner that the Opera House expresses itself through its original purpose, through

OPERNHAUS | OPERA HOUSE | 2000

Szenerie der Besucher, die in den großzügig
verglasten, über das Wasser auskragenden
Foyers auf- und abgehen.

Die vorgeschlagene öffentliche Promenade
ist weitgehend frei von funktionalen Zwängen;
sie beginnt am Hauptbahnhof und an der
zentralen Fußgängerzone, kreuzt nach leich-
tem Anstieg den Christian Fredriks Plads und
belebte Geschäftsstraßen, erreicht dann die
Foyers der Oper und der Ballettbühne und
folgt von dort aus in zahlreichen Bögen der
landschaftlich neu gestalteten Uferlinie an
der bestehenden künstlichen Landzunge.

the behavior of the visiting audience. The
event itself is celebrated with the visitors
displayed over the water, where they can be
seen from afar circulating in the illuminated, generously glazed foyers.

The proposed public promenade is largely
free from functional constraints, extending
from the main railway station and the main
pedestrian thoroughfare, rising gently to
cross Christian Fredriks Plads and busy city
roads before reaching the foyers of both the
Opera and Ballet Theatre. From here the
promenade continues via series of turns
along the new landscaped shoreline of the
existing artificial headland.

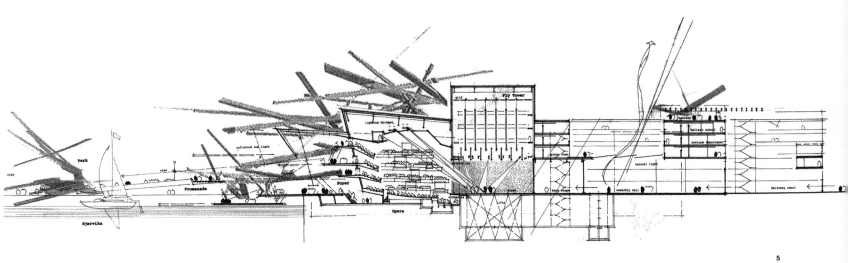

5

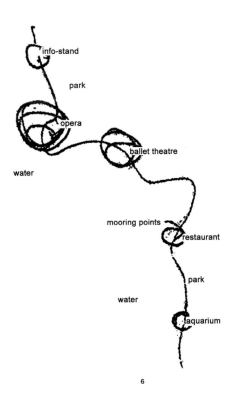

6

Das Gebäudeensemble entspricht in gewisser Weise der Anlage Oslos: Der orthogonale Grundriss des Stadtzentrums wird durch die funktionalen Elemente des Opernhauses aufgenommen – beide sind von straffen geometrischen Strukturen bestimmt. Ein strenges Grundraster dieser Art unterscheidet sich kaum von dem anderer Städte oder auch vieler anderer Gebäude. Erst durch die freie Gestaltung der Uferzone erhalten der Komplex als ganzer sowie die zur Promenade hin ausgerichteten Bereiche ihr individuelles Gepräge. Die Gestaltung der Promenade, die sowohl das Opernhaus als auch den Park mit Restaurant und Aquarium erschließt, ist die architektonische Antwort auf die Besonderheit des Standorts.

Der Entwurf berücksichtigt die verschiedenartigen funktionalen Anforderungen der sehr unterschiedlichen Bereiche des ausgedehnten Gebäudekomplexes, die sich ihrem individuellen Charakter entsprechend frei entwickeln. Es ist diese Mannigfaltigkeit der Bereiche, welche die Erscheinung des facettenreichen Gebäudes prägt und die Möglichkeit bietet, ein einzigartiges architektonisches Gebäude zu planen, dass als Landmarke wahrgenommen wird.

Der Wettbewerbsbeitrag wurde mit einem Preis (Ankauf) ausgezeichnet. ◄

In a certain way the entire building complex responds to Oslo's layout: the orthogonal pattern of the city center being reflected by the functional elements of the Opera House, both being dominated by tight geometric structures. Such a stringent grid does not differ much from that of many other towns or indeed many other buildings. However, it is the free line of the shore which gives the place its unique identity and distinguishes the layout of the front of house facilities. The form of the promenade serving both the Opera House and the new park, with its restaurant and aquarium, is a natural architectural response to the specific location.

The design takes the diverse functional requirements of the quite different areas of the large building complex into account, allowing them to develop their own individual character. It is the variety of areas which shape the appearance of the multi-faceted building and provide the opportunity to develop a true landmark in a unique situation.

This competition design was awarded a purchase. ◄

HARBOURSIDE CENTRE | THE HARBOURSIDE CENTRE

ZENTRUM FÜR DARSTELLENDE KÜNSTE – KONZERTHALLE UND TANZTHEATER
CENTRE FOR THE PERFORMING ARTS – CONCERT HALL AND DANCE THEATRE
BRISTOL, GROSSBRITANNIEN | BRISTOL, UK; 1996–1998

Im Februar 1996 erhielten wir ein Schreiben unerwarteter Herkunft. Ein Anwalt aus dem im südwestlichen England gelegenen Bristol wollte wissen, ob unser Büro daran interessiert sei, an einem Auswahlverfahren für ein Projekt, einer Art Wettbewerbsinterview, teilzunehmen. Von einem Verfahren dieser Art hörten wir zum ersten Mal, doch einer natürlichen Neugierde folgend sagten wir zu.

Nach einem ersten Kolloquium wurden wir aufgefordert, Beispiele unserer Bauten sowie unser Büro vorzustellen und darüber hinaus Präsentationspaneele vorzubereiten, die zum einen unsere Arbeitsmethode darstellen, zum anderen erläutern sollten, wie wir an die Aufgabe herangehen würden, auf einem relativ engen Innenstadtgrundstück ein großes Zentrum für darstellende Künste zu entwerfen. Ein Wettbewerbsentwurf war nicht verlangt und das Verfahren wurde von unseren Mitarbeitern unberechtigterweise schnell als »Schönheitswettbewerb« abqualifiziert.

In February 1996 we received, quite unexpectedly, a letter from an unlikely source, a solicitor in Bristol in south-west England, enquiring if we would be interested in taking part in an architects selection process, a form of competitive interview. Although such a procedure was completely new to us, our natural curiosity lead us into agreeing to take part.

Following an initial colloquium we were asked to present examples of our work, our office itself, and to prepare presentation panels illustrating both our working methods and how we would approach the task of designing a large performing arts center on a relatively constricted city center site. No actual competition design was required, and the process was quickly dubbed by our staff, quite unfairly, as being "a beauty contest."

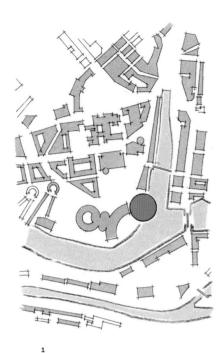

1

2

Es war sofort klar, dass der geplante Bau das Potenzial bot, zu einem besonderen Anziehungspunkt zu werden, nicht nur wegen der außergewöhnlichen Lage, sondern auch, weil die Möglichkeit bestand, hier ein herausragendes architektonisches Werk zu schaffen. Das Projekt könnte Bristol im eigenen Land und, wenn wir Glück hätten, auch international zu einem besonderen Ruf verhelfen – eine Herausforderung, die wir einfach annehmen mussten.

Da uns die Situation neu war, entschlossen wir uns für ein einfaches und sehr direktes Vorgehen: Wir würden unsere Antwort strikt

It was immediately apparent to us that the new performing arts center had the potential to become a landmark, both as an element in the urban landscape and as a unique architectural creation. It was a project which offered Bristol potential national, or even, if we were lucky, international prominence. It was a challenge we had to take up.

Having never been in such a position before we decided that our response would be simple and very direct, we would present the materials asked for and nothing else. To our surprise this approach was

1 Lageplan 2 Präsentationsmodell Ansicht Nord 3 Silhouette
1 Site plan 2 Presentation model, view from north 3 Silhouette

HARBOURSIDE CENTRE | 1996–1998

auf die Vorlage des verlangten Materials beschränken. Zu unserer Überraschung war diese Herangehensweise erfolgreich, denn anders als die anderen Teilnehmer hatten wir auch durch die Beschränkung auf Situationsanalysen dargestellt, dass mögliche Entwürfe das Ergebnis eines fortgesetzten Dialogs sein würden und alle Beteiligten gut daran täten, sich, zumal in dieser Frühphase des Projekts, nicht von vorgefassten Ideen leiten zu lassen.

Der Auswahl sehr guter Fachplaner folgte die Ausarbeitung des Projekts – von Grund auf, in einem Prozess, bei dem Entwurfsvorgaben und Entwurfsmethode in einem Lernprozess ineinander griffen.

successful, as unlike all other competitors, we had demonstrated that the eventual designs would be the result of an ongoing dialogue and that all parties should be wary of any preconceived notions, particularly at such a very early stage in the project.

Subsequent to appointment of a strong team of consultants the project was then developed from the "bottom-up," with design brief and design approach/response literally learning from one another.

4

Aus dem Standort des Harbourside Centre im Stadtkern und seiner vorgesehenen Funktion als Brennpunkt einer umfangreichen Revitalisierung des Hafens ergeben sich gewisse Anforderungen an den Entwurf aus dem Kontext heraus. Dazu gehören die Kaianlagen mit den sehr unterschiedlichen Gegebenheiten an den Grundstücksgrenzen, die Beziehung zum Hafengelände, der Ausblick auf markante Wahrzeichen der Stadt Bristol, die Lage zwischen zwei weiträumigen öffentlichen Plätzen, sowie die außerordentlich vielfältige städtische Topografie. Außer Industriegebäuden und denkmalgeschützten Lagerhäusern, von denen einige nach sorgfältiger Restauration neu genutzt werden, gehören zum Hafengelände ein großes Verwaltungsgebäude, verschiedene Kleingewerbebetriebe, ein Gasometer und eine große Freifläche, die als Parkplatz dient. Die Uferanlage wird bei der Neugestaltung des Geländes zur Attraktion. Geplant sind ein Park, Wohneinheiten, Büros und, um einen neu zu schaffenden Platz gruppiert, drei bedeutende kulturelle Anziehungspunkte – ein Technikmuseum, ein Naturkundemuseum, sowie ein Zentrum für darstellende Künste – das Harbourside Centre.

Located at the heart of the city and intended as the focus of a large redevelopment of the harbor, certain obligations for the design of the Harbourside Centre (HC) are inherent to its harbor district context. These include the rather different conditions at the site boundaries, the relationship to the harbor quayside, views to important Bristol landmarks, the location between two large and possibly competitive public squares and Bristol's remarkably varying topography. In addition to industrial buildings and listed warehouses, some of which have been painstakingly restored and converted for other uses, the harborside district also contains a large administration building, various small businesses, a gasometer and extensive vacant space used for carparking. Taking full advantage of the waterfront location the redevelopment includes a public park, residential units, offices and, gathered around a new public square, three important cultural attractions – a science center, an education facility and a performing arts center, the HC.

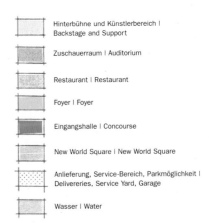

Hinterbühne und Künstlerbereich | Backstage and Support

Zuschauerraum | Auditorium

Restaurant | Restaurant

Foyer | Foyer

Eingangshalle | Concourse

New World Square | New World Square

Anlieferung, Service-Bereich, Parkmöglichkeit | Delivereries, Service Yard, Garage

Wasser | Water

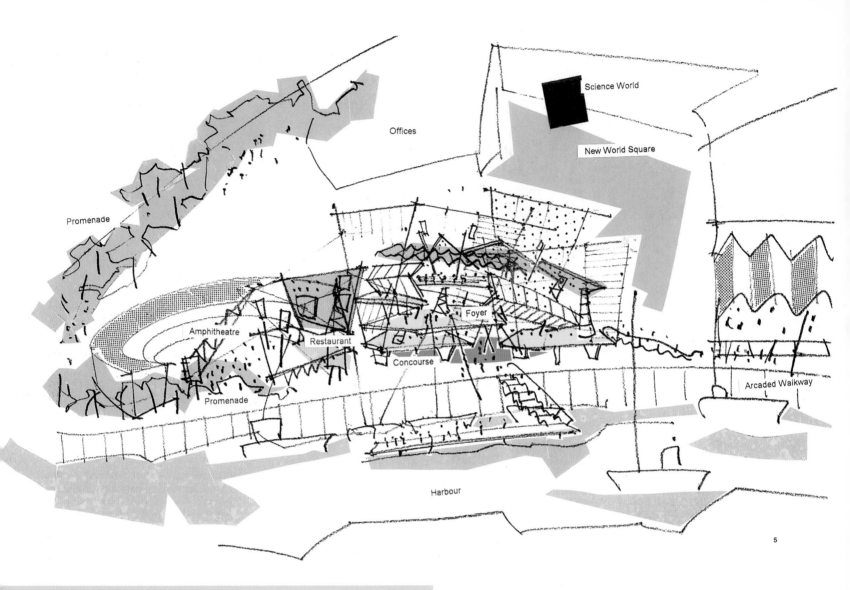

Offices

Science World

New World Square

Promenade

Foyer

Amphitheatre

Restaurant

Concourse

Promenade

Arcaded Walkway

Harbour

5

4, 6 Funktionsschema **5** Konzeptskizze
4, 6 Functional diagrams **5** Conceptual sketch

HARBOURSIDE CENTRE | 1996–1998

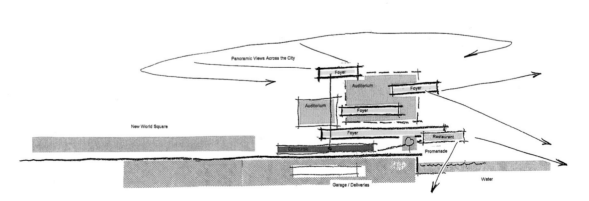

Panoramic Views Across the City

Foyer

Auditorium

Foyer

Auditorium

Foyer

Foyer

New World Square

Restaurant

Concourse

Promenade

Garage / Deliveries

Water

6

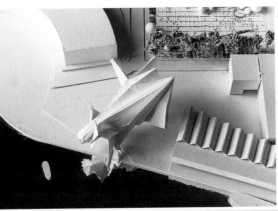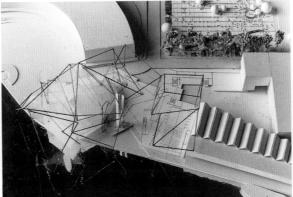

Vom Stadtzentrum aus betrachtet ist das Grundstück durch die historischen Lagerhäuser am Kai verdeckt, doch verlangen die Größe des Programms und die kulturelle Bedeutung des neuen Gebäudes, dass es die benachbarten Bauwerke überragt, über die Uferkante in das Hafenbecken auskragt und damit aus den Grundstückgrenzen und aus dem Schatten der restlichen Uferbebauung heraustritt. Einzelne Elemente des Raumprogramms bieten sich für eine derart exponierte Lage geradezu an. Mit der Auslagerung der Foyers und des Restaurants aus dem Volumen des Hauptgebäudes wird nicht nur der Bedeutung der Lage und der zu erwartenden Szenerie entsprochen; es eröffnen sich damit auf einem relativ bescheiden dimensionierten Grundstück auch reizvolle neue Sichtbezüge und zahlreiche Möglichkeiten.

Blickt man von der hoch gelegenen Universität auf das neue Hafengelände hinunter, sind Form und Anlage klar ablesbar. Durch die prägnante, plastische Form des Harbourside Centre erhält das Gesamtbild ein eigenständiges Profil. Als Ergänzung eines Ensembles kultureller Institutionen im Herzen der Stadt reagiert das Harbourside Centre flexibel auf den unmittelbar anschließenden Bestand. Auf Grund der Komplexität seiner äußeren Form präsentiert sich das Gebäude in unterschiedli-

Seen from the city center, the site is concealed by the historic waterside warehouses, however both the scale and cultural importance of the new building demands that it rises above its neighbors or projects out over the water, extending beyond the site boundary and out of the shadow of the other quayside developments. Certain elements of the building program lend themselves naturally to such exposed positions. Positioning the foyers or restaurant out beyond the main building volume responds not only to the importance of the site and the potential spectacle, but creates exciting new vistas, provides numerous opportunities on what is a relatively constricted site.

Whilst seen from the university, which occupies Bristol's high ground, the form and layout of the new harborside district are clearly understood. The HC contributes a special, sculptural shape which describes a distinct and recognisable image for it. Completing a significant ensemble of cultural buildings at the heart of the city the HC responds in a flexible manner to its immediate neighbors. The complexity of the exterior form allows the building to present itself at various differing scales when viewed either from the hills above the city, from the harbor or from street level. The building

cher Größe, je nachdem ob es von den Hügeln herunter, vom Hafen aus oder auf Straßenniveau wahrgenommen wird. Das Gebäude hat drei in ihrer Erscheinung und Wirkung unterschiedliche Ansichten. Diese passen das Gebäude an die unterschiedlichen Maßstäbe der Umgebung an.

Am New World Square, dem neuen öffentlichen Platz, zeigt sich das Gebäude in zurückhaltender Klarheit. Es bildet zunächst den formalen Abschluss des Platzes und »springt« dann Richtung Hafen vor, wodurch ein großzügiger frontseitiger Hofraum mit Vorfahrt und Besuchereingang entsteht. Südlich des Platzes ist das Amphitheater des bestehenden Verwaltungsgebäudes ebenfalls zum Hafen orientiert. Jenseits des Hafenbeckens liegen ein Kunstzentrum sowie ein Industriemuseum mit Kränen, historischen Eisenbahnwagen und alten Schiffen.

Die dem Amphitheater zugewandte Fassade bietet sich für Open-Air- und Festival-Veranstaltungen an. Das Gebäude soll als Kulisse und gelegentlich als Bühne dienen. Eine große Projektionsfläche, Element der Fassade, wirkt als Blickfang und gibt dem Außenraum den Charakter eines Vorführungssaals.

offers three visually and experientially different fronts. These fronts regulate the building within the differing scales and situations offered by the site itself.

Along New World Square, the new public square, the building assumes a modest and direct appearance. The building first closes the formal edge of the square, before "springing" towards the harbor to create a generous forecourt space for vehicle reception and visitor entrance. South of New World Square and also fronting onto the harbor is the semi-circular amphitheater of the existing administration building, whilst on the opposite side of the harbor are an arts center and an industrial museum with its cranes, historic railway wagons and old ships.

The character of the facade towards the amphitheater further promotes open-air and festival events. The building is intended as a backdrop or on occasion as a stage. A large projection screen, employed as an element within the facade, establishes a focus and provides a performance room quality to the exterior space.

Aus südlicher und östlicher Richtung betrachtet erscheint das Gebäude in größerer Distanz; Maßstab, Komposition und Lichtbrechungseffekte der kaiseitigen Ansicht fesseln den Blick des Betrachters – das Zusammenspiel von Transparenz, Tiefe, Licht, Farbe, Aktivität und Spannung ergibt ein Bild von ungewöhnlichem Reiz. Tagsüber von kristalliner Härte, abends mit Bildern der leuchtenden Foyers voller Besucher und Gäste, setzt das Konzerthaus ein bauliches Zeichen voll Leuchtkraft und Lebendigkeit, das den Hafen verwandelt.

Die drei Hauptelemente des Baukomplexes sind:

· ein Konzertsaal mit Foyers, Restaurant, Café, einer weiträumigen Hinterbühne und Garderoben,
· ein Tanztheater mit eigenen Foyers, Vestibül, Bar, Räumlichkeiten zum Eintanzen und separater Hinterbühne
· ein Verwaltungsgebäude mit Versammlungssaal bzw. Probenraum, Backstage-Bereichen, Unterrichtsräumen und Büros. Auf dem Dach sind Sitzungssäle und eine Kantine untergebracht.

From locations south and east of the site, the building is seen from a greater distance; the scale, composition and reflective qualities of the quayside elevation offers an engaging range of qualities, transparency, depth, light, color, activity and suspense, all contributing to the creation of a unique attraction; by day bright and crystalline, in the evenings the illuminated foyers full with guests and visitors, the waterside will be transformed by a luminous and lively landmark.

The building complex consists of three principal elements:

· a concert hall — including foyers, a restaurant, a café, large backstage areas and dressing rooms
· a dance theater — including dedicated foyers, lobby space, a bar, warm-up facilities and a separate backstage area
· an administration building — including a community hall/rehearsal space, backstage areas, teaching facilities, and offices. Located on the roof are boardroom facilities and a staff canteen.

8

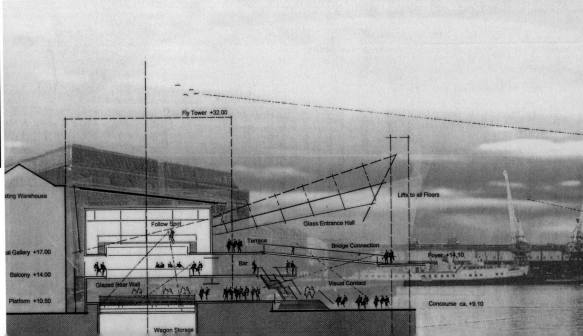

Diese drei Funktionsbereiche zeichnen sich nach außen nicht als Individuen ab. Sie sind unter einem gemeinsamen Dach und über eine sich frei entwickelnde Foyerebene zusammengefasst.

Die großzügigen gläsernen Fassaden schaffen ein hohes Maß an Transparenz. Sie lassen neben den beschriebenen Funktionsbereichen noch Raum für eine eigenständige Eingangshalle entstehen. Durch diese hindurch kann der Passant vom New World Square aus die Atmosphäre des Hafens auf der anderen Seite des Gebäudes erahnen. Zahlreiche ganz unterschiedliche Situationen gewähren Ausblick auf die Stadt, das Kunstzentrum Arnolfini, das Industriemuseum und das Laubwerk der Bäume, die die gegenüberliegenden Kaianlagen säumen.

These elements are not individually evident in the external appearance of the building; they are united overhead by a large, common roof and below by the undulating form of the public concourse.

The extent of glazing together with the physical separation between the concert hall, the dance theater and administrative areas also permits the building a significant transparency and creates a distinct entrance hall. Through this separation, the visitor can indirectly experience the qualities of the harbor from New World Square, and the entrance hall and foyers are further enlivened. A multitude of quite different sightlines through the building allow for views of the city, the Arnolfini arts center, the industrial museum and the foliage lining the opposite quayside.

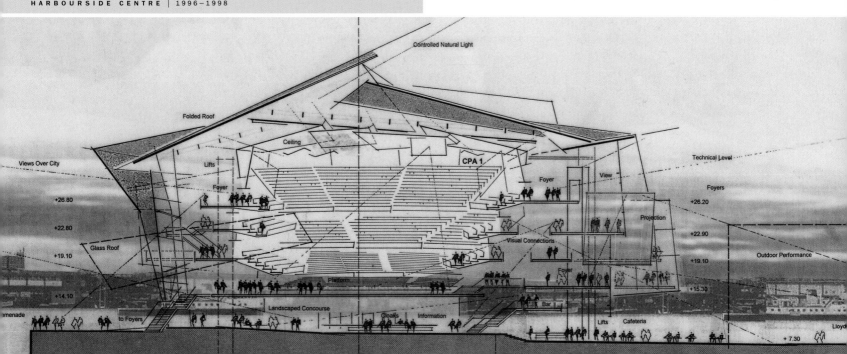

Die kaiseitigen Fassaden sind im Wesentlichen durch die Eingangshalle, Foyers und das Restaurant bestimmt. Hier nimmt sich das Gebäude größere Freiheit und greift über das Grundstück hinaus in den Hafenraum. Im Erdgeschoss tritt die Fassade zurück und schafft so Raum für eine Uferpromenade. Neue Anlegestege bieten den Besuchern Zugang vom Wasser her.

Die Unterseite von Geschossdecken und Dachelementen, die über die Wasserfläche auskragen, werden von Lichtreflexen der Wasseroberfläche erhellt. Durch die Ausrichtung dieser Flächen wird vom Wasser reflektiertes Licht unmittelbar ins Gebäudeinnere gelenkt. Die freie Dachlandschaft überspannt das gesamte Gebäude und folgt in ihrer Entwicklung formalen Gesichtspunkten. Sie ist als fünfte Fassade des Gebäudes ausgebildet und kommt von den Hügeln Bristols gesehen am besten zur Geltung. Das Dach besteht aus blechverkleideten Flächen, die über einen Konstruktionsraster gespannt sind. Die Metallhaut ist zum Teil reflektie-

The quayside elevations are largely determined by the spaces of the entrance hall, the foyers and the restaurant. Here, the building form assumes a greater degree of freedom and extends into the space of the harbor. The ground floor facade is pulled back to provide a generous space for a waterside promenade. New jetties provide visitors with the possibility of a waterside landing.

The undersides of floorplates and roof elements extending over the water are illuminated by light reflecting off the surface of the water. The orientation of these surfaces naturally directs reflected natural light towards the interior of the building. The undulating landscape of the roof spans across the whole of the building and is freely developed according to formal considerations. It is developed as an elevation of the building — one which is best viewed from the hills above Bristol. The roof consists of large plate surfaces spanned across a structural grid. The skin material is

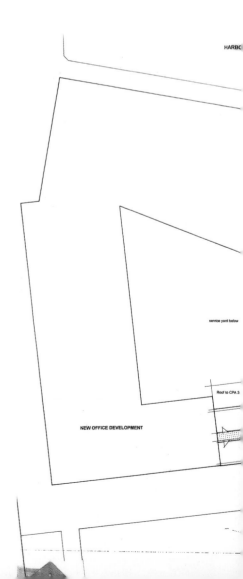

10 Grundriss obere Foyerebene 11 Grundriss Bühnenebene 12 Modellansicht Ost
10 Plan, upper foyer level 11 Plan, stage level 12 Model, view from east

HARBOURSIDE CENTRE | 1996–1998

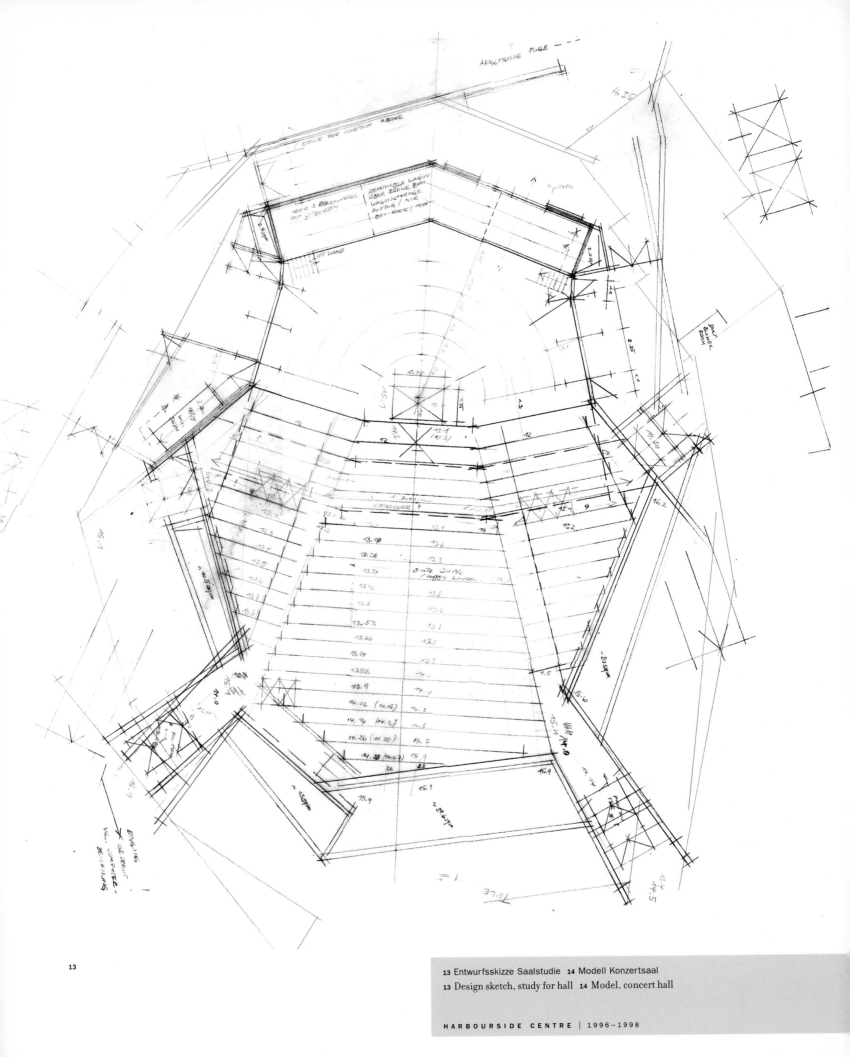

13 Entwurfsskizze Saalstudie **14** Modell Konzertsaal
13 Design sketch, study for hall **14** Model, concert hall

HARBOURSIDE CENTRE | 1996–1998

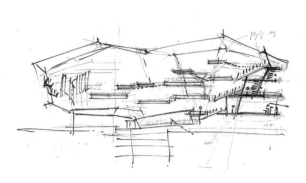

rend, zum Teil durch Farbanstrich gedämpft, wo reflektiertes Licht zu grell wäre. Die Oberfläche verläuft als Reihe von Faltungen, die den Bühnenturm des Tanztheaters in die Dachlandschaft einbeziehen. In die blechverkleidete Dachfläche sind großzügig verglaste Oberlichter eingelassen, die einen kontrollierten Lichteinfall erlauben.

Das Projekt sollte über Lotteriegelder und von der Stadt Bristol finanziert werden. Es war seinerzeit eines der größeren Lotterie-Projekte, das eine Reihe komplexer Verfahren und Präsentationen erforderte.

Wegen finanzieller Probleme des Lotterie-Fonds wurde das Projekt 1999 nach Abschluss der detaillierten Entwurfsplanung eingestellt. ◄

metallic, partly reflective or tempered through the use of color where reflection would otherwise be too severe. The surface develops in a series of folds which conceal the dance theater fly tower within the landscape of the roof. Generous glazed rooflights complement the areas of metallic panels and allow controlled light into both the foyers and performance spaces.

The project is an example of what is commonly referred to as a "Lottery Project" partly financed by the City of Bristol. At the time this was one of the larger Lottery Projects requiring a series of complex submission procedures and presentations.

Due to financial shortfalls within the Lottery Funding, this project was cancelled in 1999. ◄

Chronologie | Chronology 1989–2003

ERWEITERUNG DER DEUTSCHEN BUNDESBANK | EXTENSION OF THE GERMAN FEDERAL BANK
Wettbewerb 1989, 1. Preis. Ausführungsplanung 1989–1992, Planung nicht realisiert
Competition 1989, 1st Prize. Detail Design 1989–1992, not realised
ORT | LOCATION Frankfurt (Main), Germany
AUSLOBER | CLIENT Deutsche Bundesbank, Frankfurt (Main)
ARCHITEKTEN | ARCHITECTS Behnisch & Partner, Büro Reithalle
PROJEKTLEITUNG | PROJECT LEADER Jens Wittfoht

HAUPTVERWALTUNGSGEBÄUDE DER LANDESGIROKASSE AM HOPPENLAU-FRIEDHOF | STATE CLEARING BANK ADMINISTRATION BUILDING AT HOPPENLAU CEMETERY
Wettbewerb 1989, 1. Preis. Vorentwurf 1990, Planung nicht realisiert
Competition 1989, 1st Prize. Preliminary Design 1990, not realised
ORT | LOCATION Stuttgart, Germany
AUSLOBER | CLIENT Landesgirokasse Stuttgart
ARCHITEKTEN | ARCHITECTS Behnisch & Partner, Büro Reithalle
PROJEKTLEITUNG | PROJECT LEADERS Stefan Behnisch, Eberhard Pritzer

TECHNISCHES ZENTRUM DER LANDESZENTRALBANK BAYERN | TECHNICAL CENTER OF THE CENTRAL BANK OF BAVARIA
Wettbewerb 1989, 1. Preis. Ausführungsplanung 1992
Competition 1989, 1st Prize. Detail Design 1992
ORT | LOCATION München | Munich, Germany
AUSLOBER | CLIENT Landeszentralbank in Bayern | Central Bank of Bavaria
ARCHITEKTEN | ARCHITECTS Behnisch & Partner, Büro Innenstadt
PROJEKTLEITUNG | PROJECT LEADERS Petra Behnisch, Stefan Behnisch

FILMPALAST AM OLYMPIAPARK | MOVIE PALACE AT THE OLYMPIC PARK
Gutachten 1990, Vorentwurf
Design study 1990, Preliminary Design
ORT | LOCATION München | Munich, Germany
AUSLOBER | CLIENT Neue-Constantin-Film, München
ARCHITEKTEN | ARCHITECTS Behnisch & Partner, Büro Reithalle
PROJEKTLEITUNG | PROJECT LEADERS Stefan Behnisch, Eberhard Pritzer

SCHÖNRAINBAD | PUBLIC SWIMMING POOL COMPLEX
Wettbewerb 1990, 1. Preis, Vorentwurf 1991
Competition 1990, 1st Prize. Preliminary Design 1991
ORT | LOCATION Reutlingen, Germany
AUSLOBER | CLIENT Stadt Reutlingen
ARCHITEKTEN | ARCHITECTS Behnisch & Partner, Büro Innenstadt
PROJEKTLEITUNG | PROJECT LEADER Ken Radtkey

MEDIAPARK
Wettbewerb 1991, 3. Preis
Competition 1991, 3rd Prize
ORT | LOCATION Köln | Cologne, Germany
ARCHITEKTEN | ARCHITECTS Behnisch & Partner, Büro Innenstadt

DIENSTLEISTUNGSZENTRUM DER LANDESGIROKASSE AM BOLLWERK, HEUTE LBBW | CENTRAL ADMINISTRATION BUILDING FOR THE STATE CLEARING BANK AT THE "BOLLWERK", NOW LBBW
Wettbewerb und Realisierung
Competition and Realisation
ORT | LOCATION Stuttgart, Germany
BAUHERR | CLIENT Landesgirokasse Grundstücksanlagengesellschaft mbH + Co. KG, Stuttgart
ARCHITEKTEN | ARCHITECTS Behnisch, Sabatke, Behnisch
WETTBEWERB | COMPETITION 1991, 1. Preis | 1st Prize
PROJEKTPARTNER UND PROJEKTLEITUNG | PROJECT PARTNER AND PROJECT LEADER Günther Schaller
FARBKONZEPTION | COLOR CONSULTANT Christian Kandzia
LANDSCHAFT MIT | LANDSCAPING WITH Luz Landschaftsarchitektur, Stuttgart
TRAGWERKSPLANUNG/STRUCTURAL ENGINEERING Leonhardt, Andrä und Partner, Beratende Ingenieure VBI GmbH, Stuttgart
HAUSTECHNIK HLS | MECHANICAL ENGINEERING Rentschler und Riedesser Ingenieurgesellschaft mbH für Technik im Bau, Stuttgart
ELEKTROTECHNIK | ELECTRICAL ENGINEERING Ingenieurbüro für Elektrotechnik, Werner Schwarz GmbH, Stuttgart
LICHTPLANUNG | LIGHTING Ingenieurbüro Walter Bamberger, Pfünz
OBJEKTÜBERWACHUNG | SITE SUPERVISION Hans-Joachim Maile, Stuttgart
BRUTTOGESCHOSSFLÄCHE | GROSS 48.000 m² | 48,000 m²
UMBAUTER RAUM | VOLUME 188.000 m³ | 188,000 m³
PLANUNGS- UND BAUZEIT | PLANNING AND CONSTRUCTION 1992−1997
AUSZEICHNUNGEN | AWARDS
1997 Auszeichnung der | Award from the Architektenkammer
1998 The RIBA Award for Architecture
1999 Ausgezeichnet vom | Award from the BDA Baden-Württemberg
        Deutscher Naturstein-Preis. Lobende Erwähnung | Honorable Mention
ADRESSE | ADDRESS Fritz-Elsas-Straße 31; 70174 Stuttgart

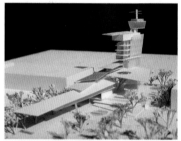

FLUGHAFEN TOWER | AIR TRAFFIC CONTROL SERVICES BUILDING
Wettbewerb 1991, 1. Preis. Planung und Realisierung Behnisch & Partner, Büro Sillenbuch
Competition 1991, 1st Prize. Planning and Realisation by Behnisch & Partner, Büro Sillenbuch
ORT | LOCATION Nürnberg | Nuremberg, Germany
AUSLOBER | CLIENT Flughafen Nürnberg GmbH
ARCHITEKTEN | ARCHITECTS Behnisch & Partner, Büro Innenstadt
AUSZEICHNUNGEN | AWARDS
2000 BDA-Preis Franken Anerkennung

NEUE MESSE | NEW EXHIBITION CENTER
Wettbewerb 1991
Competition 1991
ORT | LOCATION Leipzig, Germany
ARCHITEKTEN | ARCHITECTS Behnisch & Partner, Büro Innenstadt

1992

FLUGHAFEN, TERMINAL-ERWEITERUNG | EXTENSION OF AIRPORT TERMINAL
Wettbewerb 1992, 4. Preis
Competition 1992, 4th Prize
ORT | LOCATION Köln-Bonn | Cologne-Bonn, Germany
ARCHITEKTEN | ARCHITECTS Behnisch & Partner, Büro Innenstadt

NEUORDNUNG DES STADTZENTRUMS | NEW CITY CENTER
Gutachten 1992
Design study 1992
ORT | LOCATION Gera, Germany
ARCHITEKTEN | ARCHITECTS Behnisch & Partner, Büro Innenstadt

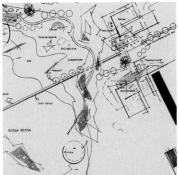

STÄDTEBAULICHER WETTBEWERB HOCHSCHULSTADTTEIL | URBAN PLANNING COMPETITION UNIVERSITY DISTRICT
Wettbewerb 1992
Competition 1992
ORT | LOCATION Lübeck, Germany
ARCHITEKTEN | ARCHITECTS Behnisch & Partner, Büro Innenstadt

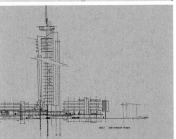

LANDESBAUSPARKASSE | STATE SAVINGS BANK
Wettbewerb 1992
Competition 1992
ORT | LOCATION Potsdam, Germany
ARCHITEKTEN | ARCHITECTS Behnisch & Partner, Büro Innenstadt

INSTITUT DER TECHNISCHEN HOCHSCHULE | INSTITUTE FOR THE TECHNICAL UNIVERSITY
Wettbewerb 1992, 1. Preis (mit Überarbeitung)
Competition 1992, 1st Prize (with revision)
ORT | LOCATION Darmstadt, Germany
ARCHITEKTEN | ARCHITECTS Behnisch & Partner, Büro Innenstadt

ERWEITERUNG DER WIRTSCHAFTSWISSENSCHAFTLICHEN FAKULTÄT | EXTENSION OF THE FACULTY OF ECONOMICS
Wettbewerb 1992, Ankauf
Competition 1992, Purchase
ORT | LOCATION Ingolstadt, Germany
ARCHITEKTEN | ARCHITECTS Behnisch & Partner, Büro Innenstadt

ST. BENNO-GYMNASIUM | ST. BENNO SECONDARY SCHOOL
Wettbewerb und Realisierung
Competition and Realisation
ORT | LOCATION Dresden, Germany
BAUHERR | CLIENT Bistum Dresden-Meißen, Bischöfliches Ordinariat, Dresden
ARCHITEKTEN | ARCHITECTS Behnisch & Behnisch
WETTBEWERB | COMPETITION 1992, 1. Preis | 1st Prize
PROJEKTLEITUNG | PROJECT LEADER Martin Werminghausen
LANDSCHAFT MIT | LANDSCAPING WITH Michaela Noack Landschaftsarchitekten, Dresden
TRAGWERKSPLANUNG | STRUCTURAL ENGINEERING Büro für Baukonstruktionen Fritz Wenzel, Karlsruhe
HAUSTECHNIK HLS | MECHANICAL ENGINEERING Rentschler und Riedesser Ingenieurgesellschaft mbH für Technik im Bau, Stuttgart
ELEKTROTECHNIK | ELECTRICAL ENGINEERING Ingenieurbüro für Elektrotechnik, Werner Schwarz GmbH, Stuttgart
LICHTPLANUNG | LIGHTING Ingenieurbüro Walter Bamberger, Pfünz
FARBEN | COLORS Erich Wiesner, Berlin
BRUTTOGESCHOSSFLÄCHE | GROSS 10.771 m² | 10,771 m²
UMBAUTER RAUM | VOLUME 45.742 m³ | 45,742 m³
EINWEIHUNG | OFFICIAL OPENING 1996
AUSZEICHNUNGEN | AWARDS
1996 Preis des Neuen Sächsischen Kunstvereins e.V. Dresden, Anerkennung | Acknowledgement
1997 Deutscher Architekturpreis. Anerkennung | Acknowledgement
    Special Prize of the Union of Russian Architects. Gold Medal.
    Interarch' Silver medal and diploma Sofia
1998 The RIBA Award for Architecture
    BDA-Preis Sachsen. Anerkennung | Acknowledgement
ADRESSE | ADDRESS Pillnitzer Straße 39; 01069 Dresden

HAUPTVERWALTUNGSGEBÄUDE DER LANDESVERSICHERUNGSANSTALT SCHLESWIG-HOLSTEIN (LVA 2000) |
ADMINISTRATION BUILDING FOR THE STATE INSURANCE AGENCY SCHLESWIG-HOLSTEIN (LVA 2000)
Wettbewerb und Realisierung
Competition and Realisation
ORT | LOCATION Lübeck, Germany
BAUHERR | CLIENT Landesversicherungsanstalt Schleswig-Holstein, Lübeck
ARCHITEKTEN | ARCHITECTS Behnisch & Partner, Büro Innenstadt
WETTBEWERB | COMPETITION 1992, 1. Preis | 1st Prize
FERTIGSTELLUNG | COMPLETION 1997
PROJEKTLEITUNG | PROJECT LEADER Gunnar Ramsfjell
FARBKONZEPTION | COLOR CONSULTANT Christian Kandzia
LANDSCHAFT MIT | LANDSCAPING WITH WES & Partner Landschaftsarchitekten, Hamburg
TRAGWERKSPLANUNG | STRUCTURAL ENGINEERING Weischede und Partner Planungen im Bauwesen GmbH, Stuttgart; Wetzel & von Seht Ingenieurbüro für Bauwesen, Hamburg
HAUSTECHNIK HLS | MECHANICAL ENGINEERING Rentschler und Riedesser Ingenieurgesellschaft mbH für Technik im Bau, Stuttgart
ELEKTROTECHNIK, OBJEKTÜBERWACHUNG, HAUSTECHNIK | ELECTRICAL ENGINEERING, SITE SUPERVISION, MECHANICAL ENGINEERING Planungsgruppe KMO Ingenieurgesellschaft mbH, Eutin
OBJEKTÜBERWACHUNG MIT | SITE SUPERVISION WITH Cronauer Beratung + Planung, München
BRUTTOGESCHOSSFLÄCHE | GROSS 37.109 m² | 37,109 m²
UMBAUTER RAUM | VOLUME 128.102 m³ | 128,102 m³
AUSZEICHNUNGEN | AWARDS
1998 The RIBA Award for Architecture
1999 BDA-Preis Schleswig-Holstein
2002 Trophée Sommet de la Terre et Bâtiment Paris
ADRESSE | ADDRESS
Ziegelstraße 150; 23558 Lübeck

1993

ROHSTOFFRÜCKGEWINNUNGSZENTRUM | RAW MATERIAL RECOVERY CENTER
Wettbewerb 1993, 2. Preis
Competition 1993, 2nd Prize
ORT | LOCATION Herten, Germany
ARCHITEKTEN | ARCHITECTS Behnisch & Partner, Büro Innenstadt

STÄDTEBAULICHER UND IDEENWETTBEWERB SPARKASSE AM BAHNHOFSGELÄNDE | URBAN PLANNING AND IDEAS COMPETITION SAVINGS BANK, RAILWAY AREA
Wettbewerb 1993, 5. Preis
Competition 1993, 5th Prize
ORT | LOCATION Fürstenfeldbruck, Germany
ARCHITEKTEN | ARCHITECTS Behnisch & Partner, Büro Innenstadt

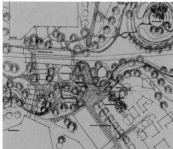

ZENTRALE HALTESTELLE ÖFFENTLICHER NAHVERKEHR | PUBLIC TRANSPORT CENTRAL STATION
Wettbewerb 1993
Competition 1993
ORT | LOCATION Oberhausen, Germany
ARCHITEKTEN | ARCHITECTS Behnisch & Partner, Büro Innenstadt

BAUREFERAT DER LANDESHAUPTSTADT | BUILDING DEPARTMENT OF THE STATE CAPITAL
Wettbewerb 1993, 4. Preis
Competition 1993, 4th Prize
ORT | LOCATION München | Munich, Germany
ARCHITEKTEN | ARCHITECTS Behnisch & Partner, Büro Innenstadt

IDEENWETTBEWERB FÜR DEN WESTLICHEN ANSCHLUSS DER STADTMITTE | IDEAS COMPETITION WESTERN URBAN CONNECTION TO THE CITY CENTER

Wettbewerb 1993, Preis ohne Rangfolge
Competition 1993, Prize without ranking
ORT | LOCATION Bremerhaven, Germany
ARCHITEKTEN | ARCHITECTS Behnisch & Partner, Büro Innenstadt

INSTITUT FÜR FORST- UND NATURFORSCHUNG (I.B.N.), HEUTE ALTERRA | INSTITUTE FOR FORESTRY AND NATURE RESEARCH (I.B.N.), NOW ALTERRA

Wettbewerb und Realisierung
Competition and Realisation
ORT | LOCATION Wageningen, Niederlande | Netherlands
BAUHERR | CLIENT Rijksgebouwdienst Direktie Oost Arnheim, Niederlande
ARCHITEKTEN | ARCHITECTS Behnisch & Behnisch
WETTBEWERB | COMPETITION 1993, 1. Preis | 1st Prize
FERTIGSTELLUNG | COMPLETION 1998
PROJEKTLEITUNG | PROJECT LEADERS Ton Gilissen, Ken Radtkey
LANDSCHAFT MIT | LANDSCAPING WITH Copijn Garten und Landschaftsarchitekten/Architects: bv, Utrecht, Niederlande (Atrien); Van Hees, Garten und Landschaftsarchitektur, Gouda, Niederlande (Außengarten)
TRAGWERKSPLANUNG | STRUCTURAL ENGINEERING Aronsohn V.O.F., Amsterdam
HAUSTECHNIK HLS | MECHANICAL ENGINEERING Deerns R.I., Rijkswijk
BAUPHYSIK UND KLIMAKONZEPT | BUILDING PHYSICS AND ENERGY STRATEGY Fraunhofer-Institut, Stuttgart
KUNST | ART Michael Singer, USA; Krijn Giessen
BRUTTOGESCHOSSFLÄCHE OHNE ATRIEN | GROSS WITHOUT ATRIA 11.250 m² | 11,250 m²
UMBAUTER RAUM INKL. ATRIEN | VOLUME INCL. ATRIA 70.200 m³ | 70,200 m³
AUSZEICHNUNGEN | AWARDS
2000 Finalist für Architectural Record | Business Week Award, USA
2001 Honorable Mention. Bienal Miami + Beach
2002 Trophée Sommet de la Terre et Bâtiment Paris
ADRESSE | ADDRESS Droevendaals Steeg 3a, 6708 Wageningen, Niederlande | Netherlands

IDEENWETTBEWERB WIENER PLATZ | IDEAS COMPETITION WIENER PLATZ

Wettbewerb 1993
Competition 1993
ORT | LOCATION Dresden, Germany
ARCHITEKTEN | ARCHITECTS Behnisch & Partner, Büro Innenstadt

1994

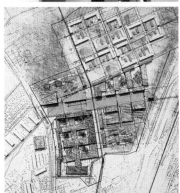

ERWEITERUNG DER TECHNISCHEN UNIVERSITÄT CHEMNITZ-ZWICKAU | EXTENSION OF THE TECHNICAL UNIVERSITY OF CHEMNITZ-ZWICKAU

Wettbewerb 1994
Competition 1994
ORT | LOCATION Chemnitz, Germany
ARCHITEKTEN | ARCHITECTS Behnisch & Partner, Büro Innenstadt

IDEEN- UND REALISIERUNGSWETTBEWERB TECHNISCHE UNIVERSITÄT | COMPETITION TECHNICAL UNIVERSITY

Wettbewerb 1994, 2. Preis
Competition 1994, 2nd Prize
ORT | LOCATION Dresden, Germany
ARCHITEKTEN | ARCHITECTS Behnisch & Partner, Büro Innenstadt

UMBAU DES BÜROGEBÄUDES DER BAYERISCHEN VEREINSBANK | RECONSTRUCTION OF THE OFFICE BUILDING OF THE BAVARIAN COOPERATIVE BANK
Direktauftrag
Direct Commission
ORT | LOCATION Stuttgart, Germany
BAUHERR | CLIENT Bayerische Vereinsbank AG, München
FERTIGSTELLUNG | COMPLETION 1996
ARCHITEKTEN | ARCHITECTS Behnisch Sabatke Behnisch
PROJEKTLEITUNG | PROJECT LEADER Carmen Lenz
FARBKONZEPTION | COLOR CONSULTANT Christian Kandzia
BRUTTOGESCHOSSFLÄCHE | GROSS 1.358 m² | 1,358 m²
UMBAUTER RAUM | VOLUME 4.401 m³ | 4,401 m³
AUSZEICHNUNGEN | AWARDS
1996 Ausgezeichnet vom/Award from the BDA Baden-Württemberg
1997 Auszeichnung der/Award from the Architektenkammer
ADRESSE | ADDRESS Kronprinzstraße 22; 70173 Stuttgart

1995

REALISIERUNGSWETTBEWERB WASSER- UND SCHIFFFAHRTSDIREKTION OST | COMPETITION WATER AND SHIPPING AGENCY EAST
Wettbewerb 1995
Competition 1995
ORT | LOCATION Magdeburg, Germany
ARCHITEKTEN | ARCHITECTS Behnisch & Behnisch

IDEENWETTBEWERB INTERNATIONALE GARTENAUSSTELLUNG | IDEAS COMPETITION INTERNATIONAL GARDEN SHOW
Wettbewerb 1995
Competition 1995
ORT | LOCATION Dresden, Germany
ARCHITEKTEN | ARCHITECTS Behnisch & Behnisch

INSTITUT FÜR TELEKOMMUNIKATION VON PORTUGAL | INSTITUTE OF TELECOMMUNICATIONS OF PORTUGAL
Wettbewerb 1995
Competition 1995
ORT | LOCATION Barcarena, Portugal
ARCHITEKTEN | ARCHITECTS Behnisch & Behnisch

MUSICON KONZERTHALLE | MUSICON CONCERT HALL
Wettbewerb 1995, 2. Preis
Competition 1995, 2nd Prize
ORT | LOCATION Bremen, Germany
ARCHITEKTEN | ARCHITECTS Behnisch & Behnisch

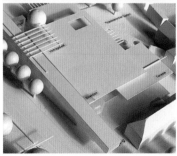

THÜRINGER UNIVERSITÄTS- UND LANDESBIBLIOTHEK | UNIVERSITY AND STATE LIBRARY OF THURINGIA
Wettbewerb 1995, 2. Preis
Competition 1995, 2nd Prize
ORT | LOCATION Jena, Germany
ARCHITEKTEN | ARCHITECTS Behnisch & Behnisch

KLINIKUM | HOSPITAL
Wettbewerb 1996
Competition 1996
ORT | LOCATION Greifswald, Germany
ARCHITEKTEN | ARCHITECTS Behnisch & Behnisch

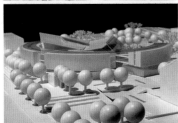

SÄCHSISCHE LANDESBIBLIOTHEK, STAATS- UND UNIVERSITÄTSBIBLIOTHEK | STATE, NATIONAL AND UNIVERSITY LIBRARY OF SAXONY
Wettbewerb 1996
Competition 1996
ORT | LOCATION Dresden, Germany
ARCHITEKTEN | ARCHITECTS Behnisch & Behnisch

NEUBAU VEREINIGTE SPEZIALMÖBELFABRIKEN (VS) – BÜRO UND AUSSTELLUNGSGEBÄUDE | NEW DEVELOPMENT FOR THE VEREINIGTE SPEZIALMÖBELFABRIKEN (VS) – OFFICE AND EXHIBITION BUILDING
Gutachten und Realisierung
Design study and Realisation
ORT | LOCATION Tauberbischofsheim, Germany
BAUHERR | CLIENT VS – Vereinigte Spezialmöbelfabriken GmbH & Co., Tauberbischofsheim
ARCHITEKTEN | ARCHITECTS Behnisch, Behnisch & Partner
GUTACHTERVERFAHREN | EXPERTISE 1996
FERTIGSTELLUNG | COMPLETION 1998
PROJEKTLEITUNG | PROJECT LEADERS Volker Biermann, Dieter Ludwig
FARBKONZEPTION | COLOR CONSULTANT Christian Kandzia
LANDSCHAFT MIT | LANDSCAPING WITH Luz Landschaftsarchitektur, Stuttgart
TRAGWERKSPLANUNG UND OBJEKTÜBERWACHUNG | STRUCTURAL ENGINEERING AND SITE SUPERVISION
Gey + Partner, Tauberbischofsheim
ELEKTROTECHNIK | ELECTRICAL ENGINEERING Ingenieurbüro für Elektrotechnik, Werner Schwarz GmbH, Stuttgart
HAUSTECHNIK HLS | MECHANICAL ENGINEERING Datzer und Partner beratende Ingenieure, Würzburg
BRUTTOGESCHOSSFLÄCHE | GROSS 250 m² | 250 m²
UMBAUTER RAUM | VOLUME 32.315 m³ | 32,315 m³
AUSZEICHNUNGEN | AWARDS
1999 Ausgezeichnet vom/Award from the BDA Baden-Württemberg
ADRESSE | ADDRESS Hochhäuser Straße 8, 97941 Tauberbischofsheim, Deutschland | Germany

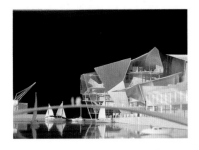

HARBOURSIDE CENTRE – ZENTRUM FÜR DARSTELLENDE KÜNSTE – KONZERTHALLE UND TANZTHEATER | THE HARBOURSIDE CENTRE FOR THE PERFORMING ARTS – CONCERT HALL AND DANCE THEATRE
Wettbewerb und Planung, nicht realisiert
Competition and Planning, not realised
ORT | LOCATION Bristol, UK
BAUHERR | CLIENT The Harbourside Centre Ltd.
ARCHITEKTEN | ARCHITECTS Behnisch & Behnisch
WETTBEWERB | COMPETITION 1996, 1. Preis | 1st Prize
PLANUNG | PLANNING 1997–1998
PROJEKTLEITUNG | PROJECT LEADER David Cook
TRAGWERKSPLANUNG | STRUCTURAL ENGINEERING Buro Happold Bath
ENERGIEKONZEPT, HAUSTECHNIK HLS | ENERGY STRATEGY, MECHANICAL ENGINEERING Max Fordham & Partners, London
AKUSTIK | ACOUSTICS Müller BBM GmbH, Schalltechnisches Beratungsbüro, Planegg
THEATERPLANUNG | THEATER CONSULTANT Theatre Project Consultants, London

NEUBAU VERTRIEBSCENTER FÜR ERNESTING'S FAMILY | NEW SALES CENTER FOR ERNESTING'S FAMILY
Wettbewerb 1996
Competition 1996
ORT | LOCATION Coesfeld-Lette, Germany
ARCHITEKTEN | ARCHITECTS Behnisch & Behnisch

MUSEUM DER PHANTASIE, SAMMLUNG BUCHHEIM | MUSEUM OF FANTASY, BUCHHEIM COLLECTION
Wettbewerb und Realisierung
Competition and Realisation
ORT | LOCATION Bernried am Starnberger See, Germany
BAUHERR | CLIENT Freistaat Bayern, vertreten durch das Staatliche Hochbauamt München; Roland Ernst, Heidelberg
ARCHITEKTEN | ARCHITECTS Behnisch, Behnisch & Partner
WETTBEWERB | COMPETITION 1996, 1. Preis | 1st Prize
FERTIGSTELLUNG | COMPLETION 2001
PROJEKTPARTNER UND PROJEKTLEITER | PROJECT PARTNER AND PROJECT LEADER Martin Werminghausen
LANDSCHAFT MIT | LANDSCAPING WITH Luz Landschaftsarchitektur, Stuttgart
TRAGWERKSPLANUNG | STRUCTURAL ENGINEERING Pfefferkorn + Partner, Stuttgart
LICHTPLANUNG SONDERBEREICHE | LIGHTING SPECIAL AREAS Bartenbach Lichtlabor GmbH, Aldrans/Innsbruck
HAUSTECHNIK HLS | MECHANICAL ENGINEERING Ingenieurbüro Schreiber, Ulm
ELEKTROTECHNIK | ELECTRICAL ENGINEERING Ingenieurbüro für Elektrotechnik, Werner Schwarz GmbH, Stuttgart
BRUTTOGESCHOSSFLÄCHE | GROSS 6.450 m² | 6,450m²
UMBAUTER RAUM | VOLUME 30.850 m³ | 30,850m³
AUSZEICHNUNGEN | AWARDS
2001 BDA Preis Bayern
2002 Jurypreis des Wessobrunner Architekturpreises
ADRESSE | ADDRESS Am Hirschgarten 1, 82347 Bernried, Deutschland | Germany

BERUFSSCHULE | VOCATIONAL SCHOOL
Wettbewerb 1996, 5. Preis
Competition 1996, 5. Prize
ORT | LOCATION Meißen, Germany
ARCHITEKTEN | ARCHITECTS Behnisch & Behnisch

SCHWIMMHALLE, LEIPZIG-GRÜNAU | INDOOR POOL COMPLEX, LEIPZIG-GRÜNAU
Wettbewerb und Realisierung
Competition and Realisation
ORT | LOCATION Leipzig-Grünau, Germany
BAUHERR | CLIENT Sport- und Bäderamt Leipzig, vertreten durch das Hochbauamt
ARCHITEKTEN | ARCHITECTS Behnisch, Behnisch & Partner
WETTBEWERB | COMPETITION 1996
FERTIGSTELLUNG | COMPLETION 1999
PROJEKTLEITUNG | PROJECT LEADER Andrea Crumbach, Christine Stroh-Mocek
FARBKONZEPTION | COLOR CONSULTANT Christian Kandzia
LANDSCHAFT | LANDSCAPING Luz Landschaftsarchitektur, Stuttgart
TRAGWERKSPLANUNG | STRUCTURAL ENGINEERING Weischede + Partner, Stuttgart
HAUSTECHNIK HLS | MECHANICAL ENGINEERING Brendel Ingenieure, Leipzig
ELEKTROTECHNIK UND LICHTPLANUNG | ELECTRICAL ENGINEERING AND LIGHTING Zimmermann + Schrage, Leipzig, Ingenieurbüro Walter Bamberger, Pfünz
ENERGIEKONZEPT | ENERGY STRATEGY Transsolar Energietechnik GmbH, Stuttgart
WASSERFLÄCHE | WATER BASINS 675 m² | 675m²
BRUTTOGESCHOSSFLÄCHE | GROSS 5.160 m² | 5,160m²
UMBAUTER RAUM | VOLUME 23.000 m³ | 23,000m³
ADRESSE | ADDRESS Prager Straße 20–28, 04103 Leipzig, Deutschland | Germany

WERKSTATT FÜR BEHINDERTE | WORKSHOP FOR THE DISABLED
Wettbewerb 1996, 2. Preis
Competition 1996, 2nd Prize
ORT | LOCATION Köthen, Germany
ARCHITEKTEN | ARCHITECTS Behnisch & Behnisch

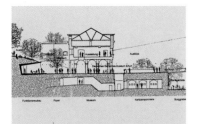

GUTACHTEN DEUTSCHES GARTENBAUMUSEUM | EXPERTISE GERMAN HORTICULTURE MUSEUM
Gutachten 1996, 1. Preis
Design study 1996, 1st Prize
ORT | LOCATION Erfurt, Germany
ARCHITEKTEN | ARCHITECTS Behnisch & Behnisch

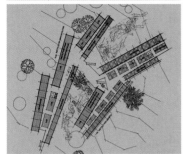

NEUBAU FACHBEREICH BIOLOGIE DER UNIVERSITÄT | NEW UNIVERSITY BUILDING FOR THE FACULTY OF BIOLOGY
Wettbewerb 1996, Ankauf
Competition 1996, Purchase
ORT | LOCATION Halle, Germany
ARCHITEKTEN | ARCHITECTS Behnisch & Behnisch

NORDDEUTSCHE LANDESBANK AM FRIEDRICHSWALL (NORD/LB) | NORTH GERMAN STATE CLEARING BANK ON FRIEDRICHSWALL (NORD/LB)
Wettbewerb und Realisierung
Competition and Realisation
ORT | LOCATION Hannover | Hanover, Germany
AUFTRAGGEBER | CLIENT Norddeutsche Landesbank, Hannover; Baubetreuung/Project Management NILEG, Hannover
ARCHITEKTEN | ARCHITECTS Behnisch, Behnisch & Partner
WETTBEWERB | COMPETITION 1996, 1. Preis | 1st Prize
FERTIGSTELLUNG | COMPLETION 2002
PROJEKTLEITUNG | PROJECT LEADERS Martin Haas, Jörn Genkel
LANDSCHAFT MIT | LANDSCAPING WITH Nagel & Schonhoff, Hannover
TRAGWERKSPLANUNG | STRUCTURAL ENGINEERING Arge Tragwerksplanung: Wetzel & von Seht Ingenieurbüro für Bauwesen, Hamburg, Pfefferkorn + Partner, Stuttgart
ENERGIEKONZEPT | ENERGY STRATEGY Transsolar Energietechnik GmbH, Stuttgart
HAUSTECHNIK HLS | MECHANICAL/ELECTRICAL ENGINEERING Arge TGA; Becker + Becker, Braunschweig; Lindhorst, Braunschweig; Grabe, Hannover; Taube-Goerz-Liegat, Hannover; Federführung: Ingenieurbüro Gierke, Braunschweig
LICHTTECHNIK/TAGESLICHTTECHNIK | LIGHTING Bartenbach Lichtlabor GmbH, Aldrans/Innsbruck
FARBKONZEPTION | COLOR CONSULTANT Christian Kandzia
BRUTTOGESCHOSSFLÄCHE | GROSS 75.000 m² | 75,000 m²
UMBAUTER RAUM | VOLUME 295.000 m³ | 295,000 m³
BÜROARBEITSPLÄTZE | WORK PLACES 1.500 | 1,500
STELLPLÄTZE | PARKING SPACES 500
ADRESSE | ADDRESS Am Friedrichswall 10, 30159 Hannover, Deutschland | Germany

NEUBAU LANDESZENTRALBANK | NEW BUILDING FOR THE CENTRAL BANK OF SAXONY
Wettbewerb 1996, Ankauf
Competition 1996, Purchase
ORT | LOCATION Chemnitz, Germany
ARCHITEKTEN | ARCHITECTS Behnisch & Behnisch

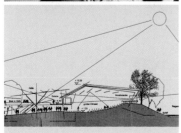

HÖRSAALZENTRUM FÜR DIE MEDIZINUNIVERSITÄT UND DIE FACHHOCHSCHULE | LECTURE HALL CENTER FOR MEDICAL UNIVERSITY AND TECHNICAL COLLEGE
Wettbewerb 1996, 2. Preis
Competition 1996, 2nd Prize
ORT | LOCATION Lübeck, Germany
ARCHITEKTEN | ARCHITECTS Behnisch & Behnisch

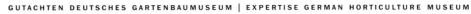

NATIONAL- UND PROVINZIALARCHIVE | NATIONAL AND PROVINCIAL ARCHIVES
Wettbewerb und Planung, nicht realisiert
Competition and Planning, not realised
ORT | LOCATION Kopenhagen, Dänemark | Copenhagen, Denmark
AUFTRAGGEBER | CLIENT Slots- og Ejendomsstyrelsen (SES), Kopenhagen
NUTZER | USER Statens Arkiver, Rigsarkivet, Kopenhagen
ARCHITEKTEN UND GENERALPLANER | ARCHITECTS AND GENERAL PLANNER Behnisch, Behnisch & Partner
WETTBEWERB | COMPETITION 1996
PLANUNG | PLANNING 1998–2002
PROJEKTPARTNER UND PROJEKTLEITUNG | PROJECT PARTNER AND PROJECT LEADER David Cook
PROJEKTLEITUNG | PROJECT LEADER Ton Gilissen
PARTNERARCHITEKT IN DÄNEMARK | PARTNER ARCHITECT IN DENMARK Niels Fuglsang ApS, Kopenhagen
LANDSCHAFT MIT | LANDSCAPING WITH WES + Partner, Hamburg
TRAGWERKSPLANUNG | STRUCTURAL ENGINEERING Cowi Consulting Engineers, Lyngby
HLS MIT | MECHANICAL ENGINEERING WITH Cowi Consulting, Lyngby, Dänemark, with Birch & Krogboe Consulting Engineers, Virum
PROGRAMMFLÄCHE | 54.000 m² | 54,000 m²
UMBAUTER RAUM | VOLUME 243.750 m³ | 243,750 m³
ADRESSE | ADDRESS Grønjordsvej Kopenhagen-Ørestad, Dänemark | Denmark

BUNDESGARTENSCHAU | NATIONAL HORTICULTURAL SHOW
Wettbewerb 1997, Ankauf
Competition 1997, Purchase
ORT | LOCATION Potsdam, Germany
ARCHITEKTEN | ARCHITECTS Behnisch, Behnisch & Partner

HAUPTVERWALTUNG DER LANDESVERSICHERUNGSANSTALT | HEADQUARTERS OF THE STATE INSURANCE AGENCY
Wettbewerb 1997, 2. Preis
Competition 1997, 2nd Prize
ORT | LOCATION Hamburg, Germany
ARCHITEKTEN | ARCHITECTS Behnisch, Behnisch & Partner

TECHNOLOGIEGEBÄUDE DER TU ILMENAU | TECHNOLOGY BUILDING FOR THE TECHNICAL UNIVERSITY OF ILMENAU
Wettbewerb und Realisierung
Competition and Realisation
ORT | LOCATION Ilmenau, Germany
BAUHERR | CLIENT Thüringer Finanzministerium, vertreten durch das Staatsbauamt Erfurt
ARCHITEKTEN | ARCHITECTS Behnisch, Behnisch & Partner
VERHANDLUNGSVERFAHREN | COMPETITIVE INTERVIEW 1997
FERTIGSTELLUNG | COMPLETION 2002
PROJEKTLEITUNG | PROJECT LEADERS Andreas Ditschuneit, Wibke Dirksen, Roland Stölzle
OBJEKTÜBERWACHUNG MIT | SITE SUPERVISION WITH Winkler + Dehnel, Erfurt
LANDSCHAFT MIT | LANDSCAPING WITH Stock & Partner, Jena
TRAGWERKSPLANUNG | STRUCTURAL ENGINEERING Leonhardt, Andrä und Partner; Beratende Ingenieure VBI GmbH, Erfurt; Büro für Baudynamik GmbH, Stuttgart
HAUS- UND LABORTECHNIK | MECHANICAL ENGINEERING AND LABORATORY TECHNOLOGY CRC - Clean Room Consulting GmbH, Freiburg
BRUTTOGESCHOSSFLÄCHE | GROSS 6.000 m² | 6,000 m²
UMBAUTER RAUM | VOLUME 19.877 m³ | 19,877 m³
ADRESSE | ADDRESS Gustav-Kirchhoff-Straße 7, 98693 Ilmenau, Deutschland | Germany

MESSEGELÄNDE, HALLE 8/9 | EXHIBITION CENTER, HALL 8/9
Wettbewerb 1997
Competition 1997
ORT | LOCATION
Hannover | Hanover, Germany
ARCHITEKTEN | ARCHITECTS
Behnisch, Behnisch & Partner

FREIBAD | OPEN-AIR SWIMMING POOL COMPLEX
Wettbewerb 1997
Competition 1997
ORT | LOCATION Deggendorf, Germany
ARCHITEKTEN | ARCHITECTS Behnisch, Behnisch & Partner

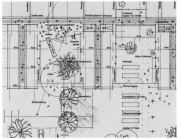

ZENTRUM FÜR ENERGIE UND TECHNIK | CENTER FOR ENERGY AND TECHNOLOGY
Wettbewerb 1997
Competition 1997
ORT | LOCATION Rendsburg, Germany
ARCHITEKTEN | ARCHITECTS Behnisch, Behnisch & Partner

SYNAGOGE | SYNAGOGUE
Wettbewerb 1997
Competition 1997
ORT | LOCATION Dresden, Germany
ARCHITEKTEN | ARCHITECTS Behnisch, Behnisch & Partner

KOMBIBAD | SWIMMING POOL COMPLEX
Wettbewerb 1997, 2. Preis
Competition 1997, 2nd Prize
ORT | LOCATION Nürtingen, Germany
ARCHITEKTEN | ARCHITECTS Behnisch, Behnisch & Partner

UNIVERSITÄTSGEBÄUDE, FAKULTÄT DER GEISTESWISSENSCHAFTEN | UNIVERSITY BUILDING,
FACULTY OF HUMANITIES
Wettbewerb 1997
Competition 1997
ORT | LOCATION Leipzig, Germany
ARCHITEKTEN | ARCHITECTS Behnisch, Behnisch & Partner

KINDERTAGESSTÄTTE DES DEUTSCHEN BUNDESTAGES IN BERLIN | CHILDREN'S DAY CARE CENTER,
GERMAN PARLIAMENT IN BERLIN
Wettbewerb 1997, 2. Preis
Competition 1997, 2nd Prize
ORT | LOCATION Berlin, Germany
ARCHITEKTEN | ARCHITECTS Behnisch, Behnisch & Partner

CONSTANTINI MUSEUM
Wettbewerb 1997
Competition 1997
ORT | LOCATION
Buenos Aires, Argentinien | Buenos Aires, Argentina
ARCHITEKTEN | ARCHITECTS
Behnisch, Behnisch & Partner

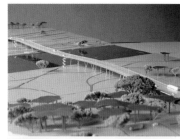

NEUE ELBBRÜCKE | NEW ELBE BRIDGE
Wettbewerb 1997
Competition 1997
ORT | LOCATION Dresden, Germany
ARCHITEKTEN | ARCHITECTS Behnisch, Behnisch & Partner

INSTITUT DE SCIENCE ET D'INGÉNIERIE SUPRAMOLÉCULAIRES | INSTITUTE OF SCIENCE AND SUPRA-MOLECULAR ENGINEERING
Wettbewerb 1998
Competition 1998
ORT | LOCATION Straßburg, Frankreich | Strasbourg, France
ARCHITEKTEN | ARCHITECTS Behnisch, Behnisch & Partner

ERWEITERUNG GEMEINDEZENTRUM | EXTENSION OF COMMUNITY CENTER
Wettbewerb 1998, 1. Preis. Behnisch, Behnisch & Partner
Competition 1998, 1st Prize. Behnisch, Behnisch & Partner
FERTIGSTELLUNG | COMPLETION 2001
ORT | LOCATION Radebeul, Germany
ARCHITEKTEN | ARCHITECTS Günter Behnisch und Gerald Staib

GESAMTSCHULE AREAL MOLTKEBAHNHOF | COMPREHENSIVE SCHOOL "AREAL MOLTKEBAHNHOF"
Wettbewerb 1998, 3. Preis
Competition 1998, 3rd Prize
ORT | LOCATION Aachen, Germany
ARCHITEKTEN | ARCHITECTS Behnisch, Behnisch & Partner

»AU-VISION« – STADTPLANUNG | URBAN REDEVELOPMENT
Wettbewerb 1998
Competition 1998
ORT | LOCATION Leoben, Austria
ARCHITEKTEN | ARCHITECTS Behnisch, Behnisch & Partner

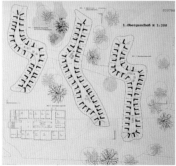

THÜRINGER MINISTERIUM FÜR LANDWIRTSCHAFT, NATURSCHUTZ UND UMWELT | MINISTRY OF AGRICULTURE, NATURE CONSERVATION AND ENVIRONMENT OF THE STATE OF THURINGIA
Wettbewerb 1998
Competition 1998
ORT | LOCATION Erfurt, Germany
ARCHITEKTEN | ARCHITECTS Behnisch, Behnisch & Partner

WISSENSCHAFTSZENTRUM | SCIENCE CENTER
Wettbewerb 1998
Competition 1998
ORT | LOCATION Göteborg, Schweden | Gothenburg, Sweden
ARCHITEKTEN | ARCHITECTS Behnisch, Behnisch & Partner

KONGRESSZENTRUM | CONGRESS CENTER
Wettbewerb 1998
Competition 1998
ORT | LOCATION Rom, Italien | Rome, Italy
ARCHITEKTEN | ARCHITECTS Behnisch, Behnisch & Partner

GRUNDSCHULE PANZERWIESE | PRIMARY SCHOOL PANZERWIESE
Wettbewerb 1999, 5. Preis
Competition 1999, 5th Prize
ORT | LOCATION München | Munich, Germany
ARCHITEKTEN | ARCHITECTS Behnisch, Behnisch & Partner

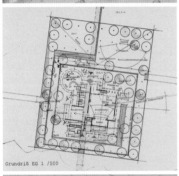

KULTUR- UND BÜRGERHAUS | CULTURAL AND COMMUNITY CENTER
Wettbewerb 1999
Competition 1999
ORT | LOCATION Denzlingen, Germany
ARCHITEKTEN | ARCHITECTS Behnisch, Behnisch & Partner

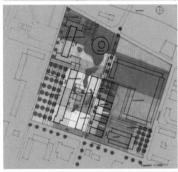

HOCHSCHULE FÜR TECHNIK UND WIRTSCHAFT | COLLEGE OF TECHNOLOGY AND ECONOMY
Wettbewerb 1999
Competition 1999
ORT | LOCATION Dresden, Germany
ARCHITEKTEN | ARCHITECTS Behnisch, Behnisch & Partner

NEUBAU DER ENTORY AG | NEW ADMINISTRATION BUILDING OF ENTORY AG
Wettbewerb und Realisierung
Competition and Realisation
ORT | LOCATION Ettlingen, Germany
AUFTRAGGEBER | CLIENT LVM Lebensversicherungs-AG, Münster
NUTZER | USER entory AG, Karlsbad
ARCHITEKTEN UND GENERALPLANER | ARCHITECTS AND GENERAL PLANER Behnisch, Behnisch & Partner
WETTBEWERB | COMPETITION 1999, 1. Preis | 1st Prize
FERTIGSTELLUNG | COMPLETION 2003
PROJEKTLEITUNG | PROJECT LEADER Christoph Mischke
FARBKONZEPTION | COLOR CONSULTANT Christian Kandzia
OBJEKTÜBERWACHUNG MIT | SITE SUPERVISION WITH Architekturbüro Wörner, Stuttgart
FREIANLAGEN | LANDSCAPING Stötzer-Neher Landschaftsarchitekten, Sindelfingen
TRAGWERKSPLANUNG | STRUCTURAL ENGINEERING Buschlinger + Partner GmbH, Ingenieurbüro für Baustatik, Haßloch
ENERGIEKONZEPT | ENERGY STRATEGY Planungsbüro Dr. Dippel, Vaihingen (Enz)
HAUSTECHNIK HLS | MECHANICAL ENGINEERING IBS Ingenieurbüro Schuler GmbH, Bietigheim-Bissingen
BRUTTOGESCHOSSFLÄCHE | GROSS 11.160 m² | 11,160 m²
UMBAUTER RAUM | VOLUME 35.000 m³ | 35,000 m³
BÜROARBEITSPLÄTZE | OFFICE WORK PLACES 350
STELLPLÄTZE | PARKING SPACES 200
ADRESSE | ADDRESS Ludwig-Erhard-Straße 2, 76275 Ettlingen, Deutschland | Germany

LANDESMESSE BADEN-WÜRTTEMBERG | EXHIBITION CENTER OF THE STATE OF BADEN-WÜRTTEMBERG
Wettbewerb 1999, 2. Phase Weiterbearbeitung
Competition 1999, admitted to 2nd phase
ORT | LOCATION Stuttgart, Germany
AUSLOBER | CLIENT Projektgesellschaft Neue Messe GmbH & Co. KG, Stuttgart
ARCHITEKTEN | ARCHITECTS Behnisch, Behnisch & Partner

WORLD INTELLECTUAL PROPERTY ORGANIZATION (WIPO) — VERWALTUNGSGEBÄUDE MIT KONFERENZZENTRUM | ADMINISTRATION BUILDING WITH CONFERENCE CENTER
Wettbewerb und Realisierung
Competition and Realisation
ORT | LOCATION Genf, Schweiz | Geneva, Switzerland
BAUHERR | CLIENT Organisation Mondiale de la Propriété Intellectuelle, Genf (OMPI)
ARCHITEKTEN | ARCHITECTS Behnisch, Behnisch & Partner
WETTBEWERB | COMPETITION 1999, 1. Preis | 1st Prize
BAUBEGINN | START OF CONSTRUCTION 2003
VORAUSSICHTLICHE FERTIGSTELLUNG | SCHEDULED FOR COMPLETION 2005
PROJEKTLEITUNG | PROJECT LEADER Stefan Rappold
LANDSCHAFT MIT | LANDSCAPING WITH Oxalis, Veyrier, Schweiz; LOG ID, Tübingen
TRAGWERKSPLANUNG | STRUCTURAL ENGINEERING Schlaich, Bergermann & Partner, Stuttgart; Tremblet S.A., Genf
Erricos Lygdopoulos, Genf
KLIMAKONZEPTION | ENERGY STRATEGY Transsolar Energietechnik GmbH, Stuttgart
HAUSTECHNIK HLS | MECHANICAL ENGINEERING Transsolar Energietechnik GmbH, Stuttgart;
Sorane S.A., Lausanne, Schweiz; Riedweg & Gendre S.A., Genf
ELEKTROTECHNIK | ELECTRICAL ENGINEERING Amstein + Walthert S.A., Genf, Schweiz; t.e. électricité SA, Genf
t.e. sanitaire SA, Genf
LICHTPLANUNG | LIGHTING Ingenieurbüro Walter Bamberger, Pfünz (Kunstlicht); Transsolar Energietechnik GmbH,
Stuttgart (Tageslicht)
BRUTTOGESCHOSSFLÄCHE | GROSS 56.538 m² | 56,538 m²
UMBAUTER RAUM | VOLUME 227.471 m³ | 227,471 m³
ADRESSE | ADDRESS 34 chemin des Colombettes, 1211 Genf, Schweiz | Switzerland

BUNDESOBERSTUFENGYMNASIUM | SECONDARY SCHOOL
Wettbewerb 1999, 3. Preis
Competition 1999, 3rd Prize
ORT | LOCATION Graz, Österreich | Graz, Austria
ARCHITEKTEN | ARCHITECTS Behnisch, Behnisch & Partner

HOCHHAUS MAX | MAX HIGH-RISE
Wettbewerb 1999
Competition 1999
ORT | LOCATION Frankfurt (Main), Germany
ARCHITEKTEN | ARCHITECTS Behnisch, Behnisch & Partner

MUSIKZENTRUM | MUSIC CENTER
Wettbewerb 1999
Competition 1999
ORT | LOCATION Helsinki, Finnland/Helsinki, Finland
ARCHITEKTEN | ARCHITECTS Behnisch, Behnisch & Partner

MULTIFUNKTIONALES SPORT- UND VERANSTALTUNGSZENTRUM | MULTI-FUNCTIONAL CENTER FOR SPORTS AND CULTURAL EVENTS
Wettbewerb 1999, 2. Preis
Competition 1999, 2nd Prize
ORT | LOCATION Stuttgart, Germany
ARCHITEKTEN | ARCHITECTS Behnisch, Behnisch & Partner

PLENARSAAL LANDESHAUS | PLENARY ASSEMBLY HALL
Wettbewerb 1999, Ankauf
Competition 1999, Purchase
ORT | LOCATION Kiel, Germany
ARCHITEKTEN | ARCHITECTS Behnisch, Behnisch & Partner

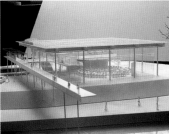

ARCHITEKTUR-/KUNSTOBJEKTE AM AEGIDIENTORPLATZ | ARCHITECTURAL/ARTISTIC OBJECTS AT AEGIDIENTORPLATZ
Wettbewerb und Planung, nicht realisiert
Competition and Planning, not realised
ORT | LOCATION Hannover | Hanover, Germany
AUSLOBER | CLIENT Stadt Hannover und Sponsoren
ARCHITEKTEN | ARCHITECTS Behnisch, Behnisch & Partner
WETTBEWERB | COMPETITION 1999, 1. Preis | 1st Prize
PLANUNGSZEIT | PLANNING 1999–2001, nicht realisiert | not realised
PROJEKTLEITUNG | PROJECT LEADER Martin Werminghausen
BERATUNG KUNST | ART CONSULTANT Heinz Mack, Mönchengladbach
TRAGWERKSPLANUNG | STRUCTURAL ENGINEERING Schlaich, Bergermann und Partner, Stuttgart; Jan Knippers, Stuttgart
LICHTTECHNIK | LIGHTING Ingenieurbüro Walter Bamberger, Pfünz
HÖHE | HEIGHT ca. 30 m/approx. 30m

EINKAUFSZENTRUM AM HIRSCHGARTEN | SHOPPING CENTER AT "HIRSCHGARTEN"
Wettbewerb 1999
Competition 1999
ORT | LOCATION Erfurt, Germany
ARCHITEKTEN | ARCHITECTS Behnisch, Behnisch & Partner

2000

HAUPTSITZ DER ITALIENISCHEN RAUMFAHRT ORGANISATION ASI | HEADQUARTERS OF THE ITALIAN SPACE AGENCY ASI
Wettbewerb 2000
Competition 2000
ORT | LOCATION Rom, Italien | Rome, Italy
ARCHITEKTEN | ARCHITECTS Behnisch, Behnisch & Partner

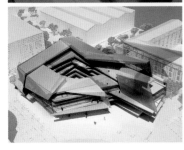

SITE 2, LANYON PLACE
Wettbewerb 2000
Competition 2000
ORT | LOCATION Belfast, Irland | Belfast, Ireland
ARCHITEKTEN | ARCHITECTS Behnisch, Behnisch & Partner

PORSCHE FORSCHUNGS- UND ENTWICKLUNGSZENTRUM | PORSCHE RESEARCH AND DEVELOPMENT CENTER
Gutachten 2000
Design study 2000
ORT | LOCATION Bietigheim-Bissingen, Germany
ARCHITEKTEN | ARCHITECTS Behnisch, Behnisch & Partner

OPERNHAUS | OPERA HOUSE
Wettbewerb 2000, Ankauf
Competition 2000, Purchase
ORT | LOCATION Oslo, Norwegen | Oslo, Norway
ARCHITEKTEN | ARCHITECTS Behnisch, Behnisch & Partner

UNIVERSITÄTSBIBLIOTHEK | UNIVERSITY LIBRARY
Wettbewerb 2000, Ankauf
Competition 2000, Purchase
ORT | LOCATION Rostock, Germany
ARCHITEKTEN | ARCHITECTS Behnisch, Behnisch & Partner

GENZYME CENTER – NEUBAU EINER HAUPTVERWALTUNG | NEW HEAD OFFICE BUILDING
Wettbewerb und Realisierung
Competition and Realisation
ORT | LOCATION Cambridge, MA, USA
BAUHERR GEBÄUDE | CLIENT BASE BUILDING Lyme Properties, LLC, Cambridge, MA
BAUHERR INNENAUSBAU | CLIENT Genzyme Corporation, Framington, NH
ARCHITEKTEN UND GENERALPLANER | ARCHITECTS AND GENERAL PLANER Behnisch, Behnisch & Partner, Inc., Venice, CA
WETTBEWERB | COMPETITION 2000, 1. Preis | 1st prize
FERTIGSTELLUNG | COMPLETION 2003
PROJEKTLEITUNG | PROJECT LEADER Christof Jantzen
ENTWURF UND ARCHITEKTONISCHE LEITUNG | DESIGN Behnisch, Behnisch & Partner, Stuttgart
PROJEKTLEITUNG | PROJECT LEADERS Maik Neumann, Martin Werminghausen
AUSFÜHRUNG GEBÄUDE MIT | ARCHITECT OF RECORD BASE BUILDING House & Robertson, Architects Los Angeles, CA
AUSFÜHRUNG INNENAUSBAU MIT | ARCHITECT OF RECORD Next Phase Studios Inc., Richard Ames, Scott Payette, Boston, MA
STATIK, HAUSTECHNIK | STRUCTURAL AND MECHANICAL ENGINEERING Buro Happold, New York City, NY, mit Laszlo Bodak
LICHTTECHNIK, TAGESLICHTTECHNIK | LIGHTING Bartenbach Lichtlabor GmbH, Aldrans/Innsbruck, Österreich
INNENGÄRTEN | INTERIOR GARDENS LOG ID, Tübingen
BRUTTOGESCHOSSFLÄCHE | GROSS 35.000 m² | 35,000 m²
ADRESSE | ADDRESS 364 Third Street Cambridge, MA 02142, USA

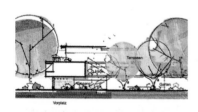

KINDERTAGESSTÄTTE JERUSALEMER STRASSE | CHILDREN'S DAY CARE CENTER JERUSALEMER STRASSE
Wettbewerb 2000
Competition 2000
ORT | LOCATION Berlin, Germany
ARCHITEKTEN | ARCHITECTS Behnisch, Behnisch & Partner

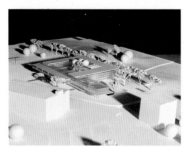

EUROPEAN HEADQUARTER KRYSTALTECH LYNX
Wettbewerb 2000
Competition 2000
ORT | LOCATION Reutlingen, Germany
ARCHITEKTEN | ARCHITECTS Behnisch, Behnisch & Partner

SPORT CAMPUS IRLAND | SPORTS CAMPUS IRELAND
Wettbewerb und Planung
Competition and Planning
ORT | LOCATION Dublin, Irland | Dublin, Ireland
AUFTRAGGEBER | CLIENT Campus and Stadium Ireland Development Ltd.
ARCHITEKTEN UND GENERALPLANER | ARCHITECTS AND GENERAL PLANER Behnisch, Behnisch & Partner
WETTBEWERB | COMPETITION 2001
MASTERPLAN | MASTERPLANNING 2001–2002
PROJEKTLEITUNG | PROJECT LEADER Eberhard Pritzer, Michael Holms Coats
INFRASTRUKTUR, TRAGWERKSPLANUNG, ENERGIE UND UMWELT | INFRASTRUCTURE, STRUCTURAL ENGINEERING AND ENVIRONMENT
Buro Happold, Bath, UK
LANDSCHAFT MIT | LANDSCAPING WITH Stötzer·Neher Landschaftsarchitekten, Sindelfingen
BRUTTOFLÄCHE | GROSS 200 ha
ADRESSE | ADDRESS Abbotstown Dublin 15, Irland

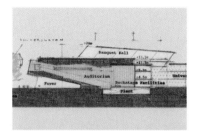

KONGRESSHALLE | CONGRESS HALL
Projektstudie 2001
Project Study 2001
ORT | LOCATION Visby, Schweden | Visby, Sweden
ARCHITEKTEN | ARCHITECTS Behnisch, Behnisch & Partner
PROJEKTARCHITEKT | PROJECT ARCHITECT Martin Arvidsson

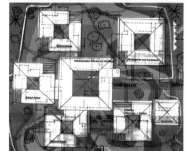

SCHULZENTRUM | SCHOOL COMPLEX
Wettbewerb 2001
Competition 2001
ORT | LOCATION Chicago, USA
ARCHITEKTEN | ARCHITECTS Behnisch, Behnisch & Partner

INDUSTRIEGEBIET FASANENHOF | INDUSTRIAL AREA FASANENHOF
Gutachten 2001
Design study 2001
ORT | LOCATION Stuttgart, Germany
ARCHITEKTEN | ARCHITECTS Behnisch, Behnisch & Partner

BÜROKOMPLEX HARDENBERGSTRASSE | OFFICE COMPLEX HARDENBERGSTRASSE
Wettbewerb 2001
Competition 2001
ORT | LOCATION Saarbrücken, Germany
ARCHITEKTEN | ARCHITECTS Behnisch, Behnisch & Partner

INDUSTRIE- UND HANDELSKAMMER | CHAMBER OF INDUSTRY AND COMMERCE
Wettbewerb 2001, 4. Preis
Competition 2001, 4. Prize
ORT | LOCATION Kiel, Germany
ARCHITEKTEN | ARCHITECTS Behnisch, Behnisch & Partner

ZENTRUM FÜR ANWENDUNGEN DER INFORMATIK UND FÜR INTERNATIONALE BEZIEHUNGEN DER UNIVERSITÄT |
CENTER FOR INFORMATION TECHNOLOGY APPLICATIONS AND INTERNATIONAL RELATIONS OF THE UNIVERSITY
Wettbewerb 2001
Competition 2001
ORT | LOCATION Passau, Germany
ARCHITEKTEN | ARCHITECTS Behnisch, Behnisch & Partner

GYMNASIUM | SECONDARY SCHOOL
Wettbewerb 2001
Competition 2001
ORT | LOCATION Erding, Germany
ARCHITEKTEN | ARCHITECTS Behnisch, Behnisch & Partner

PALUCCASCHULE | PALUCCA SCHOOL
Wettbewerb 2001
Competition 2001
ORT | LOCATION Dresden, Germany
ARCHITEKTEN | ARCHITECTS Behnisch, Behnisch & Partner

WOHN- UND GESCHÄFTSHAUS NEUMARKT | APARTMENTS, SHOPS AND OFFICES AT NEUMARKT
Projektstudie und Planung
Project Study and Planning
ORT | LOCATION Dresden, Germany
AUFTRAGGEBER | CLIENT Columbus Bauprojekt GmbH, Dresden
ARCHITEKTEN | ARCHITECTS Behnisch, Behnisch & Partner
PROJEKTLEITER | PROJECT LEADER Martin Arvidsson
BRUTTOGESCHOSSFLÄCHE | GROSS 6.229 m² | 6,229 m²
UMBAUTER RAUM | VOLUME 21.404 m³ | 21,404 m³
ADRESSE | ADDRESS Frauenstraße 4–12, 01067 Dresden, Deutschland | Germany

PLENARSAAL HESSISCHER LANDTAG | PLENARY ASSEMBLY HALL OF THE HESSIAN LANDTAG
Wettbewerb 2001
Competition 2001
ORT | LOCATION Wiesbaden, Germany
ARCHITEKTEN | ARCHITECTS Behnisch, Behnisch & Partner

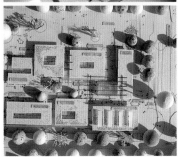

SCHULE FÜR GEISTIG- UND KÖRPERBEHINDERTE | SCHOOL FOR DISABLED CHILDREN
Wettbewerb und Realisierung
Competition and Realisation
ORT | LOCATION Herbrechtingen, Germany
BAUHERR | CLIENT Landkreis Heidenheim
ARCHITEKTEN | ARCHITECTS Behnisch, Behnisch & Partner
WETTBEWERB | COMPETITION 2001, 1. Preis | 1st Prize
VORAUSSICHTLICHE FERTIGSTELLUNG | SCHEDULED FOR COMPLETION 2004
PROJEKTLEITUNG | PROJECT LEADER Alexandra Burkard
TRAGWERKSPLANUNG | STRUCTURAL ENGINEERING Knippers und Helbig, Stuttgart
LANDSCHAFT MIT | LANDSCAPING WITH Luz Landschaftsarchitekten, Stuttgart
HAUSTECHNIK HLS | MECHANICAL ENGINEERING H+H Ingenieurpartnerschaft, Stuttgart
ELEKTROTECHNIK | ELECTRICAL ENGINEERING Ingenieurbüro für Elektrotechnik, Werner Schwarz GmbH, Stuttgart
BRUTTOGESCHOSSFLÄCHE | GROSS 4.450 m² | 4,450 m²
UMBAUTER RAUM | VOLUME 19.200 m³ | 19,200 m³
ADRESSE | ADDRESS Brückenstraße , 89542 Herbrechtingen, Deutschland | Germany

LITERATURMUSEUM DER MODERNE | MUSEUM OF MODERN LITERATURE
Wettbewerb 2001
Competition 2001
ORT | LOCATION Marbach, Germany
ARCHITEKTEN | ARCHITECTS Behnisch, Behnisch & Partner

LBBW FASSADE | FACADE OF LBBW BANK BUILDING
Gutachten 2001
Design study 2001
ORT | LOCATION Heilbronn, Germany
ARCHITEKTEN | ARCHITECTS Behnisch, Behnisch & Partner

ZENTRUM FÜR ZELL- UND BIOMOLEKULARFORSCHUNG DER UNIVERSITÄT TORONTO (CCBR) | CENTRE FOR CELLULAR AND BIOMOLECULAR RESEARCH (CCBR)
Verhandlungsverfahren und Realisierung
Competitive Interview and Realisation
ORT | LOCATION Toronto, Kanada | Toronto, Canada
BAUHERR | CLIENT University of Toronto, Toronto, Ontario
ARCHITEKTEN | ARCHITECTS Behnisch, Behnisch & Partner
MIT | WITH architects Alliance, Toronto
AUSWAHLVERFAHREN | SELECTION PROCESS 2001
VORAUSSICHTLICHE FERTIGSTELLUNG | SCHEDULED FOR COMPLETION 2005
PROJEKTLEITUNG | PROJECT LEADER Volker Biermann (für B, B & P | for B, B & P)
TRAGWERKSPLANUNG | STRUCTURAL ENGINEERING Yolles Partnership, Toronto
MIT | WITH Knippers & Helbig, Stuttgart
HAUSTECHNIK HLS | MECHANICAL ENGINEERING H.H. Angus & Associates, Don Mills
LABORPLANUNG | LAB CONSULTANT Flad & Associates, Madison, WI
BRUTTOGESCHOSSFLÄCHE | GROSS 20.500 m² | 20,500 m²
ADRESSE | ADDRESS 150 College Street, Toronto, ON M5T 1R2, Canada

GESCHÄFTSHAUS TRITSCHLER AM MARKTPLATZ STUTTGART | TRITSCHLER BUILDING AT MARKTPLATZ STUTTGART
Gutachten 2001
Design study 2001
ORT | LOCATION Stuttgart, Germany
ARCHITEKTEN | ARCHITECTS Behnisch, Behnisch & Partner

SCHAUSPIELHAUS, ROYAL THEATRE | PLAYHOUSE, ROYAL THEATRE
Wettbewerb 2001
Competition 2001
ORT | LOCATION Kopenhagen, Dänemark | Copenhagen, Denmark
ARCHITEKTEN | ARCHITECTS Behnisch, Behnisch & Partner

ZIVILJUSTIZZENTRUM | CIVIL LAW CENTER
Wettbewerb 2001
Competition 2001
ORT | LOCATION München | Munich, Germany
ARCHITEKTEN | ARCHITECTS Behnisch, Behnisch & Partner

RÖDL CAMPUS
Wettbewerb und Planung
Competition and Planning
ORT | LOCATION Nürnberg | Nuremberg, Germany
BAUHERR | CLIENT Rödl Campus GbR, Nürnberg
ARCHITEKTEN | ARCHITECTS Behnisch, Behnisch & Partner
WETTBEWERB | COMPETITION 2001, 1. Preis | 1st Prize
VORAUSSICHTLICHE FERTIGSTELLUNG | SCHEDULED FOR COMPLETION 2005
PROJEKTLEITUNG | PROJECT LEADER Dominik Heni
BRUTTOGESCHOSSFLÄCHE | GROSS 12.000 m² | 12,000 m²
UMBAUTER RAUM | VOLUME 45.440 m³ | 45,440 m³
BÜROARBEITSPLÄTZE | WORK PLACES 350
ADRESSE | ADDRESS Äußere Sulzbacher Straße 100, 90491 Nürnberg, Deutschland | Germany

2002

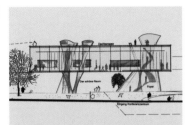

SANIERUNG UND ERWEITERUNG SCHWEIZERISCHES LANDESMUSEUM | REDEVELOPMENT AND EXTENSION OF THE SWISS NATIONAL MUSEUM
Wettbewerb 2002
Competition 2002
ORT | LOCATION Zürich, Schweiz | Zurich, Switzerland
ARCHITEKTEN | ARCHITECTS Behnisch, Behnisch & Partner

GROSSPORTHALLE SINSHEIM | SPORTS COMPLEX SINSHEIM
Wettbewerb 2002
Competition 2002
ORT | LOCATION Sinsheim, Germany
ARCHITEKTEN | ARCHITECTS Behnisch, Behnisch & Partner

KASINO, KONZERT-, KONGRESSZENTRUM UND HOTEL KLEIN VENEDIG | CASINO, CONCERT/CONGRESS CENTER AND HOTEL LITTLE VENICE
Wettbewerb 2002
Competition 2002
ORT | LOCATION Konstanz | Constance, Germany
ARCHITEKTEN | ARCHITECTS Behnisch, Behnisch & Partner

GEMEINDEZENTRUM ST. ANTONIUS | ST. ANTONIUS COMMUNITY CENTER
Wettbewerb 2002
Competition 2002
ORT | LOCATION Waiblingen, Germany
ARCHITEKTEN | ARCHITECTS Behnisch, Behnisch & Partner

STADTTEILZENTRUM LÜBECK | COMMUNITY CENTER LÜBECK
Wettbewerb 2002, Ankauf
Competition 2002, Purchase
ORT | LOCATION Lübeck, Germany
ARCHITEKTEN | ARCHITECTS Behnisch, Behnisch & Partner

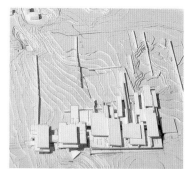

THE GRAND EGYPTIAN MUSEUM
Wettbewerb 2002
Competition 2002
ORT | LOCATION Giza, Ägypten | Giza, Egypt
ARCHITEKTEN | ARCHITECTS Behnisch, Behnisch & Partner

HAUPTVERWALTUNG ALTANA PHARMA KONSTANZ | HEADQUARTERS ALTANA PHARMA CONSTANCE
Wettbewerb 2002
Competition 2002
ORT | LOCATION Konstanz | Constance, Germany
ARCHITEKTEN | ARCHITECTS Behnisch, Behnisch & Partner

KOMPETENZZENTRUM GARTENBAU | HORTICULTURAL CENTER
Wettbewerb 2002, Ankauf
Competition 2002, Purchase
ORT | LOCATION Thiensen, Germany
ARCHITEKTEN | ARCHITECTS Behnisch, Behnisch & Partner

LANDESMUSIKAKADEMIE UND JUGENDGÄSTEHAUS | MUSIC ACADEMY OF THE STATE AND YOUTH HOTEL
Wettbewerb 2002
Competition 2002
ORT | LOCATION Wolfenbüttel, Germany
ARCHITEKTEN | ARCHITECTS Behnisch, Behnisch & Partner

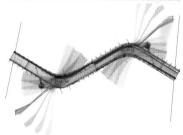

FUSSGÄNGERBRÜCKE | PEDESTRIAN BRIDGE
Wettbewerb 2002
Competition 2002
ORT | LOCATION Dublin, Irland | Dublin, Ireland
ARCHITEKTEN | ARCHITECTS Behnisch, Behnisch & Partner

ANNEN-GYMNASIUM DRESDEN | GERMAN INTERNATIONAL SCHOOL DRESDEN
Projektstudie 2002
Project Study 2002
ORT | LOCATION Dresden, Germany
ARCHITEKTEN | ARCHITECTS Behnisch, Behnisch & Partner

U2-STUDIOS — EINE LANDMARKE | LANDMARK TOWER AND U2 STUDIOS
Wettbewerb 2003
Competition 2003
ORT | LOCATION Dublin, Irland | Dublin, Ireland
ARCHITEKTEN | ARCHITECTS Behnisch, Behnisch & Partner

FINANZZENTRUM AACHEN | FINANCIAL CENTER AACHEN
Wettbewerb 2003
Competition 2003
ORT | LOCATION Aachen, Germany
ARCHITEKTEN | ARCHITECTS Behnisch, Behnisch & Partner

UMGESTALTUNG UND ERWEITERUNG GUTENBERGGYMNASIUM ERFURT | RE-MODELLING AND EXTENSION GUTENBERG GRAMMAR SCHOOL ERFURT
Wettbewerb 2003, Ankauf
Competition 2003, Purchase
ORT | LOCATION Erfurt, Germany
ARCHITEKTEN | ARCHITECTS Behnisch, Behnisch & Partner

BÜROGEBÄUDE UND HOTEL HAMBURG — ST. PAULI | COMMERCIAL DEVELOPMENT HAMBURG — ST. PAULI
Wettbewerb 2003
Competition 2003
ORT | LOCATION Hamburg, Germany
ARCHITEKTEN | ARCHITECTS Behnisch, Behnisch & Partner

KRONPRINZBAU STUTTGART | KRONPRINZ-BUILDING STUTTGART
Gutachten 2003
Design study 2003
ORT | LOCATION Stuttgart, Germany
ARCHITEKTEN | ARCHITECTS Behnisch, Behnisch & Partner

ANLEGER FÜR MISSISSIPPI-DAMPFER »MEMPHIS WAVE« | MISSISSIPPI VESSEL LANDING "MEMPHIS WAVE"
Wettbewerb 2003
Competition 2003
ORT | LOCATION Memphis, TN, USA
ARCHITEKTEN | ARCHITECTS Behnisch, Behnisch & Partner

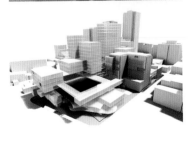

KULTUR- UND VERWALTUNGSZENTRUM MONTREAL | CULTURAL AND ADMINISTRATIVE COMPLEX MONTREAL
Wettbewerb 2003
Competition 2003
ORT | LOCATION Montreal, Kanada | Montreal, Canada
ARCHITEKTEN | ARCHITECTS Behnisch, Behnisch & Partner

FORSCHUNGS- UND VERWALTUNGSZENTRUM | MOBILE SOLUTION CENTER BREMEN
Wettbewerb 2003
Competition 2003
ORT | LOCATION Bremen, Germany
ARCHITEKTEN | ARCHITECTS Behnisch, Behnisch & Partner

OSAKA STÄDTEBAU | OSAKA INTERNATIONAL CONCEPT
Wettbwerb 2003
Competition 2003
ORT | LOCATION Osaka, Japan
ARCHITEKTEN | ARCHITECTS Behnisch, Behnisch & Partner

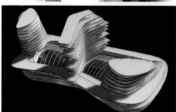

REGIONALES AUSBILDUNGSZENTRUM | ROC LEIDEN — REGIONAL EDUCATION CENTER
Wettbwerb 2003
Competition 2003
ORT | LOCATION Leiden, Niederlande | Leiden, Netherlands
ARCHITEKTEN | ARCHITECTS Behnisch, Behnisch & Partner

MUSEUM DER UNIVERSITÄT SAN JOSÉ | SAN JOSÉ STATE UNIVERSITY MUSEUM
Wettbewerb 2003
Competition 2003
ORT | LOCATION San José, CA, USA
ARCHITEKTEN | ARCHITECTS Behnisch, Behnisch & Partner

NEUBAU EINER SONDERPÄDAGOGISCHEN FÖRDERSCHULE IN ILLERTISSEN | NEW SCHOOL FOR CHILDREN WITH SPECIAL LEARNING NEEDS
Wettbewerb 2003, 1. Preis
Competition 2003, 1. Prize
ORT | LOCATION Illertissen, Germany
ARCHITEKTEN | ARCHITECTS Behnisch, Behnisch & Partner

LABORGEBÄUDE KLINIKUM UNIVERSITÄT KÖLN | LABORATORY BUILDING FOR THE UNIVERSITY HOSPITAL COLOGNE
Wettbewerb 2003, Ankauf
Competition 2003, Purchase
ORT | LOCATION Köln | Cologne, Germany
ARCHITEKTEN | ARCHITECTS Behnisch, Behnisch & Partner

Ahrens, Birgit
Altenburger, Elke
Amato, Manuel
Amft, Holger
Anhorn, Dirk
Arndt, Susanne
Arvidsson, Martin

Mitarbeiter | List of Staff 1991–2003

Baccarini, Chiara
Baksic, Natascha
Balke, Thomas
Balz, Verena
Bamberger, Michael
Bandy, Vincent
Baske, Manuela
Bassin, Delia
Baum, Martina
Baumann, Vera
Bayer, Karin
Beaugier, Marie-Alix
Behnisch, Petra
Behnisch, Stefan
Bembe, Felix
Bender, Stephanie
Benkel, Rainer
Benz, Marc
Betz, Oliver
Bhandary, Birger
Bidlingmaier, Irene
Biermann, Volker

Bilger, Joachim
Bischof, Arndt
Bittcher, Eberhard
Blank, Michael
Blauth, Renate
Blessing, Ulrich
Bodamer, Achim
Bode, Kerstin
Bökeler, Nicola
Borkowska, Aneta
Borrock-Stondzik, Petra
Bösch, Christoph
Boualam, Abdelhaq
Brandstetter, Florian
Braunger, Boris
Brenner, Christoph
Broad, Helena
Brockhaus, Mathias

Callahan, Patricia
Carrara, Federico
Chagny, Maiti
Charisius, Achim
Charlot, Jean Kekoa
Choong, Min Sang
Cook, David Howard
Corsellis, Thomas
Croé, Andrea
Crumbach, Andrea

Falk, Beate
Fecskes, Julianna
Feldmaier, Werner
Felke, Wolfram
Felsinger, Bernd
Fentz, Nicolaj
Feuerstein, Gerhard
Fields, Jeremy
Figura, Antonio
Finckh, Chris
Finnan, Gavin
Flaubert, Stefanie
Fowke, John
Frank, Sophie
Franke-Höltzermann, Carola
Fraser, Laurence
Freeman, Petra
Frese, Wolfgang
Fritsch, Jutta
Frommeyer, Elsbeth
Fuchs, Christina
Fuchs, Matthias

Haas, Martin
Haberer, Willy
Haberzettl, Simon
Hadzimujic, Sanela
Hahn, Werner
Handt, Steffen
Hannen, Katharina
Hanselmann, Ulrich
Hansen, Birgitta
Hansen, Lars
Hansjosten, Sigrid
Harder, Ruth
Hartung, Matthias
Heerlein, Christian
Helander, Henna Maria
Heni, Dominik
Henrik, Tilja
Herdt, Julia
Herrich, Philipp
Herrmann, Ulrich
Hidayat, Victor

Broszeit, Ingelore
Brown, Lucy Jane
Bruchmann, Axel
Brüchner-Huttemann, Kai
Brüggemann, Beate
Bulla, Iris
Burkard, Alexandra
Burmester, Kerstin
Butzke, Katja

Daller, Joachim
De Montgolfier, Alexis
Dehnel, Arne
Deichsel, Dieter
Delgado, Yolanda
Dengler, Roswitha
Dennig, Kathrin
Diehm, Stefanie
Dinges, Miriam
Dirksen, Wibke
Ditschuneit, Andreas Hans
Doulis, Yianni
Dunkl, Jakob

Eberhardt, Verena
Egger, Josef
Eggert, Jochen
Eichstädt, Berenice
Erkmen, Semra

Genkel, Jörn
Gerhardt, Ulrich
Gerken, Karen
Giesel, Matthias
Giesen, Veit
Gilenko, Yanika
Gilissen, Antonius
Godwin, Audrey
Göhringer, Annette Käthe
Gramm, Annette
Graniola, Pietro
Gräter, Markus
Greif, Maria
Gremmel, Martin
Grou, Christian
Grün, Simone
Guimaraes, Silvia Helena
Guym, Unjoo

Himmler, Isabella
Hinkel, Rochus
Höchstädter, Peter
Hockova, Diana
Hofmeister, Malte
Höh, Martina
Höhle, Eva
Höhn, Hans-Peter
Holms Coats, Michael
Holst, Max
Hoppe, Thomas
Hörenz, Marion
Horst-Kaiser, Jan
Hübner, Olaf
Huck, Peter
Huenefeld, Christoph
Huge, John Ilijah
Huiss, Michael
Hurt, Tom Hamilton

Ikas, Melanie
Imbach, Herbert
Iscimen, Yavus

Jablonka, Heidrun
Jäger, Pamela
Janik, Susanne
Jantzen, Christof
Janzen, Anke
Jatsch, Markus
Jedelhauser, Ulrich
Jertschewske, Peter
Johnson, Daniel
Jungmann-Brito, Adriana

Kammer, Armin
Kamogawa, Tatiana
Kerschkamp, Heidi
Kirk, Adam
Kling, Peter

Langer, Brigitte
Läufer, Jan
Lechler, Jonas
Lee, Yeoun Mi
Lehmann, Ralf
Lenz, Carmen
Leukel, Wolfgang
Lewis, Emma
Li, Fangyuan
Lienhart, Tanja
Liepold, Rosemarie
Lindahl Kristin
Lindel, Birgit
Link, Thomas
Linsenmaier, Maria
Lopez, Claudia
Lübbers, Werner
Ludwig, Andreas
Ludwig, Dieter
Lurz, Christine

Mihm, Claus
Min, Sang Choong
Minder, Dorothee
Minx, Alexander
Mischke, Christoph
Möller, Claudia
Monclin, Jean-Pierre
Monnerjan, Frauke
Morten, Nielsen
Mortensen, Trine
Muller, Brook
Müller, Horst
Müller, Markus
Müller, Moritz
Müller-Welt, Christine
Müller-Welt, Sigrid
Mullins, Richard
Mundel, Dorea
Mundel, Kai
Münster, Bettina
Munz, Brigitte
Murais, Maria

Passek, Anja
Perez, Maria Cecilia
Perrier, Marilyne
Peter, Christian
Petzel, Lena-Sophie
Pfrommer, Simon
Piatkowska, Ksenia
Pollak, Stefan
Pope, Thomas David
Popert, Arno
Potthoff, Jörg
Pötzschmann, Nicole
Pozas Guzman, Josefina
Pritzer, Eberhard

Klein, Helmut
Klöpfer, Hagen
Kobler, Tobias
Koch Daniela
Koch, Constance
Koch, Gisela
Koch, Matthias
Kohler, Xandra
Koller, Peter
Koller, Stefan
König, Janke
Kores, Daniela
Krampe, Heiko
Krause, Ellen Kristina
Krebs, Tim
Krepold, Evelyn
Krüger, Eckart
Kulbych, Tetjana
Kuhle, Sylvia
Kunz, Annett
Kuorelathi, Leena
Kurooka, Kiyomi
Kurz, Philip

Mack, Matthias
Maecki, Pekka
Maier, Bettina
Makkonen, Leena
Mallon, Terence J.
Mangold-Möbius, Ulrich
Mannsdörfer, Birgit
Manschot, Joep
Marx, Ingrid
Mastroyannis, Maria
Mathias, David
Matthiessen, David
Matthiessen-Behnisch, Charlotte
Mattmann, Jürgen
Mayr, Christoph
McCulloch, Moira
Meisel, Franziska
Mena-Quezada, Maria-Victoria
Mertins, Katrin
Meyer, Lür
Meyn, Matthias
Michael, Diana

Nadansky, Martina
Nagel, Hanne
Neubig, Stefan
Neufeld, Willi
Neumann, Maik
Neumann, Ulrich
Neureuther, Hans-Ulrich
Niehoff, Wolfgang
Nienhaus, Agnes
Nosbusch, Frederic

Ockert, Frank
Oehring, Ute
Oezcan, Oezlem
Okashi, Yifat
Ostrop, Patrick
Oyuntulhuur, Ulrii
Özdemir, Özlem

Radtkey, Ken
Ramsfjell, Gunnar
Randazzo, Antonio
Rappold, Stefan
Rashied, Magdi
Räuchle, Eberhard
Rauschke, Armin
Reischböck, Christoph
Rietzler, Markus
Rilsky, Plamen
Roegels, Kay
Römisch-Vikner, Ramona
Romoli, Chiara
Roper, Michael
Rovelli, Laura
Ruff, Hagen
Rüßmann, Severin

Saeger, Susanne
Saller, Timo
Sangster, Bonnie
Sargeson, Alex
Sauerhammer, Birgit
Sayer, Justin Lawrence
Schaab, Martina
Schäfer, Daniel
Schäfer, Anja
Schaller, Günther
Scharabi, Karim
Scherhorn, Philip
Schilling, Anna Katharina
Schilling, Julia
Schlindenbuch, Martina
Schlüßler, Constance
Schmid, Stephan
Schmidt, Matthias
Schmidthammer, Anja

Shatzmiller, Noa
Siemoneit, Oliver
Sikiaridi, Elisabeth
Soltau, Jan
Sonek, Michael
Song, Linn
Sorensen, Dorte
Späh, Jill
Späth, Silke
Stamm, Isolde
Stamminger, Iris
Stark, Bettina
Staudenmaier, Ursula
Steinhagen, Katrin
Sterr, Wolfgang
Sterzenbach, Ludger
Stick, Gernot
Stiegler, Ralph
Stjern, Audun
Stölzle, Barbara
Stölzle, Roland
Stötzler, Helmut

Taxhet, Georg
Teichert, Claudia
Teige, Christof
Tellier, Alexander
Teufel, Gerrit
Thierfelder, Anja
Thuong, Dam Viet
Tovar, Hendrik
Tovor, Bernd
Tümmler, Simon
Tuonisto, Riika
Turrian, Alexis

Wachmeister, Anna
Wagner, Petra
Wallnöfer, Jürgen
Walz, Steffen
Wang, Xiaohong
Waters, Ian
Webb, James
Wedel, Tanja
Weger, Ingrid
Weigang, Karin
Weiss, Stephanie
Wendel, Thilo
Wenzler, Susanne
Wermke, Stephanie
Werminghausen, Martin
Wichmann, Matthias
Willburger, Edelgard
Winden, Monika
Wiren, Timo
Wittfoht, Jens
Woziank, Zofia

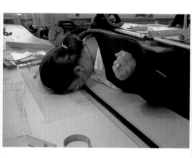

Schnitzer, Ulrike
Schoch, Ralf
Schodder, Martin
Scholl, Frank
Scholl, Karin
Scholz, Yvonne
Schreiber, Tim
Schroth, Martin
Schuch, Michael
Schuchardt, Andreas
Schulte, Pascale
Schultz, Jutta
Schünke, Gabriele
Schütte, Eckard
Schwägerl, Klaus
Schwarz, Antonia
Schwertfeger, Hannes
Schwind, Jochen
Seidel, Andrea
Seipel, Thomas
Seitz, Frank
Shagirin, Samdan
Shah, Vandana Kishor Chandra

Strähle, Thomas
Straubenmüller, Sarah
Strauß, Christian
Strittmatter, Thomas
Stroh-Mocek, Christine
Strom, Michael
Stubgaard, Mikkel
Szczesny, Elke

Uchiyama, Thais
Uebele, Andreas
Uhlendorff, Katrin
Unold, Tina
Usinger, Jörg

Vangsoe, Sally
Van der Sluijs, Jeroen
Venzke, Petra
Vettermann, Markus
Voelki, Peter
Voll, Anne Christiane
Vollmann, Marcus
Vukorep, Ilija
Vuorio, Eca Kaatariina

Yarkin, Devrim

Zapf, John
Zeleny, Barbara
Ziegenbein, Brigitta
Zimmermann, Roland
Zimmermanns, Ute
Zorlu, Akay

Ausstellungen | Exhibitions 1996–2003

BEHNISCH & PARTNER,
BÜRO INNENSTADT
ABOUT OUR PRACTICE
Leadworks
Bristol, Großbritannien | United
Kingdom
Mai | May 1996

BRISTOL CENTRE FOR THE
PERFORMING ARTS
Leadworks
Bristol, Großbritannien | United
Kingdom
September – Oktober 1996
September – October 1996

AN ARCHITECTURE OF
SITUATION – CENTRAL HALL
SPACES
Architectural Association
School of Architecture
London, Großbritannien | United
Kingdom
Februar – März 1997
February – March 1997

BEHNISCH & PARTNER, BÜRO
INNENSTADT
Dansk Arkitektur Center-Gammel Dok
Kopenhagen, Dänemark | Copenhagen,
Denmark
März – Mai 1997
March – May 1997

GÜNTER BEHNISCH:
ARCHITEKTURMODELLE
mit: Modellen des Museums der
Phantasie, Bernried, Landesgirokasse
am Bollwerk, Stuttgart, und St. Benno-
Gymnasium, Dresden
Städtische Kunstsammlungen Chemnitz
Chemnitz, Deutschland | Germany
November 1997 – Januar 1998
November 1997 – January 1998

FOUR STORIES
St. Benno Secondary School, Dresden
The Architecture Centre
Bristol, Großbritannien | United
Kingdom
Frühling | Spring 1998

Northern Architecture Centre
Newcastle upon Tyne
Großbritannien | United Kingdom
Sommer | Summer 1998

The Welsh School of Architecture
Cardiff, Großbritannien | United
Kingdom
Herbst | Autumn 1998

10 JAHRE ZENTRALBIBLIOTHEK EICHSTÄTT
Behnisch & Partner und
Behnisch, Behnisch & Partner
Universitätsbibliothek Eichstätt
Eichstätt, Deutschland | Germany
Mai–Juli 1998
May–July 1998

DESIGN DEVELOPMENTS AT THE HARBOURSIDE CENTRE
Behnisch, Behnisch & Partner
The Architecture Centre
Bristol, Großbritannien | United Kingdom
Juli–August 1998
July–August 1998

4TH BIENAL INTERNACIONAL DE ARQUITETURA DE SAO PAULO
Museum der Phantasie, Bernried, und The Harbourside Centre, Bristol
Sao Paulo, Brasilien | Brazil
Dezember 1999 – Februar 2000
December 1999 – February 2000

SITUATIONS ARCHITECTURE
Behnisch & Partner
Behnisch, Behnisch & Partner
Form Zero Gallery
Santa Monica, California, USA
Februar – März 2000
February – March 2000

TOURING EXHIBITION OF THE EU EQUINOX CONFERENCE
Institute for Forestry and Nature Research
Royal Institute of British Architects, London
University of Westminster, London
Millenium Dome, Greenwich
Technion, Israel
ADEME Paris
EU Parliament Brussels
Delft University
März – Oktober 2000
March – October 2000

SITUATIONS ARCHITECTURE
Behnisch & Partner
Behnisch, Behnisch & Partner
Arizona State University
Tempe, Arizona, USA
Oktober – November 2000
October – November 2000

FIFTY PROJECTS
Behnisch, Behnisch & Partner:
New Opera House Competition, Oslo, Norway
Art Gallery Antonella Nicola
Turin, Italien | Torino, Italy
November 2000

TENDENCIES
Behnisch, Behnisch & Partner
School of Architecture, Shephard Hall
The City College of New York
New York, USA
Februar – März 2001
February – March 2001

TENDENCIES
Behnisch, Behnisch & Partner
Hartell Gallery/Sibley Hall
Cornell University
Ithaca, New York, USA
April 2001

SITUATIONAL ARCHITECTURE
Behnisch, Behnisch & Partner
Wolk Gallery
Massachusetts Institute of Technology
Cambridge, Massachusetts, USA
Februar – März 2001
February – March 2001

SITUATIONAL ARCHITECTURE
Behnisch, Behnisch & Partner
Margaret Morrison Carnegie Hall
Carnegie Mellon University
Pittsburgh, Pennsylvania, USA
April – Mai 2001
April – May 2001

VERSCHIEDENE PROJEKTE VON BEHNISCH & PARTNER UND BEHNISCH, BEHNISCH & PARTNER
Ausstellung anlässlich der Verleihung der Wolfgang-Hirsch-Auszeichnung an Günter Behnisch
Architektenkammer Rheinland-Pfalz
Lobby des Landtages von Rheinland-Pfalz
Geschäftsstelle der Architektenkammer
Mainz, Deutschland | Germany
Mai – Juni 2001
May – June 2001

SELECTED WORKS 1990–2001
Behnisch, Behnisch & Partner
School of Architecture
Mebane Gallery. Goldsmith Hall
The University of Texas at Austin.
Austin, Texas, USA
Juni – September 2001
June – September 2001

BEHNISCH, BEHNISCH & PARTNER
Chaplin Hall
Norwich University
Norwich, Vermont, USA
August – Oktober 2001
August – October 2001

BEHNISCH, BEHNISCH & PARTNER
School of Fine Arts, Alumni Hall
Miami University,
Oxford, Ohio, USA
Oktober 2001 | October 2001

BAUPROJEKTE IN MITTEL-DEUTSCHLAND
Messe BauFach – Sonderausstellung
Technologiegebäude für die TU Ilmenau
Messegelände
Leipzig, Deutschland | Germany
Oktober 2001 | October 2001

BEHNISCH & PARTNER/BEHNISCH, BEHNISCH & PARTNER
Various Projects
Busan International Architectural Culture Festival 2001
Busan, Korea | Corea
Oktober 2001 | October 2001

SITUATIONAL ARCHITECTURE
Behnisch, Behnisch & Partner
Museo Nacional de Bellas Artes
Buenos Aires, Argentinien | Argentina
Februar – März 2002
February – March 2002

AKTIONSSCHAU FARBE 2002
Fotos vom: St. Benno-Gymnasium Dresden; Museum der Phantasie, Bernried; Dienstleistungszentrum der Landesgirokasse am Bollwerk, Stuttgart
Neue Messe, Halle B2
München, Deutschland | Munich, Germany
April 2002

FIFTY:FIFTY. Gebaute und nicht gebaute Architektur in Berlin
1990–2000
Wettbewerb KITA für den Deutschen Bundestag
Berlinische Galerie
Martin-Gropius-Bau
Berlin, Deutschland | Germany
Mai – August 2002
May – August 2002

GÜNTER BEHNISCH: »Mit der Absicht, das Vielfältige unserer Welt in der Architektur widerzuspiegeln, sitzen wir vor dem leeren Papier« (Zitat 1999)
Günter Behnisch: "In attempting to translate the variety of our world into architecture, we are sitting in front of a blank sheet" (quotation, 1999)
Ausstellung zum 80. Geburtstag von Günter Behnisch
Aedes-Galerie West
Berlin, Deutschland | Germany
Juni – August 2002
June – August 2002

Katalog | Catalogue

DIESSEITS VON EDEN
Behnisch, Behnisch & Partner
Bauten und Projekte
Aedes-Galerie Ost
Berlin, Deutschland | Germany
Juni – August 2002
June – August 2002

Katalog | Catalogue

CENTRE FOR CELLULAR AND BIOMOLECULAR RESEARCH
Behnisch, Behnisch & Partner and architects Alliance
Eric Arthur Gallery
Faculty of Architecture, Landscape and Design
University of Toronto
Toronto, Kanada | Canada
September – November 2002

BIENNALE DER ARCHITEKTUR
WIPO Genf
Modell und Tafeln
Venedig, Italien | Venice, Italy
September – November 2002

BAUFACHMESSE SAIE
Institut für Forst- und Naturforschung,
Wageningen, und LVA 2000, Lübeck
Bologna, Italien | Italy
Oktober 2002 | October 2002

**CITYSCAPE — THE INTERNATIONAL
COMMERCIAL ARCHITECTURE,
PROPERTY INVESTMENT &
DEVELOPMENT EVENT**
Behnisch, Behnisch & Partner,
selected projects
Emirates Towers Hotel
Dubai, Vereinigte Arabische Emirate |
United Arab Emirates
14.–16. Dezember 2002
14th to 16th December 2002

**»NEUES BAUEN ZWISCHEN
SALZACH UND LECH«**
Ausstellung des 1. Wessobrunner
Architekturpreises
Behnisch, Behnisch & Partner:
Museum der Phantasie
Landsberg am Lech,
Deutschland | Germany
16. November – 8. Dezember 2002
16th November to 8th December 2002

BUILDINGS & PROJECTS
Behnisch, Behnisch & Partner
Hennessey & Ingalls
Santa Monica, USA
Mai 2003 | May 2003

**BIENNALE DE VALENCIA,
CONTAINER EXHIBITION**
Norddeutsche Landesbank in Hannover
Valencia, Spanien | Spain
September 2003

**DAS VIELFÄLTIGE, DAS DIFFEREN-
ZIERTE UND AUCH DAS WENIGER
VOLLKOMMENE | VARIETY,
DIFFERENTIATION AND THE
IMPERFECT**
Ausstellung im Rahmen des Hamburger
Architektursommers 2003 | Exhibition
on the occasion of Hamburg's
Architecture Summer 2003
Hamburg, Deutschland | Germany
Juli – September 2003
July – September 2003

BEHNISCH & PARTNER
BEHNISCH, BEHNISCH & PARTNER
Galerie Six Box
Peking | Beijing, China
September 2003

Preise und Auszeichnungen

Prizes and Awards

1996

Umbau des Bürogebäudes der
Bayerischen Vereinsbank |
Reconstruction of the Office Building of
the Bavarian Cooperative Bank
Stuttgart, Deutschland | Germany
Ausgezeichnet vom | Award from the
BDA Baden-Württemberg 1996
Auszeichnung der | Award from the
Architektenkammer 1997

St. Benno-Gymnasium | St. Benno
Secondary School
Dresden, Deutschland | Germany
Architekturpreis des Neuen
Sächsischen Kunstvereins e.V. Dresden
Anerkennung 1996
Special Prize of the Union of Russian
Architects
Gold Medal 1997
Interarch' Silver Medal and Diploma
Sofia 1997
Deutscher Architekturpreis
Anerkennung 1997
BDA-Preis Sachsen Anerkennung 1998
The RIBA Award for Architecture 1998

1997

Dienstleistungszentrum der Landes-
girokasse am Bollwerk |
Central Administration Building for the
State Clearing Bank at the "Bollwerk"
Stuttgart, Deutschland | Germany
Auszeichnung der | Award from the
Architektenkammer 1997
The RIBA Award for Architecture 1998
Deutscher Naturstein-Preis Lobende
Erwähnung | Honorable Mention 1999
Ausgezeichnet vom | Award from the
BDA Baden-Württemberg 1999

Hauptverwaltungsgebäude der
Landesversicherungsanstalt Schleswig-
Holstein (LVA 2000) |
Administration Building for the State
Insurance Agency Schleswig-Holstein
(LVA 2000)
Lübeck, Deutschland | Germany
The RIBA Award for Architecture 1998
BDA-Preis Schleswig-Holstein 1999
Trophée Sommet de la Terre et Bâtiment
Paris 2002

1998

Neubau Vereinigte Spezialmöbel-
fabriken (VS) – Büro- und
Ausstellungsgebäude |
New Development for the "Vereinigte
Spezialmöbelfabriken" (VS) – Office
and Exhibition Building
Tauberbischofsheim, Deutschland |
Germany
Ausgezeichnet vom | Award from the
BDA Baden-Württemberg 1999

1998

Institut für Forst- und Naturforschung
(I.B.N.) | Institute for Forestry and
Nature Research (I.B.N.)
Wageningen, Niederlande | Netherlands
Honorable Mention. Bienal Miami +
Beach, 2001
Trophée Sommet de la Terre et
Bâtiment, Paris, 2002
Finalist Architectural Record/Business
Week Award, USA, 2000

2000

Museum der Phantasie, Sammlung
Buchheim | Museum of Fantasy,
Buchheim Collection
Bernried, Deutschland | Germany
Ausgezeichnet vom | Award from the
BDA Bayern 2001
Sonderpreis des Wessobrunner
Architekturpreises 2002

2002

Norddeutsche Landesbank am
Friedrichswall (Nord/LB) |
North German State Clearing Bank at
Friedrichswall (Nord/LB)
Hannover, Deutschland |
Hanover, Germany
Niedersächsischer Staatspreis für
Architektur 2002

2003

Norddeutsche Landesbank am
Friedrichswall (Nord/LB) |
North German State Clearing Bank at
Friedrichswall (Nord/LB)
Hannover, Deutschland |
Hanover, Germany
Nominiert für den
Mies-van-der-Rohe-Preis 2003
DuPont Benedictus Awards, Honorable
Mention 2003
Exhibition Interarch' 2003 Sofia,
Special Prize
Deutscher Architekturpreis 2003
Boston Society of Architects Sustainable
Design Awards 2003, honorable mention

Bildnachweis

Nicht genannte Abbildungen:
Archiv, Behnisch, Behnisch & Partner.

Illustration Credits

BEHNISCH, STEFAN

p. 59, ill.15; p. 103, ill.7; p. 110, ill.17;
p. 112, ill.19; p. 117, ill.24; p. 144/145;
p. 146; p. 147, ill.2; p. 149, ill.6;
p. 152, ill.13; p. 154, ill.16; p. 159, ill.25;
p. 220, ill.13

BEMBÉ, FELIX

p. 12/13; p. 23

HALBE, ROLAND

p. 184, ill.4; p. 188, ill.12; p. 197, ill.3;
p. 210/211; p. 212/213, ill.1; p. 216, ill.6;
p. 218–219; p. 222, ill.17, 18; p. 224, 225,
ill.22; p. 228, 229, ill.27, 29, 31;
p. 230, 231, ill.32, 33, 35

HECHT, HEINRICH K.-M.

p. 216, ill.7

KANDZIA, CHRISTIAN

p. 14/15, ill.1; p. 16; p.17, ill.5, 7;
p. 18/19, ill.9; p. 20, ill.12; p. 21; p. 22,
ill.16, 17; p. 24, ill.22; p. 25, ill. 25; p. 27,
ill.29, 30, 31; p. 28, ill.32, 33, 34, 35;
p. 29, ill.36, 38, 39; p. 32 ill.9; p. 34/35;
p. 36; p. 38, ill.5; p. 40, ill.6; p. 41,
ill.7,8; p. 43; p. 44, ill.14, 15; p. 46,
ill.18, 19; p. 49, ill.22, 23, 24; p. 50/51;
p. 52–53; p. 54, 55, ill.4, 5; p. 56, 57,
ill.8, 9; p. 58, 59, ill.11, 12, 14; p. 60–62;
p. 63, ill.23; p. 103, ill.8; p. 109; p. 110,
ill.16; p. 113, ill.21; p. 118, ill.26;
p. 134/135, ill.1; p. 164/165; p. 166, 167,
ill.2, 3; p. 168, 169, ill.4, 5; p. 171, ill.9;
p. 173, ill.12, 13, 14; p. 180/181; p. 183;
p. 185, ill.7; p. 186, ill.8; p. 188, ill.13,
14; p. 189; p. 193; p. 195, ill.26, 27;
p. 224, ill.21; p. 226–227; p. 260;
p. 268–269; p. 273, ill.7; p. 280, ill.6;
p. 281, ill.10; p. 284/285; p. 288–289;
p. 290, ill.5; p. 291, ill.6; p. 292–293;
p. 294–295; p. 296, 297, ill.15, 16, 17

MEYER, LÜR

p. 261, ill.3; p. 265, ill.9; p. 271, ill.2

REINECKE, ULI

p. 232, ill.36, 37

SCHINK, H.-CH., PUNCTUM

p. 258–259; p. 262/263, ill.6; p. 264

SCHODDER, MARTIN

p. 17, ill.6; p. 18, ill.8; p. 20, ill.11; p. 24,
ill. 23; p. 25, ill.24; p. 26, ill.27;
p. 38–39, ill.3, 4; p. 44, ill.13; p. 46/47,
ill.20; p. 48; p. 98–99; p. 101, ill.2;
p. 102, ill.5; p. 105, ill.10; p. 106–107;
p. 111; p. 112, 113, ill.20, 22; p. 114,
ill.23; p. 117, ill.25; p. 182, ill.1; p. 185,
ill.6; p. 186, ill.9; p. 187, ill.10; p. 190,
ill.17, 18; p.191, ill.19, 20; p. 192; p. 195,
ill.25, 28; p. 199, ill.13; p. 213, ill.3;
p. 224, ill.23; p. 228, ill.28; p. 230,
ill.34; p. 232, ill.38; p. 270–271, ill.1;
p. 275; p. 276–277, ill.10, 12

WEBER, RUDI

p. 122, ill.2

All other illustrations: Archive of
Behnisch, Behnisch & Partner.

ÜBERSETZUNG INS ENGLISCHE |
TRANSLATION INTO ENGLISH
Ian Pepper, Berlin (alle Texte mit
Ausnahme der unten genannten |
all texts except those mentioned below)
Robin Benson, Berlin (S. 115–119 |
pp. 115–119)

ÜBERSETZUNG INS DEUTSCHE |
TRANSLATION INTO GERMAN
Dr. Ute Spengler, Zürich (S. 82–87,
126–131, 236–257, 312–329 |
pp. 82–87, 126–131, 236–257, 312–329)
Sebastian Fischer Baling, Arnhem
(S. 160–163 | pp. 160–163)

REDAKTION FÜR | COPY-EDITING FOR
BEHNISCH, BEHNISCH & PARTNER
Petra Behnisch
Ingrid Weger

GRAFISCHE GESTALTUNG |
LAYOUT AND COVER DESIGN
SeidlCluss, Stuttgart

LITHOGRAFIE UND DRUCK |
LITHOGRAPHY AND PRINTING
Raff digital GmbH, Riederich

TEXTE | TEXTS
Behnisch, Behnisch & Partner
    Günter Behnisch,
    Stefan Behnisch,
    Günther Schaller
    (Projektbeschreibungen |
    Project descriptions)
Stefan Behnisch
    (Exkurse | Digressions)
Hans Erhorn (Erläuterungen zum
    Energiekonzept des I.B.N. |
    Explanation of the
    Energy Concept of I.B.N.)
Tony McLaughlin (Energiekonzept des
    Genzyme Centers |
    Environmental Design Narrative
    of the Genzyme Center)
Robert Müller (Konzept für die Tages-
    lichtnutzung und für das System
    der Lichtverstärkung des Genzyme
    Centers | Natural Lighting Concept
    and Enhancement Systems of the
    Genzyme Center)

A CIP catalogue record for this book is
available from the Library of Congress,
Washington D.C., USA

Bibliographic information published by
Die Deutsche Bibliothek
Die Deutsche Bibliothek lists this
publication in the Deutsche
Nationalbibliografie; detailed
bibliographic data is available in the
Internet at <http://dnb.ddb.de>.

© 2003 Birkhäuser – Publishers for
Architecture, P.O.Box 133,
CH-4010 Basel, Switzerland
A member of the BertelsmannSpringer
Publishing Group

Printed on acid-free paper produced
from chlorine-free pulp. TCF ∞
Printed in Germany

ISBN 3-7643-6931-0

9 8 7 6 5 4 3 2 1   www.birkhauser.ch